BALMORAL
AND THE
BRISTOL CHANNEL

CAMPBELLS SAILINGS   CAMPBELLS SAILINGS

Travel by the
**WHITE FUNNEL
FLEET**

© Mike Tedstone and Black Dwarf Publications 2011
Designed by Ian Pope
British Library Cataloguing-in-Publication Data. A catalogue record for this
book is available from the British Library
ISBN 13: 9781903599 18 1

**Black Dwarf
Publications**

Black Dwarf is an imprint of Black Dwarf Lightmoor Publications Limited
144b Lydney Industrial Estate, Harbour Road
Lydney, Gloucestershire, GL15 4EJ
Printed and bound by Gutenberg Press Limited, Malta
www.gutenberg.com.mt

WHITE FUNNEL STEAMER SERVICES

FROM SOUTH WALES PORTS

BETWEEN

CARDIFF AND WESTON	WESTON AND BARRY
CARDIFF, PENARTH, BARRY	NEWPORT AND WESTON
LYNMOUTH & ILFRACOMBE	CARDIFF & LUNDY ISLAND
SWANSEA & ILFRACOMBE	SWANSEA & LUNDY ISLAND
CARDIFF & MINEHEAD	CARDIFF & CLEVEDON
CARDIFF & CLOVELLY	CARDIFF & BRISTOL

For additional Trips apply

P.   &   A.   CAMPBELL   LTD.

PIER HEAD, CARDIFF. Tel. 32621
LANDING STAGE, NEWPORT. Tel. 3889.
THE PONTOON, BARRY. Tel. 50.
SOUTH DOCK ENTRANCE, SWANSEA.   Tel. 3845.
CUMBERLAND BASIN BRISTOL. Tel. 23112.

BALMORAL
AND THE
BRISTOL CHANNEL

The late years of P. & A. Campbell Ltd

Passenger Steamship Owners

Following the demise of P. & A. Campbell Ltd as described in this volume the revival of Balmoral *took place in time for the 1986 season. It was decided that she would have a new image unconnected with her previous life as a P. & A. Campbell Ltd ship and she was painted white overall with a buff funnel. Seen here at anchor off Lundy, with the 'Lundy doors' (as they are still known) in use.* Author

Mike Tedstone

Cardiff Queen approaching Penarth Pier on the flood, 1964.

A. K. Pope

P.&A. CAMPBELL LIMITED

BRITANNIA BUILDINGS, CUMBERLAND BASIN BRISTOL 8 · TELEPHONE : 23112

Passenger Steamship Owners

CONTENTS

WHITE FUNNEL FLEET SAILINGS IN THE BRISTOL CHANNEL·CRUISES ALONG THE SOUTH COAST·DAY TRIPS TO FRANCE

Balmoral leaving Ilfracombe, early-1970s.   Ilfracombe Museum

... Ilfracombe is the holiday Mecca of many thousands from South Wales,
Bristol and more distant places who come to enjoy the pleasures of
this beautiful resort, which nature seems to have intended for the purpose,
with its bathing coves, its wooded glens, turf-covered heights and glorious coast line.
It has not been a case of constructing this delightful place but rather of
adapting it to its natural surroundings ...
Extract from *The White Funnel Handbook*, 1957 edition

INTRODUCTION

The title of this book is a tribute to a series of articles entitled The Bristol Channel and **Bristol Queen** which were published in 1968-1969 in seven parts in *Ship Ahoy*, the quarterly journal of the South Wales Branch of the World Ship Society. Written by Norman Bird this was, in the author's opinion, some of the best material ever published about the penultimate purpose-built Bristol Channel paddle-steamer, **Bristol Queen**, which had entered service in 1946. Norman wrote candidly not just about his experiences on board her and the other, mostly veteran White Funnel Fleet paddlers in the postwar era, but he also described the wider activities and practices of the old-established company of P. & A. Campbell Ltd, whose Clyde roots went back as far as 1854. His writing went a long way towards satisfying my desire to learn about the P. & A. Campbell Ltd 'White Funnel Fleet', which was stimulated by the comeback of the classic motor-vessel **Balmoral** in 1986. At that time, very little existed in print about the company which had intrigued me since a first meeting with the one-time dual-purpose Isle of Wight car-ferry and excursion ship in 1974, when I arrived in Cardiff as a student. From that first occasion of setting foot on her deck and sailing from Penarth up to Bristol and back, I had the strong impression that there was much more here than met the eye. Not having known the Bristol Channel paddle-steamers personally, my first impressions of the solitary white-funnelled **Balmoral** in the muddy waters off Penarth were coloured by the forlorn sight of her predecessor motor-vessels **St. Trillo** abandoned a few miles away in the Graving Dock at Barry awaiting the final trip to the breakers and, further afield, the static **Westward Ho** serving as a pub of sorts in a corner of Salford Docks.

Friends in the Bristol Channel Branch of the Paddle Steamer Preservation Society (PSPS) lent me their own collections of P. & A. Campbell Ltd newspaper cuttings and the like, and eventually put me on to the *Ship Ahoy* articles as the source that might answer my continuing questions. These questions were more to do with how the business of P. & A. Campbell Ltd had actually operated, and the territory of the company, rather than just about the white-funnelled vessels themselves, and about which some details did then exist in the classic works of Farr, Duckworth & Langmuir, Grimshaw, and Thornton. The Bristol Channel and **Bristol Queen** dealt with what might be termed the postwar paddle-steamer years of P. & A. Campbell Ltd, that is, from the resumption of excursion activities in 1946 through until the sad, arguably premature withdrawal in 1967 of the beautiful **Bristol Queen**, the last of the line, hard on the heels of her half-sister **Cardiff Queen** after the 1966 season. Avid reading of Norman's account of this era, full of insight and astute observation, made me want to know more about what happened after 1967, as I had only experienced the White Funnel Fleet at firsthand during the final few years of the life of the company until the withdrawal of **Balmoral** after the 1980 season. P. & A. Campbell Ltd were of course involved with the Bristol Channel operations of **Prince Ivanhoe** during the 1981 season, but the shocking loss of that vessel more or less coincided with my own departure from South Wales believing, quite wrongly as it turned out, that Bristol Channel cruising had practically ended. It was not until a few seasons after **Balmoral** had made her remarkable comeback in 1986 that I was prompted to think about undertaking some P. & A. Campbell Ltd research of my own. This was greatly facilitated once the surviving company records were made available for public scrutiny, a few years after the closedown of operations.

It was my privilege to get to know three most affable gentlemen who, between them, had practically constituted much of the management team of P. & A. Campbell Ltd during the late years. All three were prepared to meet me to answer my questions, talk about their old company, and make available documents they had preserved in order that I could attempt to assemble an account of the business that had run from the late 1950s until the final winding-up proceedings in 1986. Sidney Clifton Smith-Cox, or SCSC as he sometimes signed himself, became Managing Director in 1954, and was very much in overall charge right up until the end. When researching the background to the

acquisition by P. & A. Campbell Ltd of the former Isles of Scilly ferry **Scillonian** in 1977 which duly became, as **Devonia**, the very last ship to join the Campbell fleet, he had courteously replied to my questions. When I first met him I regarded it as something of an honour to sit in the study at his beautiful Victorian house in Clevedon, surrounded by oil-paintings of celebrated Bristol Channel paddle-steamers, and hear at first-hand of his own beginnings with the company which he had served for almost thirty years. Peter Southcombe, as Passenger Manager, had been involved since 1963 and had particular responsibility for operations away from the Bristol Channel for many of his years of service. Thirdly, Tony McGinnity had been both a close friend of Clifton Smith-Cox and a professional adviser to the company since the 1960s as a shipbroker, and for a period in the 1970s acted as Joint Managing Director with him.

A few years later, I also got to know well Captain George Gunn, whose involvement stretched back even further than that of Clifton Smith-Cox, and who had commanded, at one time or another, all of the postwar Campbell steamers as well as an element of managerial and advisory input. These enormously stimulating acquaintances really brought to life the company that all four had known and served. The postwar paddle-steamer years of P. & A. Campbell Ltd between 1946-1967 are now rather better documented than they were when I initially embarked upon my researches, and I have been encouraged by fellow writers Nigel Coombes, Richard Clammer, Chris Collard, Richard Danielson and the late H. G. Owen and Captain Gunn to tackle the later years in order to try and complete the P. & A. Campbell Ltd story, and augment their contributions.

In so doing, I have actually gone back to the mid-1950s to set the scene, as it was the near-collapse of the old Bristol-based business after the 1956 season that led to financial reconstruction. This created a company structure in a form that somehow enabled survival for a further two decades, albeit sometimes by different means than the traditional, fairly straightforward operation of paddle-steamers. One could say that after the Second World War, the old company had tried to pick things up from where they had left off, abruptly, at the outbreak of hostilities in 1939, and that this approach did indeed keep them going for a few difficult and varied seasons from 1946 onwards. But following the move to Cardiff after 1956 and the abandonment of the traditional Bristol headquarters, it was a much leaner company that then had to struggle through a period of great change, yet managed to become one which was not unwilling to experiment, and to try and find new sources of income. The white funnel persisted and a 'new order' of sorts emerged. Becoming a part of the George Nott/Townsend, and later, European Ferries empire was not entirely apparent, at least to passengers in the Bristol Channel. Even if the paddlers were destined to disappear, there was an Indian Summer where Bristol Channel cruising was possible long after all-day excursion vessels gradually disappeared elsewhere around Britain.

For me, much of the fascination of researching the later years of the life of the company has lain in the way in which I was able to discover how business was transacted beyond the confines of just the Bristol Channel, and seeing how the postwar P. & A. Campbell Ltd territory was at times not much less extensive than at its heyday in 1914, before the Great War. A key theme of this book is indeed to do with the modest expansion of activities that got underway in the 1960s, once business had reached a rock-bottom level after the turbulence of the late-1950s, and then underwent a lean period, rather than the capitulation to changing tastes that characterised certain other coastal regions of Britain.

In the words of Norman Bird, it was a very different scene after 1967 once the last paddle-steamer had been withdrawn and departed for the breakers:

'For me, the passing of **Bristol Queen** is the end of the traditional firm of P. & A. Campbell Ltd. The firm ceased to be independent when Nott Industries took it over, but the ships remaining in service were at least a link with past glories and the high reputation established by Peter and Alexander Campbell, even though, in the remaining paddlers, that glory was somewhat faded. But *Bristol Queen* was the last ship in service to have been built for Bristol Channel work and the last in service to have been part of the company before Nott days. Now, it seems, P. & A. Campbell Ltd is chiefly a pawn in the financial operations of Nott Industries Ltd and does not, even theoretically, own any ships for *Westward Ho* and *St. Trillo* are registered in the ownership of another Nott subsidiary, Townsend Ferries Ltd (according to *Lloyd's Register*) and *Balmoral* is merely chartered from Red Funnel. *Bristol Queen* was (at the time of writing, 1969) in every way the last ship owned by P. & A. Campbell Ltd R.I.P. !'

Having myself missed out on the Campbell paddle-steamer era, when I first set eyes on *Balmoral* in 1974 it never crossed my mind that over thirty years later she would still be sailing, revitalised with new engines and looking just as good as when she was launched back in 1949. There can be little doubt that she has kept alive a Bristol Channel – and elsewhere – coastal cruising tradition which might otherwise have lapsed, and so although the title of this book might strictly be a little misleading, its purpose is to take the P. & A. Campbell Ltd story beyond where others have already described it in different ways, and perhaps also to set the scene for the successful preservation movement which, with *Waverley*, started in Scotland at virtually the same time that I was able to experience at least the late years of the once great White Funnel Fleet.

Westward Ho, *the former Isle of Wight ferry* **Vecta.**

A. K. Pope

"Westward Ho"

Chapter 1
SEVENTY-FIVE YEARS OF P. & A. CAMPBELL LTD

Setting the scene to 1958

The three phases of P. & A. Campbell Ltd

It is, perhaps, only natural that a long-lived company should undergo distinct phases during its existence. P. & A. Campbell Ltd was created as a limited company in 1893 after the Campbell brothers commenced their operation of excursions by paddle-steamer in the Bristol Channel with the first *Waverley* in 1887, and much happened in the period until the start of this story in the mid-1950s, after the business had developed and grown but gradually gone into decline. Throughout the first sixty years of life of P. & A. Campbell Ltd and, indeed on into the 1960s, successive company letterheads proudly (and accurately) proclaimed the purpose of the business as being Passenger Steamship Owners, and the term 'The White Funnel Fleet' gradually came into use, which projected a very definite image to the travelling public. Destined to not quite make its century, the business could be said to have been through three distinct phases up until its effective demise in 1980, punctuated by two wars. The Great War in 1914 ended the first phase during which the company reached its greatest fleet size ever, with a remarkable fourteen paddle-steamers on the books at one point, operating across an impressive territory which took in the South Coast and trips to France as well as being dominant in the home waters of the Bristol Channel.

In its second phase, a somewhat smaller fleet of eleven vessels was operated in most seasons between the wars, and the continuing influence of both Peter and Alec Campbell as the founders of the company was still significant for much of the inter-war years period, and who respectively survived until 1938 and 1928 and personified this 'old order'. During this second phase South Coast operations continued to be a significant part of company turnover, and the white

funnel was also seen in the south-west for a couple of seasons with excursions provided from various ports and harbours between Dorset & Cornwall, whilst Bristol Channel traffic remained as the core business of P. & A. Campbell Ltd.

After the end of the Second World War the depleted fleet that had survived was only initially able to offer a very limited range of excursions in the Bristol Channel in 1946, and South Coast services did not recommence until the following year. In the third phase of the existence of P. & A. Campbell Ltd, reduced to a fleet of just half a dozen paddle-steamers, the influence of the 'old order' to some extent was still initially apparent. Much of the management of the company and its practices were those which had characterised the business before the outbreak of hostilities in 1939, which had brought about the cessation of normal operations. This third phase, however, can be seen as dividing into two, rather different eras. Although the 'old order' re-established itself in 1946 as excursions by the veteran *Ravenswood* (dating from 1891) were resumed, it was obvious that new tonnage was needed to make good at least some of the lost capacity. Only three other paddle-steamers had survived the conflict such that restoration was feasible, in addition to a substantial, turbine-steamer which had only been completed after World War Two was underway, and which was never deployed as intended on cross-channel excursions to France. These vessels were, respectively, *Britannia* (b.1896), *Glen Usk* (b.1914), *Glen Gower* (b.1922) and *Empress Queen* (b.1940). To this fleet of five surviving ships, it was intended that four new vessels be added, all traditional paddle-steamers, but in the event only two of these were constructed.

Tastes and trends were changing and although there were three postwar seasons, 1948-1950, during which P. & A. Campbell Ltd did run seven vessels, in the Bristol Channel and along the Sussex coast,

*A postcard view of a nearly-new **Cardiff Queen** at Ilfracombe, franked in 1949: note the orderly parking.*   Author's collection

9

CAMPBELL'S SAILINGS

(Weather and circumstances permitting)

DAY TRIPS AND AFTERNOON CRUISES
in the Bristol Channel
FROM
THE PIER, ILFRACOMBE
DURING THE SUMMER SEASON.

CATERING ON BOARD.

FOR PARTICULARS APPLY

P. & A. Campbell, Ltd., 10 The Quay, Ilfracombe.   Tel. 687.

or Head Office :

1 Britannia Buildings, Cumberland Basin, Bristol 8.

Typical early postwar years style of publicity.
Ilfracombe Official Guidebook for 1950

plus another foray in the south-west in 1951 with *Empress Queen*, trading circumstances became progressively more difficult. Declining results led to drastic changes after the 1956 season, when the company withdrew from its traditional Bristol operational headquarters and engineering base. This represented the end of the 'old order', as I have defined it. Thus, the second era of the third phase was that where a 'new order' supplanted the old, with changed management, greatly slimmed-down operations and an element of austerity. Somehow these tactics enabled the company to survive rather than succumb, as did various other excursion-steamer operators in the 1960s and 1970s. The main focus of this book is therefore on the business of P. & A. Campbell Ltd during the latter part of this third and final phase of existence, spanning a little more than the two decades of the 1960s and 1970s.

These two decades cannot really be considered in isolation from the turbulent events of the earlier, very different era of the 1950s, which marked the transition from the old ways to the new. The two new postwar paddle-steamers *Bristol Queen* and *Cardiff Queen*, which had entered service in 1946 and 1947 respectively, were the continuity with the past, albeit with the concession to modernity of being oil-fired rather than coal-burners. It was basically these ships which kept the company going through the very lean period of the early-1960s, after all the old-timers had departed one by one to the breakers. The transition from the old order to the new was personified through Clifton Smith-Cox, who initially joined the Board in 1952, and became Joint Managing Director after the 1954 season, which had been designated as 'The Centenary Year' in recognition of the beginnings of Campbell operations in the Holy Loch trade on the Firth of Clyde with the paddle-steamer *Express* in 1854. A century later, the P. & A. Campbell Ltd territory had more or less developed to its maximum postwar extent, and so the 1954 season perhaps provides the optimal starting-point for this study of the last two decades of the company.

Turning point - The Centenary Year, 1954

A very brief thumbnail sketch here of the early-1950s points the way towards what was to follow. After the withdrawal in 1951 of the turbine-steamer *Empress Queen*, which had been based at Torquay in another attempt to generate traffic there and which ultimately failed, P. & A. Campbell Ltd were left with half-a-dozen paddle-steamers for 1952 and thereafter. The newest, *Cardiff Queen*, was used in 1952 and 1953 on the Sussex coast station, primarily running trips from Brighton's two piers, whilst the other five vessels remained in the Bristol Channel. This fleet size basically permitted one each to be based at Bristol, Newport and Swansea with two at Cardiff, although much inter-working

CAMPBELL'S SAILINGS

By P.S. "CARDIFF QUEEN"

(Weather and circumstances permitting)

From
EASTBOURNE
PIER

Another example of early postwar years publicity, South Coast 1952/1953 when **Cardiff Queen** *(and not* **Bristol Queen** *as per the block) was the Brighton steamer.*

Author's collection

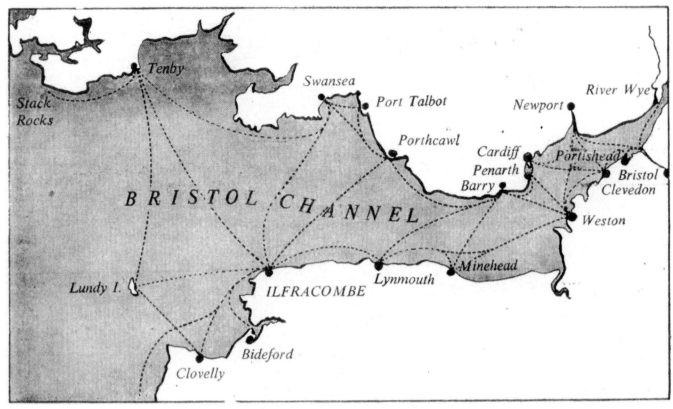

1954 'Centenary Year' map of the Bristol Channel area. This map was then correct inasmuch as Mumbles was omitted, but the connection between Tenby and Lundy was somewhat tenuous.
Author's collection

took place. With their carefully tailored schedules the management of P. & A. Campbell Ltd had always been adept in dealing with tidal constraints, and positioning their ships in the right place for fuelling to avoid dead mileage. **Cardiff Queen** was recalled to the Bristol Channel for the 1954 'Centenary Year', whilst **Glen Gower** was sent around to be the Brighton steamer. It was not until 1954 that cross-channel trips could restart, for which **Glen Gower** had the requisite certification: immediately prior to this, postwar South Coast trips from the Sussex piers had been confined to more or less following the coastline, either eastwards towards Folkestone or westwards towards the Isle of Wight, which was a rather less extensive range than that which had been operated with a bigger fleet before the Second World War.

In this manner, an extensive service could still be offered throughout the Bristol Channel in 1954 by **Ravenswood**, **Britannia**, **Glen Usk** and the newer **Bristol Queen** and **Cardiff Queen**. This fleet size enabled practically daily sailings from all main ports and piers, and when

required on busier days a goodly number of trips from the other up-Channel ships would augment those offered by whichever vessel was allocated to Cardiff-Weston 'ferry' duties. The territory of the White Funnel Fleet then embraced the destinations of Clevedon, Weston, Minehead harbour (from 1951), Ilfracombe, Lundy, Penarth, Barry and Porthcawl, but not Mumbles Pier which had closed after damage sustained in 1939 and then awaited the re-opening of the landing-stage. Swansea publicity therefore referred to the times at which one could catch a tram from Mumbles around the bay to catch a Swansea steamer departure from the South Dock entrance. Under the banner of 'The Centenary Year' calls were reinstated in 1954 at a number of extra locations in the Bristol Channel, namely Portishead, Lynmouth, Bideford, Clovelly, Tenby and Port Talbot; of these half-dozen (except at Lynmouth) calls would tend to be offered occasionally rather than regularly. It so happened that Sandown Pier, on the Isle of Wight, again became available for traffic in 1954, and that location conveniently

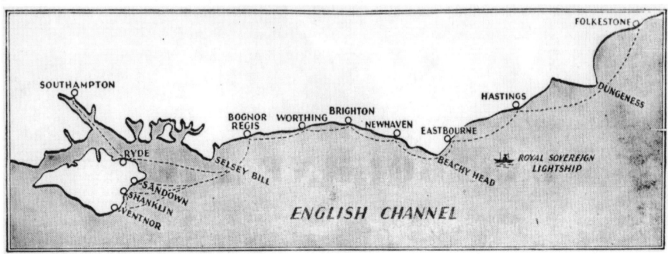

1954 'Centenary Year' map of the South Coast area.
Author's collection

11

became an additional South Coast excursion destination that year. A rather wider range of trips could now be advertised from the regular White Funnel Fleet ports of call as well as from these extra calling-points. Publicity material was then produced generally at weekly intervals for individual locations to advertise the range of cruises, and handbills incorporated summary descriptions of scenic highlights along the coastline on all the main routes followed by the steamers. New route maps were incorporated into 1954 handbills to illustrate this very substantial territory, and they make a useful point of reference for the gradual contraction of activity that followed this postwar high-point of White Funnel Fleet excursions.

Regrettably, the trading results of the 1954 season were not good, and the attempt at expansion was somewhat dulled. After being in prolonged lay-up since the end of the 1951 season *Empress Queen* was finally sold to the Greeks early in 1955, but fetched rather less than had she been disposed of when still in fully operational condition four years earlier. Although it had been intended that *Ravenswood* would run in 1955, she failed a pre-season inspection, and was thus withdrawn before entering service that year. There was therefore a slight thinning of services around the upper Bristol Channel in 1955, but circumstances were still not good for the company. Increasingly, the influence of Clifton Smith-Cox would now be felt as more drastic measures became necessary.

Sidney Clifton Smith-Cox, CBE, TD, FCA, FHCI, JP, 1911-1991

Clifton Smith-Cox was an accountant by profession, and his first formal involvement with P. & A. Campbell Ltd can be dated back to well before the 'old order' gave way to the new. The first mention of him in the Minute Books of Directors Meetings is recorded on 25th March 1952, when he accepted an invitation to join the Board, having been proposed by the then Chairman, G. H. Boucher. At this stage W. G. Banks occupied the position of Managing Director, in succession to Peter Campbell after his retirement at the end of 1935, whilst G. H. Boucher had occupied the post of Chairman since 1934

after the death of Ivie Dunlop. It is probably accurate to state that whilst he had more than a passing interest in the steamers themselves, Clifton Smith-Cox was a businessman first and foremost, as well as being a prominent Clevedon resident. Educated at Clifton College in Bristol, and with a wartime record involving service as a Lieutenant-Colonel in Malaya and taking part in the invasion of Normandy, becoming a Director of P. & A. Campbell Ltd only initially required attendance at periodic Board meetings, typically monthly, in a company structure where a full management team got on with the basic task of running its day-to-day affairs. He was an imposing character, urbane and politically astute, active and well-connected, yet he described his Directorship to the author as being his 'hobby', albeit in a slightly tongue-in-cheek manner. He had interests as a shareholder, and in reality a serious intent to run a business above all else. He had a range of business interests, some of which were based in Bristol, and which included the theatre as well as Bristol Zoo, and at one point, as a JP, was Chairman of the Long Ashton Bench.

His influence soon became considerable, and he was appointed as Joint Managing Director (with W. G. Banks) in March 1954. W. G. Banks (i.e. Bill Banks 'Junior') had succeeded his father W. J. Banks as Managing Director following his retirement in 1953 after distinguished long service with the company going back to 1897, almost the very beginning. By the end of the 'Centenary Year' season of 1954, for which it had been considered prudent to form a Management Committee in which Clifton Smith-Cox presided as Chairman, power changed hands quickly, and at the Directors Meeting on 16th December 1954 it was recorded that the services of W. G. Banks were terminated. At the same time Clifton Smith-Cox was authorised to borrow up to £150,000 from the Westminster Bank, a very considerable sum of money, and, as a qualified Accountant, his appointment was linked to a condition being imposed by the Bank to safeguard their interests as a 'clean pair of hands', in a company whose financial performance had been drifting steadily downhill. There was no instant cure in 1955, although better weather mitigated matters somewhat.

A sad occasion as **Empress Queen** *left Bristol for the last time on 3rd April 1955, after her sale to Kavounides for further service after extensive conversion to become a Greek cruise ship. This view admirably illustrates the pontoon at Hotwells then still in regular use by P. & A. Campbell Ltd for Bristol sailings.*

late George Owen collection

The 'Centenary Year', 1954, proved to be the last year in which **Ravenswood** *was operated. Built in 1891, she was rebuilt on a number of occasions over the years, the last such being in 1946 when she acquired concealed paddle-boxes. She is seen here approaching Clevedon Pier from Newport, Cardiff and Weston-super-Mare in June 1949, in this final form.* C. Hawkins Garrington, via the late George Owen

One of the postwar Queens calls off Lynmouth, where passengers were landed by launch on the slip (to the extreme right of the picture). After the flood disaster in 1952 which led to the cessation of steamer calls, Lynmouth was 're-opened' in 1954 as part of the Centenary Year initiative. Author's collection

Sailings from
PORTHCAWL
by the Steamers of the
White Funnel Fleet

P. & A. CAMPBELL, LTD.

CENTENARY YEAR 1854—1954

A 1954 'Centenary Year' billhead.   Author's collection

The 1950s were difficult times and it fell to the new MD to steer the company through receivership and subsequently into new ownership, when any management prevarication may well have led to outright failure, and where strong leadership and resolution were necessary. This quick canter through the early years of his tenure illustrates the combined effects of a declining market and an ageing fleet, which had left some to infer that cessation of trading was practically a certainty, but in fact others believed that perseverance would bring dividends and that the business could continue if some form of financial reconstruction could be arranged to give a new foundation to such a reduced scale of activities. This is my own conjecture, but I believe that Clifton Smith-Cox would have produced detailed cash-flow projections which demonstrated that, shorn of practically all overheads, and with a drastically thinned management structure, there was still just enough business about to make a return on capital if the assets were used intensively, and he thereby satisfied the Receiver. Through these difficult years an old order had gradually been superseded by a new one. Clifton Smith-Cox became virtually the sole person making the decisions, albeit supported by a handful of others. His creative skills as an accountant were undoubtedly put to good use behind the scenes throughout 1959 as details emerged of a complex financial reconstruction package, which was put to shareholders at the end of the year.

George Nott Industries, who owned the expanding Townsend Ferries business which had been established at Dover to compete with the railway-owned cross-channel steamers, were to take on the debt of P. & A. Campbell Ltd and inject new capital, and tied in with this deal was a requirement that Clifton Smith-Cox should remain as sole Managing Director to take the new venture forward. The bottoming-out of the affairs of the company had arrived, old shares had been traded for new, but few could have accurately predicted the way in which the next two decades would see modest expansion, the substitution of motor-vessels for paddle-steamers, and an expedient business relationship developed with Townsend Ferries and their successors which was to provide a vital source of income in the 1960s. This involved business being transacted from old South Coast ports-of-call, in the name of P. & A. Campbell Ltd, on the first *Free Enterprise* and later car-ferry vessels. Other coastal excursion operators, such as the Liverpool and North Wales Steamship Company, were to succumb but there was now a determination that P. & A. Campbell Ltd should survive.

We go back now, to look a little more closely at how the enormous changes wrought by the 1950s were, on the one hand, presented to shareholders and, on the other, at just what it was that became the foundation of effectively a new company, albeit with the old name and continuity of operation. It may still have been called P. & A. Campbell Ltd, but after financial restructuring, more visible changes were being shaped. Some would not have agreed with the scale of change imposed, but on balance it appears that the inevitability of radical change was acknowledged. Inevitably the name of Clifton Smith-Cox thus recurs frequently throughout this story: others had vital management roles but for practically thirty years he was to be the constant and the one most frequently giving the information to the media and to passengers. Often in the spotlight, too, as the embodiment of the company, he was there until the end, in the early-1980s.

Financial problems accrue

In many ways the 1954 season could be said to have marked a turning point in the fortunes of the White Funnel Fleet. There had been positive attempts to stimulate interest in paddle-steamer excursions as well as a genuine effort to boost carryings of people going to and from their holidays in the West of England. The effect of board-room changes were evident in the new publicity styles to promote the additional locations now served, and heightened direct sales efforts. As things turned out, 1954 was to be the last year in which five vessels continued to operate in the Bristol Channel, although more effort had been made to use these assets to better commercial advantage. However, there is little evidence that the results were analysed during the season itself: the Management Committee met on a number of occasions during the season and on 20th August 1954, despite what was described as a long discussion that went on until after lunchtime (sic) still no decisions

P. & A. CAMPBELL LTD. & BRITISH RAILWAYS
PERIOD BOOKINGS
by DAILY SERVICE from
CARDIFF via WESTON-super-MARE
to the undermentioned Stations in
SOMERSET, DORSET, DEVON and CORNWALL
Commencing June 1st, 1950, and continuing until Sept. 30th, 1950
or such later date as the service may be in operation.

For particulars of the Sailings between Cardiff and Weston (weather and circumstances permitting), See Special Bills.

From CARDIFF to	THROUGH MONTHLY RETURN FARES. Saloon on Steamer.		From CARDIFF to	THROUGH MONTHLY RETURN FARES. Saloon on Steamer.	
	1st Class Rail	3rd Class Rail		1st Class Rail	3rd Class Rail
	s. d.	s. d.		s. d.	s. d.
BARNSTAPLE	38 9	29 0	MINEHEAD	30 11	23 9
BIDEFORD			NEWQUAY	77 5	54 9
via Dulverton	43 0	31 10	NEWTON ABBOT	41 3	30 8
BODMIN	66 11	47 9	PAIGNTON	45 0	33 2
BRIDPORT	35 8	26 11	PENRYN	79 8	56 3
BRIDGWATER	16 3	14 0	PENZANCE	87 0	61 2
CHARD	26 0	20 6	PERRANPORTH	82 2	57 11
CHEDDAR	16 11	14 5	PLYMOUTH	54 8	39 7
CLEVEDON	14 2	12 7	REDRUTH	80 3	56 8
DARTMOUTH	47 11	35 1	SIDMOUTH	38 9	29 0
DAWLISH	38 2	28 7	ST. AGNES	79 8	56 3
DEVONPORT	54 8	39 7	ST. AUSTELL	70 6	50 2
DORCHESTER	35 2	26 7	ST. IVES	86 5	60 9
EXETER	33 5		TAUNTON	21 2	17 3
FALMOUTH	81	57 7	TEIGNMOUTH	39 5	29 5
FOWEY	69 5	49 5	TORQUAY	43 8	32 3
HELSTON	86 5	60 9	TOTNES	45 0	33 2
ILFRACOMBE			TRURO	76 9	54 4
via Dulverton	45 6	33 6	WADEBRIDGE	70 0	49 10
LISKEARD	62 0	44 6	WELLS	20 0	16 6
LOOE	65 2	46 7	WEYMOUTH	37 8	28 3
LOSTWITHIEL	66 11	47 9	YEOVIL	26 6	20 10
MARTOCK	23 6	18 10			

PERIOD BOOKINGS available for one calendar month will also be given to any station. Particulars of additional Fares, etc., obtainable on application.

BREAKS OF JOURNEY.—Passengers have the privilege of breaking the Outward and Homeward Journeys at any intermediate station on the direct line of route, for as long as convenient, while the tickets are available.

OUTWARD JOURNEY.—Passengers proceed from Weston-super-Mare (General Station) by any train after arrival of Steamer, and must produce both the Outward and Homeward portions of their Tickets whenever Tickets are examined on the journey broken, failing which the usual Single Journey Fare will become payable. The partially used Outward portion of a Ticket is not available when the Homeward half of the Ticket has been used for any part of the backward journey.

The Fares do not include Pier Tolls at Weston-super-Mare (4d. each way), nor the cost of conveyance between the Steamer and Station at Weston-super-Mare or vice versa. The Tickets are available by all Ordinary and Express trains, and for one journey only, to the Destination Stations and back, but passengers are permitted to break the journey as shewn above. For times of trains see the British Railways Time Tables.

LUGGAGE.—The following weights of personal luggage are allowed free of charge:—1st Class, 150lbs.; 3rd Class, 100lbs.

NOTICE.—The Company will not hold themselves responsible for the safety of any Passengers or intending Passenger before embarking on or after disembarking from any of their Steamers; reserve to themselves the right of calling at any ports or places for any purposes whatsoever, and do not hold themselves responsible to sail at the advertised times of departure or guarantee punctuality of arrival of Steamers, but will use every endeavour to carry out the sailings as announced.

The issuing of Through Tickets is subject to the Conditions and Regulations referred to in the Timetables, Books, Bills and Notices of the Steamboat Company, the Railway Executive and Proprietors on whose Steamboats, Railways, Coaches or Piers they are available; and the holder, by accepting a Through Ticket, agrees that the respective Undertakings and Proprietors are not liable for any loss, damage, injury, delay or detention caused or arising off their respective Steamboats, Railways, Coaches or Piers. The contract and liability of each Undertaking and Proprietor are limited to their own Steamboats, Railways, Coaches or Piers.

Tickets are to be obtained on board Steamers, or at the following British Railways (Western Region) Stations—Cardiff (General); Cardiff (Queen Street); Cardiff (Bute Road).

For further particulars, etc., apply to:
BRITISH RLYS. INQUIRY OFFICE, Cardiff (General) Station.
P. & A. CAMPBELL Ltd., Pier Head, Cardiff.
P. & A. CAMPBELL Ltd., Cumberland Basin, Bristol.

Telephones : Cardiff 3031. Weston 6784. Bristol 23112.
Telegrams : "Pier, Weston." "Ravenswood, Phone, Bristol."

Dates, Ltd., Printers, Cardiff—3,000

Comprehensive through-booking arrangements between the steamers of P. & A. Campbell Ltd and British Railways existed for holidaymakers, and others requiring period return tickets. This 1950 handbill typifies such arrangements for passengers.   Author's collection

WHITE FUNNEL FLEET

Sailings from
FOLKESTONE
HARBOUR

By **P.S.**
"GLEN
GOWER"

(Weather and circumstances permitting)

Cruise through the
STRAITS
OF DOVER

WEDNESDAY
↓
Aug. 11th
" **25th**
Sept. 8th

Leave Folkestone   Back at
3 p.m.   4.30 p.m.

Fare 5/-
(Children over 3 and under 14 years, Half Fare)

Circular trip to HASTINGS
(Out by Steamer, back by Train)

Leave Folkestone 4.45 p.m.   Due Hastings 7.0 p.m.
(Trains leave Hastings for Folkestone at 8.28 and 9.30 p.m.)

Return Fare **10/6**   (Single **6/6**)

Also Single Journey to **EASTBOURNE** (Fare **8/6**)
and **BRIGHTON** (Fare **11/-**)

Tickets to be obtained at Railway Booking Office, Folkestone Harbour Station
(Passengers should allow a margin of 10 minutes for boarding Steamer)

All Tickets are issued subject to P. & A. CAMPBELL'S conditions of carriage as exhibited on Steamer and to the Bye-Laws, Regulations and Conditions contained in the Publications and Notices of, or applicable to, the British Transport Commission

Further particulars from :

P. & A. CAMPBELL, Ltd., 25, Old Steine, Brighton. 'Phone 20711

Hastings Printing Co., Portland Place, Hastings. Telephone: 2450.

were taken at this stage. Indeed, little was thought to be amiss as late as 17th September 1954, the date of the next and what proved to be the last of the Management Committee meetings, and these particular records within the Minute Book stop abruptly here. At this point it was intended that, in view of the unsatisfactory results of the operation of *Glen Gower* on the South Coast the service would be suspended, and that – remarkably – six vessels would operate again in the Bristol Channel in 1955.

With the benefit of hindsight it is difficult to avoid the conclusion that Clifton Smith-Cox had become frustrated after his first few months as joint Managing Director, and had perhaps formed an opinion about which of his colleagues were effective, rather than those who were reluctant to face facts and tackle the trading difficulties being faced. The weather experienced in 1954 was not good and when the financial results became available later in the year, it was clear that losses had again been sustained despite the enhanced efforts that had been made, and it was felt necessary to send an explanatory letter to all shareholders. (A copy of this letter, dated 24th September 1954 is reproduced in the Appendix as item 1). The next event of note took place at the 16th December 1954 Board Meeting, which was to prove highly significant as this was the point at which Bill Banks (Junior) was, in effect, ousted and power substantially transferred to Clifton Smith-Cox, who then became sole Managing Director. One could reasonably assume that a minor coup of sorts took place, and that Mr Banks (Jnr) became a scapegoat for the fifth successive season of operating losses.

Left: Despite the standardisation of advertising styles for the 1954 'Centenary Year', this particular handbill appears to have been overlooked.   Author's collection

Below: **Bristol Queen**, *dressed overall, departing from Mumbles Pier on the day the pier finally re-opened for traffic, 9th June 1956. A late change of plan had meant that* **Cardiff Queen**, *the regular Swansea steamer, had been switched with* **Bristol Queen** *that day and an engraved silver cigarette case intended to be presented by the Mayor to Captain Gunn was instead received by Captain George.*   late George Owen collection

*Practically a timeless scene: **Britannia**, built in 1896, steams majestically along the Avon Gorge. No traffic is in sight on the road behind her. However, the two funnels marked her 1948 rebuild, which left her bereft of deckhouse accommodation. She is seen here on 20th July 1955.*

Chris Collard collection

The 1954 Accounts, when presented on 5th July 1955, were accompanied by a Statement by the Chairman, Arthur Roy Boucher, who had succeeded his father G. H. Boucher. This contained a curiously low-key reference to the better results of the 1954 season that the innovations had been expected to bring, but cited the poor weather as a major factor:

'It is very disappointing to me year after year to have to make animadversions about the bad weather which now appears to characterise the English summer and which is so crippling to the efforts which are being made to make the Company's business a success. The unfortunate fact remains, however, that of five successive stormy summers 1954 proved to be quite the worst. I think it speaks well for the management and employees of the Company that their enthusiasm and optimism remains undiminished in spite of what many people are beginning to regard as an alteration in the summer normally enjoyed by these islands.'

In going on to review particular features of the innovations of the 1954 season Mr Boucher stated that of the Bristol Channel re-openings, those at Bideford and Tenby had been best received: mention was also made of Sandown in the Isle of Wight which had re-opened to steamers as planned, and the disposal of the turbine steamer **Empress Queen** was noted. Details were given of the better prospects expected for South Coast business in 1955, compared to 1954, now

that negotiations had taken place which would permit the resumption of cross-channel excursions, after the company had had to contemplate bringing **Glen Gower** back to Bristol Channel traffic duties. On-board entertainment was cited as being successful, as was the incorporation of pier tolls in steamer fares at most locations, a practice which the Chairman hoped would become universal. Perhaps the most telling remarks were not made until the end of the statement, however:

'Your Directors are now satisfied that a start has been made upon the major operation of modernising the administration and outlook of the Company. Whereas we hardly expected any beneficial results from the innovations effected to be shown to any great extent in 1954, I cannot deny that the adverse season was a cruel blow and might well have been a fatal one but for the goodwill of the Company's Bankers ... no-one is under any illusion about the magnitude of the task before the Company or as to the probability of some form of capital reconstruction being necessary before too long.'

The recognition of the probable need for capital reconstruction was ominous. Mr Boucher concluded by alluding to the more promising start which had been made to the 1955 season on account of better weather, and he expressed optimism regarding the likely effect of actions in hand to try and improve the fortunes of the Company. As an aside, one might not nowadays expect to conjoin the words goodwill and bankers, but times were clearly very different then.

An unplanned event

The withdrawal of the veteran paddle-steamer *Ravenswood* before the start of the 1955 season was the first of several unplanned events which characterised much of the rest of the decade for the Company. As previously stated, it had been the firm intention that five steamers would again trade in the Bristol Channel during 1955. *Ravenswood* held a vital place in the history of the White Funnel Fleet, having been the first vessel specifically built – in 1891, at Ayr – for the Bristol Channel trade. She also had a fine wartime service record including minesweeping and, in the Second World War, anti-aircraft ship duties. Her appearance had undergone a number of changes over the years but she remained a coal-burner to the end, rather slower than her newer and larger oil-fired sisters **Bristol Queen** and **Cardiff Queen**. She was generally confined in her last years to up-channel duties, rarely if ever proceeding any further down-channel than Minehead and had in 1954 been much associated with Newport sailings. Her premature demise was all the more regrettable as it had been intended that during neap-tide periods in 1955, she was to be based at Ilfracombe for a number of three- or four-day spells, in order to offer long days ashore on Lundy and cruises additional to those normally offered by the steamers which had come down-channel.

Ravenswood in her original form had possessed two funnels and a single-cylinder engine. Re-engined and re-boilered in 1909 her appearance changed considerably as she then lost one funnel and had her bridge repositioned to be forward of the remaining funnel. Serving in both wars, an extensive refit was needed before she returned to P. & A. Campbell Ltd service in 1946, and this saw her acquire 'enclosed' paddle-boxes, although she retained her compound diagonal machinery from the 1909 alterations and remained a coal-burner. She was, therefore, the last open-foredeck type of steamer in the Campbell fleet, and rather shorter than the other paddlers. She looked delightful, especially so when she had proudly returned to service in 1946 to re-open the White Funnel Fleet's postwar business. When *Ravenswood* was dry-docked, prior to the 1955 season, it was discovered that there was extensive deterioration of her hull-plating and, quite simply, the cost of repairs estimated at £10,000 could not be justified. At the Meeting of Directors held on 19th May 1955 the decision to scrap *Ravenswood* was recorded on account of her hull-condition as '...*the mortgagees ... (were) ... not prepared to provide money for repairs*'. This was hardly surprising after five seasons of losses, between 1950 and 1954, and after the company had had to negotiate overdraft facilities with their Bankers. It must have been a severe disappointment that, having had such a substantial rebuild only nine years beforehand, the ship had to be put aside like this. George Owen described the scenario thus:

'...in 1945-46 she would have been subject to a most rigorous inspection by the M.o.T. surveyor before being granted a passenger certificate. After the war the bottoms of the ships were not so carefully looked after as hithertofore. It was the custom to give the underwater bodies two coats of anti-corrosive and two coats of anti-fouling. After the war, it was one coat of black bituminous, this would never have been countenanced by Peter Campbell.'

On announcing that *Ravenswood* would not feature in 1955 Bristol Channel operations, it was stated in one newspaper that the overall level of sailings offered would scarcely be affected by her withdrawal, and that her place would be taken by another steamer. However no evidence can be traced to substantiate this opinion, and it is hardly likely that *Empress Queen* could have been contemplated as a direct replacement since her sale to Greek interests had been virtually completed. More likely might have been the return of *Glen Gower* to the Bristol Channel, but that vessel was to stay at Brighton for another couple of seasons. What actually happened in 1955 was that the company's capacity to handle occasional peaks in traffic – especially at Bank Holidays - was reduced as the remaining up-Channel steamers were worked harder to fill the gaps.

There was considerable sadness in the announcement that her days had ended and she lay, for the duration of the 1955 season, in Merchants Dock at Bristol awaiting her future. An offer by the British Iron & Steel Corporation of £3,300 in the autumn to break up *Ravenswood* had already been accepted. She left the Cumberland Basin under tow for the last time early in the morning on Friday 21st October, and by 0930 she was tied up alongside Cashmore's wharf on the River Usk at Newport for breaking. Little time was lost in starting the scrapping process and by the end of the month a photograph in the local newspapers showed her bereft of all structures above the promenade deck. The Chairman wrote to shareholders on 5th July 1955 to report on the 1954 season and developments therein, and briefly commented upon the withdrawal of *Ravenswood*, in these terms:

'... your Directors are now satisfied that a start has been made upon the major operation of modernising the administration and outlook of the Company ... it was a disappointment, though not altogether a surprise, in view of her age and service in two world wars, to have to reach a decision to take *Ravenswood* out of service. I can however assure shareholders that the effect of these reverses on the Board and Management has been stimulation and not despair.'

Despite earning a modest profit in 1955 things were still not right. Losses had been successively incurred during a number of successive postwar seasons and finances were still on a knife-edge. Attempts were being made to squeeze more out of less, so to speak, as the operating territory had been expanded whilst the fleet strength had started to decline. One positive factor was the use of Avonmouth to give better sailing-times when tides were adverse for Bristol, and which had required an agreement with British Railways locally for the provision of rail connections and through ticketing arrangements. Less satisfactory for the trading position was the continued non-availability of Mumbles Pier, which reduced the earning potential of the Swansea steamer, with poor weather cited as the reason behind prolonged delays in reconstruction of the pier landing-stage. The weather which, as ever, was fundamental in influencing results, had been better in 1955. Norman Bird described the results very succinctly:

'... the Company's trading profit was £26,761, but, by the time depreciation, bank charges and other charges were allowed for, the net profit was only £8,742. If this was all five ships could make in a glorious summer, with capacity crowds on all popular sailings, it should have been fairly clear that there were too many ships and, somewhere, either (a) expenses which were too high and/or unnecessary, and/or (b) sailings which were a dead loss.'

As it turned out, 1956 was to be the greatest year of change for the affairs of P. & A. Campbell Ltd and these changes were to be threefold. Firstly, there was the almost unthinkable withdrawal from Bristol itself as both the headquarters of the Company and the place where the ships wintered and were maintained. Secondly, there was the withdrawal of another vessel, which also was the last link with the 1890s, and the laying-up of a third paddle-steamer. Thirdly, there was a substantial cutback to the territory in which operations had been carried out practically since the very earliest days. Whilst the withdrawal of *Ravenswood* had been unplanned, it is clear from statements made to shareholders that a realisation was dawning that more drastic cutbacks were going to be needed, and the 1956 changes, when they came, had to a degree been foreseen and planned for. A few weeks before the AGM was due to be held, a particularly detailed Statement by the Chairman was issued to shareholders, dated 3rd July 1956, and which was quite explicit in stating the inevitability of change. (This statement is reproduced in full in Appendix One as Item 2). With the critical peak-season months of July and August – during which the steamers normally earned as much as in April-June and September-October put together – everyone was hoping that income could be maximised by a spell of kind weather. As it happened the weather was cold and wet, and by the time set for the AGM on Thursday 26th July, it had become clear that changes were going to be effected sooner rather than later. Shareholders would have received all of this information at the point at which the season would have been getting into full swing with four paddle-steamers active in the Bristol Channel. The fifth, **Glen Gower**, had started up another South Coast season with the confidence that would have been generated by the welcome news that 'No-Passport' trips could at last be resumed from Brighton to the Continent, though this easement had been a long time coming and was arguably too late to really help the company's prospects there.

Withdrawal from Bristol

Described as a 'surprise announcement' in newspaper reports of the Shareholders Meeting at the Grand Hotel in Bristol, Mr Boucher spoke to reporters afterwards to enlarge upon his statement that the Company had decided to move their headquarters from Bristol to Cardiff to save costs, having been '... *sending their steamers from Bristol since 1887...*'. The announcement was coupled with the information that the Company was not in a position to pay any dividend on either the Preference or Ordinary shares, and that operating costs were soaring.

The *Bristol Evening World* summed up the position, as follows:

CAMPBELL'S WILL MOVE TO CARDIFF
City's Poor Support

P. & A. Campbell ... are transferring their business from Bristol to Cardiff. Mr A. Roy Boucher, Chairman of the company, told the Evening World 'I know that this will come as a big shock for Bristol, but we must think of the company's financial position. We will save a lot of money by moving to Cardiff'. But this is not the only reason why Campbells have decided to break the long link with Bristol. Said Mr Boucher: 'It is a sad fact that we carry 12 people from Wales for every one from Bristol'.

For many months the company's directors have been discussing the prospect of a move to Wales and today Mr Boucher put the proposal to shareholders in this way: 'I don't like having to say this and I must emphasise that we have no quarrel with Bristol or the Port of Bristol Authority. But I cannot help being disappointed with the small number of people we take from Bristol. It is a costly business making the long journey down the river. To carry on here would be expensive in overheads. I understand that all the facilities we need for our ships are available to us in Cardiff.' How will Bristolians be affected? Mr S. Smith-Cox, a director, said: "The number of sailings from Bristol next year - that is when we intend to move - will depend entirely on the number of people who support Bristol sailings for the rest of the year. I know that sounds like a threat, but we must obviously base our plans on something". The shareholders sat quietly while the announcement was made, but when Mr Boucher sat down there was a buzz of conversation. Then a vote of thanks to Mr Boucher and the directors for the way they are handling the company's business was passed unanimously.

On a positive note, it was hoped and expected that the takings of the Swansea steamer would improve as a result of the eventual re-opening in 1956 of Mumbles Pier, which had not been used by Campbell steamers since 1939 on account of its condition, but which was now repaired and resumed its rightful place again in the territory of the White Funnel Fleet.

It is clear from Company records that withdrawal from Bristol had actually been under consideration at Board level for some time, and had first been mentioned in the Company Minutes for 19th May 1955, when the Board had agreed that it was necessary to investigate '... *income and expenditure in connection with the works ...*' and that this '... *should be dealt with after ... the last winter overhaul completed*'. This decision was taken at the same time as the sale of **Empress Queen** had gone through, and the withdrawal of **Ravenswood** confirmed. It is reasonable to assume that such a fleet reduction would inevitably have left the ship repair side of the business seeming somewhat exposed, with fewer vessels across which to spread remaining overheads.

Having forewarned their customers in July 1956 of what was in store, matters did not improve for the White Funnel Fleet later that season. The Board Meeting held on 5th October 1956 was particularly significant in terms of the magnitude of the decisions taken, and which were to profoundly influence the future of the Company. Describing the 1956 summer as '... *disastrous due to the bad weather ...*' and recording a trading loss of £35,000, it was noted that the number of Boulogne passengers had fallen from 16,000 in 1955 to 12,000 in 1956, and that twelve trips had to be cancelled. At this point however, no decision was taken to suspend South Coast sailings, of which more anon. The cutbacks were not spelt out in any particular order but what they amounted to was that P. & A. Campbell Ltd would cease to be a Bristol company, which meant that the Bristol office (i.e. No's 1 & 2, Britannia Buildings) would be sold (to the Bristol Mutual Meat Traders, for a sum of £3,250), and that alternative office premises at Dock Chambers, Cardiff would be leased, at £275 p.a. rent. The 'in-house' maintenance of the fleet at Bristol would end, and the Underfall Yard and associated premises were to be disposed of. An arrangement with the Penarth Pontoon Co. for winter lay-up of the fleet was to be entered into, on the understanding that the ship's engineers would work by the steamers in Penarth Dock during the winter. There would be redundancies of Officers, in particular Captain Murphy and Chief Engineers Soloman and Taylor, with

Britannia Buildings, Bristol, close to the Cumberland Basin and the former Underfall Yard, were the offices of P. & A. Campbell Ltd until 1956. Seen here in 1996. Author

BRISTOL

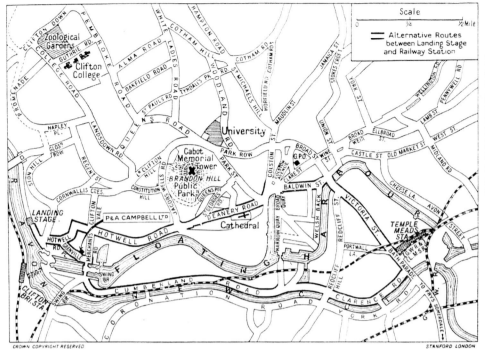

*Town map of Bristol, from the 1939 edition of the **Bristol Channel District Guide**, showing the location of the pontoon at Hotwells. This map also pinpointed the company offices. The Underfall Yard maintenance facility was located on the south side of the Floating Harbour, very close to the Swing Bridge marked. The pontoon landing-stage continued in use until 1971, whereafter occasional calls would generally be made in the Cumberland Basin entrance-lock.*
Author's collection

provision for compensation, and the Newport office would close. The veteran paddle-steamer **Britannia** would be withdrawn. As a gesture of goodwill towards the Bristol-based shipwrights it was agreed that **Glen Gower** would in fact remain in Bristol for the winter, to be maintained by Charles Hill. The intention at this stage was that three steamers would operate in the Bristol Channel in 1957 (including one stationed at Swansea), and that **Glen Gower** would return to the south coast again.

By any reckoning this was a big package of changes but, despite the cutbacks that were to affect the Bristol maritime scene, a degree of understanding was apparent by the media even after the announcements of the move to Cardiff and associated cutbacks had been made. The *Western Daily Press*, on 27th July 1956, had commented:

KEEPING THE FLAG FLYING

'... this is not a sentimental world and ships, particularly a fleet such as Campbells, catering solely for the holidaymaker, cannot be run on happy memories and good wishes. The ships ... have given magnificent service ... their record on war-service is well-known, for not only the local ships but local men, too, were on active service. The post-war years especially brought almost complete revolution to the holiday habits of the British public. "Relaxation" today, for the vast majority of people, demands something fast and furious, with speed, "snap" and constant variety ... Campbell's have fought hard to keep their flag flying. We have watched with sympathy their efforts by modern innovation and adventurous ideas, to win back the popularity which once packed their ships in every port and resort.

The latest move, a regrettable one from Bristol's point of view, could only have been taken after serious consideration. The sorry fact is that this city with its half-million people has lost the right to be the home port of the fleet, for it has not supported local enterprise as it should have done. In going to South Wales P. & A. Campbell go over, with every justification, to the population from whence it draws its main source of present livelihood and hope. At least we can wish them well, not only for old times sake, but because such local courage and enterprise against heavy odds deserves to triumph.'

However, events had moved on rapidly as the season progressed and when the Board reconvened again, on Wednesday 31st October 1956, further economies were to be decided upon.

4, Dock Chambers, Bute Street, Cardiff became the offices of P. & A. Campbell Ltd after withdrawal from Bristol in 1956, for much of the subsequent life of the company. Seen here in the late-1990s. Author

A charming publicity picture from the 1950s showing the White Funnel Fleet excursion steamer at Boulogne after arrival from the Sussex coast, with one of the Eagle steamers on the other side of the harbour, and a railway ferry. At low water it was quite a descent to this berth. **Glen Gower** *ran such cross-channel trips as there were in the period 1954-56, initially just from Newhaven until restrictions at the pleasure piers were eased.*

Peter Southcombe collection

Further economies

It appears that the first 'package' of economies had been insufficient to satisfy the bankers of P. & A. Campbell Ltd, and at this second Board Meeting they agreed to the continuing £150,000 overdraft provision on condition that South Coast sailings were abandoned, that **Britannia** was disposed of (rather than be merely held in reserve, as had been mooted) and that the Company needed to '... *dispense with the services of certain employees and cut out all unnecessary employment ...*'. The sale of the goodwill of the Campbell & Banks engineering concern was

recorded at £5,500, and further redundancies included those of Captain Harris, two mates and two pursers. As a consequence of the decision by R. J. T. (Bob) Campbell to take retirement from his position as the Company's Agent at Weston-super-Mare, the South Coast Agent was to be transferred to Weston, and the abandonment of Newport sailings was decided upon. As a consequence of this further package of cuts, fleet deployment plans were altered so that **Bristol Queen** was expected in 1957 to become the principal long-distance steamer based at Cardiff, and **Cardiff Queen** would stay as the Swansea steamer.

Glen Usk would go into reserve and the slightly younger *Glen Gower* take her place on 'ferry' duties. It only remained that year to note, at the December 21st 1956 Board Meeting, that apart from the sale of *Britannia* the long-serving Company Secretary Joseph W. J. (Joe) Jenkins would retire on 31st December after forty-nine years of service with the Company, twenty-one of them as Secretary.

Even if it appeared to some that running excursion steamers was a service rooted in tradition, and that any type of cutback was regrettable, the necessity to run a viable business remained in terms of the duty of the directors towards their shareholders and – more fundamentally, by this point – their creditors. Whilst the withdrawal of venerable steamships like *Ravenswood* and *Britannia* was very sad to those who had known them all their lives, the facilities they offered were perhaps becoming to be seen as rather basic compared to either the modern vessels or indeed completely alternative types of leisure amenities on offer then. In contrast to the sentiment and nostalgia evident in the media, there was an awareness that things had to change, and Norman Bird again succintly captured the issues in his writings in *Ship Ahoy* when analysing the 1956 season:

'... 1956 was not a good year for weather and the company trading loss was £56,725 - an all-time record. The ship's behaviour (i.e. that of *Bristol Queen*) during the season seemed to indicate that the standard of maintenance of the ships was declining. I have no doubt that the minimum requirements for survey and safety were complied with, but a certain shabbiness was creeping in, breakdowns were more prevalent and, indeed, the Company's financial situation was such that the most stringent economies had to be effected.'

To this end the Company decided to close down its own repair yard at Bristol, transfer its head office to Cardiff, as operations from Bristol had been declining, and lay up the ships in Penarth Dock, where officers and crew would carry out as much maintenance as possible but slipping and mechanical work would be contracted out. To minimise hardship at Bristol *Glen Gower* spent the winter there, for lay-up and overhaul, but all the other ships retired to Penarth. *Bristol Queen* went to Bristol when she finished on September 12th but kept steam up until the 17th when she was used to transfer as much P. & A. Campbell equipment as needed to be moved from Bristol to South Wales. This gave her the nickname of the 'furniture

van' among the enthusiasts for a couple of years – a derisory epithet, as not only was her accommodation still somewhat austere, if spacious, but it was now also shabby, and was not helped by the reduction in basket chair seating in the after deck-saloon. The chairs were, it is believed, removed for her to carry the 'furniture' but were never replaced! She was thus the first P. & A. C. Ltd ship to enter Penarth Dock.

The serious loss convinced the management that there were too many ships. *Glen Gower* had done badly on the South Coast, and the pontoon at Newport needed heavy repairs which the Newport Harbour Commissioners were unwilling to pay for. The effect of all this was:

a. *Britannia*, (60 years old, heavy on oil consumption, but having a relatively low passenger capacity, and wearing very thin) was scrapped three months after she finished sailing. In spite of her drawbacks she had been the stalwart of the 1956 season having maintained reliable high speeds during her last three seasons and I was very sad to see her going although I fully realised the inevitability of this even at the time.

b. The South Coast service was abandoned, apart from the experimental charter of G.S.N.'s twin screw diesel ship *Crested Eagle* for 1957 only and mainly on short cruises.

c. The cessation of sailings from Newport. *Glen Usk's* departure from Newport on 20th September 1956 was, thus, the last sailing from the pontoon.

d. *Glen Usk* was laid up for the season in 1957.'

Farewell *Britannia*

The farewell voyage of *Britannia* on 19th September 1956 received much attention by the press, which played heavily on the long and happy association between Bristol and what was thought of as very much a ship belonging to the city. It was a significant event for a number of reasons. Firstly, at 60 years of age, she was a venerable ship in her own right, and possibly better known – specifically as a celebrated Bristol ship - than her elder sister *Ravenswood*, whose earlier demise had not been pre-planned in any way and thus not marked by any sense of occasion. Secondly, she was the only postwar Campbell vessel, as things turned out, to have any kind of conscious send-off, as the other paddlers came to an end in later years either by way of breakdown (*Bristol Queen*) or by fading away after an uncertain period of lay-up (*Glen Gower*, and later *Glen Usk*) or even just being withdrawn without any finality being made apparent (*Cardiff Queen*). Even the latter-day motor-vessels had no particular send-off, and *Britannia* was probably unique amongst British coastal excursion ships in having occasioned a fly-past by the Bristol-built 'Whispering Giant' aircraft Britannia on her last planned day in service, on a trip sponsored by the *Bristol Evening World*. This brief quote from the *Bristol Evening Post* on her last day captured the scene:

'The Whispering Giant, the Britannia airliner, kept her promised rendezvous with her namesake, the veteran paddle-steamer, in dramatic fashion yesterday. Poor flying conditions had prevented the airliner paying a planned salute to the steamer off Weston. But just as passengers were landing from the steamer at Ilfracombe, the aircraft appeared over Capstone Hill. With Bill Pegg at the controls, the plane banked and flew down towards the pier. Then at 200ft., the aircraft flew low across the old steamer and turned for a second saluting run, which the steamer answered with a hoot of her siren. The famous old ship drew into Ilfracombe dead on time. Throughout her long career the veteran had a high reputation for punctuality.

Almost as if to salute the old *Britannia* on her last trip of all, the sun came out and passengers were able to sunbathe. Everywhere on her last voyage, there were waves and cheers from spectators ashore, and sirens sounded in salute from other vessels ... the steamer was given a memorable send-off at the Hotwells Landing-Stage. Crowds lined the river-wall and some cheered and clapped as she moved away to the strains of "Auld Lang Syne" from the Albion Dockyard Silver Band. Earlier, the Lord Mayor, Ald. G. A. Watson-Allan, accompanied by the

Advertisement to announce disposal of the 1896-built paddle-steamer **Britannia**, *placed in* **Lloyds List** *very shortly after the end of the 1956 season.* Miss Gwyneth White

Britannia *at Clovelly,*
19th July 1955.
Norman Bird

Lady Mayoress, made a farewell speech on board. He said " The long association of the Campbell's steamers, in particular the *Britannia*, is something one has come to believe to be permanent, but through all the tides of humanity, things change and circumstances alter".'

Notwithstanding this grand send-off, the following day **Britannia** was in service again taking over the sailings of **Glen Usk**, which had developed boiler trouble, until 26th September 1956, her final trip being on the Weston ferry late on that Wednesday evening. After this brief stay of execution she duly entered Penarth Dock to lay-up and was put up for sale. Her final voyage was from Penarth Dock on Friday 7th December 1956 at about 0730 to Newport, in fog, under tow by the tugs **Boxmoor** and **Rose**. It was expected that demolition would not take long.

Other matters, 1956

The retirement of Bob Campbell, who for the previous ten years had occupied the position of Agent at Weston, took place on 31st October 1956. One of two sons of Captain Peter Campbell who had founded the company, Bob Campbell had joined in 1913 as an apprentice marine engineer, serving in the First World War when commissioned in the Argyle & Sutherland Highlanders. Born in 1894, Robert John Turner Campbell became a director in January 1929, and did not finally relinquish this directorship until 23rd January 1960. The vacation of the post of Weston Agent meant that John MacDougall, the South Coast Agent at Brighton displaced by the cessation of services there, could continue in P. & A. Campbell Ltd employment, albeit at a new location.

Not all was total despondency, however, as it was announced that some Bristol trips would still be offered in 1957, and that although they were vacating No's 1 & 2 Britannia Buildings as their Headquarters, an enquiry office would remain at No. 3. Although all Avonmouth calls were to cease, and with them the useful connecting all-stations train services from Parson Street to Avonmouth Dock station which catered for a large area of Bristol on low-tide days, more combined ship and coach excursions to the Welsh Mountains were to be inaugurated, and more Ilfracombe trips were to be run, it being stated that the White Funnel Fleet was now carrying more people in and out of the North Devon resort than at any time in its history. Finally,

the company planned a special December issue of coupon books, at three-quarters of normal fares, where such tickets could be used not just by the purchasers but by any members of their families. Pointing out that three steamers would be used in the Bristol Channel in 1957, this statement confirmed that in addition to the two **Queens** being in service **Glen Usk** might be out but more probably it would be **Glen Gower**, then being 'conditioned' in Bristol. Neither of the two **Glens** were in particularly good shape at that stage, it being rumoured that the boiler of **Glen Usk** was 'half-full of mud', as the late H. G. Owen put it. In the event, 1957 proved to be the final year for **Glen Gower**, somewhat unusually on the 'ferry' as it turned out.

Closure of the Newport station

Mention had been made, at the 31st October 1956 Board meeting, of the abandonment of sailings from the long-established landing stage on the River Usk at Newport, very well sited just below the main road and railway bridges, and easily accessible to a large catchment in the Eastern and Western Valleys that looked to Newport rather than Cardiff. The Newport agency had been set up in the early days of the limited company, in 1895, when the fleet grew in strength, and after a Cardiff presence had been established. After the earlier fleet cutback in 1955, when **Ravenswood** had not re-appeared in service, the landing stage at Newport had continued to enjoy excursion sailings but inevitably no longer on a broadly daily basis after the fleet had been slimmed from five vessels on Bristol Channel duties to four. In effect Newport in the 1955 and 1956 seasons 'shared' the services of one of the Cardiff-based steamers, often **Glen Usk** or **Britannia**, whilst **Bristol Queen** usually resided at Bristol and **Cardiff Queen** at Swansea. It is worth considering this cutback of the Bristol Channel territory of P. & A. Campbell Ltd in some detail, as it typified the difficulties that the company would continue to experience into the 1960s before business levels stabilised again.

Owned by the Newport Harbour Commissioners and operated to all intents and purposes exclusively for the benefit of the excursion steamers in the season, the floating pontoon-berth was staffed by Harbour Commissioners personnel. In addition to an annual fee paid by P. & A. Campbell Ltd for the use of this facility, as well as a modest amount for office rental for space used by the Newport Agent, pier-tolls

NEWPORT

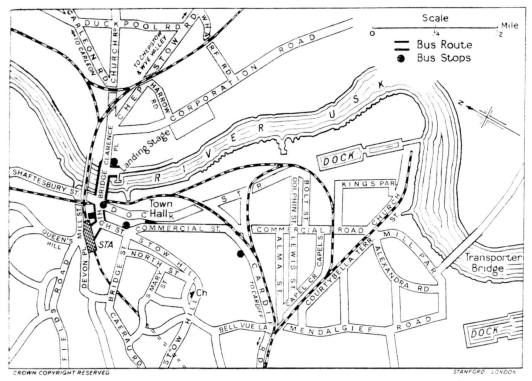

STANFORD LONDON

The town map of Newport, from the 1939 edition of the **Bristol Channel District Guide,** *showing the central location of the Landing Stage, which was operated by the Newport Harbour Commissioners mainly for the use of P. & A. Campbell Ltd passengers. The guide-book pointed out that the distance down the river to the Bristol Channel was around four miles, with much of interest to be seen on the way, including the spectacular Transporter Bridge.*
Author's collection

were charged by the Commissioners, who also raised charges for the supply of water to the steamers. Each year the operations of the landing stage were dealt with as an almost 'stand-alone' item in the Harbour Commissioners Report & Account documents, where a subsidiary profit and loss statement recorded income and expenditure and the number of steamer calls made each year as an indication to the Commissioners of the worth of this aspect of their responsibilities for the tidal river, its buoyage, and towage & wharfage activities. The landing-stage was clearly expected to 'pay its way' by the Commissioners who liked to think that their asset was being both properly utilised and providing an adequate level of service to the folk of Newport and Monmouthshire. Their relationship over the decades with P. & A. Campbell Ltd was of much interest, not least in the annual charter of a ship for the Harbour Commissioners inspection cruise. This would set off each year from the Newport landing-stage, in grand style, with the Commissioners and their guests on what would now be described as a 'hospitality' or corporate entertaining event, to stimulate trade with Newport and Monmouthshire shipping and industrial interests.

On the matter of throughput and service levels, the failure of **Britannia** in traffic in August 1954 had prompted some interesting comments in the south Wales newspapers of the period, and the consequent cancellation of a few Newport sailings seems to have caused a hardening of attitude in the minds of certain of the Harbour Commissioners when the time came for decisions to be made regarding this part of their business. After the veteran paddle-steamer sustained paddle-wheel damage on 24th August 1954, temporary repairs proved ineffective, and so she ended the season prematurely and sailed to Bristol to lay-up for the winter. Thus followed a number of days when, seemingly, Newport sailings were often cancelled but services from Cardiff were seen as being much less affected, causing a degree of ill-feeling that Newport was being shabbily treated by P. & A. Campbell Ltd. Writing in protest to the steamer company, Mr Arthur James, MBE, JP, said on behalf of the Commissioners that this was '... *a very dirty trick. It is bad for the town of Newport and for passengers who came down from the valleys and had to join the ship at Cardiff. We should point out this very bad treatment of Newport which accounts for the big decrease in passengers*'. To illustrate the point it was mentioned that the number of passengers paying toll at the Commissioner's

Newport landing-stage during August 1954 was 9,416, a decrease of 5,326 on August 1953. The company provided a full explanation to the Commissioners, which was made public, and which pointed out the comparatively greater operational restrictions on serving Newport for tidal reasons than applied at Cardiff, and stressed that Newport had not borne all of the cancellations as Cardiff and Bristol had suffered reductions too. Attributing much of the fall in passenger numbers to the weather, the company sought to repair the public relations damage caused, adding that in 1955 they were planning to not only improve the frequency of Newport sailings but also the times of their departure and return.

Another newspaper article of the time entitled 'Not So Sunny for Mr Hale' touched on the problems faced by Mr John Hale, the P. & A. Campbell Ltd Newport Agent. Perhaps the pun in the title was not entirely intentional, but the piece did sadly highlight the basic problem of adverse weather being experienced generally by the White Funnel Fleet:

'Almost every day this wet, miserable summer, Mr John Hale, the Newport Manager of Messrs. P. & A. Campbell's pleasure steamers, has peered through the window of his Usk-side office in search of the sun. He has had trips galore to offer, but the passengers have asked for the sun too. So, almost every day, John Hale has philosophically returned to the "office work" piling up on his desk - sun or no sun - hoping for better weather and bigger crowds. On Thursday, John Hale had to look twice – the sun was there ! To his assistant he whispered, "We're in for a busy weekend". But on Saturday, with the sun still shining, John Hale still had to return, philosophically, to his "office work". Mr Hale told a *South Wales Argus* reporter: "We had trips scheduled for Saturday and Sunday from Newport, but the *Britannia* which was heavily booked from Cardiff, broke down in the week and could not be repaired in time. So our ship, the *Ravenswood*, had to be transferred to Cardiff – and we are without one until Monday ... Mr Hale estimated that the firm lost about 500 customers on Saturday and about 600 on the attractive sailing to Weston, Lynmouth, Ilfracombe and Bideford arranged for Sunday. Said Mr Hale: "I am disappointed, of course. You would be surprised how fed up you can get when you have a steamer just itching to be packed with laughing kids - and the sun's let them down. Then, when you have got the sun, the ship has a bit of bad luck". Mr Hale added, in resignation, "Anyway, there's plenty of office work to do".'

The condition of the pontoon was starting to become a cause for concern in the early 1950s, largely because it had only received minimal maintenance since before the war, yet as a floating structure it was subject to considerable stresses and strains given the tremendous tidal range it was built to handle. A survey had been undertaken by a consulting engineer on behalf of the Newport Harbour Commissioners, and the 1954/55 Report of the Harbourmaster noted that deterioration was setting in. Although the overall condition of the landing-stage and the assembly-area was at that point thought to be satisfactory for the forthcoming season, the report (dated 1st May 1955) was ominous regarding the pontoons themselves:

'... Following a thorough examination of the pontoons, your Consulting Engineer submitted a report together with his recommendations, when it was decided that no further expenditure should be incurred, and the future of these properties is to be decided at the end of the present passenger boat season. The pontoons will adequately meet the needs of the coming season, but I cannot recommend that the two large pontoons should remain in position after the end of this year without extensive repair to the bottoms. It is 17 years since they were last repaired below the waterline.'

The Harbour Commissioners Records suggest that this advice was ignored for one more season, as a year later the 1955/56 Report, given on 1st May 1956 for the twelve months ended 31st March 1956 noted that '... it is expected that the pontoon will meet the needs of the coming season ...'. Profitability of the landing-stage operation, however, was in decline compared to the situation of a few years earlier, and evidently the situation became critical to the Commissioners in July of that year when a sub-committee was formed to address the matter of an increase in steamer dues, doubtless with the purpose of raising more cash to fund overdue remedial works as safety fears increased. An 'interview' with P. & A. Campbell Ltd took place in September 1956, the outcome of which was that the Commissioners found themselves unable to accept what was offered, and thus decided to dispose of the landing-stage. The Commissioners, though doubtless aware of the difficulties the company were experiencing that year, would have approached P. & A. Campbell Ltd at a very bad time, when the company was under pressure from its bankers to make cuts. The Newport station had for many years effectively fully occupied one vessel of the White Funnel Fleet as virtually daily trips were normally offered, and as the fleet-size had to be cut then Newport was an obvious port-of-call to eliminate at the same time, given the requirement there for essential repairs. The Newport Harbour Commissioners accounts suggest that the annual amount paid for the use of the landing-stage, £600, had not been reviewed for many years and this factor, together with falling pier-toll receipts they collected themselves directly, would not have aided the cause of the pontoon-berth as there would have been less and less each year to spend on full maintenance.

The handbill for sailings from the Newport Landing Stage for the period 2nd August to 20th September 1956 was a substantial affair, and despite the absence of a steamer dedicated to the provision of daily excursions, showed that out of the fifty days spanned by the bill, there were nineteen on which no trips were advertised, the maximum length of time between sailing days usually not exceeding two days. Of the thirty-one days on which sailings were offered, most were booked to depart on the morning tide between around 0800-1000, some of which were down-Channel to Ilfracombe, and occasionally beyond, and others were up-Channel to Weston, Clevedon or Bristol. On some days connections might be advertised, such as at Weston into the boat proceeding down-Channel from Bristol, and there were some days when the sailing outwards had no return, requiring passengers to use a bus or train from Cardiff or Barry. On nine days in the period, the tidal pattern permitted two departures from Newport, and on occasions when there were sailings on two consecutive days from Newport the

steamer arriving back at around 2200 could lie at Newport overnight on the mud. Thus there was still a reasonable level of service provided, to many of the destinations all around the Channel, in what was to be the final year for the Monmouthshire port, even if frequencies were reduced compared to the past.

Being such a visible part of the Newport scene, the loss of the White Funnel Fleet steamers there caused considerable concern, but which was mingled with an awareness of the difficulties of the times. The Newport paper on 22nd October 1956 carried this valedictory article, entitled Farewell to the Ships, some weeks after the last sailing had been taken by **Glen Usk** on 20th September:

'... It is a sad thought that no more shall we see the White Funnel steamers gracefully thrashing their way up and down the River Usk. The chairman of Newport Harbour Commissioners (Councillor H. R. Nock) puts the reason for the end of trips from Newport in a nutshell when he says: "It is a sign of the times. As a business we could not accept the terms offered." For some years the service from Newport has failed to pay its way, and no one would expect the commissioners to continue subsidising the trips in such circumstances. And so another public service dies because of soaring costs. Several wretched summers have also not helped to ease the financial burden of the company. After sixty years it is difficult to say "Goodbye" to old friends, for that is how Monmouthshire people had grown to look upon the ships of the White Funnel fleet. The Commissioners, regretfully, but rightly, have realised there is no alternative but to say "Goodbye". To them and to P. & A. Campbell Limited - for perhaps they will understand it better - the feelings of Monmouthshire people can best be summed up in the words of Robert Burns "What dire events have taken place! Of what enjoyments thou has reft us ! In what a pickle thou has left us!'

Written as part of an editorial piece this item was an interesting one for three reasons. Firstly, the Commissioners had not been subsidising trips, as their own accounts recorded profits on the Landing-Stage operation, albeit on a very modest scale, and in gradual decline up until the closure decision. Secondly, the perception that White Funnel trips were then 'another public service' was noteworthy, given that one would now see paddle-steamer trips as an optional, leisure activity. Thirdly, the reference to 'wretched summers' probably summed up what many felt, and which had aided the decline of the White Funnel Fleet. Elsewhere, the company was quoted as saying that alternative arrangements would in future be made for Newport and Monmouthshire trippers, in the form of special coach and train facilities to connect with the steamers at Cardiff and Barry. Considerable problems were subsequently encountered by the contractors engaged to dispose of the landing-stage, the floating pontoons eventually being towed away in 1957, for further use in Holland. The final mention of the landing-stage in the Records of the Newport Harbour Commissioners, in a Report dated 1st May 1958 read as follows:

'... on 29th May, the three pontoons with the two bridges lashed to the decks, left Newport in tow and arrived safely in Holland. Great difficulties were experienced by the purchasers in demolishing the dolphins and pontoons and it was not until October that the keys of the assembly areas were handed over to Newport Corporation, who had purchased these properties.'

Thus ended a symbolic chapter in White Funnel Fleet history – but Newport had perhaps been the obvious first target for cuts in services as a result of the combination of the capital expenditure needed to stay in business there against the tidal constraints, which meant that on most days only one sailing was offered, with obvious implications for potential earnings. Yet further cuts to Bristol Channel services were to come, however, and on the south coast an era had also ended after **Glen Gower** had made the last 'Round Trip' from Brighton back to her home port. Whereas the truncation of Newport activities was final, P. & A. Campbell Ltd had not altogether finished with the south coast, as we shall discover in due course.

1957: A transitional year

The steamers were still important in north Devon, and were seen to contribute significantly to the local economy, by dint of the relatively large number of visitors they still brought in to the premier resort of Ilfracombe, where the Council cooperated with P. & A. Campbell Ltd in various ways. There, one could scarcely overlook the ubiquitous image of a White Funnel Fleet paddle-steamer sweeping into the picturesque harbour, and tourism publicity was relatively generous in promoting marine excursions as a key element of a holiday. Regrettably this factor was less so on the Sussex coast, and the steamers there had perhaps succumbed accordingly. These few words, quoted from an official Guidebook from around 1951, *Focus on Brighton & Hove*, which was published by the Publicity Committees of the Corporations of Brighton and Hove, were the only mention of sea trips. No pictures of the coastline or the ships on which to view it from were featured, and the text perhaps illustrated the lesser role that the White Funnel Fleet steamers were then seen to play along the south coast of England:

STEAMER TRIPS: Paddle and screw steamers are operated from both the Palace and West Piers. Trips daily, weather permitting, to Worthing, Littlehampton, Southampton and the Solent, the Isle of Wight, Bournemouth, Newhaven, Beachy Head and Eastbourne, Hastings and Folkestone

Whereas in north Devon the steamers went back a long way and fulfilled a cross-channel ferry role from Wales, the P. & A. Campbell Ltd south coast presence was less deeply engrained. The coastal trips suffered from more competition, as the rail or coach alternatives were both feasible and more plentiful. The complete withdrawal by the company from Brighton in 1951 would have tended to dent public confidence. It had taken a long time to reinstate 'No Passport' day-excursions to France, and when these had eventually resumed in 1954 advance booking was required, passport-sized photographs had to be

provided, and there were currency restrictions. The stated position of the company after the 1956 season was that the dreadful weather had finally brought about the decision to withdraw, but the failure to re-establish the cross-Channel trips to prewar levels of popularity was self-evident.

Whereas 1956 was the season that saw the greatest amount of change and cutbacks in the White Funnel Fleet in the postwar years, 1957 can perhaps be regarded as the season in which the transition was made from having been a sizeable, established pleasure-steamer company – carrying on substantially in the manner of the prewar years, with its own dedicated maintenance facilities and repair-yard and traditional headquarters – to an altogether leaner organisation. Instead of managing and supporting five paddle-steamers and operating on two fronts, at home in the Bristol Channel and further afield on the south coast (and across the English Channel to France), a more compact business was now being run from the new headquarters at Dock Chambers in Cardiff's Butetown district. Nonetheless a degree of financial nervousness would still have existed. In spite of the severity of the economies made after the 1956 season, experience was still needed of running the slimmer, three-vessel Bristol Channel operation. The Directors hoped that this would be viable, and might fix the pattern before any further radical financial restructuring was to take place. The 1957 season opened with two vessels in operation at Easter, although not the pair intended. Unusually **Bristol Queen** commenced service on the Cardiff-Weston 'ferry' as **Glen Gower** was trapped in Bristol as a result of a shipyard strike. **Cardiff Queen** was therefore also fetched out of Penarth Dock after her winter lay-up, to join **Bristol Queen**. Meanwhile, the oldest fleet-member **Glen Usk** lay idle, and was stated to be on standby and available at 48 hours notice if required.

Despite the closure of the Brighton Agency, and the withdrawal of the traditional coastal excursions and cross-Channel sailings that had been carried out by **Glen Gower** in 1956, the south coast was not entirely without a P. & A. Campbell Ltd presence in 1957, as the little motor-vessel **Crested Eagle** was operated on charter on short

An official postcard view of the 1922-built paddle-steamer **Glen Gower** *approaching Ilfracombe. After three years down south as the Brighton steamer, between 1954-56, she came back to the Bristol Channel for the 1957 season but was laid up thereafter. In the early-1950s she would often have been found on the Cardiff to Ilfracombe run, possibly calling at Penarth, Barry, Minehead and Lynmouth, and going on to Clovelly or Lundy, in the time honoured manner.*

Author's collection

In her final year of 1957, Glen Gower spent much of her time on the Cardiff to Weston ferry. The Pier Head Dock Offices building is one of only a few such old buildings still standing in Bute Town, latterly Cardiff Bay. There were four berths at the Pier Head, one either side of a pair of pontoon structures, once known respectively as the Burnham and Bristol berths, a reminder of when Cardiff had packet links to those places in Victorian times.

Howard Jones

coastal excursions. This enterprise was of an experimental nature, and the rationale which lay behind it is not entirely clear from the Minute Books. With hindsight it seems perverse that it went ahead at all when, only a year previously, Campbell's bankers had insisted on the disposal of **Britannia** and a reduction in the overall fleet size. The company evidently believed that residual, if reduced, commercial potential remained at the key Sussex coast resorts, and felt the charter fee was worth the risk. They may have been keen to gain experience in operating motor-vessels, if this was the key motive. Perhaps it put Campbells off, as it was not until over five years later that **St. Trillo** was purchased, mainly for continuing north Wales use, and after which the operation of motor-vessels became a regular feature of White Funnel operations. Aspects of this charter of **Crested Eagle** are returned to later, when the decision was made to re-enter the market on the south coast, but in a distinctly different manner.

The basic fleet deployment in the Bristol Channel in 1957, after Whitsuntide when the season got fully underway, was thus for **Bristol Queen** to carry on doing much as she had always done, namely providing the long-distance down-channel trips, now mainly from Cardiff but still, to a lesser extent, from Bristol. **Cardiff Queen** remained on the Swansea-based duties to which she had become accustomed since her own recall from the South Coast after the 1952/53 seasons. Finally, whilst **Glen Usk** had been relieved of her traditional up-channel role and slumbered throughout the year in Penarth Dock, **Glen Gower** carried out ferry duties between Cardiff and Weston. She was to experience boiler trouble intermittently that year, and Norman Bird recorded that it was thought on occasions that **Glen Usk** might have had to have been pulled out of her lay-up to take the place of **Glen Gower** – known affectionately by some as 'Galloping Gertie' – because of her problems. During the early part of the 1957 season it seemed that matters were proceeding tolerably, but an unusually lengthy statement by the Chairman accompanied the publication of the 1956 Accounts, on 1st August 1957, and reminded shareholders

of his warnings during the previous year regarding the consequences of so many successive seasons of adverse weather, and the actions the company had been obliged to take in an endeavour to rectify matters. (This statement is reproduced in full in the Appendix as Item 3).

The death occurred in April of William James Banks, who had ten years earlier retired as the Managing Director of P. & A. Campbell Ltd after service with the company which went back almost to its very beginnings. Mainly involved with the engineering side he had joined P. & A. Campbell Ltd in 1897, after an apprenticeship commenced in 1892 with Messrs Mark Whitwill & Jones, Ship Repairers, of Bristol, and had risen to become a Director in 1925. After the death of Captain Alec Campbell in 1928 he became joint MD with Captain Peter Campbell, thereafter becoming sole Managing Director shortly after the death of the latter in 1938. The Banks family connection with White Funnel ships ceased after the departure of Mr (Bill) Banks' son W. G. (Billy) Banks in 1954, and the subsequent ascendancy of Clifton Smith-Cox.

Bristol Queen made a rare appearance at Newport in June 1957 as she was the vessel booked to carry out the annual charter cruise, of long-standing tradition, for the Newport Harbour Commissioners. For the first time this was obliged to depart from the south quay of the Alexandra Dock, which was a much less straightforward arrangement than had been possible when departure instead took place from the far more convenient landing-stage in the centre of town, and necessitated a fleet of buses to be laid on for the Commissioners and their guests. The cruise proceeded out through the sea-lock and towards Avonmouth, and thence to Weston for a lunch-stop at the Grand Atlantic Hotel. The cruise continued towards Minehead in the afternoon and returned to Newport by around 2100: Captain George commanded **Bristol Queen** that day. Later that summer, explosives were used in an attempt to obliterate the last remains of the timber piles in the River Usk, which had formed part of that most useful facility, not entirely successfully it would seem as some evidence of these could still be detected over forty years later!

Occasional calls at the Pembrokeshire port of Tenby were revived during the 1954 'Centenary Year', and it often fell to **Cardiff Queen** *as the Swansea steamer for much of the 1950s to carry out these trips. The pier had been demolished by this time which necessitated the use of the harbour, very well located for the delights of the beautiful old town of Tenby. Calls at Tenby were fewer in number after the withdrawal of the Swansea steamer at the end of the 1958 season.*

Author's collection

A classic view of Cardiff Queen carrying out the role of the Swansea steamer, seen here after setting off from the old 'Pockett's Wharf' past the eastern docks complex, then full of shipping. Captain George Gunn had command of Cardiff Queen for much of the period in the 1950s when she was based at Swansea.

courtesy Nick James

Glen Gower settled down to her new 'ferry' duties in 1957 with only very occasional trips away from the Cardiff to Weston route, and the odd Clevedon call, without the diversity that trips up the River Usk to the Newport Landing Stage had provided in previous years for up-channel vessels. Her restaurant had been converted into a milk-bar, and a sweet-shop was provided where her foreign-currency exchange facility had been on Boulogne trips. *Glen Gower* stayed out the longest of the three ships in 1957, continuing on the ferry until 14th October, some time after *Cardiff Queen* closed down the 'Swansea station' on 17th September and *Bristol Queen* had run the last Ilfracombe trips on 29th September. Enthusiasts and others could only then speculate that *Glen Gower* might now in fact have reached the end of her Campbell service, at the age of thirty-five years. Her engines, of course, were much older, having originally been installed in *Albion*, which had been built in 1893 as *Slieve Donard* for the Belfast & County Down Railway. The traditional end-of-season farewells on the last ferry crossing of the season from Weston duly took place, and something of the atmosphere was captured by a local newspaper in a piece entitled:

LIVELY FAREWELL FOR LAST BOAT OF SEASON

'A colourful scene was witnessed by a large crowd on Birnbeck Pier, Weston-super-Mare on Monday evening, when Messrs. P. & A. Campbell's steamer *Glen Gower*, left Weston for Cardiff on the last cross-Channel trip of the season. People lined the seaward end of the pier and the jetty itself as the last of the passengers went aboard. Near the end of the jetty Weston British Legion Silver Band under its conductor, Mr C. H. Cotton, played "Now is the hour" and, just before the steamer drew away, "We'll keep a welcome". Cheers and singing mingled as the craft drew away from the jetty. Capt. E. J. Wide (Piermaster) and pier staff released numerous rockets, and a farewell in Morse was sounded over the "loud-hailer". From the steamer came answering blasts from her siren, as well as rockets and fireworks, which could be seen searing through the Channel mist as the brightly-lit boat headed for Wales.'

Chief Engineer in the paddle-steamer *Glen Gower* in her last year was the last member of the Campbell family actively involved in the Company, Alexander Campbell, who himself was then in his forty-second year of service. Interviewed by a newspaper reporter as *Glen Gower* arrived back at Cardiff for the last time, he described the winter workload of maintenance that faced the small number of employees who stayed on after the season ended. He had served his engineering apprenticeship under his father, and at the age of sixty, still felt that he could not yet afford to contemplate retirement. Rounding up the same newspaper article, Clifton Smith-Cox was quoted as saying that considering the bad weather experienced in July and August that year, the passenger figures were as good as could be expected.

To sum up, then, it had become clear that things had changed considerably and that the prospects for P. & A. Campbell Ltd were not now likely to suddenly improve. The fleet was depleted, being at less than half its strength of just six years earlier, when seven vessels had operated compared to the three paddle-steamers left by 1957, if one discounts the charter of *Crested Eagle* on account of its experimental nature. Nevertheless, if the market for paddle-steamer excursions had shrunk, then the territory of the White Funnel Fleet, at least in its home waters, had not. Excepting the loss of Newport departures, the Bristol Channel still offered an immense variety of scenery and character, with its sheer size, and the compelling appearance of what were still two, modern, purposeful steamers built for long-distance running in open-sea conditions. Frequencies of sailings had been reduced across the piece, though, but an evocative reference to this powerful image of character was made by Norman Bird in describing his feelings about some of the more outstanding recollections he had of 1957, prompted by having made a visit to a rather different area where coastal steamer excursions, by turbine- and paddle-steamers, were still operated extensively:

'... I paid my first visit to the Clyde this year and was impressed very favourably by much of what I saw of the area and the C. S. P. ships. But how I enjoyed my first trip on the Bristol Channel when I returned to 'Combe in *Bristol Queen* on 8th September. I remember

Cardiff Queen at the jetty just below 'Pockett's Wharf', Swansea. This view was taken on 9th September 1947, as the last White Funnel Fleet paddle-steamer built approached the end of her first season. This area in barely recognisable following extensive redevelopment after the 1990s, and the former berth is some way upstream from the River Tawe barrage, and thus no longer accessible to shipping.
George Owen

lying on the Tunnels Beaches, at 'Combe, watching **Bristol Queen** pass by on a cruise and being distinctly moved by her dignity and the stately elegance of those two, tall, raked, white funnels. I remarked to my companion that whatever advantages the Clyde and its steamers had to offer, there was nothing to touch the sight of **Bristol Queen** at speed or the excitement of the Bristol Channel ...'.

Not forgetting that a reasonably full service was still provided on the Cardiff to Weston ferry, another quote from the same article adds substance to the general remark earlier about the scale of operations in the Bristol Channel when on 2nd July 1957, a day of glorious weather, it was possible with a little ingenuity to use both of the *Queens* to see virtually all of the Bristol Channel in one rather lengthy day:

'...A really full day's sailing in which, most unusually, it was possible ... to "do" the extreme ports of the Channel in the same day - viz., Bristol on the English side and Tenby on the Welsh. We had a lift down to Swansea where we boarded **Cardiff Queen** for Tenby and Ilfracombe. A few hours ashore, and we boarded **Bristol Queen**

for Barry, Weston, Clevedon, Bristol and Cardiff. We thus saw most of the Bristol Channel, enjoyed over twelve hours actually afloat, and had a really exhausting eighteen-hour day!...'.

And so the 1957 season ended with the two newest paddlers **Bristol Queen** and **Cardiff Queen** both having completed a little over a decade in service, and seemingly still with a reasonable life-expectancy ahead of them. An ailing **Glen Gower** was set to be replaced by her older sibling **Glen Usk** for the following season, after wintering in Penarth Dock. The south coast was now abandoned, along with the Underfall Yard too. In the Bristol Channel all the ports of call which had comprised the full White Funnel Fleet territory in the 1954 'Centenary Year' – plus Mumbles Pier, which had featured again from 1956, after prolonged reconstruction – were still served, with the notable exception of Newport. It was fervently hoped that there would now be a degree of stability in operations, and that the economies that had been effected would be sufficient to let the business go ahead viably, albeit on a reduced basis compared to how things had been a decade earlier after the postwar resumption of sailings.

Captain George Gunn and guest on the bridge of **Cardiff Queen** *in a late-1950s publicity shot.*
Peter Southcombe collection

The 1958 season

Fears that **Glen Gower's** end-of-season trips in 1957 were her last proved to be sadly accurate for admirers of that elegant, much-travelled vessel with such graceful lines. She was put up for sale and *Lloyds List* that November carried an advertisement by shipbrokers C. W. Kellock (the same agents that had handled the disposal of **Britannia** a year earlier) inviting offers for her. The description of **Glen Gower** mentioned her speed of about 17 knots, her Class II certificated capacity of 500 passengers on short international voyages, and domestic Class IV capacity of 'just over' 1,100. **Glen Gower** was not, however, destined to operate again, and she lingered on throughout 1958 in Penarth Dock. Failing to attract suitable offers for her purchase she was nominally available on standby, but she inevitably deteriorated and was finally taken away for scrapping some years later. Some slight alterations were made to **Glen Usk**, including the fitting of one new furnace and, in a similar manner to the way in which **Glen Gower** had been adapted for the short ferry crossings, the aft lower-deck dining saloon was altered to become a large bar, whilst the smaller bar on the main deck aft was adapted to become the officers' dining saloon. Clifton Smith-Cox had decided to review the timings that would be on offer by the three Bristol Channel vessels **Bristol Queen**, **Cardiff Queen** and **Glen Usk** during 1958 and, speaking to the press on board an early-season trip by the latter at Easter, somehow managed to convey a positive message about greater reliability through what was intended to be an announcement about a modest general deceleration of schedules. The piece was entitled:

PUNCTUAL STEAMERS

'... *speed-up of their Bristol Channel pleasure steamers this season*' was announced by Mr S. C. Smith-Cox, managing director of P. & A. Campbell Ltd "It's not a question of getting them to their destinations even faster ... but to ensure that the ships are not late," he said on board the steamer **Glen Usk**. Announcing plans for 1958, Mr Smith-Cox said they would be running special late-evening services from Cardiff to Weston during the Empire Games. "It is an almost impossible feat to do this over a ten-day period, but on this occasion we have been blessed with perfect tides" he said. Other Campbell's news: Two Sunday trips during the season from PORT TALBOT, first time ever Easter services from SWANSEA to ILFRACOMBE, improved services between ILFRACOMBE and LUNDY ISLAND, and three "SHOWBOATS" during the year ...'

Elsewhere in the press, much useful publicity was obtained as a result of the good weather on the first day of sailings (the Wednesday preceding Easter 1958) by **Glen Usk**, captained by Neville Cottman. Clifton Smith-Cox was quoted as saying that the company was hoping for a much better year's weather than the previous few seasons had yielded, and stated – perhaps somewhat disarmingly – that they had not had a really successful season since 1949. Emphasising the greater punctuality that was expected he also mentioned an expanded range of motor-coach tours, better train connections at Barry Pier for Cardiff and the Welsh Valleys, and improved catering in the longer-distance steamers. One of these new tours was provided on certain days for Ilfracombe passengers, who were to be offered the possibility of travelling across to Mumbles for a 'Combined Steamer and Coach Tour of the WELSH MOUNTAINS with their glorious and unsurpassed Panoramic Views of four counties'. For the fare of twenty-two shillings and sixpence, it was not altogether clear which four counties one might see, nor to what extent this might be dependent on visibility, and the tour-route was somewhat casually described, as follows:

'Coach will leave Mumbles Pier Head and proceed via Sketty and over Townhill, and then proceed via Morriston, Pontardawe, Black

The atmosphere of the late-1950s is nicely captured in this view of **Glen Usk** *with a good crowd on board, almost certainly on Cardiff-Weston 'ferry' duties. She gave good years of generally reliable service after the Second World War and was laid up after the 1960 season, only going for scrap in 1963 after plans for her re-boilering had been abandoned.*

Photographer unknown

Mountains, Llangadock, Llandilo, Cross Hands, Pontardulais etc. and back to Mumbles. Steamer leaves Mumbles 5.10 pm, due Ilfracombe about 6.50 pm. Tickets can only be booked at Office, 10 The Quay or kiosk on Sea-Front, Ilfracombe for combined tour.'

The optimism was high before Easter, but the fickle weather was soon to dash the hopes of the Company, during the Bank Holiday weekend and afterwards. Only thirty-three people were said to have braved the sleet and rain on board the sailing of **Bristol Queen** from Hotwells that Easter Saturday. Cancellations occurred, owing to east winds and bitterly cold weather: the sailings by **Cardiff Queen** to Porthcawl on Easter Sunday and from Ilfracombe to Lundy on Easter Monday, which should have earned useful early-season revenue for P. & A. Campbell Ltd, were unable to operate.

As Norman Bird observed:

' ... after four good Easters in succession with two steamers, P. & A. Campbell Ltd tempted providence by bringing out three steamers for Easter 1958, *Glen Usk* on "ferry" work, *Bristol Queen* (on Bristol-Cardiff-'Combe) and *Cardiff Queen* on the first ever Easter trips from Swansea. The weather was very poor, however, and traffic was poor. Both "Queens" were scheduled to lay up at Penarth after Easter Tuesday, but *Bristol Queen* remained in service for an extra couple of days in order than *Glen Usk* could have some minor troubles attended to. During these days *Bristol Queen* performed the earliest postwar sailing of the season to Minehead on April 10th'.

As 1958 continued, it appeared that whilst **Glen Usk** performed erratically, **Bristol Queen** behaved generally satisfactorily, and that **Cardiff Queen** did not always keep good time. If one scrutinises timetables and other publicity material of the late-1950s, it seems clear that P. & A. Campbell Ltd had been making considerable efforts to improve the range of excursions on offer, in an attempt to maximise earnings, and in which endeavour the coach trips in conjunction with steamer trips had taken on a greater significance than hitherto. Nevertheless, the poor weather was again making trading conditions difficult, and even before the month of August was out it became known that drastic measures had been resorted to. Behind the scenes, urgent discussions between P. & A. Campbell Ltd and their bankers would have been taking place as outgoings started to exceed income. The company had now ceased to be solvent and a suitably-worded letter to Members and Creditors was sent out on Monday, 18th August 1958 by the company Chairman A. R. Boucher from the Cardiff HQ. (This is reproduced in full as Appendix Item 4). This alerted addressees to the momentuous decision which had been made to call in the Receiver, a Mr W. Walker, F.A.C.C.A. We will return to this more fully in due course.

A turning-point is reached

For a company which had been operating steamships for over seventy years this state of affairs, if not wholly surprising to the regulars, some of whom were also shareholders, would still have come as a profound shock to many passengers. Although the letter explained that services were to continue as advertised for the remainder of the season, it seemed to observers that the writing was now on the wall for the Swansea steamer, and it was only a matter of days before the company made further statements which indicated what might lie ahead if the Receiver was able to do his job in a manner that would permit the White Funnel Fleet to sail on at all. The announcement happened on a day with good tides, when the three-strong fleet was planned to be fully utilised, and it is worth setting out in some detail just what was advertised as being on offer to the public at that precise moment when the big decision was communicated, the repercussions of which were to shape the destiny of the company for the next two decades or so.

There was no sailing from Bristol that day, but a convenient late-morning tide permitted the Swansea boat – **Cardiff Queen** – to leave Swansea at a fairly normal departure time of 0845 for Ilfracombe and Clovelly, taking in the customary Mumbles Pier call at 0905 and Porthcawl at 1005. Unusually, after departure from Ilfracombe

at 1150, a 'double-run' to Clovelly was offered with departure from the North Devon fishing village back to Ilfracombe at 1330. This was advertised from Clovelly as a North Devon coastal cruise, returning from Ilfracombe at 1500 to Clovelly, after which the second departure took place at 1645 for Ilfracombe, Porthcawl, Mumbles and Swansea. **Bristol Queen** had a fairly routine 0900 start from Cardiff (which almost replicated the 'Railway Run' of old performed by the Barry 'Red Funnel Line' steamers) and made her way down-Channel, calling at Penarth, Barry, Minehead and Lynmouth to Ilfracombe, on this day adding on the leg at 1235 from Ilfracombe to Lundy. An option was thereby possible for passengers on the Swansea steamer to go to Lundy for the afternoon, rather than Clovelly, if they so chose. Departure from Lundy was at 1635, after which the Cardiff boat retraced its steps back up-Channel, leaving Ilfracombe at 1815 for Lynmouth, Minehead, Barry, Penarth and Cardiff.

The more humdrum roster for **Glen Usk** on that day was a couple of ferry runs from Cardiff to Weston at 0930 and 1140, followed by a low-water crossing (from Weston) to Barry Pier. A train connection brought folk from Cardiff down to Barry for a 1445 cruise to the Breaksea Light-Vessel, returning at 1645, and a 1725 crossing from Barry to Weston repositioned **Glen Usk** for two more ferry crossings to Cardiff that evening, finishing up at the Welsh capital almost exactly 12 hours after her day had started. To complete the picture, the Swansea, Mumbles & Porthcawl contingent were offered the option of a coach tour from Ilfracombe to Lynton and the Valley of the Rocks, and the Cardiff, Penarth & Barry contingent could if they wished avail themselves of a coach tour of Exmoor from Minehead. Not to be left out of this range of road and sea trips, Clovelly bills offered passengers joining there the possibility of travelling on a 'Circular Tour' by bus in the morning to Ilfracombe, with a choice of return times by steamer.

It was not long before the withdrawal of the Swansea steamer would be confirmed, and it is worth considering how Messrs Boucher and Smith-Cox were to handle the communication of such unpalatable news. The tone of this letter (see Appendix item 4) was significant, in terms of its reference to the efforts made by the Directors in foregoing their entitlements, their apparent frankness at what amounted to the failure of earlier restructuring to put the company on an even keel, and the plea for patience and understanding for the Receiver to try and sort it all out. If this view – too little, too late – seems a little harsh it only emphasises what, in the personal opinion of the author, amounts to one explanation of the philosophy underlying a company that had ceased to behave entirely rationally in a strict financial and economic sense, which survived against the odds having failed to pay any dividend for a number of successive years and whose fixed assets were clearly of limited worth if the company had been liquidated any earlier. The poor weather, however, was self-evidently a very major factor in exacerbating such a financially critical situation where there was little room for manoeuvre if the expense of running the fleet in the high summer - in terms of cash needed to meet immediate outgoings on crew wages, fuel bills, and dock dues – exceeded overall ticket revenues.

The news of receivership spread quickly and, in very much the same way as the announcement that the White Funnel Fleet was to abandon its Bristol base two years before, the reaction of the media was a blend of sympathy for the plight of the company and an acknowledgement of the dreadful weather which had caused passenger numbers to be so depressed. This was coupled with an expression of hope that somehow the steamers might yet still be kept running, at Cardiff at least, by some providential means. An editorial article in the local *South Wales Argus* entitled 'Cloud over the Severn' published in Newport on Wednesday 20th August 1958 eloquently summed up the more emotive side of the announcement, and was notable in its recognition then of the benefits that a transport operation conferred on the area it served, aside from the harsher realities of the profit and loss account. The reference to an 'older generation of Monmouthshire people' needs to be explained as, by 1958, the early P. & A. Campbell Ltd paddle-steamers **Bonnie Doon** and **Albion** had been gone for the larger part of five decades or so:

HALLADALE CAR FERRY AT DOVER.   D/9623

At the point at which P. & A. Campbell Ltd entered receivership in 1958, a pioneering car-ferry service from Dover to Calais was being operated by Townsend Brothers, deploying the steam-turbine powered **Halladale**. *A former 'River' Class frigate, built in 1944, she had been rebuilt into a car-ferry for her new service in 1950. When George Nott Industries (who had taken over Townsends in 1957) acquired the Campbell business and its four paddle-steamers in 1960, this part of their new maritime portfolio initially exceeded the scale of Townsend operations by a considerable factor.*
Author's collection

'For more than half a century the handsome white-funnelled ships of P. & A. Campbell Ltd have busily paddled their way through the Severn Sea, bringing the delights of Somerset and Devonshire within easy reach, with a pleasant sea-trip thrown into the bargain. Over all these years, boat trips have seemed an integral part of the summer. So the news that a succession of disastrously wet summers had put the Campbells in financial difficulty was greeted with widespread regret and a sympathy that would be extended to few industrial concerns. The older generation of Monmouthshire people recall with affection the days when the old **Bonnie Doon** and **Albion** provided virtually the only opportunity for an excursion and so, legend had it, they had crossed from Newport to Weston so often that they could find their way without the aid of captain or compass. Since those early days Campbells' modernised and improved their fleet and for a long time prospered. The company survived two wars, during which their ships and their crews fought gallantly for England with heavy casualties. Now there will be widespread hope that the remainder of this holiday season will prove profitable enough for Campbells' to decide to take one more chance next year, and so preserve for the people of both sides of the channel an amenity which once lost would be sadly missed. That hope will be echoed by traders – particularly the small traders – and the boarding-house keepers of Weston-super-Mare, Minehead, Lynmouth and Ilfracombe, whose prosperity in the past has depended upon the Welsh excursionists and holidaymakers, and for whom the end of White Funnel boat trips would mean financial ruin. We hope the sun will shine for Campbells. The possibility of their passing has cast a heavy cloud over the Severn.'

With the announcement of Receivership it had thus become apparent that the fortunes of P. & A. Campbell Ltd had reached a more parlous state than ever before. The end of 1958 should be seen for what it was: another substantial 'downsizing' of the once-great Campbell empire to a level which would now endure for quite some time to come. At the tail-end of that season, as if to add to the miseries then being suffered, **Glen Usk** made the headlines shortly before the end of her 1958 deployment. Running late on the last ferry trip of the evening from Weston to Cardiff on Wednesday August 27th, she became stuck on the mud just fifty yards or so away from the 'Burnham Berth' at the Pier Head with around 150 passengers and her crew of twenty-six on board. She had been scheduled to arrive on the last of the water at 2215 but had been delayed almost an hour, the newspapers reporting that her engines were 'running slower than usual'. The passengers spent an uncomfortable night aboard, although reports stressed that every effort was made by the crew to ease the situation. A few were still awake when she slid off the mud at 0358 the next morning, and a few minutes later passengers came ashore to what was later described in *Ship Ahoy* as 'a battery of reporters and cameras', and were able to buy a special edition of the *Western Mail* which featured their plight as front-page news before going home to bed. The media also went to some length to emphasise that at no point was anyone in any danger, and what could have been a very poor piece of public relations was somehow presented in a remarkably positive way, with no blame being attached to the ships' officers, and passengers being quoted as saying how much fun they had, and how it really had been a trip with a difference. It is hard to imagine such generous media treatment nowadays if similar circumstances arose. It might also be noted that at this time no vision existed to turn what was then known to some as 'the Drain', the tidal mudflats off the Pier Head at Cardiff, into the modern-day tide-free lagoon of what is now marketed as Cardiff Bay, or its waterfront.

Glen Usk made the headlines again shortly after this escapade, being withdrawn prematurely on 21st September from ferry duties. Arriving at Cardiff from Weston, and scheduled to turn round and return with another load of passengers, the coal-fired steamer developed a mechanical fault described subsequently as being due to a faulty feed-pipe. Thirty-five passengers who were due to return to Weston by sea were sent home instead by rail, and it was promptly decided to substitute the oil-fired *Cardiff Queen* (which would herself have been due to lay up for the winter at about that time) for the remainder of the season that *Glen Usk* would have operated. This was in sad contrast to the smart spectacle she had presented a couple of months earlier, on 23rd July, when – dressed overall – she had greeted the arrival of the Royal Yacht *Britannia* at Cardiff. As had been the practice since the early years of the company, occasional visits by the Royal Yacht were noteworthy in the Bristol Channel in that timetables drew attention to them, and cruises were run to view her.

The threat to the Swansea presence was now, perhaps, inevitable as affairs moved towards reducing operations to a bare minimum. However, the adjustment to reduced circumstances implied by the slide into Receivership did not happen immediately. After the appointment of Mr Walker as the Receiver, he evidently decided that some income was better than none at all. He might well have been made aware by the Managing Director that some prospect of salvation for the company could yet be to hand if further economies were made, rather than insisting on liquidation there and then, and finding that the suspension of trading and an immediate sale of the assets might have yielded an even less satisfactory financial result. Clifton Smith-Cox was himself a qualified Accountant, and whilst neither he nor anyone else could control the fluctuations of the weather, he had by then had five or so years experience of running P. & A. Campbell Ltd, and doubtless considered that further economies and increased utilisation of a trimmed fleet could yet turn the balance of the company's trading position. When looking to see what else could be cut out to reduce expenses further, it was almost inevitable that the continuing operation of the Swansea steamer would come under scrutiny, and the reasons for this attitude by the Company were to be set out later in the year, in another lengthy statement from the Chairman which was to accompany the belated publication of the 1957 Report and Accounts. (See Appendix Item 5).

Cardiff Queen was advertised to run the 'Last Trips of the Season' from Swansea on Tuesday 16th September 1958. The schedule that day was a routine one, with the steamer leaving Swansea at 0900, and Mumbles twenty minutes later for Ilfracombe, via Porthcawl, from where departure across the Channel was scheduled at 1020. On arrival at Ilfracombe, *Cardiff Queen* was to proceed at noon to Lundy Island to land. Passengers from south Wales were offered the alternative of a Lynmouth cruise if they preferred, by changing steamers at Ilfracombe. The return departure from Ilfracombe for Mumbles and Swansea was due at 1750, and for good measure the final run back up-channel to Cardiff was advertised to passengers that night, leaving Swansea at 2000, with a final call at Porthcawl at 2110 before heading home, via Barry and Penarth. The trip appears to have gone off uneventfully, and the *South Wales Evening Post* that day carried a substantial story accompanied by a photograph of *Cardiff Queen* setting off from Mumbles Pier with the caption: '*Will this be the last time the cross-channel service will operate?*'. Perhaps appropriately, the weather that morning was gloomy and overcast. Appearing a couple of weeks before it was to be officially made known that the Swansea steamer would be taken off, the headline was a little more dramatic. Perceptively written, after recounting the early highlights of the Campbell fleet in general terms the article – entitled NO ILFRACOMBE TRIPS - UNTHINKABLE – succinctly summed up the postwar problems the company had suffered, and read as follows:

> '... Those were halcyon days indeed, and the decks and saloons of the White Funnel steamers had never been more consistently crowded with happy voyagers between South Wales and the North Devon coast. On summer mornings, streams of holidaymakers, many with luggage for a long stay, could be seen below Wind Street bridge, making their way to Pockett's Wharf to join already long queues waiting to board the steamer for Ilfracombe ... a Second World War again closed down the

cross-channel services, the steamers being requisitioned as before for a more necessary and urgent traffic. Three White Funnel ships were sunk in the Dunkirk evacuations, another by attack from the air, and a fifth the *Glen Avon*, came to grief off the Normandy beaches soon after D-Day. In the year following the end of the war the company resumed their Bristol Channel sailings, but trips from Swansea did not start until the summer of 1947 ... then followed a few years of quite busy traffic, with a re-establishing of social and family contacts between South Wales and North Devon, and it developed into something like a reunion. Barnstaple's ancient September Fair once more came into its own, and there were regular crossings and re-crossings of exiles, particularly among those North Devon families who had been settled for generations in the Swansea district.

> It did not continue for long, however, and this postwar decade has been, on the whole, a very trying period for the White Funnel Fleet. Operating costs have soared enormously, people's holiday-making tastes have changed, the motor-car and motor-coach have provided increasing competition and, worse than all, a succession of abnormally bad summers has seriously reduced their payloads. During the past few years the company has done quite a lot to reduce running costs and it has been announced that, even now, a belated spell of real summer weather might go a long-way towards retrieving the position. Possibly this may be too much to hope for, so late in the year, but there is evidence of a real and widespread concern over the possibility of services being withdrawn or curtailed. To most of us it is unthinkable that there should be no pleasure boats between Swansea and Ilfracombe, no-one having any recollection of a period, except during two world wars, when there was not a regular service between the two towns.'

A little later on that week, on Thursday 18th September 1958 a somewhat different angle on the demise of the Swansea steamer, and what it had represented was given, again by the *South Wales Evening Post*. Written before withdrawal of the Swansea steamer had been confirmed, it is interesting in the way in which recognition of the difficulties facing North Devon resorts was acknowledged. A degree of economic interdependence on the steamers was noted, together with a implicit plea for the needs of holidaymakers and residents of Swansea, Mumbles and thereabouts. A broader picture was painted, before the era of widespread car ownership:

> **CLOUDS ACROSS THE CHANNEL**
> ' ... this week an event occurred that begins a period of intense anxiety for Ilfracombe, Lynton and the coastal resorts in their area. It is uncertain whether excursion steamers from South Wales, the only near mass population region, will continue their summer visits. The circumstances are well known. If there is to be a total discontinuance, it will strike a double blow. There will be the loss of daily tripper custom, and the reduction of the attractiveness of these resorts to visitors from Southern England if they cannot offer short sea excursions such as plied from 'Combe to Lundy, along the Devon Coast and occasionally across the Bristol Channel.

> Weston has the advantage of proximity to the Bristol area, and very easy access to Cardiff and Newport. But Ilfracombe and its sister resorts are too far down the coastline. In the past many people there let annually for a week or fortnight to the same family patrons in turn: with the loss of that holiday habit ... some compensation could be found with the trippers, but that solid help may now disappear. There are no alternatives in sight.

> Distant visitors who came to North Devon from the Midlands and found the sea route from Swansea and Cardiff a saving of time and money will likewise be cut off. A new distressed area could easily arise - with the added handicap that a proportion of the distressed people are not the type one can visualise as taking up any industries that may be established.'

The end of the Swansea steamer

Following a period of uncertainty raised by these articles a statement released in early October confirmed the permanent withdrawal, together with the closure of the office premises occupying what had once been the headquarters of the celebrated 'Pockett Packets' before the First War, at Pockett's Wharf in Swansea's South Dock. The reduction of the fleet to two vessels for 1959 was clearly not the absolute minimum of downsizing that could have been implemented, and it was not immediately stated which vessel would actually be withdrawn. Nor was Swansea to be totally eradicated from the White Funnel territory, as it was announced that on summer Saturdays, a service would still run between Swansea, Mumbles and Ilfracombe, primarily for the benefit of south Wales holidaymakers, so as to retain a weekly link with the North Devon resort. Such sailings were to be operated by the surviving long-distance steamer, the other vessel predictably being retained on established Cardiff-Weston ferry duties.

A front-page article in the *South Wales Echo* on Friday 3rd, October 1958 was prompted by this announcement. It started with the positive news that P. & A. Campbell Ltd steamers would again operate in 1959, but on a reduced scale and after the weeks of speculation that had followed the Receivers' appointment the article confirmed that one fewer ship would operate:

Regular service from Swansea ends
'P. & A. Campbell's White Funnel Fleet of pleasure-steamers will be running again in the Bristol Channel next summer. The company announced this today, thus ending weeks of speculation following their statement last month that they were faced by a critical financial situation. They then told shareholders and creditors that they had appointed a Receiver through their bank. Bad summers were blamed for the crisis.
Some will be unchanged
Today, P. & A. Campbell stated that, though they were continuing operations, there would be no regular service from Swansea to the North Devon coast next summer. And there might be fewer sailings from Bristol and Porthcawl. Services from Cardiff, Penarth, Barry and Weston are likely to be unchanged. The full statement, which followed a meeting of the company's directors, read:
"The Board understand that it is the Receiver's intention, in the absence of any unforeseen circumstances and subject to it being possible to make satisfactory arrangements with the various authorities concerned, to continue the operation of Bristol Channel passenger steamers during the summer of 1959. The scale of operations, however, will in some cases be restricted, in particular in that no regular service will operate from Swansea to the North Devon coast. As far as the remaining resorts are concerned there is not likely to be any great change in the service provided, except for a possible diminution in the number of sailings from Bristol and Porthcawl. So far as Cardiff, Penarth, Barry and Weston are concerned the service is likely to be very similar to that in operation during 1958.
Excursions will continue to be run from Minehead, and there will be a service from Ilfracombe to Lundy Island, Clovelly and elsewhere, but some reduction in the number of afternoon cruises operating from that resort. It is hoped that, on occasions during the summer, a day trip from Mumbles to Ilfracombe will take place, and that a Saturday service will operate between Ilfracombe and Mumbles and vice-versa. In addition, occasional afternoon cruises will be made from Mumbles. The number of excursions carried out jointly with coach companies and facilities for through bookings are likely to remain very similar to what they were in 1958".'

Although it was still not apparent which vessel was to be cut out, yet another White Funnel Fleet steamer now seemingly appeared to have reached its ignominious end, bringing the total number of withdrawals to five ships in the seven years since 1951 (when the turbine *Empress Queen* ended her brief UK career in British waters). As it turned out, P. & A. Campbell Ltd did not do what seemed to many to be the obvious thing to do given that the fleet at this point consisted of two more comfortable, modern oil-fired steamers and one coal-burner dating from 1914, relative fuel prices still dictating that economies could be obtained by sticking with coal.

The withdrawal of the Swansea steamer led to the displacement of Captain George Gunn who had by this time been employed by P. & A. Campbell Ltd for around ten years, and was closely associated in the latter period with the Swansea steamer. However he was to continue his employment with the company, having been asked by Clifton Smith-Cox to act as a part-time Agent in the area. Captain Gunn was to now become a full-time Swansea pilot and combined this profession with occasional relief duties for the White Funnel Fleet during the 1960s, of which we will hear more in due course.

The 66th Ordinary General Meeting, Friday 14th November 1958

This was held at the Grand Hotel at Bristol and the Directors Report, which accompanied the Accounts for the year ended 31st December 1957 alluded to the 'rather exceptional circumstances' which had affected the Company's operations in 1957. The details of these were given to shareholders in a copy of the Chairman's Speech (reproduced as Appendix item 5) circulated with the Report and Accounts. After recording events such as the shipyard strike at the beginning of the season, bus & coach strikes which reduced the number of potential steamer passengers, the Suez crisis which led to fuel price increases, the losses sustained on the south coast by the charter of *Crested Eagle*, and exceptional maintenance expenditures on all steamers, Mr Boucher concluded that while 1957 had been a year of extremely bad weather, 1958 had proved 'infinitely worse'. He had elaborated further on the decision that had been made regarding the Swansea steamer but hoped that the Company still had some future ahead of it if costs were tightly controlled, and the weather did not intervene to depress demand.

So ended the regular operation of the Swansea steamer, and it is pertinent to mention here what went with it: Mumbles Pier, the landing-stage of which had been re-opened for steamer traffic after considerable effort and expense in 1956, was the main casualty, and lost a large proportion of its steamer revenue virtually overnight. Porthcawl was probably the next largest place to lose out, as it had been largely the preserve of the Swansea steamer where calls were made alongside the harbour breakwater as the tidal cycle permitted. To a lesser extent Tenby lost out too as a consequence of the demise of the Swansea steamer and, although calls were subsequently made by the up-channel boats, frequencies were inevitably reduced. Finally, some of the other 1954 'Centenary Year' initiative ports would lose out too, particularly Clovelly, but also Bideford. Port Talbot, albeit of only peripheral importance to P. & A. Campbell Ltd, ceased to be served after the 1958 season.

As all four steamers (only three of which could by this point be described as active) faced another winter at their moorings in Penarth Dock, there was inevitably a degree of sorrow felt by many regarding the loss of the 'Swansea Steamer'. Perhaps a turning point in the fortunes of the White Funnel Fleet had now finally been reached, as the Chairman had hoped for in his speech. As 1959 approached discussions carried on behind the scenes as attempts were made to put the business on a firm footing, with its slim-line fleet, minimal overheads and intensified utilisation of just two of the three remaining assets, the two postwar and the one veteran paddle-steamers *Bristol Queen*, *Cardiff Queen* and *Glen Usk*. The fourth vessel *Glen Gower* languished, unwanted and unsold. The 1950s had been a turbulent era for the business of P. & A. Campbell Ltd, and after a number of difficult seasons which brought worsening trading conditions the company had gone into Receivership – and the Lean Years now lay ahead …

The commencement of the period here styled as the Lean Years': **Bristol Queen** *is seen here laid-up in Penarth Dock on 18th September 1958, prior to spending the next two seasons out of commission. The larger steamer behind her is* **St. Andrew**, *then a Western Region railway steamer often deployed at Fishguard or Weymouth.* Miss Gwyneth White

The Lean Years

The turbulent fifties

The mid-fifties era had been characterised by the degree of change in operations between each successive season, reflecting a steadily declining position. P. & A. Campbell Ltd had been in Receivership since August 1958, and this situation was now set to continue for an indefinite period until some solution to the company's financial problems could be found. Despite statements made late in 1958 it was, therefore, by no means a complete certainty that any white-funnelled ships would emerge out of winter lay-up to resume trading on excursion duties in the Bristol Channel in 1959. Later Company Reports and Accounts were to reveal that the Receiver, Mr Walker, had already been acting as the financial controller for some years before Receivership became a fact, and one could say that the bankers to P. & A. Campbell Ltd had, by 1959, been seriously concerned for around five years or so beforehand. A solution to the company's deep-seated financial problems was urgently needed, yet in 1959 operations were to resume virtually unchanged, the brand-image (on publicity, and on related material) unaltered, but services spread yet more thinly. This pattern would utilise just a very modest, two-vessel fleet. The 1922-built **Glen Gower**, idle since the end of the 1957 season, lingered on in Penarth Dock, ostensibly open to offers of purchase, but in reality simply deteriorating pending the last, one-way voyage to the breakers yard.

A theme that would be evident throughout the next phase of the history of the company was that of the intensified utilisation of the two surviving operational steamers, where three had previously been deployed. This was accompanied by an increased emphasis on optional coach-tours and rail & bus ticketing inter-availability, and rather more pressure was now placed on personnel afloat through working long hours on busier, more complex schedules. Morale amongst those still employed may well have reached its lowest ebb when it had been decided, late in 1958, that for 1959 the favourite of many enthusiasts,

the 13-year old oil-fired paddle-steamer and flagship **Bristol Queen** would not emerge from her winter lay-up. Instead, the veteran coal-burner **Glen Usk** was to soldier on, carrying out upper Bristol Channel and ferry duties, leaving longer-distance excursion work largely to the newest steamer **Cardiff Queen**. A remark that Clifton Smith-Cox had made in late-1958 throws interesting light on the logic behind the new arrangements: '... *the vessels which are being used will have to carry about twice as many passengers as they did before the war if they are to be economic. Costs have risen six times, but fares have gone up only by three times* ...'.

This period has been styled 'The Lean Years' because, seen in the context of what had gone before, and now just operating two vessels after the cutbacks that had been endured, they were just that: there was no likelihood of new investment until a basic level of stability was reached and a period of calm experienced after the turbulent years. During this period, it was reasoned, if P. & A. Campbell Ltd could just survive and demonstrate sufficient profitability then better times might lie ahead. The company was still – despite being in Receivership – actually trading after all its misfortunes, and talks were taking place behind the scenes throughout 1959 regarding the shape that financial reconstruction might take. Sailings were still being offered at all the main piers and harbours around the Bristol Channel (except at Newport) and by working the ships harder, Swansea – or at least via calls at Mumbles Pier, as calls at the South Dock diminished in frequency – still retained a limited P. & A. Campbell Ltd presence, even if the Swansea office had been had closed down and the regular steamer providing the long-established daily trips cut out. Bristol retained occasional calls just on favourable tides, and the Cardiff-Weston ferry continued throughout the season which roundly commenced at Easter, paused in late-April & May before resuming in readiness for Whitsuntide, and continued until late-September or early-October. This is therefore perhaps an opportune point at which to look further afield at factors which were ultimately to shape the destiny of the company.

Beyond the Bristol Channel

Behind the scenes, things were happening far away from the Bristol Channel which were to have a profound effect upon the business outlook for P. & A. Campbell Ltd. Clifton Smith-Cox had connections with various businesses through his professional capacity as an accountant, actively seeking a purchaser for the struggling business. Survival ultimately rested upon shedding an old financial structure, where income could no longer pay the dividends expected by shareholders, and virtually wiping the slate clean. This pre-supposed that, shorn of most overheads, a slender excursion-steamer operation could generate sufficient income, over a relatively short season, to be profitable to such an extent that the providers of any new capital could be satisfied with the return on their investment. If a suitable investor were identified, then maybe the business of P. & A. Campbell Ltd could be taken over, and operations continued. Although this is awkward to define nowadays, what was needed then was for such an investor to be able to take advantage, in taxation terms, of the losses that P. & A. Campbell Ltd had steadily been accumulating for some years, in order to reduce their own taxation liability by offsetting these losses against new profits, to advantage. Surviving P. & A. Campbell Ltd published accounts from this era do not in themselves clearly show how this approach worked, but documents from the Receiver and subsequent published Court of Chancery proceedings – plus the interpretation of a qualified Accountant – have enabled a picture to be built up of the way in which both the assets and the accumulated debts of the old Bristol company were purchased. The creditors and shareholders were dealt with, and a new business created – albeit with the same name as before. This naturally took time, and we need to look beyond the confines of the Bristol Channel in order to consider what was happening in the south-east of England, at Dover, in order to understand how the rescue of P. & A. Campbell Ltd eventually came about.

Captain Stuart Townsend had, in the 1920s, effectively challenged the railway providers of channel ferry services from Dover on the most expedient means of shipping cars to France. The Southern Railway naturally concentrated on its foot-passenger traffic, bringing boat-trains alongside their 'classic' passenger-only ships for simple interchange, mostly from London to either Dover Western Docks or to Folkestone Harbour. Captain Townsend placed a ship called *Forde* on a new Dover-Calais car-carrying service in 1930 and, in simple terms, this venture was to survive and eventually prosper. The immediate Southern Railway response to this was to have a freight vessel, due to

be delivered in 1931, converted to carry a small number of cars, and this was duly named *Autocarrier*. A larger vessel, *Halladale*, provided the Townsend service from 1950 and not long after this, the loading of cars via what we now know as a link-span superseded more labour-intensive crane-loading methods. The advantages were abundantly obvious, and in order to expand his working capital Captain Townsend decided to go public in 1956. He was not alone in his endeavour, as Dover Eastern Docks as it is known today had then started to take shape. The Belgians had already introduced car-ferries after World War Two, on the Ostend service, and one of the first British purpose-built railway car-ferries *Lord Warden* appeared in 1952, on the Dover to Boulogne route. The French introduced their first car-ferry *Compiegne* in 1958, but at this time 'classic' passenger ferries still predominated in the short-sea ferry routes between England and the continent.

A company called George Nott Industries, based in Coventry, took control of the Townsend interests and after a short period of time decided in 1957 to take matters in hand to develop the car-carrying business as they saw fit. The nationalised railway industry, through its shipping division, was not seen by Notts as fully capable of rising to the challenge of the burgeoning car-carrying market at this time. Although it is documented that Notts had initially considered an 'asset-stripping' approach to the business that Capt. Townsend had built up, an opening for a private sector operator to cater for motorists at Dover was recognised and after a short period of time – which more or less happened to coincide with that of the Receivership of P. & A. Campbell Ltd – an order was placed in 1961 for a radical new design of car-ferry for the Dover-Calais route, to replace the ageing *Halladale*. This vessel was to be called *Free Enterprise*. Before this order was placed, Clifton Smith-Cox had been working with George Nott Industries to devise a capital reconstruction scheme whereby Notts proposed to 'purchase' the accumulated debts of P. & A. Campbell Ltd with their own, new capital. The roots of this relationship were created during the season of 1959, during which time a sort of silence prevailed in the Bristol Channel pending any release of details of any definite arrangements for the future of the White Funnel Fleet. Roland Wickenden, then the Accountant to Notts, was to become a key player in this development, becoming a close acquaintance of Clifton Smith-Cox. He would later join the P. & A. Campbell Ltd board in 1960 to represent the interests of the new backers. His name became a fundamental part of the broader Townsend-Thoresen (latterly European Ferries) short-sea business which grew out of these roots at Dover as the wider car-ferry market took off during the 1960s.

The 'Lean Years' were when **Bristol Queen** *had gone into prolonged lay-up after the 1958 season, and this view perhaps exemplifies this period, where* **Cardiff Queen** *was captured at anchor off Lundy on 4th August 1959. Her schedule that day was 0900 from Cardiff, 0910 from Penarth and 0945 from Barry Pier for Ilfracombe and Lundy, returning at 1630 from the island back up-Channel. This was much in the manner of the old 'Railway Run' which the Barry Railway Company steamers had carried out daily in the 1905-1909 period, with a train connection from Cardiff (Riverside) to Barry Pier station in the morning, and meeting the returning steamer again in the evening.*
Norman Bird

Above: *Although* **Glen Usk** *was in her twilight years in the late-1950s her elegant lines still graced the landing-stage at Weston-super-Mare's Birnbeck Pier in Somerset. She has just arrived on another 'ferry' crossing from Cardiff and Penarth, less than an hour away on the other, Welsh side of the Bristol Channel.* Peter Southcombe collection

Left: *'Alec' – Alexander Campbell, (son of Peter Campbell), Chief Engineer of* **Cardiff Queen**, *seen on board his ship on 28th September 1958.* Pat Murrell collection

For the commercial success of a reconstructed P. & A. Campbell Ltd to ensue, it would need the company to deliver profits after the injection of the new funds enabled the period in Receivership to be ended, and this is what duly happened. The 'losers' were, of course, the ordinary shareholders as well as some of the creditors. We have, however, jumped ahead here, and we now need to go back to look at what was on offer to passengers in the Bristol Channel in 1959, which was not quite "business as usual", as the pressure was now on to earn the maximum possible income from the surviving two operational vessels. 1959 was also to be an eventful year in other ways …

The 1959 season commences

As the year dawned, all four surviving P. & A. Campbell Ltd paddle-steamers were to be found laid up in Penarth Docks, **Glen Gower** destined never to see commercial service again and **Bristol Queen**, a mere thirteen years old, humiliatingly put aside as an ominous sign of those difficult times. **Glen Usk** was the first steamer to be activated, and her crew joined her on 24th March 1959 to take her out into the channel for the customary pre-season compass adjusting. She was prepared for service the next day, and ferry duties commenced on Thursday 26th March, the day before Good Friday, when minor mechanical difficulties were incurred which shortened her planned day. She made a run down-Channel to Ilfracombe on Easter Monday as well as ferry trips, and thereafter stayed in service throughout the season. The youngest fleet member **Cardiff Queen** went on to the pontoon at Penarth Dock for underwater treatment between Monday 13th - Friday 17th April 1959, but her crew were not signed on until a month later, on Wednesday 13th May. The following day saw her move round to the Pier Head at Cardiff in readiness for entry into traffic on Friday 15th May 1959, on ferry duties. She was off to Mumbles and elsewhere the following day, and opened Lundy sailings on Sunday 17th May, landing singles only. The normal routine for the older **Glen Usk** was the Cardiff-Weston ferry, but she made odd trips further afield as well as continuing to call at Barry Pier at times of low water when Cardiff was inaccessible, often at least once per day. Drama would befall her later in the season but in the meantime, together with her younger consort **Cardiff Queen**, it was basically a matter of both steamers running intensively around the Bristol Channel trying to pick up what traffic was to be had where, in the previous season, three vessels had done the job.

A wide range of trips was advertised on handbills for 1959, in the customary style where the block at the top gave the impression to the travelling public that the active White Funnel Fleet still consisted of four vessels, rather than just two. A good range of optional coach trips were offered in conjunction with the services and although there was now no 'resident' steamer berthing overnight at Bristol or at Swansea, the former place would often have a coach-departure to Weston-super-Mare to connect with a steamer trip on days when no steamer came up the River Avon. On most summer Saturdays Devon holidaymakers were provided with a service between west Wales and Ilfracombe, as had been pledged when the demise of the Swansea steamer had taken place at the end of the 1958 season. Mostly it was just Mumbles Pier rather than Swansea (South Dock Entrance) where the calls took place. Ticket inter-availability between steamer and railway was offered, for example when a steamer which had started out from Swansea only returned to Mumbles Pier, and by way of connection from & to Swansea, the White Funnel Fleet bills in the 1959 season could still refer to the frequent service of 'electric trains' on the venerable Swansea & Mumbles Railway, which had been there since well before Mumbles Pier had opened back in 1898.

During the month of August, Bristol saw two periods of about a week where favourable tides allowed five trips on almost consecutive days, giving ten long-day excursion opportunities, in addition to which there was one day, the 30th, where there was advertised to be a short Walton Bay cruise taken by a steamer coming up the river from Cardiff, before its return to Cardiff later on the same tide. Right back in the early days of Campbell steamers this pattern of operation was a regular occurrence, utilising a period of about two hours whilst there was sufficient water to make the double river voyage from the Hotwells Pontoon. This day turned out to be a fateful one, and we will return to it shortly. It was still considered appropriate to publish a separate bill for the small number of calls that were made at Portishead (at the Dock Entrance), and which generally took place on days when a steamer was starting out from Bristol to go down-Channel. Clovelly enjoyed something like fifteen advertised days of sailings in the 1959 season, and on three days these were to the old pattern of schedules when a 'Swansea boat' would proceed to Lundy calling at both Ilfracombe and Clovelly en-route, except that now the starting-point would just be Mumbles Pier.

Minehead bills advertised a small number of coach-tours to the Welsh Mountains, on occasions when a steamer was scheduled to depart from the Harbour to Cardiff in the morning. The same coach-tour excursion was also popular for passengers originating at Weston-super-Mare in connection with 'ferry' sailings across the channel. Porthcawl bills continued to offer a good variety of sailings and most weeks usually saw two trips on offer from the breakwater there. From Cardiff itself the greatest volume and variety of trips was advertised, and for coach-excursions the choice was considerable, the more common examples being to Cheddar Gorge (via sailings to Weston-super-Mare), Exmoor & Dunkery Beacon (via Minehead) and Saunton & Arlington (via Ilfracombe). An afternoon tea stop was, naturally, allowed for in many of these coach-excursions. Yet further variety could be had if sailing from Mumbles, one notable offering (on 27th August) being

via Ilfracombe to the 'English Switzerland', namely the Valley of the Rocks at Lynton, outwards by road via Two Potts and Blackmoor Gate, and returning via Combe Martin. Rather more tenuously the Mumbles/Swansea combined bills also promoted through rail & steamer fares for intending passengers to travel by train to Cardiff in order to catch a late-morning 'ferry' sailing from the Pier Head to Weston-super-Mare, returning the same way, but were somewhat vague on interchange arrangements between Cardiff (General) station and the Pier Head some little distance away in Bute Town, down in Cardiff's docklands.

The Tenby bill was straightforward: on three Sundays during August in 1959 a Cardiff steamer was advertised to proceed to Tenby, whence a cruise lasting around one and three-quarter hours was offered to the Stack Rocks from Tenby Harbour (the pier had by now been dismantled), before the steamer returned to Barry. On such a schedule there would not be sufficient water to get back all the way to Cardiff and so the usefulness of Barry Pier and a train-connection homewards to Cardiff was underscored. Finally, in this resume of bills in 1959, one enterprising specimen was that assembled for Burnham on Sea and Brean: in connection with the WEMS Coaches company, a number of Weston-super-Mare sailings were designated to be provided with buses from these places. The most common end-destination offered to folk wanting a day-out by coach, steamer and coach from this part of the Somerset coast was that provided by the Welsh Mountains tour, and one wonders now whether Clifton Smith-Cox composed the advertising copy himself in a spare moment or contracted an advertising agency of the day to carry out the task:

> '… A steamer may not seem the most likely mode of transport in which to start a Mountain Tour – nor the Old Pier at Weston the most probable point of departure. But Wales, after all, really is another country – a fact very often overlooked – and what more appropriate way of "going foreign" than by crossing the busy shipping-lanes of the Bristol Channel to reach the country's capital – Cardiff – where coaches meet the steamer at the Pier Head …'

There may have been a little nervousness as the 1959 season opened, after the sweeping changes of the previous few years, and in recognition of the fact that the bankers – who were now strictly in control – would require proof of the viability of the new regime of services based on two-vessel operations. It is instructive to look in depth at a typical week for **Cardiff Queen** and **Glen Usk** in 1959, to portray what was to become the norm throughout the rest of the ensuing seven-year period. The first four of these, 1959-1962 inclusive, have been defined as 'The Lean Years' as it was only in 1962 that the first signs of some resurgence became apparent, after a period when modest profitability was restored after many earlier years of consecutive losses.

The weather in 1959 was mercifully rather better than in previous years, and passengers were turned away on occasions during the season, notably at Mumbles, Weston and Ilfracombe. The timetables for a typical week in the high summer of 1959 illustrated the very considerable range of options that could still be squeezed out utilising just two vessels, with a degree of imagination applied to create both planned interchanges between steamers, and combined steamer and coach or steamer/bus circular tours, of the type that had been promised after the end of the 1958 season. The week commencing Monday 24th August 1959 has been singled out for analysis, and illustrates the long hours of both vessels in traffic and the relative complexity of the individual schedules devised to offer this variety, vital to earn the maximum possible revenues from the two steamers **Glen Usk** and **Cardiff Queen**. Appendix Two fully sets out the schedules for that week together with extracts from log-books to compare planned and actual times, for reference.

Picked out here are the main characteristics of a week in the life of the White Funnel Fleet, typifying the 'Lean Years'. Although **Glen Usk** was mostly the steamer which took 'ferry' duties and **Cardiff Queen** the one generally associated with longer-distance duties, the vessels interchanged to some extent and when the former was due for an off-service day, the latter could be switched to ferry duties in order to maintain a daily ferry operation. Conversely, *Glen Usk* would tend to stay on ferry duties when *Cardiff Queen* had an off-service day, and no long-distance trips would run that day as a consequence. The ferry service pattern in 1959 typically involved *Glen Usk* performing three or four round trips daily from Cardiff Pier Head to Weston's Birnbeck Pier as tides permitted, and she would often fit in a round trip from Weston to Barry Pier at low water when Cardiff would be inaccessible, exploiting the tidal range of Barry Pier to the full. On some of these occasions special trains would be provided between Cardiff and Barry Pier to connect, as a substitute for direct Cardiff sailings, and the degree of co-operation with the railways locally was notable. For most ferry journeys throughout the day, it was normal to call at Penarth when outward bound from Cardiff, but not on the way back if the tide was on the ebb and another trip due straightaway from Cardiff to Weston, which would again serve Penarth. Ten minutes was allowed between Cardiff Pier Head and Penarth Pier. The steamers were often but not always berthed overnight at Cardiff, and there were odd occasions, such as Tuesday 7th July when *Cardiff Queen* ran the last ferry from Cardiff to Weston and, rather than return to Wales, anchored in Walton Bay for the night, so as to be positioned ready to run up the River Avon the following morning for an 0900 departure from Hotwells to Clovelly. It was a particularly interesting week in that a degree of light running was necessitated to position *Cardiff Queen* overnight for her next day's duties, which were varied and widespread, but it was probably a fairly typical week in terms of the long hours worked by both vessels.

A week of two-vessel operations in 1959

Monday 24th August 1959. *Glen Usk* was the ferry steamer, but also made two round trips between Cardiff and Minehead to offer an unusual Up-Channel trip from the latter. Such trips seem to have run at approximately monthly intervals during the 1959 season. *Cardiff Queen*, as the long-distance vessel, was Bristol-based for the day and served Clevedon, Weston, Barry, Lynmouth and Ilfracombe in the time-honoured manner. A coastal cruise from Ilfracombe to Lynmouth and Porlock Bay, described on the Ilfracombe handbill as the 'Ilfracombe Publicity Cruise' was provided in the time that would otherwise have been spent alongside at Ilfracombe. Whilst it had been common until the early '50s for steamers to lie at anchor for a couple of hours off Ilfracombe between duties, or stay alongside the pier if circumstances permitted, this practice gradually became less common as the remaining vessels were worked more intensively.

Tuesday 25th August 1959. *Glen Usk* carried out a straightforward ferry roster, which combined four round trips between Cardiff, Penarth & Weston with one round trip between Weston and Barry. The couple of hours spent alongside Barry Pier at low water between trips were not idle, as the time was used for carrying out lifeboat drill and various checks and inspections. A variety of afternoon non-landing cruises from Barry were also offered during the season, but not during this particular week. *Cardiff Queen* was engaged on a Cardiff-Lundy duty which involved the normal calls at Penarth, Barry, and Ilfracombe but which also included morning and evening calls at Porthcawl Harbour as the tides were favourable that day.

Wednesday 26th August 1959. *Glen Usk* enjoyed her off-service day at Cardiff whilst *Cardiff Queen* covered 'ferry' duties and combined three round trips with one between Weston and Barry. On arrival at Cardiff after the last trip of the day from Weston (via Penarth), she set off light to Swansea where she was to spend the night, in readiness for the next day.

Thursday 27th August 1959. This was a somewhat less usual day, as *Cardiff Queen* was Swansea-based, leaving there at 0830 for an advertised schedule exactly like that which had been regularly on offer more frequently in 1958 and before, when there had been a regular Swansea-based steamer, namely to Mumbles, Ilfracombe, Clovelly and then across to Lundy Island to land. However she ran late after leaving Ilfracombe and was so late leaving Clovelly that a cruise to the North End of the island ran instead (the log suggests that only 'single' passengers were landed, as she was only in Lundy Roads for 25 minutes) before she returned to Clovelly and Ilfracombe and thence recovered her schedule. On arrival at Swansea she promptly

discharged her passengers before returning light to Barry, spending the night moored inside the Docks at 19 Berth. *Glen Usk* as the ferry steamer that day ran a full roster of four Cardiff-Weston round trips and one Weston-Barry return trip, albeit not without incident: the log recalls that on approaching the 'Burnham Berth' at Cardiff Pier Head at 1115, an incorrect order was given from the bridge to the engine-room, and that a minor collision was sustained. No apparent damage was recorded, and no voyages were lost.

Friday 28th August 1959. It was the turn of *Cardiff Queen* (which had maintained the Cardiff-Weston ferry on Wednesday, when *Glen Usk* had enjoyed her off-service day) to be off-service on this Friday, and this duly took place at Barry Dock. However her engineers were not entirely at rest that day, as workmen were present attending to the bushes of her starboard paddle-wheel. *Glen Usk* carried out the normal three round trips on the ferry before a final round-trip which ended at Barry Pier, where she then spent the night, not far away from her younger sister, within Barry Dock itself.

Saturday 29th August 1959. Some rather more complicated rostering was necessitated on this Saturday, in order to provide the weekly Swansea/Mumbles to Ilfracombe holidaymakers link that had been promised the previous year by the company when the regular Swansea steamer had been withdrawn, and which had previously provided virtually daily crossings of that somewhat more exposed end of the Bristol Channel. After their day off on Friday 28th August, the crew of *Cardiff Queen* were rewarded with an exceptionally early start on Saturday 29th at 0515 off the berth at Barry Dock, to lock out and proceed light to Swansea in readiness for the 0930 crossing to Ilfracombe, calling twenty minutes later at Mumbles Pier. On arrival at Ilfracombe she then proceeded to Lynmouth, Barry, Penarth and Cardiff, thereupon changing places with *Glen Usk* which had been on ferry duties during the morning. As *Cardiff Queen* approached Cardiff, *Glen Usk* had already set off from there to Penarth, Barry, Lynmouth and Ilfracombe. Unusually, *Glen Usk* then took the evening crossing from Ilfracombe just to Mumbles Pier where, pausing only briefly, she then turned her bow up-channel for Barry, Penarth and Cardiff where she finally tied up at 0120 on the Sunday morning. The fun was not over for all of the crew, though, as bunkering then commenced. This splendid piece of scheduling permitted, amongst other possibilities, an unusual up-channel cruise to be offered from either Swansea, Ilfracombe or Lynmouth to Barry, with a change of steamers thrown in for the return voyage.

Sunday August 30th 1959 The real drama was to unfold the next day as *Glen Usk* was to hit the headlines in a spectacular manner. Her schedule was a comparatively leisurely cruise at 1240 from Cardiff to Penarth, Weston, Clevedon and Bristol, followed by a 2-hr Walton Bay cruise from Hotwells on the afternoon tide (High Water at Cardiff was at 1701), before returning to Cardiff the way she came at 1815. *Cardiff Queen* was merely scheduled to be on ferry duties all day, starting at Barry for Weston at a civilised 1115 before taking just two round trips between Cardiff, Penarth & Weston. It would be an understatement to say that things did not quite go to plan for the older vessel on that fateful day.

The grounding of *Glen Usk*

A considerable amount of publicity, albeit not wholly adverse, was generated by the events that took place on the evening of Sunday 30th August 1959 when *Glen Usk* was returning down-river on a falling tide from Bristol to Clevedon, Penarth and Cardiff after having operated the Walton Bay afternoon cruise. She had got a little behind schedule whilst en route up-river from Cardiff to Bristol earlier on in the afternoon, and had not arrived at Hotwells until 1615, fifteen minutes after the scheduled 1600 departure. Leaving at 1630 on the cruise she passed Avonmouth at 1706 and turned outside the river mouth at 1727, passing Avonmouth again shortly afterwards heading back up-river. Despite a quick turnround at Hotwells between 1836-1845 she was then half an hour late leaving on an ebbing tide.

She went aground on the Horseshoe Bend at 1910, her starboard side having caught the river bank, in calm conditions with visibility described as fine & clear. Subsequent log-entries recorded the following:

1930	Passengers started going ashore
2000	All passengers ashore safely
2030	'Abandon Ship' order given to crew
2100	All crew ashore, vessel keeling over at (est.) 40°-45°
2359	Bosun plus 3 AB's aboard closing portholes on port side.
0300	(Monday) Vessel began to right herself
0345	Afloat
0410	Taken in hand by tugs, to Avonmouth Pier Head
0930	To Cardiff
1655	Entered Penarth Dock
1815	On Pontoon at Penarth Dock
1900	On blocks, for inspection.

Remarkably, little damage appeared to have been sustained by the elderly vessel, then 45 years old, and after repairs that took all day on the Tuesday she locked out early on the morning of Wednesday 2nd September and made her way across to Cardiff Pier Head. After bunkering, ferry duties were resumed at 0948. The way in which this incident caused publicity is of considerable interest. The image presented to the public was one that inspired confidence through the calm, professional way in which the incident was handled by the officers and crew of *Glen Usk*. It had however been an unlucky event, but no heavy criticism was implied. Given that there was no loss of life, one does wonder if the wisdom of having decided to run the cruise late, and consequently be unavoidably late on leaving Bristol for Cardiff against a falling tide, would now be challenged. The 'Comment' editorial of the *Bristol Evening Post* for Monday August 31st, 1959 made a calm assessment of the events that had taken place the night before. The theme of a strong public fondness in Bristol for the activities of what had been a favourite local company was ever-present, and there was no hint of criticism that *Glen Usk* had run aground with around 600 passengers on board.

The piece was entitled 'Happy Ending to Avon drama':

> '...The *Glen Usk* drama in the twisting River Avon has had a happy ending - and we are glad to know that this grand old sea-lady is likely to be back in service quite soon. Rescue services all went smoothly. Everyone buckled down to the job admirably - not least the scores of local people who volunteered their help in bringing the passengers across the mud and up the cliff to the roadway in safety. We hope a full-scale examination will serve to bear out the present hopes that *Glen Usk* is not too seriously damaged - and that the whole episode will not be a blow to her owners. The tide has been running against Campbell's for some years, but this season has been the best since the war. We trust that the White Funnel Fleet will be with us for a long time yet.'

Death of Alexander Campbell, and the end of the season

A second drama during the 1959 season was the tragic death of Alexander Campbell, then the last surviving member of the Campbell family involved in the business since the retirement of Bob Campbell had taken place a couple of years before. He had held various engineering positions in the Company and was Chief Engineer in *Cardiff Queen* at the time of his death on Sunday 13th September 1959. He had already suffered ill-health. A well-known character, his death was recorded in the *Bristol Evening Post* on 14th September 1959 as follows:

> #### ENGINEER IS FOUND DEAD ON STEAMER
> 'Mr Alexander Campbell, (62) of 32, Effingham Road, Bristol, Chief Engineer of the P. & A. Campbell Ltd pleasure-steamer *Cardiff Queen*, was found dead in her control room by a ships' fireman at Ilfracombe yesterday morning. Mr Campbell – who leaves a widow - was the son of one of the founders of P. & A. Campbell Ltd, Capt. Peter Campbell. A Campbell's spokesman at Cardiff told the Evening Post today that the body was discovered at 8.45 a.m. yesterday, when the ship was moored at Ilfracombe Pier awaiting the return journey to Cardiff. Mr

> Campbell had had breakfast, the spokesman said, and had gone alone to the control room to turn the engine over before the Cardiff run. Minutes later a ship's fireman, Mr Roy Ferrier, found him slumped over the controls. Mr Campbell worked a five-year apprenticeship in the company's Bristol fitting shop before going to sea and taking his engineers ticket. He was Chief Engineer of various ships operated by the company for about 30 years.'

Tribute was paid to Alex Campbell in the *White Funnel News and Views* section of the journal *Ship Ahoy*. This referred to '... *his robust sense of humour and his jovial personality ... combined to make him one of the best loved characters on the Bristol Channel. He will be sadly missed by the regular passengers and those who have known him during his forty years of service to the firm* ...'. The funeral was held in Bristol on 17th September 1959. The Second Engineer with Alex Campbell on *Cardiff Queen* was Jack Rowles, and the sudden passing of her Chief Engineer led to Jack taking on that role once he had gained the necessary ticket a few days later. Like his erstwhile Chief Engineer, Jack had served an apprenticeship at the Underfall Yard after joining the company in 1939, followed by a spell in the Royal Navy and then going deep-sea, but he had returned to a job ashore with P. & A. Campbell Ltd in the early-1950s. He soon switched to a sea-going position as Second Engineer on *Glen Usk*, moving to *Cardiff Queen* in 1955. He was destined to be her last Chief Engineer, and we will hear more of him in due course.

The events of the 1959 season have been dealt with at some length, as in many ways that initial year of two-vessel operations created the basic pattern of excursion services that was to last for broadly the next decade or so. A basic 'ferry' operation between Cardiff, Penarth and Weston-super-Mare was supplemented by as wide a variety of longer-distance excursions as could possibly be squeezed out of a second vessel around the Channel, and complemented by the ancillary business of the provision of Coach Tours and sustaining more humdrum road/rail inter-availability options for tickets. *Cardiff Queen* was the first vessel to be taken out of service at the end of the 1959 season, running her last sailing from Cardiff to Lundy on Sunday 27th September. On the following afternoon she proceeded the short distance from Cardiff Pier Head across to Penarth Dock to lay up, and her final log-book entry that year recorded an incident with the steam tug Cardiff inside the dock on Saturday 3rd October, with the prosaic entry 'damage unknown'. Her master throughout 1959 had been Jack George, and her Mate Phil Power. *Glen Usk* remained in service a little longer, but ran the last ferry service, at 2240 from Weston to Cardiff, on Monday 5th October, proceeding the next day into Penarth Dock. Her master had been Neville Cottman and her mate Leslie Brooks, and the closing log-book entry revealed that her mileage steamed had been 16,724 during the 1959 season.

Financial Reconstruction

Whilst the 1959 season had run its course for the company the next major event would be the 'financial reconstruction' of P. & A. Campbell Ltd, an event which was to largely determine the future shape of the business in 1960 and afterwards. The company had now been in Receivership for well over a year already and there was a something of a paradox here, as operations had continued with seemingly little visible change, but to a slightly more rapid tempo, and the average passenger may well have neither known nor cared that a transformation of the business structure was being undertaken behind the scenes. For regular travellers, some of whom were also shareholders, there had been no news of what might be the likely outcome of the deliberations of the Receiver. But it was reasonable to hope that the 1959 season had, at long last, been a better summer for the company, and that perhaps a turning point had been reached. The effects of the reconstruction were to be tangible, however, and the result of the injection of fresh capital into the ailing business was to give a continued ability to the public to cruise in the waters of the Severn Sea for another twenty years or so, not necessarily in the well-cared for paddlers that had once been the norm, but most importantly the White Funnel Fleet would still soldier on as other steamer operators fell by the wayside. We thus momentarily step aside from the pattern of sailings, steamers and incidents in order to consider the circumstances which lay behind the terms that were to be offered to creditors and shareholders by the Receiver at the very end of 1959 and which, when agreed, were to shape the longer-term survival of P. & A. Campbell Ltd. This requires us to come back to when the connection with George Nott Industries was first forged.

The basic chain of events that was to lead to the eventual salvation of the White Funnel Fleet stemmed from the fact that one of the favourite outings of the George Nott directors was to go down to Weston-super-Mare (traditionally popular with visitors from Birmingham and the Midlands) and spend a day on board a P. & A. Campbell Ltd steamer in the Bristol Channel. These individuals would have been George Nott himself, Roland Wickenden and Colin Fenn and possibly Ken Siddle plus guests of the directors, but at this point all were unknown to Clifton Smith-Cox and his fellow directors. As Peter Southcombe (who joined the company as its Passenger Manager in 1963, and of whom we will hear more) explained it to the author, the story that Clifton Smith-Cox later told was that it was a lucky coincidence that had put him in touch with Notts. P. & A. Campbell Ltd had been a member of the old Coastal Passenger Steamship Operators Association, and in that context he had written to the other member companies looking for support to help him keep the White Funnel Fleet afloat as its financial position deteriorated after bad summer succeeded bad summer. The letter sent to Captain Townsend had courteously been forwarded by that gentleman to George Nott, whilst its author had then been advised by Captain Townsend that this was what he had done as his own circumstances within the business at that time were clearly changing rapidly. This being the case, Notts gave a degree of careful thought to acquiring P. & A. Campbell Ltd, in the same manner as they had already acquired Townsend Bros. Ferries. Aside from the way in which Tax Law – in layman terms – permitted the losses of a subsidiary company to be offset against the profits of a parent body, there was doubtless some sentimental attachment too, and thus it came about that a useful relationship between the politically well-connected Clifton Smith-Cox and George Nott Industries was forged. Another shipping subsidiary was thus acquired by Notts and although exactly what was intended at the outset is not recorded, it can be assumed that the relationship was commercial rather than philanthropic – and not necessarily to be of a permanent nature.

The author was fortunate to acquire, via the late H. G. Owen, some of the papers of the late Cyril Hawkins-Garrington, who had been a P. & A. Campbell Ltd shareholder of long-standing and who took a lively interest in Bristol's shipping affairs in general, and paddle-steamer operations in particular during the 1950s. He was also a freelance artist, and before the Second World War had occasionally advertised his work in the annual Bristol Channel District Guide books published by the company. These papers included an extensive set of official letters to shareholders, which complemented the statutory Accounts of the company and Chairman's Reports that shareholders would have received. (It is worth mentioning that attendance at the Ordinary General Meetings during the 1950s was often confined to no more than 20 or 30 shareholders, and that a large proportion of the ordinary shares in the Company were held in relatively small blocks, by a comparatively large number of private individuals, not changing much year by year). From study of these official communications (a number of which have already been referred to, and are reproduced in full or in part in Appendix One) a picture emerges of what shareholders were told as the Company went through the periods of financial difficulty already described, culminating in Chancery proceedings and the successful conclusion to the financial reconstruction. So, here we try to take the story forward, in this context.

The build-up to the eventual takeover of P. & A. Campbell Ltd by George Nott Industries was a prolonged affair, given that the appointment of a Financial Controller by the Westminster Bank pre-dated the formality of the company entering receivership, and that it was this gentleman who became the Receiver. Thus, an early reference

to the existence of 'outside' controlling interests can be found in a letter from the Chairman, A. R. Boucher, to all Shareholders dated 9th November 1956, which described the series of cutbacks implemented earlier that year, and which stated that:

'... I may hardly add that the ... decisions have been reached after consultation with, and approval by, the Financial Controller. I believe that Shareholders must appreciate the anxiety and frustration felt by my colleagues and myself when, as has happened in six of the last seven years everyone's efforts to achieve success have been hampered by bad summer weather and I believe that all will be sympathetic with our desire to minimise this factor so far as it is humanly possible.'

As has been shown, the trading position had not got better after this position was set out, and further moves towards the eventual financial reconstruction were still quite a time in taking shape. Publication of the results for the 1957 season had been delayed and it was not until over two years later, after the 66th AGM held in Bristol on Friday 14th November 1958 that the Receiver & Manager, W. Walker, had written to all Creditors announcing his preliminary findings. This letter constituted a landmark and contained a formal admission of the behind-the-scenes talks that had been initiated to find a purchaser for P. & A. Campbell Ltd. The letter warned that the insolvent state of the company was such that in addition to the Debenture Holder (that is, the Westminster Bank through its loan) being likely to suffer a shortfall on it's financial interest there would be no surplus for unsecured creditors. In simple terms the liabilities of P. & A. Campbell Ltd exceeded the amount that could be expected by the sale of the assets – namely the four surviving paddle-steamers at that point – which was thought to be significantly less than the 'book' value recorded in the Assets side of the Balance Sheet. The crucial paragraph read as follows:

'... I am, however, happy to say that, as a result of negotiations I have just concluded with another Company and with the Debenture Holders, new working capital and control will be acquired within the framework of the present Company, which will permit not only the continuation but the expansion of the Company's business with, all other considerations being satisfactory, continuing business for the suppliers. The Directors approve the proposals. These proposals, if approved by creditors and shareholders, provide for a capital reconstruction, discharge of the present debenture, and a payment to creditors. It will take some time to work out the legal issues and documents before the scheme can be submitted for consideration".
Yours faithfully,
W.WALKER
Receiver & Manager.
4th December 1958'

This was more or less still at the beginning of the period in Receivership, and the other company referred to was, of course, George Nott Industries. One wonders how literally this letter was interpreted, in its reference to expansion after so many years of retraction, yet here was recognition that there was still thought to be life in the ailing paddle-steamer business, and that a rescue could be effected. Harder evidence which defines the actual motive of Notts is lacking now but at this point it is reasonable to conclude that the Tax-Losses potential that the Campbell business so clearly offered to Notts was a further incentive. This was sufficient to induce them to put in the necessary cash to clear the Bank Debenture – on commercial terms - and take control of the company, as legitimate diversification as well as perhaps assisting them in funding major investments elsewhere. Equally, the political connections of Clifton Smith-Cox both in the Bristol business community and more broadly were an attraction to Notts and it must have seemed a good business proposition, without necessarily having to look too far ahead then. The reference to taking '... *some time to work out the legal issues* ...' practically equated to the cautious embarkation upon and journey through the 1959 season, which we have already looked at in some detail.

The technical accountancy issues involved with the processes of receivership, insolvency, liquidation and so on are complex and not easily understood by the layman. In looking back to events which were unfolding almost fifty years ago, reliance has had to be placed on the written statements made both by the Company Chairman and subsequently the Receiver, plus Court of Chancery papers. An overview of selected extracts from the Company Accounts themselves, set alongside these other sources, is set out in the Appendix as item 6, entitled: 'An Accountancy Perspective', based on analysis by Keith Adams, a professional accountant. This considers all the available Annual Results from 1950, and other financial documents relating specifically to the period of receivership, broadly covering the five-year period 1956-1960. The phrase 'wiping the slate clean' somewhat oversimplifies what happened then, and a key factor was that a fresh start could be enabled, unburdened by past liabilities. Therefore, as 1959 gave way to 1960, what was going to be needed was to gain the formal endorsement of shareholders to what was being proposed, and this was duly forthcoming.

A turning point in the fortunes of P. & A. Campbell Ltd had now been reached, although this might not have been apparent at the time. After so many years of bad weather and deteriorating financial results, the fleet had been cut to just two operational ships after 1958 in the belief that this scale of activity was sustainable, without heavy overheads. Success would depend greatly on higher utilisation of assets and, indeed, more effective marketing to get the White Funnel Fleet to pay its way. The two-vessel operation established in 1959 has been examined at some length largely because it established the pattern that was to become the norm for the next period of the life of P. & A. Campbell Ltd. It also represented the manifestation of the concept that Clifton Smith-Cox had managed to sell to Nott Industries, and what this came down to was that after extensive surgery, the operations of P. & A. Campbell Ltd had started to turn around from losses into modest profitability, even though on the face of it little had altered in day-to-day appearances, and no change of image had been felt to be necessary.

The 67th Ordinary General Meeting of P. & A. Campbell Ltd was convened at the Grand Hotel at Bristol on 31st December 1959, to immediately follow an EGM so as to formally present the proposals to shareholders, as special resolutions. In the new year, a letter dated 6th February 1960 from Company Secretary Ernie Harris to all shareholders was circulated, and which announced that the Court of Chancery had approved the Scheme, and invited all to submit their share certificates in order that new ones could be issued. Elsewhere it was recorded that the Sanction of the Court to the scheme had been given on 25th January 1960, and that the Receiver ceased to act after 5th February 1960. The Observations of the Receiver, and the Chancery Proceedings documents describing the technicalities of the financial reconstruction were complex and lengthy. In practical terms, the proposition which had been brokered basically meant that the worth of individual shareholdings was substantially reduced, that some creditors would lose out, but that the Westminster Bank Debenture was released, and control through a new majority shareholding was now vested in George Nott Industries. Clifton Smith-Cox would remain as Managing Director after the 'Scheme of Arrangement' had been executed.

A succint explanation of up the practical effects of the exercise was given in the journal *Ship Ahoy* in the Christmas 1959 edition, one of it's then editors Donald Anderson seemingly taking a tolerant view of the greatly diminished worth of his own modest personal stake in the Campbell business before the scheme was formally approved. There appears to have been a sense that this long drawn out affair would now be ratified by the shareholders, there being little practicable alternative in sight:

'... The long awaited 'Scheme of Arrangement' to ease Campbell's financial crisis was made known to shareholders on December 8th. It is as a result of negotiations between the Company and Nott Industries Ltd (parent company of a group including Townsend Ferries). The scheme has two sections relating to (a) shareholders and (b) creditors.

Under the scheme the 200,000 £1 Ordinary shares and 30,000 £1 Preference shares of the issued capital will be converted into 4,600,000 1/- shares. Two 1/- shares for each currently-held Preference share and one 1/- share for each currently held Ordinary share will be retained by the present shareholders and these holdings will be consolidated into 5/- 6% Preference shares with interest guaranteed by Nott for three years. The vast bulk of the new shilling shares (4,340,000, equivalent to £217,000 capital) will be transferred to Nott Industries Ltd and reconverted into £1 Ordinary shares.

With regard to creditors Nott Industries undertake to purchase the Debenture, worth £135,000, under which the whole Campbell undertaking is charged to the Westminster Bank Ltd, for £95,000 plus certain other sums deposited in the Bank as at 31st December 1958. Capital will then be released to pay off the all preference creditors in full and also unsecured creditors whose claim is less than £25. Unsecured claims in excess of £25 will be settled at the rate of 5/- in the pound.

Subject to the approval of shareholders, creditors and the Chancery Division of the High Court being obtained, the scheme will be retrospective to January 1st 1959. Meetings of interested parties will be held at Bristol on December 31st 1959. Nott Industries have indicated that the present Board of Directors will remain in office and the name of the company will be unchanged. The Receiver and Manager appointed by the Westminster Bank in 1958 will be withdrawn.

Commending the scheme to those concerned the Company Chairman makes it clear in his explanatory letter that there is little choice but to accept its terms. One of your Editors is delighted ! He exchanges his £50 holding of ordinary shares (which have not yielded a dividend for years) for a £2.10/- holding of preference shares which will yield a guaranteed 3/- p.a. (less tax !) … Financial security at last!'

1960: The new company's first year

A steadier period was now to follow, yet it was only to be a couple of years before sufficient confidence would be found to justify fleet expansion and ventures in new areas, including experimentation with operating hovercraft. Although the 1960s started with the vestiges of the paddle-steamer era, much was to happen as the transition was made through that decade as paddle-steamers gave way to motor-vessels. In the meantime the season of 1960 was characterised by being substantially similar to the one that had preceded it, inasmuch as the same two vessels continued in service, with a broadly comparable range of operations. An early season press statement for 1960 referred to the circumstances of the two-vessel pattern established after 1958 and confirmed that whilst things had begun to pick up as hoped in 1959, operations would be very similar to those of the previous season, and the newest vessel **Bristol Queen** would remain out of service on the grounds of economy. The company stated at the beginning of the 1960 season the reason for her not being in commission: '*... it is not economical to run three boats, and the* **Bristol Queen***, being the largest and most expensive to run, will be kept in reserve*'. The retention of the aged, and sometimes less than punctual coal-burning **Glen Usk** as the ferry steamer seemed odd to some observers, but there was recognition that this was largely dictated by fuel price considerations.

The 1950s might have been predominantly a period of retrenchment and gloom but as the White Funnel Fleet plans for 1960 were announced, regulars and enthusiasts were assured that a good variety of sailings would still be offered, and which included occasional calls at the further-flung locations of Tenby, Clovelly and Bideford in addition to retention of the Swansea & Mumbles to Ilfracombe link, and the 'bread-and-butter' Ilfracombe and Lundy runs from up-Channel, mainly the preserve of **Cardiff Queen**. Coastal cruises from Mumbles were also occasionally still offered, as well as calls at Porthcawl and Minehead. Enthusiasts and others could still be grateful that steamer excursions were still part of the Bristol Channel way-of-life, and hope that this would continue as other companies elsewhere around Britain could be seen to be faltering.

One peripheral difference to would-be Bristol Channel passengers in 1960, mostly those travelling from west Wales, was the sad closure of the historic Swansea & Mumbles Railway, which had finally succumbed in January that year. Those Swansea folk wishing to join a steamer at Mumbles Pier now had to catch one of the replacement buses, a retrograde step in the minds of many locals.

Before the 1960 season got underway one of the first, melancholy White Funnel events of the new decade was the sight of *Glen Gower* leaving for Belgian ship-breakers from Penarth Dock on April 7th, 1960, after rumours during the previous year that she might have been purchased for further service on the Devon coast. These rumours appear to have had only limited substance as the Company Minute Book recorded that a price of £4,800 was considered for her sale, subject to the buyers undertaking not to use her in competition with Campbell sailings. A second offer was received for £5,100 although it is not entirely clear that this was actually the price paid by the breakers. H. G. Owen, writing in *Ship Ahoy*, provided an obituary notice to what had been one of his favourite P. & A. Campbell Ltd paddle-steamers, having as a young boy been privileged to see her run her maiden voyage from Swansea, back in 1922. Her last few years of service were summed up thus:

'... Returning to the Bristol Channel on June 21st (1950) she was employed out of Cardiff, occasionally on the 'ferry' and also out of Bristol. In 1951 she was similarly employed, but the next year, 1952, sailed out of Swansea for the season. 1953 saw her commence on the 'ferry' on May 22nd and sail for Brighton on June 7th from where she attended the Coronation Naval Review at Spithead. Coming back to the Bristol Channel on June 17th she again plied out of Cardiff and Bristol, occasionally running down to Ilfracombe. In 1954 she again went south ... 1956 was the last season that *Glen Gower* operated the Boulogne trips, in 1957 she ran principally on the Weston 'ferry' with a final visit to Ilfracombe on 28th September. Her boiler was now in a very bad way, steam pressure often falling as low as 80 lbs. In October of that year she

was offered for sale, but with no offers forthcoming she was laid up at Penarth and sank into squalor. The process of decay was hastened by the depredations of scrap metal thieves who removed almost every portion of brass aboard. The old ship was sold in April to Belgians, it is understood for conversion to a floating machine shop and she left Penarth on 7th April, in tow, a decrepit travesty of what had once been one of "Campbell's yachts".'

In the valleys around Newport, efforts continued to be made to promote through rail & steamer fares from a very wide range of stations, via Cardiff, thereby continuing to honour the undertaking that had been given to the public by P. & A. Campbell Ltd after the closure of the Newport Landing Stage in 1956. An agreement with British Railways locally at Cardiff underpinned the detailed accountancy and settlement arrangements necessary for such through fares, and the railway-produced bills made interesting reading as they quoted a comprehensive range of day and period fares to cross the Bristol Channel from every station on each of the lines radiating from Newport still enjoying passenger services, which in the pre-Dr Beeching era still included those to Brynmawr and Ebbw Vale via the 'western valley' and to Blaenavon via the 'eastern valley', as well as the main lines towards Abergavenny and Chepstow, via Cardiff General (latterly Cardiff Central) station. These bills even mentioned a facility at the Pier Head, for those taking a three-monthly ticket, for a 'free transit' of up to 100 lbs of luggage to the boats, but did not elaborate on exactly how to get between the railway station and the Pier Head with such an encumbrance. Another element of the combined rail & steamer ticket offerings of this era, the roots of which went back to prewar days when more or less daily boats connected Cardiff and Bristol, was the facility to take a ticket by steamer from Cardiff to Weston and then proceed via train to Bristol, or vice-versa. This facility was also offered to Bristol folk the other way round, as it were.

Intending passengers in the locality of Cardiff were still reasonably well catered for inasmuch as a trolleybus service still existed from

*The two old-timers **Ravenswood** (b.1891) and **Britannia** (b.1896) had already gone to the breakers during the 1950s. After being laid-up at the end of the 1957 season, **Glen Gower** (b.1922) slumbered awhile uncertainly until being towed away from Penarth Dock on her own one-way trip on 7th April 1960.*

Miss Gwyneth White

Right: *Another view of* **Glen Gower** *when leaving Penarth Dock under tow by the tug Tradesman, 7th April 1960.*
Miss Gwyneth White

Below: *A promotional leaflet aimed at attracting passengers from the Newport area, with through fares by train, for Cardiff sailings after the cessation of sailings from the Landing Stage at Newport following the 1956 season.*
Author's collection

WESTERN REGION

SEASON 1960.
Commencing 28th MAY
Approx. Closing Date 25th SEPTEMBER.

Combined Rail and Steamer

EXCURSIONS

in connection with
THE WHITE FUNNEL FLEET
SEASON 1960.

WEEKDAYS

Through Day and Three-Monthly Return Tickets

TO

LYNMOUTH

AND

ILFRACOMBE

Via Cardiff (General) and Messrs. P & A. Campbell's Steamers

(Weather and other circumstances permitting).

FROM	Via CARDIFF (Gen) Station and Cardiff PIER HEAD Second Class Rail & Boat Fare to Lynmouth or Ilfracombe		FROM	Via CARDIFF (Gen) Station and Cardiff PIER HEAD Second Class Rail & Boat Fare to Lynmouth or Ilfracombe	
	One Day	Three Months		One Day	Three Months
	s. d.	s. d.		s. d.	s. d.
ABERGAVENNY (Mon. Rd.) ...	30 6	49 6	BRYNMAWR ...	32 3	50 6
PONTYPOOL ROAD ...	28 9	45 10	NANTYGLO ...	31 6	49 6
			BLAINA ...	31 6	49 6
BLAENAVON ...	30 9	48 6	ABERTILLERY ...	30 6	48 -
ABERSYCHAN (L.L.) ...	29 9	47 -	SIX BELLS HALT ...	30 6	48 -
PONTNEWYNYDD ...	29 3	46 6	EBBW VALE ...	31 6	49 6
PONTYPOOL (Crane St.) ...	29 -	46 2	VICTORIA ...	31 6	49 6
PANTEG & GRIFFITHSTOWN ...	28 6	45 6	CWM ...	30 9	48 6
SEBASTOPOL ...	28 6	45 6	ABERBEEG ...	30 -	47 4
UPPER PONTNEWYDD ...	28 3	45 -	LLANHILLETH ...	30 -	47 4
CWMBRAN ...	28 -	44 8	CRUMLIN (L.L.) ...	29 3	46 6
LLANTARNAM ...	27 9	44 4	NEWBRIDGE ...	29 -	46 2
PONTHIR ...	27 -	43 6	ABERCARN ...	28 6	45 6
CAERLEON ...	26 9	43 2	CWMCARN ...	28 3	45 -
			CROSS KEYS ...	28 -	44 8
CHEPSTOW ...	30 9	48 6	RISCA ...	27 9	44 4
PORTSKEWETT ...	29 9	47 -	TYNYCWM HALT ...	27 6	44 -
SEVERN TUNNEL JCN. ...	28 9	45 10	ROGERSTONE ...	26 9	43 2
MAGOR ...	28 3	45 -	BASSALEG JUNCTION ...	26 6	42 10
LLANWERN ...	27 -	43 6			
			NEWPORT ...	24 6	42 -

NOTE—These fares do not include Pier Tolls.

For particulars of bookings to Weston-super-Mare see Handbill N4092

For details of Steamer Sailings and Notice as to Conditions etc., see overleaf.

various parts of the city to the Pier Head, and P. & A. Campbell Ltd bills stated that special Cardiff Corporation buses '… *met all steamers on arrival at Cardiff and run to all points in the City after regular services have ceased*'. At Barry Pier, it was further mentioned that on occasions when a steamer returned to Barry rather than to Cardiff, the Purser on board would issue a rail ticket to Cardiff (General) from Barry Pier station. Conversely, the bills also noted that on those occasions when passengers from Barry might have gone to Weston but the steamer only returned to Penarth, then they could use a free bus, at 2230, to get home from Penarth to Barry (Town Hall).

It fell to *Glen Usk* to open the season at Easter 1960, and a new feature mentioned on handbills was the offer of an inclusive weekend trip to Ilfracombe with hotel accommodation. This was based around her planned excursions down-Channel on two days of the Easter holiday period, the Saturday and the Monday (in addition to sustaining Weston ferry duties up-Channel), such that a two-night stay at the Grosvenor Hotel could be offered for the sum of £6.00, sailing outwards on the Saturday and returning to Cardiff on the Monday. Just for good measure an afternoon cruise out of Ilfracombe on Easter Monday was also on offer, passing Lee Bay, Bull Point lighthouse and Morte Point to turn off Woolacombe. After the busy Easter period *Glen Usk* remained on up-Channel and ferry duties, and there was a gap in Ilfracombe services until the second steamer came out in late-May in readiness for the Whitsun holidays.

'Showboat' trips in the Bristol Channel that are nowadays provided by *Waverley* and *Balmoral* are nothing new: back in 1960, one such 'Midsummer Showboat' (with Music and Entertainment on board) was advertised to be run (by *Cardiff Queen*) on Sunday 26th June leaving Bristol at 0900 and Cardiff at 1105 for Lynmouth, Ilfracombe and a Bideford Bay cruise.

Down at Bideford itself, on one of the three occasions in the 1960 season that a White Funnel Fleet ship was billed to proceed there from Ilfracombe, a short afternoon cruise out of Bideford down the River Torridge, passing Appledore and Instow, was offered. A little further afield, Lundy was promoted by a special handbill in which one could again detect the subtle humour of a copywriter – or even Clifton Smith-Cox himself - in darkly referring to the 'legal and illegal' practices with which this evocative island had been associated over the centuries, but without actually elaborating on the details of these practices.

Glen Usk – the last 'old-timer'

As the 1960 season ran its course the heartening news broke that a resurrection of *Bristol Queen* was in mind as she was inspected during July and steam raised again for the first time in almost two years. Although the initial stated intention was that she and *Cardiff Queen* would swap places in 1961, a shift in the balance of coal and oil-fuel prices was to mean that *Glen Usk* would be finally laid aside

Sailings from ILFRACOMBE to LUNDY ISLAND
and other resorts on the English and Welsh Coasts during
the summer months. Details can be obtained from:

THE WHITE FUNNEL FLEET

P. & A. CAMPBELL LTD., 4 DOCK CHAMBERS
CARDIFF 20255
10 THE QUAY, ILFRACOMBE 687

An advertisement from the 1960 Ilfracombe Guide Book, the official publication of the Ilfracombe Joint Advertising Committee, entitled On Glorious Devon's Ocean Coast. Author's collection

after the end of the 1960 season, and from 1961 to 1965 the basic Bristol Channel two-vessel operation would be undertaken – quite logically – by the two modern postwar paddlers **Bristol Queen** and **Cardiff Queen**.

1960 was not entirely a trouble-free year for **Glen Usk**, and it was reported that she hit Weston Pier on 14th April. The dramatic news headline 'Steamer hits Weston Pier' went on to explain that this occurred when 'turbulent waves' swept her against the pier, albeit whilst she was tied up, on the first trip of the season. Only slight damage to the pier was incurred, the article then admitted, but the headline certainly drew attention in a somewhat unwelcome way. A little later, in late June, **Glen Usk** developed a fault en route to Weston which led to the Glamorgan County Polo Team failing to arrive for their match and the steamer having to turn back to Barry for repairs. Some of the old public affection for the White Funnel Fleet was still expressed by the media, the newspapers quoting a Penarth headmaster (seventy-five of whose physically-handicapped schoolchildren were carried back from Barry to Penarth by special train, and then taken by a hastily-organised fleet of cars to their school) as being '… *full of praise* …' for the combined efforts of P. & A. Campbell Ltd and British Railways – '*It was a wonderful job all round*'.

There was good news, too, in what was to be the last season for **Glen Usk**, on the occasion of a Royal Visit to South Wales. She was used to run special trips to view the Royal Yacht as it sailed away from Cardiff. This article, published in the *Western Daily Press & Bristol Mirror* on Monday 8th August 1960, was rather more like the sort of media attention the White Funnel Fleet really needed:

TRIPS TO SEE THE ROYAL YACHT
Bristol Steamer takes crowds to see Queen
'Bristol and Cardiff joined hands across the Bristol Channel on Saturday to cheer the Queen and Royal Family at the end of their visit to South Wales. The link was formed by the White Funnel steamer *Glen Usk* which operated a special excursion by P. & A. Campbell Ltd to enable people from both sides of the channel to see the Royal Yacht *Britannia* set sail. Three buses were laid on to take Bristolians from Anchor Road to embark on the steamer at Weston-super-Mare. Two special buses ran from Clevedon. Hundreds of Weston's holidaymakers made the trip and well over 500 people were taken on board at Weston Old Pier.

Biggest Yet
With large numbers of Welsh holidaymakers also returning home at the same time, it was one of the biggest crowds *Glen Usk* has carried this season. About 400 people went ashore at Cardiff, but hundreds joined the ship, both to see the Royal yacht leave, and to start holidays at Weston. More passengers joined at Penarth. When *Glen Usk* stood off Penarth to await the Royal yacht her decks were crammed with people. The P. & A. Campbell Chairman Mr S. C. Smith-Cox, who was aboard, had to broadcast appeals to passengers to not crowd over to the port rail. The weight of passengers on this side had caused the ship to list. After repeated appeals, *Glen Usk* was brought on to an even keel. As *Glen Usk's* siren sounded when the *Britannia* passed the Queen smiled and acknowledged the waving passengers.'

The 'special excursion' referred to was, in fact, simply an extended "ferry" crossing from Cardiff and Panarth to Weston, advertised to leave Cardiff at 1640 and arrive at Weston 'not before 1810': meanwhile, on this day, *Cardiff Queen* was busy elsewhere operating a lengthy schedule which took her from Cardiff to Penarth, Barry, Lynmouth and Ilfracombe, Mumbles, and return.

Other matters in 1960
Rumours also circulated in 1960 that the possibility of the White Funnel Fleet going back into the operation of cross-channel trips to France (abandoned by **Glen Gower** after 1956) was being considered and, indeed, the Company Minute Book corroborates these. If a relaxation on the need for passport-photographs being required with identity cards had been forthcoming, then the foreign-going ability of **Bristol Queen** would at last have been put to use on the English Channel. It was recorded that the company would experiment 'on our old South Coast station' if the appropriate dispensation was forthcoming. When questioned by the press, Company Secretary Ernie Harris confirmed that P. & A. Campbell Ltd had applied to the Secretary of State for formalities to be cut, and had written to town clerks and mayors asking for their views. Adding that the company still had an office at Brighton Palace Pier that they had used until 1957, and that they could probably enlist the services of their former South Coast Agent again, he did admit that '*I don't think we will be in time to run trips this season, but we would be ready by 1962.*' These remarks were interesting as they hinted at the belief of the company that there was still a demand for South Coast excursions which was not being satisfied. We will see in due course how this belief was to be substantiated, in line with a low-key policy of seeking to not be solely dependent on the Bristol Channel paddle-steamer business.

Alas, the dispensation was not forthcoming, but had it been then the plan would have been to convert **Glen Usk** to oil-firing for retention on 'ferry' duties alongside *Cardiff Queen* in the Bristol Channel, with the bigger sister away making use of her Cl.II certificate. By late 1962 Clifton Smith-Cox had been endeavouring to gain the required dispensation, and emphasised that P. & A. Campbell Ltd could only operate trips if government bureaucracy was cut. At the same time he gave a shrewd insight into the marketing that then applied where cross-channel trips by car-ferry or fast-craft today are taken entirely as the norm:

'... we are aware that ... excursions operate from the Thames area but, in the case of Brighton, Eastbourne & Hastings, with their exposed piers, it is, in our opinion, essential that passengers should be able to board the steamer for France on the morning of their excursion should the weather appear to be inviting without the necessity of pre-booking ... It is our experience that passengers, unwilling as they are to book on the previous day unless the weather is very settled, are frequently none the less perfectly happy to make up their minds on the day of the excursion to travel.'

As the end of the season drew near it was again clear that trading results were likely to be satisfactory "in spite of the appalling summer", according to the Managing Director. The significance of this remark should not be overlooked, as it served to vindicate the actions that had been taken to cut the level of overheads in preceding years, and thus reduce to some extent the overall vulnerability of the undertaking. It seemed like survival with just two vessels was possible and, speaking to the press on the last day of the 1960 season, Clifton Smith-Cox confirmed that the Campbell steamers would operate again in 1961: "... There is no question about next year - they will run all right. There is no despondency at all and operations will start on the Thursday before Easter next year". He referred to the weather as having been " ... as bad as it could be ..." but stated that he was nevertheless gratified at the numbers of passengers carried which was only 10% less than the previous year.'

'Feeling all right now, love?'

Glen Usk, the oldest vessel still surviving in the fleet, was destined – after closing the Cardiff-Weston ferry on October 10th, 1960 – to be laid up, never to sail again. Unwittingly, the description in the *Western Mail* on Tuesday 11th October of the last trip of the season was to be her obituary notice. The demise of the 1914-built *Glen Usk* was just as sad as that of *Ravenswood* and *Glen Gower* in that it was an unplanned event and unmarked by any particular sentimental farewells. To fully appreciate the nuances of this item one really needs to conjure up the mellifluous Cardiff accent in which the punch-line would have been delivered on that atmospheric end-of-the-season night, out in the swirling Bristol Channel, whilst imagining the night-sky and the many decades of Campbell paddle-steamer tradition which had gone before and which many loyal passengers still then savoured:

"Farewell Weston, till next year" !

'It was 10 o'clock last night and we were aboard the steamer *Glen Usk* as she set off on the season's last P. & A. Campbell trip to Weston-super-Mare. "I always come on this trip" said Mrs. F. B. Davies, of City Road, Cardiff. It was cold, the ship was half-empty and I wondered at Mrs. Davies's staunchness. An hour and a half later I had ceased wondering. A heaving mass of Cardiff-bound passengers, some waving flagons, some waving lethal chunks of Weston rock, all of them waving, was pouring down the ship's gangway.'

Gaiety

On the pier the Weston British Legion Band, looking rather dispersed for a band, may well have been playing an appropriate hymn, but I couldn't hear. A great clanging of bells and hooting of hooters added to the general gaiety, but failed to instil a sense of urgency into those on the gangway. We cast off 15 minutes late, but who cared? The Coastguard had been notified, and now

It is easy to see from this delightful 1960s postcard just why **Bristol Queen** *had such a following and is so fondly remembered over forty years after her withdrawal: her elegant lines are seen to perfection in the snug confines of the ancient harbour at Minehead with the West Somerset coast in view, and the sun is shining.*
Author's collection

was the time for the fireworks display. Twenty-six distress flares leapt up from the pier and floated down on their parachutes. The ship's crew launched a similar effort, but with nothing like the effect; most of our flares shot straight into the sea.

Holiday

This was the ship's 650th trip of the season and Captain L. Virgo, after 31 years at sea, was philosophically looking forward to his holiday. Down below his passengers were enjoying the sensations of the moment. All the way back they kept up their singing, their dancing and, until the last legal minute, their drinking. It was all very friendly: as I leant over the side to watch landing operations at Cardiff a large lady with a kindly face caught and pinned me to the railing and said "Feeling all right now, love?"'

The 1961 & 1962 seasons

At the Directors meeting on 14th November 1960, the readiness of *Bristol Queen* to operate in 1961 had been noted, and she was earmarked to open the season at Easter and then operate at weekends until May, her crew being used in the week to complete the overhaul of *Cardiff Queen*. No Home Office decision regarding passport relaxations had yet been forthcoming and, intriguingly, it was also recorded that consideration was being given to the possibility of *Bristol Queen* being operated in the South of France! A critical point here was that additional hard cash would have been needed before the

end of the 1960 season, to pay for the attention that *Bristol Queen* required, and the performance of the company had been adjudged sufficiently strong to justify the expenditure which needed before she was to be revived and returned to service. There needed to be confidence that she could thereafter earn her keep with the higher running costs of oil-fuel, although she provided greater versatility and carrying capacity. Reducing reliance on the old techniques of finding, paying and keeping stokers for the coal-burning *Glen Usk* would of course have been a factor too, as this was self-evidently a career few were still prepared to follow.

A couple of months later, on 31st January 1961, the availability of an oil-firing installation at the premises of Cosens of Weymouth which would have been suitable for use in *Glen Usk*, was noted, at '… *a reasonable figure* …'. Also noted was an estimate of £2,000 for *Glen Usk* to undergo her quinquennial survey. The mention of an oil-firing installation was interesting inasmuch as it had belonged to a Mersey ferry named *J. Farley*, built by the Ailsa yard in 1922 as a coal-burner. After the Second World War, during which the vessel had been commandeered for naval duties, she had been converted to oil-burning and was subsequently purchased in 1952 by the Admiralty for experimental purposes at Portland. Thus her not very old oil-burning installation had been stripped out by Cosens almost a decade beforehand, and carefully put into store, long before the tentative connection with re-use in *Glen Usk* would be made. In the meantime other re-usable components of the one-time Wallasey ship found their way into various Cosens vessels.

Purser Charlie Wall was a well-known P. & A. Campbell Ltd character, and is seen here with a group of expectant passengers on board **Glen Usk** *at the Pier Head at Cardiff.*
Peter Southcombe collection

Other noteworthy items discussed by the Directors in 1961 meetings were signs of troubles ahead with the pontoon installations at Barry and at Cardiff which had been used by the paddle-steamers since the turn of the century. At Barry Docks the British Transport Commission (precursor to the British Transport Docks Board) quoted a figure of £13,000 as being necessary to effect repairs, but P. & A. Campbell Ltd maintained that these were the responsibility of the BTC. Some success must have been had with this argument as it was later recorded that it was instead agreed that the sum of £250 p.a. would be paid as '… *a special contribution …*' to the costs of the repairs, the implication being that the Campbell steamers were going to be around for a good while yet. Barry Pier featured extensively in upper Bristol Channel operations then, and its loss could not have seriously been countenanced, particularly in view of its flexibility at all states of the tide. As 1960 drew to a close the prospects for *Glen Usk* were clearly mixed. However, excitement – but uncertainty too – lay ahead in the Bristol Channel and elsewhere as the White Funnel Fleet readied itself for what was to be a new more positive era as the period of the 'Lean Years' was slowly coming to an end.

The 68th Annual General Meeting of the Company took place at 4, Dock Chambers, Bute Street, Cardiff on 31st January 1961, and the Chairman, Arthur Roy Boucher, was able to declare to shareholders and others present that the financial restructuring undertaken at the end of 1959 had been successful, profitability having been restored to such an extent that preference dividends were paid in full and that a dividend of £25,000 would be paid on the Ordinary Shares. Speaking to reporters at the AGM, he was also able to announce that there would be no fares increase in 1961 and that improved passenger comfort would be provided by the operation of the two *Queens* while *Glen Usk* remained laid-up in Penarth Docks. He also referred to slight increases in services from Swansea to be offered in the forthcoming season, and stressed that although *Glen Usk* was going to be laid-up she had not yet outlived her usefulness. '*She is the oldest ship in our fleet*' he said, '*but she is in first-class condition. After 46 years the ship is a tribute to British workmanship*'. Explaining the decision, Traffic Manager Jack Guy went on to mention comparative fuel costs as the main factor behind the decision to bring *Bristol Queen* out of her lay-up: '*As the price of oil has gone down and coal increased we felt it would be more economical to run the two Queens*' he said. '*Apart from that, the oil-burners are much cleaner in operation, and should result in improved service.*'

The rumours regarding a resuscitation of the South Coast business persisted in 1961 but as the two *Queens* settled into their Bristol Channel duties the prospect of the older *Glen Usk* being converted to oil-firing became more remote, despite her having been on the Penarth pontoon for inspection at the beginning of the year. Another story again circulated regarding *Bristol Queen* and her possible deployment somewhere off the coast of the South of France. One likes to think that perhaps Clifton Smith-Cox – or maybe Mr Nott or one of his Board members – had been on holiday in the region, spotted a possible opening for an excursion vessel, and mentioned this to colleagues – in this way rumours could so easily be spread. Needless to say, it came to nought.

An unusual trip took place early in the season when *Bristol Queen* undertook a special trip to Milford Haven from Cardiff on Monday April 17th 1961, and ran from Milford Haven to Ilfracombe the next day, prior to undertaking a charter cruise on the 20th April from Pembroke Dock in connection with the opening of the new British Petroleum Angle Bay oil terminal. This was her first trip to Milford Haven and she returned up-channel on the 20th, encountering heavy seas on the way, yet generally running well.

On a more mundane level a little more variety could be offered in the Bristol Channel in 1961, such as on 13th August when an unusual sailing from Minehead to Mumbles with Gower Coast cruise was advertised, the Bristol handbill stating that this was 'A New Excursion' (although *Ship Ahoy* explained that such trips had run before the war). Leaving Bristol at 0900, calls were made at Portishead, (outward direction only, return passengers by coach via Clevedon at night), Clevedon, Weston, Minehead and Mumbles Pier, the call at Minehead Harbour being made by motor launch in the outwards direction. This practice at Minehead in west Somerset had become slightly more

common by this time, and enabled a greater range of trips to be offered at the ancient harbour where tides prevented as much flexibility as at some of the other Bristol Channel ports of call. Bristol handbills of this period devoted much space to outlining which bus-services in Bristol could be used to gain access to Cumberland Basin when direct sailings could be offered from there, or to describing the arrangements made for special coaches to run from Anchor Road, Bristol to Weston-super-Mare to connect with sailings from Birnbeck Pier. A number of coach trips in south Wales were offered at this time for passengers from Bristol, Clevedon or Weston via Barry Pier or Cardiff to the Welsh Mountains, Porthcawl or the Wye Valley. Conversely, Welsh passengers had had an opportunity to travel by Coach Excursion earlier in the season, on Sunday 7th May, to Sidmouth via Weston-Super-Mare, a somewhat longer jaunt. Finally, it is worth recording that occasional visits to a number of the ports reopened in the 'Centenary Year', such as Clovelly and Bideford, still featured, two calls being planned to be made at the latter in 1961.

All did not run smoothly during the 1961 season, however, and an incident on Wednesday 9th August when *Bristol Queen* suffered a paddle-wheel defect generated a certain amount of media attention. In retrospect this can possibly be seen as the beginning of the era where the paddle-steamers were starting to show their age. There were no longer any in-house maintenance facilities supported by skilled staff familiar with paddle-steamer technology, such as the company had enjoyed when the staff at the Bristol Underfall Yard could be called upon to work all hours to rectify mechanical problems at short notice, in order to get vessels back in service with the minimum revenue loss during the short operating season. *Bristol Queen* had run from Cardiff to Lundy, and on returning to Ilfracombe with around 700 passengers on board suffered radius rod problems which necessitated a severe reduction in speed. Partial repairs were undertaken at Ilfracombe, taking around five hours, and she was obliged to crawl along, as the *South Wales Echo* put it, with the damaged paddle. Rather than make for Barry, she became so late after what turned out to be an all-night passage that she ended up making straight for Cardiff where buses were provided to take weary passengers home to Penarth and Barry. Despite the extent of the delays on this voyage, some of the old loyalties to the beleaguered Campbell business still seemed apparent as passengers were quoted by the newspaper reporter as being '… *full of praise for the engineers who kept the steamer going and the catering staff who provided food and drink throughout the long journey.*' Revenue losses on this occasion were mercifully contained as that day had been intended to be an off-service day anyway for *Bristol Queen*. Jack Guy, the Traffic Manager, was able to advise the public that ' … *full repairs could be made in time for its scheduled run to Weston tomorrow.*'

More significantly, the end of the season did not go as planned either as a result of mechanical failures. *Bristol Queen* had finished her duties after Monday 18th September 1961, but had to be brought back into service to cover for *Cardiff Queen* which had suffered problems, and failed to operate the last trip of the season to Ilfracombe on Sunday 1st October. Re-appearing on October 3rd, an additional certificate had to be obtained to allow *Bristol Queen* to carry passengers as hers had ceased at the end of September. A final Ilfracombe trip from Cardiff, with cruise to Bideford Bay, was hastily advertised for Sunday 8th October to compensate for the cancellation caused by *Cardiff Queen's* breakdown the previous weekend. The 1961 season finally ended the next day, on Monday 9th October 1961, when *Bristol Queen* ran from Cardiff at 1840, calling at Penarth at 1850, to Weston-super-Mare, returning at 2200 to the now traditional accompaniment of fireworks at Birnbeck Pier. The newspaper advertisement mentioned that bars would be '… *open throughout the voyage …*', and there were doubtless enthusiasts on board who would drink a fond toast or two to their beloved *Bristol Queen* after her first, sadly not quite trouble-free season back on her old Channel runs after two years of enforced idleness. To conclude this brief account of the highlights of the 1961 White Funnel season it is appropriate to record that the final Ilfracombe run had been one of the latest ever operated, and that after only a very short period of use of Penarth Dock for winter lay-up new quarters now had to be found for the fleet owing to its closure. Thus,

Cardiff Queen and her older sister were to spend the winter at the east end of Cardiff's Roath Dock, where they were joined in due course by the older vessel *Glen Usk*, towed round from Penarth on October 19th.

A key point to reiterate is that a degree of financial stability had now been attained, and at the 69th AGM on 31st January 1962 the Chairman was able to advise shareholders that Preference Dividends had been paid to date, that a dividend of £45,000 would be paid on Ordinary Shares, and that '... *the season 1961 proved profitable in respect of the Company's activities in the Bristol Channel.*' At this point the accounting date of the Company had changed and so the Accounts then presented actually covered the 1960 season, about which it was stated that '... *the summer of 1960 was depressing from a weather standpoint but notwithstanding this the service of steamers in the Bristol Channel operated profitably.*'

The 1961 season closed with more speculation that South Coast operations were still being considered for 1962, contingent upon an easement to permit No-Passport trips to be offered. On a rather more dramatic note, though, came the news that P. & A. Campbell Ltd had applied to the Air Transport Licensing Board for authority to operate hovercraft in 1962 – or such date thereafter as suitable craft would be available – within the limits of Cardiff, Swansea, Clevedon & Ilfracombe. There was just a glimmer of hope that better times lay ahead, that the trend of business levels was positive, and that confidence was coming back. The next few years for the White Funnel Fleet were, in their way, to be as eventful as earlier more prosperous times as expansion beckoned and new opportunities were exploited. The season of 1962 was much like 1961 in its use of the two *Queens*, but with slightly more variety of trips being provided in the charismatic Bristol Channel, where forceful tidal constraints made for challenging timetabling. One significant piece of news which broke in March 1962 in the Bristol and Weston-super-Mare newspapers was that P. & A. Campbell Ltd was considering the acquisition of Birnbeck Pier, otherwise known as The Old Pier, at Weston-super-Mare as the owners had been experiencing hard times and were open to offers.

One example of such timetable innovation was that on Sunday 24th June 1962 when 'The Trip of the Season' was advertised, from Cardiff to Milford Haven. This phraseology was redolent of older times, to draw the attention of the travelling public at individual piers to the most unusual or outstanding excursion of the season to be offered to them, generally of very long duration. Departure from Cardiff was advertised at 0835 with arrival at the Pembrokeshire port at 1540, something of a marathon but replicating patterns of sailings established back in the 1890s by the speedy trio of *Westward Ho*, *Cambria* and *Britannia*. Between 1550 and 1650 a short cruise out of Milford Haven was offered, down the Haven and towards St. Anns Head, before the advertised return departure at 1705 to Cardiff.

Norman Bird sampled this trip on *Bristol Queen*, and described the atmosphere vividly:

'...The first day-return trip from Cardiff to Milford Haven since prewar days was taken by *Bristol Queen* on June 24th, 1962. She sailed via Ilfracombe, and there was a short cruise out of Milford. This was one of my most exhilirating and memorable trips ever, with BQ at her finest. It was fine and sunny, but the day was cold with a strong NW wind and excellent visibility. We were some 45 minutes late into 'Combe and the possibility of cancellation existed. Any other company would have cancelled, but it is to P. & A. Campbell's credit that we continued. The seas were on the port bow and *Bristol Queen* rode them effortlessly. She was slowed down to about 35rpm (instead of her usual 43) for most of the crossing and was on "slow ahead" when particularly heavy seas were encountered at one stage. In spite of this she only lost another 15 mins. or so, to arrive at Milford an hour late. The Milford trip became an annual event after this, always performed by BQ until 1967.'

Shortly after this, on Sunday 1st July 1962, the 'first ever' excursion from Clevedon to Bideford was offered, by an enthusiastic Clifton Smith-Cox who would doubtless have been on board himself from his 'home pier'. In reality the excursion for Clevedon folk was a coach connection to Weston-super-Mare to join the steamer from Cardiff which then headed via Ilfracombe to Bideford, to be alongside there for a few minutes at 1630 after the wonderfully scenic River Torridge passage, returning up-Channel at 1640. Later in the season, on Sunday 2nd September, a Minehead 'Showboat' was offered with entertainment provided on board after a 1245 departure from the Somerset harbour to Mumbles and the Gower Coast. Bills stated that outwards embarkation would be by motor-boat but that in the homewards direction the steamer would berth in the harbour. Elsewhere in the Bristol Channel, five trips were advertised to Tenby from up-channel, each with a short afternoon cruise to Stack Rocks offered to Tenby folk, and one long-day cruise from Tenby to Ilfracombe was advertised on Tuesday 18th September. All trips to and from Tenby had to take into account the tidal limitations at the harbour wall as the last remains of the former Victoria Pier had finally been removed around a decade earlier.

At Minehead, the construction of a new Butlins holiday camp had not gone unnoticed. Prior to the opening of this facility talks had been held to ascertain what joint marketing and promotional opportunities might be possible, for the White Funnel Fleet to bring people from Wales over to Minehead to enjoy the camp facilities, or for campers already there to have the opportunity to take steamer excursions in the Bristol Channel independently from Minehead Harbour. At the Meeting of Directors on 8th June 1962 the details of commercial arrangements, in connection with this worthwhile new traffic source were agreed, and special publicity produced. This was deemed a commercial success by the Directors at the end of the 1962 season, which had featured a regular Western National bus connection from Weston to Minehead on summer Saturdays for campers crossing on the ferry from Cardiff to Weston, and vice-versa. More extensive publicity was produced for the 1963 season, leading to better results, although towards the end of the 1963 season P. & A. Campbell Ltd felt obliged to object to an application by Butlins to the Traffic Commissioners to run their own coaches from South Wales to Minehead for the benefit of their campers. After this less mention was made of the White Funnel Fleet/Butlins connection at Minehead. Although joint promotions were still mentioned on bills thereafter the Butlins traffic declined after 1966, the year in which the three-vessel experiment was launched, and which in September saw the opening of the Severn Bridge and its predictable impact on White Funnel carryings subsequently.

Also of note in August 1962 was an exhibition of models and photographs staged in Bristol to mark the 75th Anniversary of the White Funnel Fleet in the Bristol Channel, sponsored by the Paddle Steamer Preservation Society and largely arranged by Peter Southcombe of Weston-super-Mare, who went on to become a highly-respected and long serving member of the P. & A. Campbell Ltd management team, mainly involved in the south of England business activities.

At the 70th AGM of the Company held at Cardiff on 30th January 1963 the obligatory reference to the effect of the weather on the preceding season was again made, and Mr Boucher noted that whilst the summer of 1961 had been a poor one, '... *unfortunately that of 1962 was possibly the worst from a weather point of view that one can recall.*' It was, however, also observed that the indications were that '... *more passengers are tending to travel by sea than previously provided the weather is reasonable.*'

After a four-year period of two-vessel operations, there had been a return to profitability, and the 'Lean Years' drew to a close. The parent company Townsend Ferries was on the brink of a new era with the first *Free Enterprise* ferry. Capital was committed to buy the Weston-super-Mare Pier Company, and expansion beckoned. There had been the first rumblings regarding experimentation with exciting new hovercraft technology, and things were now turning round financially. Elsewhere in Britain, the affairs of the Liverpool and North Wales Steamship Company had been looking dire after 1961 and worsened drastically after the 1962 season had ended, and these would have implications for steamer enthusiasts in south Wales and the west of England.

Thus it was that these circumstances set the tone for the next part of this story.

A promotional leaflet from 1962 describing arrangements for travel to the new Butlins Holiday Camp at Minehead by steamer, as well as the attractions of cruises from Minehead Harbour.
Authors collection

At home: Sidney Clifton Smith-Cox, Managing Director of P. & A. Campbell Ltd, during the period 1954-1980.   Peter Southcombe collection

Chapter 2
NEW LIFE

Expansion: property, fleet, hovercraft and abroad

The wider picture

Seemingly wholly unconnected with the affairs of the Bristol Channel, the maiden voyage of the radical new car-ferry *Free Enterprise* took place on 22nd April 1962 from Dover to Calais, a truly momentuous day for the parent company George Nott Industries, whose vision for a more expedient means of crossing the English Channel for car-drivers was now coming to fruition. This had required new capital on a considerable scale, especially as the first of this new generation of ships would be swiftly followed by more, and bigger and better, sisters and new routes. This new generation of car-ferry was to play a part in the fortunes of the subsidiary company in the late-1960s and it is worth noting that, at this point, the P. & A. Campbell Ltd element of the George Nott empire was of greater dimensions than the Dover business, although of course this would change dramatically in due course. It was now over three years since the vote of confidence by the parent company had been given to Clifton Smith-Cox to reconstitute the ailing Bristol Channel business of P. & A. Campbell Ltd and, as has been seen, profitability had been restored. A characteristic of all of this was the extent to which he could simply get on with running P. & A. Campbell Ltd as the Managing Director, with very few other staff, with little practical intervention from Notts some distance away in Coventry, and bearing in mind that he had his own full-time professional career as an accountant to occupy his time as well. This gave continuity of management to the company and reassurance to its backers.

Three days before the launch of *Free Enterprise* on 2nd February 1962 by Mrs. Bernice Nott at Schiedam, there had been a P. & A. Campbell Ltd Directors Meeting, at which the prospective terms for the purchase of the shares of the Weston-super-Mare Pier Company had been debated, and it is clear that the requisite 'authority' would had been given by the parent company to take this step, based on a projection that it would be a profitable one for the subsidiary. Rather than pay dues to the struggling pier company, P. & A. Campbell Ltd could save cash by taking on ownership of the pier by its acquisition at a realistic price, from owners keen to divest their principal asset. The capital funding came from elsewhere in the group, at suitable rates of interest, and could be regarded as being soundly invested in property with a longer-term view.

The acquisition was significant in that it represented the first expansionary move made after the 'Lean Years' and heralded a new period of development. Rather than continue to follow the company history in a strictly chronological fashion, it is now easier to chart key events in 1962 and 1963 in three individual segments, of expansion of property interests, fleet enlargement, and experimentation with hovercraft services. Although not destined to establish any bigger pattern of property dealings, the acquisition of Birnbeck Pier at Weston-super-Mare signified that things were changing, and 1963 would see the recruitment by Clifton Smith-Cox of Peter Southcombe as the company's new Passenger Manager, and who was destined to have a major business development role over the next decade, albeit mostly away from the Bristol Channel itself.

*When **Free Enterprise** took up her duties in 1962 and replaced **Halladale** she could legitimately be promoted as 'The New Townsend Luxury Car Ferry', on the shortest route to the continent. Townsend Bros Ferries was still a one-ship operation in 1962, but was then poised to rapidly expand during that decade as the cross-channel car-ferry market evolved. The P. & A. Campbell Ltd business thus became a less significant part of the Nott empire during the 1960s, yet continued in business despite deteriorating market trends for all-day coastal excursions. When new, **Free Enterprise** offered two round trips per day between Dover and Calais in the shoulder season, rising to four in the peak season.* Author's collection

Property

Acquisition of the Weston-super-Mare Pier Company: background

Birnbeck Pier at Weston-super-Mare, a prominent location in the territory of the White Funnel Fleet, has a venerable history and easily warrants its own story, but our concern here is to document the relatively brief period of time that the pier was actually owned by P. & A. Campbell Ltd after the Second World War. The construction of Birnbeck Pier in 1867 predated the coming of the Campbells to the Bristol Channel excursion business, and Weston-super-Mare was to become one of the select few British seaside resorts to boast two piers as the Grand Pier took shape around the turn of the century, but failed to detract from the dominance of Birnbeck Pier for the steamer excursion business.

Unusual in its construction in that the steamer landing-stage was actually built off a second section pier at right angles to the main section (in effect a bridge) linking the mainland with Birnbeck Island, Birnbeck Pier prospered and was even – briefly – expanded by a second steamer jetty, on which work had commenced in 1898 but which was not opened until 1909 and turned out to be short-lived, being dismantled shortly after the Great War. A factor setting Birnbeck Pier apart from the other Bristol Channel piers used by P. & A. Campbell Ltd steamers was the extensive range of entertainments provided on Birnbeck Island and the pier itself, and which acted as a major attraction to holidaymakers generally as well as a magnet to those arriving by steamer on the frequent 'ferry' paddle-steamer services across the Channel from Cardiff and Penarth, as well as other sailings from Newport & Barry and elsewhere. In its day a very useful tramway ran from Birnbeck Pier around the seafront, of great convenience to those arriving at Weston by sea who wished to proceed a little further than Birnbeck itself.

Perhaps a little hard to imagine nowadays as Birnbeck Pier lies forlorn and forgotten, this account by John Bailey from *Weston – The Good Old Days* illustrates the charms of Birnbeck Pier for Campbell steamer passengers admirably, and probably without undue exaggeration:

> '... In its heyday Birnbeck was almost stiflingly packed with humanity. Before noon jollity's noise was tremendous and still crescendoing. Holidaymakers shrieked as they sped down the water chute, went swirling around on the switchback, or shot down the helter-skelter. Their laughter came from the sky as they circled out over the sea in the Air-o-plane's gondolas. Under cover were the roller skating rink, bioscope theatre, pavilion buffet room and, especially, the bar ... In the square was a bandstand, and dancing continued day and night – after darkness fell, under gas jet illuminations. It was said that miners from the Welsh valleys saved packets of sovereigns for the great day out. They were "primed" at paddle-steamer bars before they arrived at Weston, found all they wanted on the pier, never left it to go to town, and finally staggered, or in many cases were carried down the jetty to catch the last boat back to Cardiff.'

Although Birnbeck Pier escaped the fate of 'gapping' (which affected a number of seaside piers around Britain, but which by the nature of its unusual structural design was ruled out) during the Second World War, it succumbed to a different fate by eventually becoming the naval establishment known as HMS *Birnbeck*, the home of the Directorate of Miscellaneous Weapons Development, better known to the irreverent as the 'Wheezers & Dodgers', and where novel destructive technology could be tried out. An excellent account of this period is given in *The Secret War* by Gerald Pawle, but it suffices to say here that it was not until 1946 that it reverted to being Birnbeck Pier and was available again for steamer passengers. The Weston-super-Mare Pier Company was thus able to regain control of its principal asset, although maintenance during the war was said to have been non-existent and the condition in which the pier was handed back caused something of a drain on the company's resources. At the same time the revenue generated by the steamers fell as the number of vessels calling each postwar season was less than pre-war, and declining, and the financial situation of the Pier Company deteriorated during the 1950s. Reporting poor 1957 season results at the

Shareholder's Annual Meeting in August 1958, Campbell's reduction from four to three steamers was cited as being the cause of disappointing results, together with poor weather. No dividends could be paid, and the Chairman reported that a new deal had been struck with P. & A. Campbell Ltd where, in 1958, they would pay a fixed sum of £2,500 to use the pier plus 8d per passenger landed instead of 6d previously.

A couple of years later the situation had deteriorated further, and the Chairman of the Weston-super-Mare Pier Company Mr A. V. L. Pillinger contrasted the then state of affairs of just two paddle-steamers calling with fifty years previously when there were '... *fourteen or fifteen passenger steamers operating in the Bristol Channel ...*', going on to state that this was '... *a sad thing for the pier*'. Acknowledging that the better weather of the 1959 season had produced better results, he opined that the 1960 results would be the worst ever recorded. Clifton Smith-Cox was present at this Annual Meeting of the Pier Company on 15th September 1960 and commented that his company '... *had been able to turn a limited number of ships into a profitable business, rather than run a large number of ships unprofitably ...*', but no mention was made of any takeover at this stage.

The next reference traced to P. & A. Campbell Ltd interest in the acquisition of Birnbeck Pier (then otherwise known as the Old Pier) lies in the Minute Book of Directors Meetings when, on 31st January 1962 it was recorded that George Nott Industries was to make an offer of £5 for every £10 Ordinary or Preference Share, and £45 for every £100 of Debenture Stock of the Weston-super-Mare Pier Company. In a circular sent to pier shareholders the Directors recommended that they accept the offer, it being stated that P. & A. Campbell Ltd – through a subsidiary company, Ribnans Investments Ltd – intended to continue to operate the pier. By May 1962 reports appeared that the pier had indeed changed hands, for about £26,000, and Clifton Smith-Cox was quoted as saying that '... *Campbell's did a tremendous amount of their business from Weston, and it would be a great advantage to the company to own the landing-stage ... and approaches*'. Whilst accepting that nothing would actually change that season, he alluded to detailed plans for the development of the pier, which were intended to be actioned the following year.

P. & A. Campbell Ltd accounts of this time throw very little light on whether the acquisition of the pier was in itself deemed to be a financial success. The Chairman, in his Report accompanying the accounts submitted to shareholders at the 70th AGM on 7th January 1963 confined his remarks to a statement that '... *the acquisition, on 1st May 1962 of the Weston Pier Company by an associated company of P. & A. Campbell Ltd should in due course be of benefit ...*'. A year later, he remarked at the 71st AGM that '... *the majority interest in the Weston Pier Co. has proved to be of help to the company ...*'. No further formal references to the pier company were made in subsequent reports. However, it was the case that despite the rhetoric when the P. & A. Campbell Ltd takeover was effected, no substantive plans for pier development had really existed, and the first visible sign of change was not until 1966 when a concession was granted to Cornish businessmen to operate funfair attractions on Birnbeck Island, with some initial success. The idea did not last for long, however, and Piermaster John Wide worried about the weight of the funfair equipment, vans, etc. crossing the 'bridge' to the Island. The cafe was refurbished, and inspired by the belief of Clifton Smith-Cox that the public were motivated by islands the terminology of Weston Old Pier was dropped in favour of Birnbeck Island or Birnbeck Pier, at least on White Funnel Fleet publicity. A set of secondhand turnstiles removed from Eastbourne Pier were purchased to replace the defective ones in situ, but failed to find favour and were never installed. The condition of the shelters on the bridge part of the pier structure deteriorated, and these useful structures were gradually removed rather than repaired, which was perhaps symptomatic of the malaise that affected the whole place after the novelty of its acquisition had worn off.

On a more positive note, the White Funnel Fleet still had days in the mid-1960s when very substantial numbers of passengers were handled at Birnbeck, at least prior to the 1966 opening of the Severn Bridge. A blacksmith's shop was retained, and maintenance staff were still needed as well as staff to handle the crowds and sell tickets, and Peter

Southcombe (then the newly-appointed Passenger Manager for P. & A. Campbell Ltd) recalled occasions such as Saturday 13th June 1964 when **Cardiff Queen** on ferry duties brought across 1,379 passengers on two trips from Cardiff in pre-booked groups, in addition to ordinary passengers. Marshalling upwards of thirty coaches in the car-park at the pier-entrance was a tricky operation requiring the full cooperation of all involved to ensure passengers joined the right coach, for Bristol Zoo, Minehead, Burnham or various other excursions. Getting people away by sea was tricky, too, at busy times and an elaborate system of "pens" had been built on Birnbeck Island in earlier years to facilitate handling the crowds for the various steamers to Cardiff, Newport, Barry and other destinations: these were still in use in the 1960s but clearly becoming of less significance as passenger numbers declined and the variety of steamer destinations shrunk.

As the story of P. & A. Campbell Ltd ownership of the pier progressed towards its natural conclusion, one of the most positive occasions of the 1960s for Birnbeck Pier was when the centenary of its opening was celebrated, on Thursday 8th June 1967. **Westward Ho** was programmed to come across from Cardiff after afternoon ferry duties and operate a special cruise at 2030 around Steep Holm island. The *Bristol Evening Post* on 3rd June 1967 billed the occasion thus:

Old Pier reaches a century

'The Old Pier at Weston-super-Mare will be 100 years old on Monday. A century ago the bridge connecting the mainland with rocky Birnbeck Island provided Weston with its first pier – and one of the first bridges to be constructed in the Bristol Channel. When the pier was opened in 1867 the event provided a gala day for the then entire 10,000 population of the town.

For today's population of some 44,000 the pier provides a centre of entertainment for holiday visitors and residents during the summer months, and the port of call for the White Funnel Fleet of cross-channel and cruise steamers. To mark the centenary of the pier there will be a special "anniversary cruise" in the Channel next Thursday. Passengers in Victorian costume will travel on the steamer from Cardiff, and will be joined by passengers in similar costume at the Old Pier for an evening cruise. Amateur theatrical societies on both sides of the channel are taking part in the event and the cruise is to start from Weston at 8.30 pm.

There will be fun and games every night on the pier next week. On Monday Weston Silver Band will give a concert and on Tuesday at 7.15 pm there will be an air-sea rescue demonstration by a helicopter from RAF Chivenor and Weston lifeboat. On Wednesday evening a concert is to be given by Burnham-on-Sea Town Band and on Thursday evening music will be provided on the pier by Mr Tony Mockford and an orchestra from the Grand Spa Hotel, Bristol. A group of folk-singers, the West Country Three, are engaged to entertain on Friday night.'

Sadly the company records are silent as to why nothing ever actually happened in terms of redevelopment as initially announced. The White Funnel Fleet would obviously have gained some financial advantage by cutting out the need for payment of pier dues to a third party at what was still very much a key part of their territory, and the purchase of the company when poorly performing could be seen as a pragmatic piece of opportunism. This had, incidentally, generated a little publicity then, which was a side-benefit. The takeover of the Weston-super-Mare Pier Company can be seen, in retrospect, as part of possibly a grander plan by Clifton Smith-Cox to safeguard his fiefdom by diversification and expansion, through the hovercraft venture shortly after this, and the deft purchase of **St. Trillo** against competing bidders. That the supposed plans for pier re-development never really came to much may not have ultimately mattered in the overall picture of the fortunes of the company after the initial enthusiasm had passed.

This brief account of Birnbeck Pier in P. & A. Campbell Ltd ownership now skips past the remainder of the 1960s, when the pier had fleetingly seen rather more activity from a three-ship Bristol Channel operation in 1966. An era ended in 1971 when **Westward Ho** and **Balmoral** had consolidated the last period of two-vessel White Funnel Fleet operations

involving the daily 'ferry' and down-channel sailings (notwithstanding the brief foray of 1978 when **Devonia** briefly supported **Balmoral**). Sadly, it was the demise of **Westward Ho**, towards the end of the 1971 season, that effectively spelt the end for the continued ownership of Birnbeck Pier by P. & A. Campbell Ltd, as the reduction of the White Funnel Fleet to one vessel brought about the elimination of daily Cardiff-Weston 'ferry' services. The use of Weston for steamer calls on upper Bristol Channel schedules was thus greatly reduced, and the non-availability of nearby Clevedon Pier by that time created a very big gap in where passengers could be embarked on the English side. An editorial article in the *Weston Mercury* at the end of September 1971, contemplating the future of Birnbeck Pier after the announcement of curtailed upper Bristol Channel services asserted that '... *the owners are at present very actively concerning themselves about what can be done to increase the attractiveness and turnover of this enterprise ...*'.

The outcome of these deliberations was soon to be revealed as it became known, in January 1972, that the Weston firm of solicitors Messrs Stephen & Co. had been instructed to put Birnbeck Island up for sale by private treaty. By the summer of that year the sale had gone through to a Mr Critchley who, like P. & A. Campbell Ltd, had ideas of development for his newly-acquired pier. One source put the price paid to P. & A. Campbell Ltd for Birnbeck Pier as around £50,000, implying a reasonable capital growth in just nine years of ownership. Whilst steamer services carried on with occasional calls by **Balmoral** over the next few years, with the White Funnel Fleet continuing to be responsible for the steamer operation side of the pier activities themselves, it merely remains to mention here that P. & A. Campbell Ltd services finally ceased to call at Birnbeck Pier after the end of the 1979 season, on account of the deterioration of the landing-stage, and the inability to justify the cost of repairs and staffing. Further reference is made to the final demise of the pier subsequently.

Fleet

At around the same time that the decisions were being made to proceed with the acquisition of the Weston-super-Mare Pier Company, and to engage in experimentation with hovercraft, Clifton Smith-Cox was well aware of the parlous state of the affairs of the Liverpool and North Wales Steamship Co. Ltd. Since the late nineteenth century this undertaking had run excursion sailings from Liverpool along the coast principally to Llandudno and Menai Bridge on the island of Anglesey, and elsewhere, as well as linking Llandudno with the Isle of Man. The difficulties this company experienced lay in the declining market for the long-day excursions that, since the 1930s, had been operated by two particularly attractive and substantially-sized traditional turbine-steamers. A third, smaller motor-vessel **St. Trillo** was deployed on short runs out of Llandudno, rather more economically than her steam-powered elder sisters. The trading problems became so acute that one of the two turbine steamers had been withdrawn after the 1961 season, whilst the other persevered for the 1962 season. P. & A. Campbell Ltd would have been well aware of the difficulties another excursion ship company was facing as only a few were still in business around Britain. His business interests required him to travel around the country and he could thus see how other coastal excursion operators were faring at first hand.

Sadly, it was therefore reasonable to suppose in 1962 that the end may have been nigh for the Liverpool company. Clifton Smith-Cox may well have had his eyes specifically on **St. Trillo** as a lower-cost vessel for Bristol Channel deployment, if she were to come on the sale market. One could easily have seen how many passengers she was then carrying out of the premier north Wales resort relative to the fares then charged, and formed a tentative view on the viability of such a vessel based on experience in south Wales and the west of England. It would thus have been entirely rational to consider the principle of different, smaller types of vessel for Bristol Channel use, at least for the 'shoulder' times of the early- and late-season periods when passenger numbers were lower than between May/June and August/early September. Mention was made earlier of the use by P. & A. Campbell Ltd of a smaller motor-vessel on South Coast duties in 1957, and we now briefly return to this interlude to 'set the scene' for what was, in 1963, to become the beginning of a new phase of White Funnel Fleet history.

First motor-vessel experiences: charter of *Crested Eagle* in 1957

Despite the cessation of the use of paddle-steamers to maintain the P. & A. Campbell Ltd South Coast presence after 1956, a vessel was chartered from the General Steam Navigation Company (hereafter referred to as GSN) in 1957 to operate services in the P. & A. Campbell Ltd name. This vessel was the **Crested Eagle**, which had formerly been known as **New Royal Lady**, and which had been built in 1938 for Scarborough owners. GSN publicity for her previous (and final) season with them proclaimed that she operated on a daily basis, except Mondays, from Gravesend and Southend down the Thames estuary to Clacton, a voyage that took two and a half hours from Southend. In earlier seasons she had operated London Docks cruises for GSN with 'Cafeteria Catering' provided. During her charter to P. & A. Campbell Ltd from June to September 1957, she was programmed was to operate from Brighton (Palace Pier), Eastbourne and Hastings.

In contrast with the long day-trips and 'No-Passport' excursions to France that **Glen Gower** had offered during the 1954-1956 seasons, **Crested Eagle** operated mainly short-duration local cruises, often viewing Beachy Head or the Royal Sovereign lightship but including Fridays-only trips to the Isle of Wight. On arrival at the island, additional short cruises from Shanklin were offered viewing Sandown and the Nab Tower. The single-funnelled vessel ran with a white funnel which carried the P. & A. Campbell Ltd pennant motif: when built, she had carried twin funnels and contemporary opinion reckoned she looked better balanced in that configuration. During the 1957 South Coast season, a typical day of advertised sailings from Hastings Pier comprised the following, in this case for Whit Monday, 10th June 1957:

10.30	Morning cruise to off BEXHILL, passing St. Leonards, Bo-Peep, Bulverhythe and Galley Hill. Back at 11.30.
11.45	Cruise towards RYE BAY, passing Ecclesbourne Glen, Fairlight and Lovers Seat. Back at 12.45
14.15	EASTBOURNE (Three hours ashore). Leave Eastbourne 18.30, back at 19.40.
14.15	Cruise to off NEWHAVEN BREAKWATER passing Pevensey Bay, Eastbourne, Beachy Head, Birling Gap. Seven Sisters and Seaford Head and Town. Back at 19.40.
14.15 and 19.45	Circular trips to EASTBOURNE, returning by Road or Rail.

This scheduling was quite a neat way of selling a variety of trips along the Sussex coast when combined with road and rail options. Additionally the fourth departure that day from Hastings Pier positioned **Crested Eagle** ready for a 10.00 departure the next day from Eastbourne to Hastings, an afternoon cruise around the Royal Sovereign Lightship, and return to Eastbourne. An article written by H. A. Allen published in *Marine News* early in 1957 had welcomed the re-introduction of Campbell South Coast sailings, albeit on this very modest scale, and explained the organisation that would support the venture:

'... Campbell's former South Coast Manager, Mr MacDougall, will be in charge of all the initial arrangements for the Crested Eagle, following which he will hand over the affairs to Mr McNair prior to taking over the duties allocated to him at Weston where he will act as Agent in place of a retirement. (i.e. that of Bob Campbell) It is interesting to note that Mr McNair has been Campbell's Hastings Agent for several years, but suffered premature retirement following the previously intended withdrawal of all Sussex Coast sailings. As with the paddle-steamers in previous seasons, **Crested Eagle** will use Newhaven Harbour as her base port and will be "off-service" on Saturdays. The piers are at last co-operating; tickets will be available for the steamer at the pier entrances and will include the pier tolls.'

The charter of **Crested Eagle** by P. & A. Campbell Ltd was in part an attempt to gain experience of the operation of motor-vessels, and it is worth quoting in full the statement made by the Company Chairman at the 1957 Shareholders Meeting held on 1st August regarding this:

The chartered motor-vessel **Crested Eagle** *approaching Eastbourne, 13th June 1957, during the short time that the P. & A. Campbell Ltd coastal services were maintained at Brighton after the cutbacks of 1956.*

H. A. Allen collection

The funnel of the chartered motor-vessel Crested Eagle, *suitably modified by the P. & A. Campbell Ltd pennant, displaying the white chevron and ball, on blue.* H. A. Allen collection

'... The South Coast Service has been suspended entirely so far as Continental trips are concerned and the *Glen Gower* which previously operated on this service has been withdrawn. In it's place, as an experiment this year, we are operating a small diesel-driven twin-screw vessel, the *Crested Eagle*, chartered from the General Steam Navigation Co. of London. It is hoped that this experiment will give the Company valuable experience with this type of vessel. The cost of operation is, incidentally, only a quarter of that of the larger steamers hitherto operated by the Company on the South Coast ...'.

Sadly for South Coast excursionists, the 1957 charter of **Crested Eagle** was not a financial success. The motor-vessel suffered engine troubles whilst on charter to P. & A. Campbell Ltd, and was withdrawn and sold abroad on the termination of these seasonal sailings. The log-book of **Crested Eagle** for 1957 and the day-by-day analysis of sailings revealed an extremely unsatisfactory position hardly likely to give P. & A. Campbell Ltd any confidence in continuing with South Coast activities any longer. No more was said about the merits or otherwise of the use of diesel-powered vessels and so it was not until 1963 –

WHITE FUNNEL
Sailings by M.V. Crested Eagle

Afternoon Cruise along the Island Coast towards the Nab Tower passing Sandown, Yaverland & Culver Cliffs

EVERY FRIDAY
JUNE 7th to SEPTEMBER 27th
from
SHANKLIN PIER
Leave Shanklin 2.15 p.m.   Return 3.45 p.m.
FARE 4/-
(Children 3-14 half fare)

During the Cruise music will be provided by the George Wilkinson Trio

4.0 p.m. Single Trip to Brighton : Fare 12/-

Note : The Crested Eagle leaves Brighton at 10.0 a.m.; due Shanklin about 1.45 p.m.

SINGLE TRIPS TO EASTBOURNE
Thursday, August 8th, 3.45 p.m.: SINGLE TRIP to EASTBOURNE. Fare 15s. 0d.
Note : The Crested Eagle leaves Eastbourne 9.0 a.m.; due Shanklin about 1.45 p.m.
Thursday, August 22nd, 3.45 p.m.: SINGLE TRIP to EASTBOURNE. Fare 15s. 0d.
Note : The Crested Eagle leaves Eastbourne 9.0 a.m.; due Shanklin about 1.45 p.m.
Thursday, September 5th, 3.15 p.m. : SINGLE TRIP to EASTBOURNE. Fare 15s. 0d.
Note : The Crested Eagle leaves Eastbourne 8.30 a.m.; due Shanklin about 1.15 p.m.

GENERAL INFORMATION

CONDITIONS : Tickets can be obtained on Board the vessel or in advance at the Company's Offices at the Piers. All tickets are issued and passengers carried subject to the Company's conditions of carriage as exhibited on Piers, at the Company's Offices, Agencies, and on their vessels. Sailings are subject to weather and circumstances.

PIER TOLLS are included in the fares, except at Brighton.

SPECIAL RATES are available for parties of 12 and over.
CATERING ON BOARD. The Licensed Bar and Tea Lounge are open throughout the voyage.
DOGS on a lead and under proper control are allowed on board during Afternoon Cruises only. They cannot be carried to Brighton or Eastbourne due to the regulations prohibiting dogs, which are enforced by the respective Pier Companies.

P. & A. CAMPBELL LTD. THE MARINE BOOKING OFFICE, THE PIER GATES. 2232

WHITE FUNNEL
Sailings by M.V. Crested Eagle

...ay trips from EASTBOURNE PIER to the
...LE OF WIGHT
allowing about 2 hours at
SHANKLIN

DATE	Leave Eastbourne	Leave Shanklin	Due Back
...8th AUG.	9 am	3.45 pm	8.40 pm
...2nd AUG.	9 am	3.45 pm	8.40 pm
...th SEPT.	8.30 am	3.15 pm	8.10 pm

...urn Fare 20/-
...ingle 15/-
...ildren 3 to 14 half fare

...he ship has a fully licensed Lounge Bar and a ...omfortable Tea Room where snacks are ...vailable.

...ERMS FOR PARTIES OF 12 OR MORE

...aily Sailings see monthly handbill

...ros. and Potts Ltd., Printers, St. Leonards 1981/57

Specimen 1957 handbills advertising cruises by the chartered motor-vessel Crested Eagle. H. A. Allen collection

some six years later, and after the Company had undergone various crises resulting in a complete financial restructuring – that lower-cost motor-vessels were again to feature in White Funnel Fleet operations.

The late Roy Barclay, who became the Second Engineer on *Bristol Queen* joined the White Funnel Fleet in 1957 on *Crested Eagle* (as Second Engineer) within an Engineering Department which comprised only two engineers in total! He described vividly to the author what conditions were really like on the dilapidated ship, which was jocularly known as the 'Ruptured Duck' to those familiar with her ways. *Crested Eagle* had been brought round from London to Newhaven to commence the charter under the command of Captain Neville Cottman, with Spencer Soloman (who had been 'borrowed' from *Cardiff Queen*) acting temporarily as Chief Engineer. The twin 6-cylinder Crossley engines had a comparatively unusual salt-water cooling system which had become corroded, and therefore leaked coolant into the engine-room. 'Metalloc' engineers had been called on-board to attempt to mitigate this by welding, but having ascertained that metal fatigue had set in declined to do anything further. The weekly trips to the Isle of Wight involved extended periods of continuous running and Roy recalled occasions where the leakage exceeded the ability of the bilge-pumps to cope, necessitating him and the Chief to resort to baling out! He stayed with the ship for the whole season.

Capt. Harris stood by the vessel when she signed articles, but as stated he was relieved by Capt. Cottman after Wednesday 5th June, who remained as Master for the rest of that season. The operating season for *Crested Eagle* ran from Sunday 2nd June until Sunday 29th September 1957. This gave a total of 103 potential sailing days. Saturdays, almost inconceivably nowadays, were her regular off-service days, but were then the basic 'changeover' days for holidaymakers. The following figures clearly illustrate at least two reasons for her financial failure:

Month	Operating days planned	Cancellations owing to weather	Cancellations owing to engine failure
June	24	3	2
July	28	4	5
August	27	10	0
September	24	12	0
Total	103	29	7

These figures exclude half-day cancellations when she either failed to start the day's programme on time in the morning, or had to withdraw from service prematurely in the afternoon, and are solely days when the vessel's log book recorded a whole day of excursion sailings missed.

About a week before the end Roy Barclay discovered a party of people seemingly invading his engine-room without permission. On the point of ejecting them, he was told that the party of Maltese were in fact prospective purchasers for the vessel! At the end of the season *Crested Eagle* was advertised to carry passengers round on her 'return positioning' voyage, on Monday 30th September 1957, departing from Eastbourne at 0700 and from Hastings at 0815 to Gravesend where arrival was expected at 1800. After this she proceeded to Tower Bridge Dock to lay up, and was indeed sold abroad by GSN.

Over a third of potential revenue-earning days were thus missed on this ill-fated charter, and the episode ended the P. & A. Campbell Ltd presence on the Sussex station. This statement by the Chairman at the 66th Ordinary General Meeting, held at the Grand Hotel in Bristol on 14th November 1958, summed up the situation succinctly:

'... As shareholders will be aware, your Company entered into a new departure on the South Coast by operating a small vessel called the *Crested Eagle*. This was done with a view to ascertaining whether services in the Bristol Channel could be more economically operated with a different type of vessel. The result was unfavourable from all points of view, the vessel being confined to harbour mostly on account of bad weather upon more days than she was able to sail (sic). The resulting loss amounted to £12,736.'

The receiver had been appointed by the time these results were disclosed, and little more can be said regarding the role of *Crested Eagle* in bringing to a close in 1957 this finale of what had been a very significant chapter in White Funnel history.

Postwar South Coast operations – in retrospect

Motor-vessels were not now destined to feature in the company outlook for some years. However, a brief look at what other excursion steamer companies were doing in the south of England after the Second World War may be helpful to illustrate the relative extent of failure and, occasionally, success that the P. & A. Campbell Ltd business enjoyed compared to its neighbours in the region. The comparison is interesting inasmuch as there was no other operator in the Bristol Channel after the Second War, whereas three companies could broadly be described as being in the same excursion market as P. & A. Campbell Ltd in the south even if they did not specifically compete by trading from the same piers. These three companies were the General Steam Navigation Company operating as the 'Eagle Steamers' from Thames estuary ports, the Red Funnel undertaking at Southampton primarily serving the Isle of Wight with a year-round ferry service to Cowes, and Cosens of Weymouth whose traffic mostly lay further west, principally at Bournemouth, Swanage and Weymouth.

The services operated by the GSN 'Eagle Steamers' possibly represented the most comparable business area to that in which P. & A. Campbell Ltd traded. In the same way as their vessels were inhibited in sailing from the Sussex piers to France after the war for the reasons described earlier, the inability of the Eagle Steamers concern to use their modern, purpose-built tonnage on continental excursions severely hampered results. However once restrictions were eased, carryings from Southend, Margate etc to Calais & Boulogne picked up, and the business survived in the hands of their motor-vessels long after P. & A. Campbell Ltd had given up with their turbine-steamer *Empress Queen* (which never ran in the cross-channel trade for which she was built) and after *Glen Gower* had failed to satisfactorily re-establish the Boulogne connection, which was axed after 1956. The end came for *Royal Daffodil* (II), *Queen of the Channel* (II) and *Royal Sovereign* (III), after the close of the 1966 season. One reason for this was the effect of extensive industrial action that year which had brought a number of maritime operations to a standstill, but GSN had in effect consciously decided to terminate the Eagle Steamers operation.

The situation was a little different along the coast westwards, and whilst the Red Funnel undertaking at Southampton did not attempt to run either to France or on long-distance excursions to destinations such as Dartmouth after the war, they did acquire some tonnage to replace war-losses. However, like GSN they had started to switch to diesel propulsion in the 1930s and the acquisition of the versatile pair *Medina* and *Vecta* – principally on ferry-based duties – influenced their more selective retention and operation of pure excursion steamers. After the war they continued to acquire motor-vessels, notably the *Balmoral* in 1949 and dedicated car-ferries subsequently, but their own paddle-steamer *Princess Elizabeth* survived for some years, and outlived the two secondhand paddlers and the pair of screw steamers they acquired. The four acquired vessels – *Queen of Kent* (renamed *Lorna Doone*), *Queen of Thanet* (renamed *Solent Queen*), *Upton* and *Robina* – were not particularly successful and did not have long Red Funnel careers, all four having been withdrawn by 1951. This inevitably led to excursion sailings being extensively cut back at quite an early stage, and effectively reduced to that which the motor-vessels could offer on the margin of routine Cowes ferry services, ceasing altogether after the withdrawal of *Balmoral* after the 1968 season.

Rather less comparable in terms of territory, the Cosens fleet mirrored the White Funnel Fleet to some degree and deployed a number of older paddle-steamers. Apart from an extensive summer excursion programme the Cosens business had diversity, with engineering and towage and other activities which brought more all-year round earnings. Joining forces with the Red Funnel company in 1946, they restarted business in a small way and built up excursion operations in 1947 rather like P. & A. Campbell Ltd had done in the Bristol Channel in 1946. A peak of postwar activity was reached in the early-1950s but again, just like the rundown of the White Funnel Fleet, withdrawals became a regular and sad feature throughout the rest of the decade and afterwards as fondly-regarded paddlers such as *Victoria*, *Empress*, *Emperor of India*, *Monarch* and *Consul* came to the end of their careers, with the last survivor *Embassy* finishing after 1966, the same year that saw the demise of *Cardiff Queen*. In looking at this necessarily brief picture of the decline of the south of England excursion-steamer industry through the 1950s and 1960s it seems all the more remarkable that Bristol Channel activities stayed alive at all, and after briefly considering the remarkable classic quartet of motor-vessels acquired for use by P. & A. Campbell Ltd in the 1960s and 1970s we go on to look at the circumstances that permitted this survival, through financial crises and a general backcloth of declining demand and changing tastes.

A classic quartet of motor-vessels

With the exception of the ill-fated turbine-steamer *Empress Queen* and the brief charter of the little motor-vessel *Crested Eagle* in 1957 P. & A. Campbell Ltd had, since their beginnings in Scotland almost a century before, only ever operated paddle-steamers. As the 'lean years' – between 1959 and 1962, during which only two vessels had been operated in the Bristol Channel – came to a close, events elsewhere were such that the company was now poised, at the beginning of 1963, to take the first step towards acquisition of what would later be seen as a remarkable quartet of secondhand motor-vessels. These would come from various sources, each having their own personality and would ultimately enable the White Funnel Fleet to live on for some years after the paddle-steamers met their end. The first two ships acquired in the 1960s were built before the Second World War while the second pair, which joined Campbells a little later, dated from after the war. To set the scene for this transitional era from paddle to screw propulsion, and from steam to diesel, it is worth briefly looking at the provenance of this quartet of motor-ships before later

considering each of them in more detail, the part each one played and what their acquisition enabled the management of P. & A. Campbell Ltd to achieve during the often difficult times of the 1960s and 70s.

The liquidation of the Liverpool and North Wales Steamship Company after the end of the 1962 season appeared to bring to an end a long tradition of steamer excursions along the coast of north Wales and Anglesey, and from Llandudno to the Isle of Man. The effect of this sad ending of a once-buoyant business was to put a useful vessel on to the market, as during the postwar years a trio of vessels had served north Wales and the youngest, *St. Trillo*, which had been built in 1936 by the Fairfield Shipbuilding & Engineering Co. Ltd concern at Govan, was mainly associated with short coastal cruises from the piers at Llandudno and Menai Bridge. When built she had carried the name *St. Silio*, but she was renamed in 1945. Whilst her older, Fairfield-built turbine-steamer fleetmates were now sadly destined for the breakers, *St. Trillo* still had life left in her and Clifton Smith-Cox, recognising her qualities, persuaded Townsend Bros to purchase her with the express intention of being operated by P. & A. Campbell Ltd. Of fairly basic specification, with only rudimentary refreshment facilities, she was a neat-looking vessel with twin funnels. She commenced her White Funnel Fleet duties at the opening of the 1963 season in the Bristol Channel and was subsequently destined to remain primarily associated with her old haunts in Caernarfonshire. With this new acquisition the Campbell territory was set to expand, into north Walian waters where the company had never previously operated.

The second pre-war diesel-powered vessel to be acquired followed two years later, towards the end of the 1965 season. *Vecta* had been built in 1939 for the Red Funnel concern at Southampton and was a somewhat more substantial ship than *St. Trillo*, being conceived as a two-class vessel capable of sustaining the principal car-ferry route between Southampton and Cowes alongside an array of paddle-steamers and the rather older passenger motor-vessel *Medina* which

The first of the 'heritage quartet' of vintage motor-vessels acquired for use by the P. & A. Campbell Ltd fleet, St. Silio (b.1936), seen here in her pre-war role with the Liverpool and North Wales Steamship Company. She was renamed St. Trillo after the war, and remained with the company until their demise after the 1962 season.
Author's collection

*The second of the 'heritage quartet' of vintage motor-vessels, **Vecta** (b.1939), seen here in her pre-war role as a Red Funnel steamer on the Southampton to Cowes route of that undertaking. She was renamed **Westward Ho** for the 1966 season after she had entered White Funnel Fleet service.* Author's collection

*The third, and longest-lived, of the 'heritage quartet', **Balmoral** (b.1949), likewise seen here in her pre-war role as a Red Funnel steamer on the Southampton to Cowes route of that undertaking. The similarities with the earlier **Vecta** are notable.* Author's collection

*The fourth member of the 'heritage quartet' was **Scillonian**, (b.1956) seen here after arrival at Penzance from St. Marys on the Isles of Scilly. She was the second vessel of that name, the third (built in 1977) continuing into the 21st century. Of the four members of this quartet, **Devonia** (as she was renamed) had the shortest working life during 1977/78.* Author's collection

dated from 1931. She was also utilised for tendering duties for ocean-liners which would halt briefly in the Solent to exchange passengers and mails, but not actually stop to call at Southampton. *Vecta* was verging on the revolutionary when built, having been equipped with Voith-Schneider propulsion for maximum manoeuvrability. Equipped with full restaurant facilities, her car-ferry capacity for twelve vehicles now seems pitifully small in comparison with modern-day Raptor-class double-deck vessels on the Cowes run, but back in 1939 the Red Funnel organisation could legitimately boast about their new ship in effusive terms. As things turned out her high-tech Voith-Schneider propulsion system was not retained and by 1946 she had been rebuilt into a far more conventional, twin-screw ship. *Vecta* came to be acquired for White Funnel Fleet duties after the programme to re-equip the Cowes crossing with bigger car-ferries (***Cowes Castle**, **Carisbrooke Castle** et seq*) made her surplus to the requirements of the Southampton company. Once rebuilt to P. & A. Campbell Ltd requirements, and renamed ***Westward Ho***, she went on to give a good few years of Bristol Channel service. She was inevitably regarded by some as not quite the ideal substitute for the bigger and undoubtedly more elegant traditional-style paddle-steamers, which were in fact considerably younger than the motor-vessel which ousted them.

The third and most significant motor-vessel to be acquired was, of course, the principal subject of this study, the venerable ***Balmoral***. Ten years younger than ***Vecta***, she looked rather like her in certain respects, and when delivered in 1949 had a more or less similar multi-purpose role within the Red Funnel fleet. This involved Cowes car-ferry duties, tendering to liners and a cruising capability, often around the Isle of Wight but also further afield. Coming from the same Southampton builders, Thornycrofts, the strong visual similarities between ***Vecta*** and ***Balmoral*** were perhaps not surprising but the younger vessel carried her car-deck aft rather than forward, and in the event was never

substantially altered for P. & A. Campbell Ltd after her ownership (in fact, a demise charter) changed. Like ***Vecta***, ***Balmoral*** was equipped from the outset with full catering facilities, dining on board on Isle of Wight crossings and cruises being a feature which Red Funnel publicity had always explicitly promoted.

The fourth and final motor-vessel to be acquired was another Southampton-built vessel, the sturdy but functional ***Scillonian*** (II) which dated from 1956, and which had served as the mainstay of the Isles of Scilly Steamship Company on their Penzance to St. Marys run until being superseded in 1977 by the third vessel to carry the name ***Scillonian***. Comparable to ***St. Trillo*** inasmuch as she lacked full dining facilities, but in no other way, ***Scillonian*** (II) was destined to have the shortest career of this quartet, and was perhaps the least likely vessel of the four to have been acquired for passenger duties as she had been conceived as a passenger-cargo vessel, which showed in her lines and general ambience. Nevertheless she was renamed as ***Devonia***, and eventually was fully repainted into traditional P. & A. Campbell Ltd colours. Had things turned out differently she might well have been rebuilt and served for longer as a White Funnel Fleet vessel.

One might also mention here briefly the ***Queen of the Isles***, another Isles of Scilly Steamship Company passenger-cargo vessel, which spent much of its brief life with the Scilly company on charter to P. & A. Campbell Ltd. From the use of a first motor-vessel in 1963, then, the company thus switched from having been a wholly steamship fleet to one which was wholly based on diesel-powered ships after 1968. ***Balmoral*** would become the backbone of the fleet in the 1970s, and enable business to continue even after the demise of the 'ferry' after 1971. Two hovercraft had also operated in the P. & A. Campbell Ltd name in the 1960s as well, but this is to jump ahead rather from late-1962, and to which we now return to elaborate on what were to become the Campbell motor-vessel years.

A neat-looking motor-vessel, **Queen of the Isles** *had considerable spare time on her hands as the second Isles of Scilly Steamship Company vessel, almost from the time at which she was built in 1965, at Bristol. She was operated over considerable periods of time in the late-1960s by P. & A. Campbell Ltd.*
Author's collection

St. Trillo and the north Wales years

The demise of the Liverpool & North Wales Steamship Company Ltd.
The old-established Liverpool and North Wales Steamship Company Ltd (referred to hereafter as the LNWSSCo.) could be said to have had certain parallels with P. & A. Campbell Ltd, and the demise of the company after the end of the 1962 season was much regretted by enthusiasts of coastal cruising in north Wales and the north-west of England. The company was registered in 1891, just two years before P. & A. Campbell Ltd became a limited company and similarly traded solely as a seasonal operator of pleasure-steamers. The principal traffic source and company headquarters were at Liverpool, and the main route over the years had been the daily run from the River Mersey along the north Wales coast to Llandudno and then on to Menai Bridge pier. Shorter cruises were offered from Llandudno, as well as all-day excursions to the Isle of Man. Whereas Liverpool, as a major seaport with a large hinterland, could be likened to Cardiff or Bristol then Llandudno, similarly, could be compared with Ilfracombe as a significant seaside resort, at a broadly comparable distance by sea and with attractive coastal views in prospect when underway after leaving the River Mersey and heading along the north Wales coast.

The acquisition of the motor-vessel *St. Trillo* for use by P. & A. Campbell Ltd signified a first real step towards the operation of low-cost diesel-driven tonnage, when trading conditions were still difficult. The fleet of the LNWSSCo. was quite different to that which had evolved under P. & A. Campbell Ltd ownership for Bristol Channel duties, as was the state in which the former company found themselves after the Second World War. Geoffrey Grimshaw, author of British Pleasure Steamers (published in 1939), described the appearance of the fleet then: '*The hull colouring of the fleet of the Liverpool and North Wales Steamship Co. Ltd is black with white waterline and red underbody. The funnels of the vessels are painted yellow. In recent years the Company has become notable for the up-to-date character of its fleet: the average age of the three vessels now employed is eight years*'. In comparison the average age of the wholly paddle-steamer White Funnel Fleet in 1939 was approximately 33 years. In marked contrast to the Bristol-based concern, considerable investment by the LNWSSCo. in new tonnage, all constructed by the Fairfield shipbuilding concern on the Clyde, had taken place between the wars. As a result of this the Liverpool company found itself in 1946 with three reasonably modern vessels, all of which were in such a condition that they could be made fit for use for the first postwar season. The

youngest was a motor vessel, the 1936-built *St. Trillo*, which forms the main subject of this chapter. Paddle-steamers had disappeared from the LNWSSCo. fleet after *St. Elvies* was superseded by the then new *St. Seiriol* in 1931. A most attractive ship, *St. Seiriol* was herself a smaller version of the 1926-built *St. Tudno* and this turbine ship had been a worthy successor to the celebrated, very large paddle-steamer *La Marguerite*. She had been withdrawn at the end of 1925 after many years of domination of the north Wales coastal cruising scene, since having come to the north Wales trade from her original Thames coast duties. As the older, smaller paddle-steamers were withdrawn in the 1920s and 1930s, so calls at the smaller piers at Beaumaris (on Anglesey) and Bangor were dropped by the larger, newer vessels, thus curtailing the extent of the LNWSSCo. territory somewhat.

After the second World War, north Wales coastal cruising operations were able to be resumed almost normally in 1946, that is, with *St. Seiriol* commencing service between Liverpool and Menai Bridge on Good Friday, 19th April. The motor-vessel *St. Trillo* (II) was only to carry that name after 1945, and when launched in 1936 had been originally named *St. Silio*. Her renaming commemorated the 1876-built LNWSSCo. paddle vessel called *St. Trillo* (I), and she commenced postwar duties on 27th May 1946 carrying on virtually the same trade as she had before the war, namely short cruises between Llandudno and Menai Bridge, as well as towards other scenic destinations west and east of Llandudno such as Red Wharf Bay or Colwyn Bay. The third north Wales steamer *St. Tudno* re-entered service on Saturday June 8th, 1946 and resumed her role as the mainstay of the through Liverpool to Menai Bridge sailings. In much the same way as with P. & A. Campbell Ltd on Bristol Channel and South Coast excursions, a degree of inter-availability of ticketing between the LNWSSCo. steamers and rail or bus was an important element of what the Liverpool company was selling to the travelling public.

The territory of the LNWSSCo. Ltd
While certain comparisons with P. & A. Campbell Ltd were valid, as described above, the territory in which the LNWSSCo. traded was distinctly different. Tidal considerations had virtually no impact on timetables and it was possible to advertise an almost constant pattern of sailings, which were repeated on a weekly basis. Furthermore, the postwar pattern in north Wales was essentially a simple rather than a complex one, and unencumbered by any 'ferry' element which had noticeable peaks of demand and which in the Bristol Channel led to such complex rostering of vessels to cater for

St. Trillo *in the Mersey, 1960s.*

E. A. Nurse, Pat Murrell collection

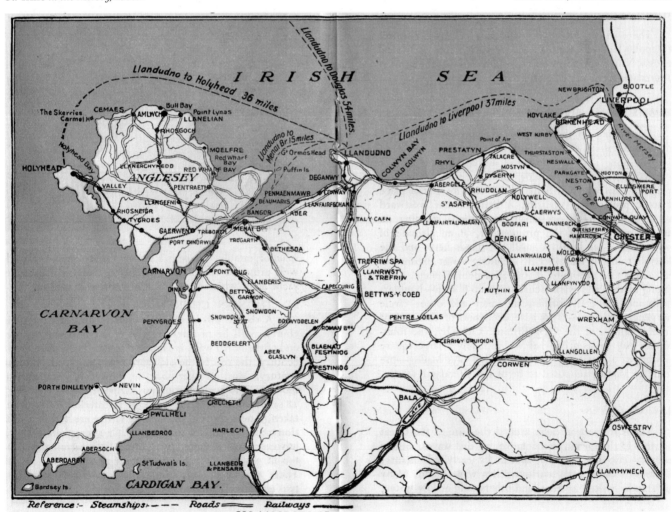

In a similar manner to the publication by P. & A. Campbell Ltd (annually until WW2) of the **Bristol Channel District Guide**, *the official guidebook of the LNWSSCo. was entitled* **North Wales Coast**. *This map was published in the 1949 (31st) edition and illustrated their routes from Liverpool via Llandudno to Menai Bridge, and from Llandudno to Douglas, Isle of Man. Excursions at weekly intervals to Holyhead were abandoned after 1949, and slightly shorter cruises from Llandudno around the Skerries likewise after 1950. After P. & A. Campbell Ltd acquired* **St. Trillo** *for the 1963 season, her principal run was between Menai Bridge and Llandudno, plus occasional non-landing cruises eastwards and westwards from the premier north Wales resort. The IoMSPCo. took on the Douglas excursions in 1962 and also ran between Liverpool and Llandudno from 1963, and into the 1970s.*

Authors collection

This striking drawing of **St. Trillo** *was used in the late-1950s publicity of the Liverpool and North Wales Steamship Company.*

demand. Through fares by rail and steamer were offered from principal stations in the north-west, such as Manchester Victoria, to Llandudno or Menai Bridge by train to Liverpool, or vice-versa. Another variant, for Wirral folk, offered a coach from either Birkenhead or Wallasey to Llandudno, with return to Liverpool by steamer, or vice-versa, although fares for the last leg home, on the Mersey ferries between Liverpool and the Wirral piers, had to be purchased individually. *St. Tudno* had remained as the main Liverpool-Menai Bridge vessel, whilst *St. Trillo* ran cruises of short duration from Llandudno in the mornings, afternoons and evenings. Isle of Man day-trips from Llandudno were also operated, usually once or twice-weekly by *St. Seiriol*. Whereas the turbine steamers were substantial vessels, longer than any of the Bristol Channel paddle-steamers, the compact *St. Trillo* had a GRT of 314t, and was of 149ft length. She tended to lie overnight mostly at Menai Bridge pier.

The LNWSSCo. published an official guidebook entitled North Wales Coast, at a price of sixpence, and the 31st edition (published c.1949) had this to say about the cruise from Llandudno to Menai Bridge, which all three vessels operated, and which the P. & A. Campbell Ltd operation of *St. Trillo* would perpetuate. The prose style was not unlike that used in similar Campbell publications to describe the scenic virtues of south Wales and north Devon coastal trips:

On To The Menai Straits

'A brief stay at Llandudno Pier, and we leave for the beautiful Menai Straits. The Great Orme towers above us as we skirt its base where the sea crashes and swirls against its limestone rocks and caves. High, on its extreme point, its white lighthouse stands sentinel ... On our left lie the low shores of the peaceful Conway estuary, showing mile after mile of yellow sand if the tide is low. Ahead lie the Snowdonian mountains. Their beauty is breathtaking, a combination of wonderful colour and massive shapes that fade into the sky beyond the towering outline of Snowdon.

Lonely Puffin Island lies in the calm waters right ahead. Its cliffs at the northern end rise sheer from the water – the nesting-place of thousands of birds, including the picturesque puffin. Recently declared a bird sanctuary, the history of this strange little island

goes back to A.D. 600 when St. Seiriol founded his monastery there ... We pass through the quiet waters of the Sound. To our left lies Penmaenmawr, a quiet seaside resort dominated by the huge mass of Trwyn-y-Wyffa – "the weeping point" ... Beyond Penmaenmawr and its neighbour Llanfairfechan lies Aber. The sun touches its misty waterfall as it drops steeply from the high slopes of Foel Fas. There is colour everywhere – the green, golden bracken and purple heather.

The straits are slowly narrowing; the quiet almost mysterious beauty of Anglesey is on our right, and the cloud-flecked line of mountains on our left. There is every type of yacht to be seen from the humble dinghy to the ocean cruiser, for the sailing here is as perfect as in any part of the British Isles ... We pass the lovely town of Beaumaris with its thirteenth century castle and Georgian front ... Our outward journey is almost over, Menai Bridge Pier lies ahead – a quiet spot set in lovely surroundings. Time is our only enemy, for there is so much one wishes to see, so many places to explore. The hour's stay here goes all too quickly.'

The postwar pattern of LNWSSCo. excursions endured with little variation in the 1950s and through until 1961, the last year of full three-vessel operations. Traffic was starting to fall off by this time and in marked contrast to the intensive utilisation of vessels exemplified increasingly by Campbell schedules as withdrawals took place throughout the 1950s, the conservative pattern of LNWSSCo. operations was such that two vessels could easily have encompassed much of the work of three towards the end. Had, say, *St. Tudno* been laid up after the 1958 season then *St. Seiriol* could have had a more productive weeks' work by perhaps running from Liverpool to Llandudno and Menai Bridge on Saturdays, Sundays & Mondays, crossing to the Isle of Man from Llandudno on Tuesdays and Wednesdays, running the Llandudno to Liverpool trip on Thursdays and still having Fridays as a regular off-service day. This would have left more of the Menai Bridge traffic to *St. Trillo*, the smallest and most economical unit of the fleet. Such a course of action might possibly have ensured the survival of the company longer than 1962, when capitulation to falling demand and rising cost trends took place.

It was only in 1962 that some move – arguably too little, and too late – towards intensified utilisation of the Liverpool company fleet took place. *St. Seiriol* had been withdrawn at the end of the 1961 season, to later be sold for demolition, and during what was to be the final season of the LNWSSCo. the two survivors *St. Tudno* and *St. Trillo* carried on with little change to their established pattern of deployment. As the LNWSSCo. had, after 1961, given up the Douglas run to their 'neighbours' the Isle of Man Steam Packet Company (hereafter the IoMSPCo.), that route was operated in 1962 by their large, postwar turbine-steamers, using spare time in their rosters. In this way revenue from Manx day-trips was inevitably lost by the LNWSSCo. and *St. Tudno* merely carried on operating her established Liverpool to Menai Bridge duties on virtually a daily basis: the main change for the little *St. Trillo* was that she took a slightly greater proportion of what Menai Bridge trade there still was, whilst the former was called on to relinquish some of her off-service Fridays as *St. Seiriol* was no longer available to take these. The end of the 1962 season for the LNWSSCo. passed unremarkably in itself, but all was not well. The IoMSPCo. appeared satisfied with their venture into Llandudno-Douglas day-excursions that year, in substitution for what *St. Seiriol* had carried out in earlier years. But by November it was announced that after over seventy years the LNWSSCo. would sadly cease to trade, and that the Manx company would take over the Liverpool-Llandudno sailings as well from 1963. *St. Tudno* and *St. Trillo* were put up for sale and, in the case of the thirty-six year-old steamship the inevitable happened as she was purchased for scrap, and eventually followed her younger sister *St. Seiriol* to the breakers.

Efforts were made locally, particularly by some of the Councils in the area who were worried about the loss of holidaymaker facilities, to keep *St. Trillo* operational by a new local company and fears were publicly expressed that she might be sold abroad. However nothing

materialised that year and *St. Trillo* wintered pending an uncertain future. Luckily for enthusiasts of coastal cruising, however, *St. Trillo* was to be spared the fate of her fleet-mates. It became apparent, in February 1963, that P. & A. Campbell Ltd were the successful bidders at auction for the little motor-vessel, at an undisclosed price but which exceeded the sum of around £17,500 known to have been the highest local bid. The two ex-seafaring Thomas brothers of Menai Bridge had offered £15,000, and raised this to £17,500 to try and prevent the ship being sold '... *to a firm from the South of England ...*', although they had publicly expressed disappointment at the lack of local support for their venture.

The capital was put up for P. & A. Campbell Ltd by their parent company George Nott Industries Ltd. Whilst it was not categorically stated at the outset that the purpose of the Cardiff company in acquiring the *St. Trillo* was to operate her on her old north Wales routes, it was soon announced that the intention was in fact for her to operate at Llandudno for the main part of the 1963 season, more or less as she had done previously for her original owners, but that in addition to this she would open Bristol Channel sailings at Easter, and return there at the end of the Llandudno season to close Cardiff-Weston ferry and other Bristol Channel services. In this way the White Funnel Fleet would benefit by exploiting the lower operating-costs of this smaller motor-vessel at times of lower demand relative to *Bristol Queen* and *Cardiff Queen*. By this time *Glen Usk* had been laid up for over three years, and it came as no surprise that the advent of *St. Trillo* effectively precipitated the demise of the last prewar paddle-steamer. In the winter of 1962/63 *St. Trillo* had remained in the north, in dock at Birkenhead: as Easter 1963 approached, her Master from LNWSSCo. days, Capt. O. C. Williams, together with some of her old crew commenced preparations for the first journey away from the familiar waters of north Wales to the foreign waters of the Bristol Channel, and a new phase in the career of the 1936-built *St. Trillo*.

Llandudno Pier in north Wales was, for a period in the 1960s jointly served by St. Trillo *for short excursions, and by the much larger turbine-steamers of the Isle of Man Steam Packet Company, which ran between Liverpool and Llandudno, and from Llandudno to the Isle of Man. The postcard view admirably illustrates the contrast offered between the White Funnel Fleet in north Wales and the Manx company.* Author's collection

St. Trillo *at the Pier Head, Cardiff.*

The first year of *St. Trillo* in the White Funnel Fleet

The use made by P. & A. Campbell Ltd of their first motor-vessel in 1963 fell into three distinct phases; firstly, after her initial trip around practically the entire Welsh coast from Liverpool to Cardiff, for early season Bristol Channel duties; secondly, her main north Wales season, running on her old route between Llandudno and Menai Bridge, and offering short cruises from Llandudno; and thirdly, her second foray back from north Wales to the Bristol Channel to close the season there.

The surviving log-book of *St. Trillo* for the first year in her new role makes fascinating reading. Activity commenced on Monday 4th March 1963 at the Egerton Dock, Birkenhead as two AB's were signed on to assist Capt. O. C. Williams to prepare *St. Trillo* for the '... *run to Cardiff* ...'. The remainder of the crew signed on during Friday 8th March and on the following day, *St. Trillo* came alongside the Princes Landing Stage at 0815 before leaving for Cardiff at 0845. However she only got as far as Menai Bridge, and had to seek shelter from the weather, tying up there at 1315 on Saturday 9th March. It was another three days before the onwards journey was recommenced, and the times of the positioning voyage are of interest as this was probably the first time a Campbell ship had ever plied a course such as this between north and south Wales:

Tuesday 12th March	Menai Bridge	dep.	1022
	Caernarvon	pass	1105
	South Bishop	pass	1856
	Skokholm	pass	2015
	St. Govans	pass	2215
Weds.13th March	Scarweather	pass	0306
	Breaksea	(await clearance)	0526
	Cardiff Pontoon	arr.	0936

The next day was occupied by berthing trials at Weston's Birnbeck Pier, and after this *St. Trillo* entered the East Dock at Cardiff on Friday 15th March 1963 where the crew were paid off. A do-it-yourself effort to transform the appearance of the little ship into partial White Funnel

Fleet colours was undertaken, for her funnels and upperworks, but not her hull. The full crew were signed on during Monday 8th April in readiness for her introduction to White Funnel service on Maundy Thursday, 11th April, when ferry sailings commenced for the 1963 season. Her spell in the Bristol Channel was to last until shortly before Whitsun, and although basically confined to ferry duties she did visit Bristol occasionally and, on one occasion, Friday 19th April, she put in an appearance at Ilfracombe. A number of sailings were lost owing to engine trouble, on 9th-10th-11th May, and on the evening of Sunday 26th May *St. Trillo* left Cardiff at 2115 for Menai Bridge, arriving there at 1827 the next day. The crew of *St. Trillo* during the 1963 season was as follows: Master, Captain O. C. Williams; Mate, Captain Power; Chief Engineer, Mr Hand; Second Engineer, Mr Parry; Purser/Chief Steward, Mr Taylor; Barman, Mr Heal; Tea Bar, Miss Carpenter; plus Officers Steward, Cook, Five deckhands, one Engineroom Cleaner and a boy – all unnamed.

After an off-service week where *St. Trillo* lay at Menai Bridge for further sprucing-up, the first north Wales trip by a ship carrying the white funnel duly took place on Saturday 1st June 1963 at 1325 from Menai Bridge pier to Llandudno. This was a special trip provided by the new owners for invited guests and representatives of local authorities and included the Mayors of Beaumaris and Caernarfon, as well as the Chairman of the Menai Bridge Urban District Council. For the month of June, Saturdays continued to be regular off-service days and the very first P. & A. Campbell Ltd handbill for Sailings from Llandudno Pier indicated that public trips would commence on Whit Sunday 2nd June 1963. The weekly schedule of *St. Trillo* was initially little changed from that which had been offered in previous years under LNWSSCo. management, consisting mostly of runs between Menai Bridge and Llandudno, using the Anglesey pier as the normal overnight berth but occasionally anchoring overnight in Llandudno Bay or Conway Bay if necessary for early starts from Llandudno pier the following day. She sailed on some Saturdays in the high summer period, whereas Saturday had generally been her regular off-service day in the LNWSSCo. era.

St. Trillo *pulls away from the Pier Head, Cardiff and generates an impressive amount of black smoke whilst getting underway*
Nigel Jones

Right: *Llandudno early-season handbill, May 1967, which advertised the **Kungsholm** visit.* Author's collection

However, the White Funnel Fleet management must have decided it was appropriate to inject a little variety into this somewhat mundane programme, and it was arranged that Caernarfon would again be visited for the first time since before the war, and that a limited number of Round Anglesey cruises would operate. Appropriate paragraphs of the old LNWSSCo. guidebook to the North Wales Coast were edited and then printed on the back of the first White Funnel Fleet handbills which were issued for both Menai Bridge & Llandudno sailings.

A short description of the various excursions
To Menai Bridge
This is undoubtedly one of the finest coastal trips of the British Isles and is an ideal sightseeing cruise and one that every holidaymaker should not miss. After leaving Llandudno Pier we pass Great Orme's Head, with the lighthouse perched high above, when a glorious view of the Menai Straits opens up with lonely Puffin Island right ahead, where seagulls, puffins and occasionally seals greet passengers as they approach. Passing through the Sound, the vessel enters the Menai Strait and as she sails through its placid waters passengers settle down comfortably in their seats to enjoy the truly magnificent scenery. On the starboard side (which lest anyone does not know is the right) all the beauties of Anglesey can be seen while on the port side are the mountains of the Snowdonian Range. Cruising past Beaumaris with its lovely setting on the right and then Bangor on the left, looking ahead passengers get their first glimpse of the Menai Suspension Bridge, an impressive structure, and finally arrive at the terminal point, Menai Bridge Pier.

"The full beauty of the Menai Strait can only be seen from the Sea."

WHITE FUNNEL FLEET

SPECIAL CHEAP EARLY SEASON EXCURSIONS
from
LLANDUDNO PIER

by the Twin Screw Vessel ST. TRILLO   FRIDAY MAY 5th—SATURDAY MAY 20th, 1967

Morning, Afternoon and Evening Cruises

Morning   On the Morning Cruises, lasting one and a half hours, the **St. Trillo** either passes the Great Orme and then sails toward Puffin Island or goes eastwards. In that case she journeys along the North Wales Coast past Colwyn Bay and towards Rhyl. The direction of the cruises is varied from day to day in order to provide the maximum variety.

Afternoon   On Sunday a special cruise takes passengers past the Great Orme, the entrance to the Menai Strait and Puffin Island. The vessel then proceeds westwards along the Anglesey coast through Red Wharf Bay, past Moelfre and towards Point Lynas. The Wednesday afternoon cruise proceeds along the same route, but not so far.

Evening   The route of the evening cruises is varied in the same way as it is in the morning.

Whichever excursion passengers may make, they will find the scenery unsurpassed and varied. And this scenery can only be seen to its full advantage from the sea.

Other handbills produced for the 1963 season went on to mention circular tickets between Llandudno and Menai Bridge involving the steamer, rail or Crosville buses in various permutations, and naturally also extolled the virtues of the 'extensive' Bristol Channel services whilst grandly listing the White Funnel Fleet as consisting of the vessels **Bristol Queen**, **Cardiff Queen**, **Glen Usk**, **St. Trillo**, **Waverley**, **Devonia**, **Lundy Queen** and **Westward Ho**, not condescending to point out that the last four named were actually launches, nor that **Glen Usk** had not sailed since 1960 and was now distinctly unlikely to do so again!

Saturday 27th July 1963 saw the first call at Caernarfon (Victoria Wharf) since prewar days, and things became even more interesting on Saturday 10th August 1963 when the first Round Anglesey cruise since 1947 was operated. At the modest speed at which the **St. Trillo** cruised perhaps this could never have become a very frequent operation - paddle-steamers in 1901, for example, took only six hours to circumnavigate the island from Llandudno - but it was the enterprise that was displayed by P. & A. Campbell Ltd after so many years of such little variety from the LNWSSCo. that was commendable.

The timings recorded for this historic trip were as follows:

Menai Bridge	dep.	0833
Llandudno		1000-1030
Menai Bridge		1214-1223
Caernarfon		1315-1325
Belan	pass	1340
South Stack	pass	1525
Pt. Lynas	pass	1733
Puffin I.	pass	1835
Great Orme	pass	1910
Llandudno		1923-1930
Menai Bridge	arr.	2103

A second trip scheduled for Saturday 24th August was disrupted by adverse weather and could not circumnavigate Anglesey as planned. Other notable events in 1963 were the charter of **St. Trillo** on Saturday 31st August by a party of anglers, leaving Llandudno pier at 1230 and returning at 1750. All sailings were cancelled on Friday 6th September on account of the weather. The season was drawing to a close by then, and **St. Trillo** completed this first White Funnel north Wales season on Thursday 12th September, being fuelled the next day before setting off at 1850 on Saturday 14th September for her second stint on Bristol Channel duties. She was to arrive, after an uneventful voyage, at the Pier Head at Cardiff on Sunday 15th September at 1505, a voyage of just under one day.

The satisfaction of the new owners with their first north Wales season was nicely expressed by this piece in the *Western Mail* published on 13th September 1963:

St. Trillo's Last Trip

'... the *St. Trillo* will be in the Menai Straits again next summer, when she returns north from her new home port, Cardiff. Thousands more – this was the promise made by Mr Smith-Cox, managing director of the company, when he stepped ashore for a few minutes to shake hands with Mr W. Lewis Williams, chairman of the local council: Mrs. Lewis Williams: Mr J. T. Richards and Mr W. Trevor Hughes, clerk. "We are glad to say the ship carried several thousand more passengers than she did last year, despite the poor weather during the summer ..." said Mr Smith-Cox "... I am also happy to say that the *St. Trillo* will return to Menai Bridge next summer.'

Spending most of Monday 16th and Tuesday 17th September 1963 alongside at Cardiff Pier Head, *St. Trillo* entered the Roath Dock for the night before operating the ferry on the Wednesday. The next few days passed uneventfully but a little variety was offered on Friday 27th September, when she was chartered to run a short trip for the Port of Bristol Authority: her log rather quaintly recorded that she had tied up at 'Bristol Town Centre' prior to departure at 1050 for Avonmouth where she put her passengers ashore at 1435 before proceeding back to Cardiff. Ferry services finished on Monday 21st October, and *St. Trillo* then bade farewell to Cardiff the next day leaving at 1139 for north Wales.

Drama ensued as she suffered bad weather during the night as she headed across Cardigan Bay, and she was to run aground off Porthdinllaen in the small hours of Wednesday 23rd October. That evening, the South Wales Echo gave extensive coverage to the incident which had taken place somewhat away from the normal area of reporting for that organ, but which was clearly justified in that the ship in question could now be thought of as a Cardiff vessel:

Welsh pleasure boat hits rocks

'The Menai Straits pleasure boat *St. Trillo* (314 tons) which in the summer was for five weeks in the Bristol Channel on the Cardiff to Weston run, struck a rock on the northern coast of the South Caernarvonshire peninsula early today. She was able to move under her own steam four hours late. The vessel was on her way from Cardiff to Port Dinorwic on the Menai Straits, for docking and re-fit. The 140 ft. long motor-vessel with accommodation for 568 passengers was bought earlier this year by P. & A. Campbell Ltd, Cardiff and Bristol, from the Liverpool and North Wales Steamship Company. In thick fog and with a 40 mph south-east wind blowing the boat ran on to the jagged rocks at Porth Ysgaden, five miles west of Nefyn. She was held fast by the bow.

Penarth man aboard

She was commanded by Captain Owen Cecil Williams, Bryn Seiriol, Garth Road, Bangor and had a crew of 16. Captain Philip Power of Penarth, skipper of *Cardiff Queen*, another Campbell boat, was acting as First Mate and he was on the bridge at the time of the incident. Porthdinllaen (Nefyn) lifeboat was launched and 15 volunteer members of the local life-saving team were rushed by lorry across country in the dark to the windswept Porth Ysgaden headland. Three members of the *St. Trillo's* crew came ashore. They scrambled down a rope ladder on to the rocks.

Cardiff Girl

The only woman on board was Miss Jean Carpenter, 21 year old stewardess, of Trafalgar Road, Roath Park, Cardiff, said: "We left Cardiff at noon yesterday and everything went well until we got to the Irish Sea. I was asleep on my bunk when at about 4.15 am I was suddenly awakened by the whole ship shuddering. I heard a scraping, rasping noise. I ran on deck in my nightdress and the rest of the crew who were below also came running up. The captain shouted orders for us to stand by. There was no panic. After I got dressed and was assured there was no immediate danger, I went below to make coffee." The vessel was refloated by the rising tide and she was guided to the entrance of the Menai Straits at Caernarvon by the lifeboat.'

A disaster was averted: *St. Trillo* refloated at 0802 and entered the conveniently-situated nearby dry-dock at Port Dinorwic for inspection, and her crew were signed off the next day. Some repairs were carried out but the damage was quite extensive and, after signing on a fresh crew on Monday 4th November, she made for ship-repairers at the Clovers Dry Dock at Birkenhead, where repairs which included the replacement of shell plating and the removal of damaged frames continued beyond Christmas and into the early part of 1964 as the opportunity was also taken to commence interior structural alterations. No costs of repairs were disclosed, but they must have made a significant impact on the profitability of *St. Trillo* in her first year as a White Funnel ship.

The White Funnel Fleet 'North Wales station', 1964-1969

The White Funnel Fleet presence in North Wales had been thus established in 1963, and was officially deemed to have been successful. The Bristol Channel had benefited to some extent by the shoulder-season availability of *St. Trillo* to maintain 'ferry' sailings, and the Chairman's Report to Shareholders at the 71st Ordinary General Meeting at Cardiff on Friday 31st January 1964 had this to say about the newly-acquired motor-vessel, prior to actual publication of the accounts for the 1963 operating season:

'…In March 1963, a Company within the George Nott Group acquired the *St. Trillo* and this vessel came under the operation of your Company. The service between Llandudno and Menai Bridge previously operated by this vessel when in the ownership of the Liverpool and North Wales Steamship Co. has proved successful and is being continued. The operation of the *St. Trillo* in the Bristol Channel in the early and late season has been of considerable help and benefit to your Company.'

How, then, had P. & A. Campbell Ltd managed to make a profit on the north Wales station when the long-established operator, the LNWSSCo., had failed to do so ? The core programme offered was virtually identical and no effort had been made to establish onwards connections from the Isle of Man steamer as she arrived at Llandudno from Liverpool although in hindsight this might have been a profitable development. P. & A. Campbell Ltd was, of course, unencumbered by the high running and maintenance costs of the large turbine steamers *St. Tudno* and *St. Seiriol* and much of the more economical running costs of *St. Trillo* could be absorbed by the existing management at Cardiff. The revival of calls at Caernarfon and cruises around Anglesey generated modest but useful additional revenue, as well as the introduction of Coach Tours, mirroring the practice in the Bristol Channel. Inter-availability of steamer tickets with road and rail options was maintained, which required the co-operation of the then dominant bus company Crosville Motor Services Ltd, whose headquarters was at Chester, and British Railways. In this way the public could be continually reminded, through a wider spread of advertising than would otherwise have been the case, of the presence of the most recent acquisition of the White Funnel Fleet on the 'North Wales station' at Llandudno, and elsewhere.

Other activities of *St. Trillo* in North Wales
Tendering
1964 was the first year in which an association began between the Swedish American Line and the White Funnel Fleet, whereby *St. Trillo* and other vessels found work as a tender to the liners *Kungsholm* or *Gripsholm* on then annual visits to Britain including calls in both the Bristol Channel and the Irish Sea. On 5th May 1964 *St. Trillo*, being of a suitable size for tendering duties, ferried passengers ashore at Avonmouth from *Kungsholm*, which had anchored in Walton Bay to enable passengers to visit Bristol and other places in the locality. When the liner made her first visit to Llandudno a couple of days later the Mersey ferry *Royal Daffodil II* acted as a tender, but *St. Trillo* undertook the task in 1965 and subsequent years. Quite apart from the money generated from tendering *Kungsholm* and her sister ship *Gripsholm* (dating from 1953 and 1957 respectively) the sheer beauty of the striking

sisterships and the attention they attracted made it a prestigious task in its own right and one with which P. & A. Campbell Ltd was keen to be associated. *St. Trillo* (and, in later years *Westward Ho* and *Balmoral*) would make the most of the annual Swedish American Line visits by also offering public cruises to view the ships at anchor. As someone that delighted in ocean liner travel himself, Clifton Smith-Cox would have had the greatest personal pleasure in ensuring that his company could provide these tendering services as a commercial proposition whilst appealing to enthusiasts as well.

Beneficial publicity was also generated by the liner visits, and the *North Wales Weekly News* was fulsome in its account of the welcome given by Llandudno to 375 passengers who came ashore from *Kungsholm* on Thursday 6th May 1965 by means of *St. Trillo*. Nine coaches and nineteen cars provided by Red Garages, Llandudno were lined up at the pier gates and the passengers visited such sights as Bodnant Gardens, the Llanberis pass and castles at Conway, Caernarfon and Penrhyn. These sights were the ones which had also been familiar to earlier generations of LNWSSCo. passengers from Liverpool and north-west England who had arrived at Llandudno Pier by sea. The President of the Swedish American Line John M. Frazer, from New York, was amongst the first ashore and said he was keen to experience for himself the warm Welsh welcome for which passengers the year before had expressed such delight, and he confirmed that the following year the slightly larger *Gripsholm* would make the round-Britain cruise.

Exactly one year later an equally successful visit was made by the newer liner and, after *St. Trillo* had again successfully carried out the tendering duties, her Captain Henry Solje was able to send a radio telegram to the Chairman of Llandudno Council which said that '*The passengers on the* Gripsholm *would like to express their heartfelt appreciation of the wonderful, spontaneous and unprecedented welcome to Wales. Never in their experience have they been so honoured or so received. Long Live Wales*'. Llandudno could clearly put on a good show and P. & A. Campbell Ltd played a key part in this valuable boost to the tourism industry through their presence on the north Wales station. The *North Wales Weekly News* could again make positive statements about this activity, and quoted a spokesman of the Swedish American Line who explained that their ship *Kungsholm* had been sold (and was renamed *Europa*) but a new ship – also to be called *Kungsholm* – would take her place in their fleet, and repeat the prestigious trip in the following year.

St. Trillo *alongside* Kungsholm, *6th May 1967, Douglas Bay, Isle of Man (see Llandudno handbill page 67, 5-20 May).* Stan Basnett

During the period of White Funnel Fleet operation in north Wales, 1963-69 inclusive, the vessel normally deployed during the 1968 season was the chartered Isles of Scilly vessel **Queen of the Isles,** *seen here pulling away from Menai Bridge pier on the island of Anglesey.*   Author's collection

The first entry on the 1967 handbill of Special Cheap Early Season Excursions from Llandudno Pier, by the Twin-Screw Vessel *St. Trillo*, covering the period Friday 5th to Saturday 20th May, made a nice reference to a one-hour cruise around ***Kungsholm*** at 1930 on Friday 5th May, at a fare of five shillings. The main advertising message on such bills emphasised that '*The full beauty of the Menai Strait can only be seen from the sea*'.

The White Funnel Fleet association with the beautiful vessels of the Swedish American Line on their round-Britain cruises lasted some ten years or so and was not without incident, the most noteworthy of which happened off Llandudno on 6th May 1968 after the cruise passengers had had a day ashore, and was vividly described in the book *Liners to the Sun* by John Maxtone-Grahame. This involved the newer ship named ***Kungsholm*** which had been commissioned in 1966: a storm was gathering and Stanley Page, an American from Carmel, California described the ordeal thus:

'A line thrown from the *St. Trillo* to the *Kungsholm* fouled the propeller of the *St. Trillo* causing us to drift into a night of rain, wind, heavy seas and terror for the 400 aboard. A lifeboat dispatched from the shore tried, without success, to pass a tow line - this went on for six hours; meantime, cold, wet, violently seasick passengers crowded the one small lounge below decks or stayed on the open decks for fear of being trapped below, while we drifted helplessly close to the rocky shore. Disaster becomes a common leveller and the passengers who had spent cruise days perusing the New York Social Register looking for "the right people" cradled other passengers in their arms, joined together in misery and fright. All aboard, including myself, would have given up all their worldly goods to get off the *St. Trillo* that night. Finally, they got a line aboard and the slicker-clad, courteous Welsh lifeboat crew towed us to the dock in Llandudno where we were met by dozens of people who escorted us

to hotels for the night: meanwhile, "our" *Kungsholm* had deserted us by sailing off to a safe haven, Liverpool; a move to avert possible disaster to her. Llandudno is a summer resort and hotels do not open until June, but that night those wonderful Welsh people opened their hotels, put hot water bottles in our beds and gave us ham and eggs at midnight: quite a job to accomplish at short notice.

The next morning, we were bussed to Liverpool where the *Kungsholm* was waiting for us, band playing, lunch ready and the Captain acting as though nothing had happened – that is a Swedish speciality. Once, en route from Panama to Tahiti, the *Kungsholm* "went dead" for 3 to 4 hours at 3 a.m. with all lights out due to generator failure, some passengers showing up on deck in their night clothes and life-jackets. The next summer when I mentioned this to the same captain, he looked me in the eye and said – "it never happened". All's well that ends well – after we sailed from Liverpool, the passengers collected almost $10,000 which was sent to the lifeboat crew, really a small amount compared to what could have been collected aboard *St. Trillo* while the rescue operation was at its height during that night of terror and misery!'

As luck would have it the timetable for the tendering operation by *St. Trillo* to *Kungsholm* the following year, on Saturday 17th May 1969, did not quite go to plan either as adverse weather intervened. Although the tendering itself took place during the daytime as scheduled, the evening trip at 1930 from Llandudno around the liner, which was also due to take local visitors off, was unable to get alongside safely. The passengers who were thus obliged to remain on board *Kungsholm* for the night were not rescued until the following day at Douglas, Isle of Man, the liners next port of call ! On this occasion *St. Trillo* was due to tender to *Kungsholm* again at Douglas, and doubtless P. & A. Campbell Ltd would have seen to it that these unfortunates got home safely, at their expense.

Charter use

A rather different type of business was also found for *St. Trillo* and a tradition evidently reinstated when she ran a programme of cruises on behalf of the Mersey Docks & Harbour Board, as was recorded in *Lloyds List*, 16th March 1964:

'... For many years the Mersey Docks and Harbour Board entertained guests on board their steam yacht *Galatea*, but these functions were discontinued in 1957 when the vessel was sold owing to her age and condition. These trips in the *Galatea* were very much appreciated and in order to maintain relations with the various trading associations and port users from all parts of the country the Board have decided to charter a vessel and to run a series of cruises during the second week in May this year. The vessel is the former Liverpool and North Wales Steamship Company's *St. Trillo*, now owned by P. & A. Campbell Ltd of Cardiff. It is intended to include parties from the London area, the Midlands and Yorkshire as well as representatives of local Associations connected with Liverpool.'

Routine matters

Aside from the increased variety of excursions offered by *St. Trillo* from 1963 onwards, the White Funnel Fleet organisation also brought combined coach tours of Anglesey to the public in their first year, which connected out of the steamer arrival at Menai Bridge from Llandudno, on Thursdays. The next year saw a modest increase in the number of these coach tours, as well as the Round Anglesey cruises which called at Caernarfon (Victoria Wharf). The 1963 pattern of early- and late-season Bristol Channel deployment of *St. Trillo* in the Bristol Channel was not repeated beyond Spring 1965, as the acquisition of the motorship *Vecta* (renamed *Westward Ho*) late in the 1965 season

made it unnecessary for the north Wales ship to venture south again for this purpose. In 1966 *St. Trillo* ventured slightly further afield when early-season sailings from Liverpool were advertised, with sailings to Llandudno on Saturday 14th May and on Sunday 15th May, the latter being extended to Menai Bridge pier.

The arrangements for the 1967 season were a little more adventurous and this year there was no IOMSPCo. presence at Llandudno as, due to the poor condition of the pier, their large turbine steamers were unable to call. P. & A. Campbell Ltd took partial advantage of this by offering a small number of Liverpool-Llandudno-Menai Bridge 'through' sailings, in the manner of that which had been provided by *St. Tudno* and *St. Seiriol* in LNWSSCo. days. The coach tour side of the operation expanded too, with advertised coaches at weekly intervals from Aberystwyth, Borth & Machynlleth to Menai Bridge to connect with the Llandudno run of the *St. Trillo*, and there were even a couple of days when a Crosville coach ran to Caernarfon in order to connect into a round-Anglesey cruise. Just for good measure, a couple of Holyhead calls were also arranged, billed as the first since 1949, although one was cancelled. A visit was advertised to be made to New Brighton too, on Wednesday 6th September 1967.

The situation changed somewhat in late-1967 as the breakdown of *Bristol Queen* on the Bristol Channel on Saturday 26th August necessitated the recall of *St. Trillo* to cover ferry duties, while *Westward Ho* switched duties to cover for the failed paddle-steamer. This major event is dealt with in more detail elsewhere, but the effect on the north Wales station was minimised by the prompt charter of an alternative vessel ensuring that Llandudno was only left without a Campbell steamer for a few days at the end of August and early September. The Isles of Scilly Steamship Company 'relief' steamer *Queen of the Isles* was chartered to cover from 2nd September, and set off northwards in order to resume services, which occupied her

Queen of the Isles, *at the Landing Stage, Liverpool, 1968.*

R. Brandreth, Pat Murrell collection

between 4th-29th September 1967. *St. Trillo* did close the Llandudno station in 1967, having returned north on 27th September after two-vessel operations in the Bristol Channel had ended. *Queen of the Isles* and *St. Trillo* were briefly together at Menai Bridge before the former returned south to her owners, leaving *St. Trillo* to close Llandudno sailings on 1st October 1967.

The situation in 1968 was a little more complicated as *St. Trillo* ostensibly was required to run alongside *Westward Ho* to provide a two-ship service on the Bristol Channel where for the first time ever there were no traditional paddle-steamers. However, the continued availability of *Queen of the Isles* meant that P. & A. Campbell Ltd were able to charter her to maintain the 1968 Llandudno services, between 30th May and 12th September. *St. Trillo* opened the early-season services on 5th May, and after the dramatic tendering experience described earlier closed her public sailings on 24th May and sailed for the Bristol Channel. By comparison with *St. Trillo*, *Queen of the Isles* had a much smaller capacity of just 300 passengers, leading to occasions when passengers were turned away. She was less suitable in terms of available deck-space, but certainly better than no steamer at all on the Menai Bridge run. Early in 1968 she spent some time on the Isles of Scilly service for which she had been designed, and, once her charter commenced and her funnel had been painted white, she returned to the islands on the now-established P. & A. Campbell Ltd weekend trip from the Bristol Channel to Penzance and St. Marys, Isles of Scilly.

After this last foray into her home waters for some time came her positioning run from Cardiff to Menai Bridge which, evidently at short notice, was advertised as a public sailing leaving the Pier Head at 0800 on Wednesday 29th May 1968 with a call en route at Mumbles Pier at 1100. As *St. Trillo* had lacked the requisite certification to carry passengers on such trips around Wales, this was a distinct novelty for enthusiasts, a few of whom were enticed despite the long overnight bus journey home from north Wales. The handbill for this special sailing contained a brief description of which landmarks would be seen after the more commonplace part of the run towards the entrance to Milford Haven, although for much of the day the vessel would have been well out to sea with not a great deal to actually see:

'... in succession the vessel passes Skokholm and Skomer Islands and crosses the mouth of St. Brides Bay until St. Davids Head can be seen on the starboard side. The next landmark is the lighthouse of Strumble Head after which the *Queen of the Isles* steams across the expanse of Cardigan Bay until Bardsey Island will be seen ahead. Following the Caernarvonshire coastline along the Lleyn Peninsular the Anglesey coast comes into view and the *Queen of the Isles* enters the Menai Straits and berths at Menai Bridge pier near the world famous Menai Suspension Bridge.'

Midway through the 1968 season, a north Wales newspaper ran a substantial feature on the new-look vessel which, ignoring the obvious errors regarding her age and a degree of harmless exaggeration, was wholly positive in tone. The article opened by asking readers if '*there was any more picturesque harbour in the world than Menai Bridge*?' and continued:

"Queen captivates a new isle and coast".
'As she sails up the narrow channel of the Menai Straits, her white paintwork gleaming in the sunshine, she looks every inch a Queen. Majestically, she turns in to berth at Menai Bridge Pier. She is *Queen of the Isles* on a cruise along the North Wales coast. She has been sailing from Llandudno for the season and the people of North Wales and the thousands of holidaymakers have fallen in love with her. As many as 2,500 passengers a week take a cruise aboard her, as she proves that cruises along this coastline can be as popular now as they were in the heyday of the Llandudno-Menai Straits or Anglesey trips.

With her for ten years
The passengers love her, but none love her more than the man who for the past ten years has spent the whole of his working days on her bridge. Welsh-born, Captain Leonard Davies, the man who is responsible this year for the pleasure of so many holidaymakers, is proud of his ship ... *Queen of the Isles* was specially built for the more strenuous and rougher passage to the Scilly Isles. For ten years (sic) she plied on this run, carrying the great and the humble, and on the return trip delicate flowers. Captain Davies is more than an ordinary skipper - he can honestly say that this is his ship. For no other captain has skippered her – and he is partly an owner. *Queen of the Isles* is owned by the Isles of Scilly Steamship Company – of which the islanders are the shareholders. And he is a shareholder, although his home is now in Penzance.

Busy life for the crew
This year she is on charter to P. & A. Campbell Ltd, the Bristol-based owners of the *St. Trillo* which has run a similar service in recent years. But now *St. Trillo* is engaged on other duties in the Bristol Channel. For the *Queen* and her crew, her North Wales sojourn is a busy life. Some days she sails as many as six times from Menai Bridge or Llandudno. Sometimes she may carry a capacity complement of 300, particularly if the weather is kind. And she has been seen on Merseyside this summer ... but her main voyages have been round Anglesey, and for afternoon and evening cruises between Llandudno & Menai Bridge. Aboard her, as Pilot, is a man who knows those waters like his own hand. He is Captain Cecil Williams, of Bangor, who was skipper of *St. Trillo* when she was on this cruise. He knows the tricky Menai Straits as well as anyone alive. Even if the navigation lights are not working he can, he told a public enquiry earlier this year, take his ship into Menai Bridge by the light of street lamps. Thus two men, each with many years of experience behind them, form a team fit to serve a Queen.'

Despite the positive tones of this report, all was not well behind the scenes. Although Llandudno pier had been repaired the financial results of the 1968 north Wales season were poor, and a company record (which was only published after the 1969 season had ended) reveals that a decision had been made to withdraw from north Wales at the end of 1968:

'... In view of it being Investiture year and our receiving repeated requests from North Wales to do so, we did undertake to try one further season of operation from Llandudno and Menai Bridge. This unfortunately proved as unsatisfactory as the previous year and as a consequence we have now decided finally to withdraw this service.'

In the event the decision had been reversed at very short notice in the Spring of 1969, and the Llandudno station was granted a reprieve. P. & A. Campbell Ltd had acquired *Balmoral*, a highly suitable former Isle of Wight vessel, to partner *Westward Ho* on the two-ship Bristol Channel service. This rendered *St. Trillo* surplus to needs there and, in view of money invested in engine repairs in 1968, it was decided to retain her and send her back to north Wales. *Queen of the Isles* was destined to be occupied elsewhere on P. & A. Campbell Ltd business in 1969.

Due to continuing repairs on Llandudno pier, *St. Trillo* opened the season rather later than usual, on 15th June 1969, having spent a few days in May on tendering duties, as already mentioned. Local interests were still concerned at the possible loss of their excursion vessel, and a Civic Reception was held in the Chambers of the Menai Bridge Council to which Mr Smith-Cox was invited, where he heard the views of Councillors at a sherry party. '... *The sailings were a tradition of long standing ... said Councillor Evans, and were valued ... as being an integral part of local life during holiday times. The boat was a delightful sight on the local waters and the trade from* her passengers was appreciated by the tradespeople'. He went on to acknowledge, however, that '... businesses are not run on sentiment and tradition and one way to guarantee that St. Trillo stays with us is for more people to support the service as passengers'.

Sadly, however, the end was in sight. **St. Trillo** was beginning to show her age, and mechanical failures in 1969 became more frequent, culminating in a three-week period in the high season, between 9th - 30th August, when she was off-service and no replacement could be chartered in. So much revenue was lost that as the season drew to a close an announcement was made that the thirty-three-year old ship was to be withdrawn.

The schedule for the last day of regular P. & A. Campbell Ltd excursion services in north Wales, Tuesday 16th September 1969, was broadly typical of what **St. Trillo** had been offering over three decades, and comprised three round trips from Menai Bridge to Llandudno, leaving the Anglesey pier at 0900, 1230 and 1830, returning from Llandudno to Menai Bridge at 1045, 1645 and 2015. In addition a short afternoon cruise was offered, at 1430, towards Colwyn Bay and Rhyl. The *Western Mail* remarked thus on 16th September 1969:

Bad Season Brings End To A Pleasure Voyage

'The pleasure boat *St. Trillo* ends her North Wales season today and she will not return next year. Her owners, P. & A. Campbell Ltd of Cardiff have announced the end of their association with the traditional link between Menai Bridge and Llandudno. In a letter to Menai Bridge Urban Council the company's managing director, Mr S. C. Smith-Cox, stated that this season had not been a successful one financially. He attributed this to the late start caused by Llandudno Pier being out of commission for a time and then *St. Trillo's* engine troubles, which meant that 18 days were lost at the height of the season. Campbell's took the run in 1963 after the Liverpool and North Wales Steamship Company went into voluntary liquidation.'

St. Trillo duly left north Wales and on arrival at Cardiff spent a few days in the Queens Dock before being reactivated for the very special occasion of the re-dedication of Lundy to mark the passage of the island from private ownership into the care of the Landmark Trust. All three vessels of the White Funnel Fleet were to be seen together at Ilfracombe on the afternoon of Saturday 27th September 1969, and on the following day (after **St. Trillo** had spent the night at Ilfracombe) her final duty was to assist **Westward Ho** in carrying well over 1,000 passengers to Lundy for the ceremony. Her master for that last day of revenue-earning service was Captain Jack George, who had been recalled from retirement especially for the occasion. **St. Trillo** was afterwards laid up and advertised for sale. She spent several years lying in Barry, in the Cadoxton Graving Dock, before being towed to shipbreakers in Dublin during 1975.

Thus with the demise of the little **St. Trillo** P. & A. Campbell Ltd lost a short-lived but useful fleet-member (their first-ever motor-vessel) and north Wales said goodbye to its constantly regular pleasure steamer service after many decades. Given good weather, good luck and an absence of expensive mechanical failures, the north Wales experiment could have been a financial success but circumstances dictated a different outcome. With hindsight it is easy to see that a combination of changing holiday fashions, elderly ships and piers, and rising maintenance costs must always have made the operation a marginal one. All was not lost at Llandudno however, as the IOMSPCo. announced that, in 1970, their vessels on the Liverpool-Llandudno service would also offer two-hour non-landing cruises from Llandudno towards Point Lynas when they would otherwise have been lying idle. These trips lasted until 1980, and once the seasonal Steam Packet connection between Llandudno and Douglas, Isle of Man was finally severed in 1982, the very last remnants of the once proud Liverpool & North Wales Steamship Company – and which had been kept alive by a vessel operated by what were then in effect South Wales owners – were thus finally abandoned. Just as in the Bristol Channel, it then fell to the operationally-preserved paddle-steamer **Waverley** to keep the flag flying in this charming territory.

The World's First Cross-Channel Hovercraft

The story of P. & A. Campbell Ltd's brief foray in 1963 into hovercraft operation in the upper Bristol Channel, between Penarth and Weston-super-Mare, illustrates a fascinating aspect of the company history, which hitherto had been based on long-established paddle-steamer operations. These were to be gradually supplanted by motor-vessels, and the pioneering use of hovercraft was in great contrast to where the company had been only shortly before. The notion of travel by hovercraft in the 1960s was visionary and especially so if a direct comparison with the more sedate steamship experience were made. The brief period of operation of the Saunders-Roe designed hovercraft which complemented traditional White Funnel Fleet sailings was basically experimental and it was claimed by the Westland Aircraft Co., manufacturers of the SRN-2 craft, that journeys of around twelve miles represented the optimum for hovercraft operation in terms of the speed offered and journey times achieved compared to conventional vessels. The SRN-2 had been notionally designed to seat seventy passengers but the presence of various items of test-equipment on board reduced this at times. Even if the Bristol Channel hovercraft venture in 1963 was to be overtly experimental it nonetheless represented a powerful means of raising awareness and getting some positive publicity for the company after the period of the 'lean years'.

However, the background to this episode in the diverse and varied postwar history of the White Funnel Fleet went back to 1960 when it was announced in the Journal of Commerce that an application to the Air Transport Licensing Board had been made by a shipping company for a licence to operate a hovercraft service for passengers, freight and vehicles between all ports in the Bristol Channel between Cardiff and Swansea, and Clevedon and Ilfracombe. In this application, P. & A. Campbell Ltd acknowledged that the craft were not yet available for commercial work, but that they had in mind a specification for a hovercraft that would accommodate 200 passengers or 20 tons of freight, or a combination of both, and which would operate in a manner that was complementary to their steamer services across the Bristol Channel. Prospective manufacturers named at this time were Vickers-Armstrong (South Marston) Limited, of Swindon, and Denny Hovercraft Ltd, a subsidiary of Wm. Denny & Bros, the celebrated Clyde shipbuilders.

Over the next couple of years plans became firmer and a preliminary announcement was made in the Western Mail in September 1962 that an experimental Bristol Channel passenger service might commence the following summer. At that time a trial service of two months duration across the Dee estuary linking the Wirral with Rhyl had just finished operating. This had deployed the Vickers-Armstrong VA3 prototype and which was then dismantled on the beach at Rhyl prior to being returned by road to their Swindon factory, having suffered storm damage and ending operations prematurely as a result. Initially intended to run from Hoylake on the Wirral peninsula westwards to Rhyl, operations actually took place between Leasowe (near Wallasey) to Rhyl with a journey time of around twenty minutes. As the VA3 craft carried passengers in 1962, this feature slightly compromised the grand advertising claims that were to be made for the 1963 Bristol Channel 'world's first' experimental operation by the SRN-2 craft, although this was in fact 'cross-channel', whereas the operation across the mouth of the River Dee could perhaps simply be described as having been along the north Wales coast.

The publicity brochure produced to advertise the high-speed trips across the Bristol Channel in 1963, which ran from the west end of the Esplanade at Penarth to the beach terminal at Weston-super-Mare, adjacent to the swimming-pool, and the subsequent comments of the Company Chairman in the Directors Report for the financial year 1962-63, suggested that greater things were envisaged for the use of this type of craft in the Bristol Channel. Announcing the new service to be provided by the SRN-2 hovercraft, which was advertised to operate at frequent intervals on Mondays to Fridays between July 23rd and August 30th, 1963, the brochure stated that: '... P. & A. Campbell Ltd look forward to the day when they will be inaugurating Hovercraft services as a regular feature of Bristol Channel travel and

The streamlined appearance of the SRN-2 hovercraft is seen to advantage at Weston super Mare, with the Grand Pier behind. Birnbeck Pier is visible, in the distance.
Author's collection

in the meantime ... they trust passengers will enjoy their crossing and remember with pleasure the summer of 1963, when they travelled on the world's most revolutionary form of travel - literally on a cushion of air - between Weston and Penarth.'

The *Penarth Times* newspaper clearly regarded as worthy of full front-page treatment the announcement in June 1963 by Campbells that Penarth had been selected as the hovercraft terminal for this '... *experimental cross-channel service between Somerset and Glamorgan* ...'. The enthusiastic support of Penarth Council was given to the venture, its Chairman announcing that the hovercraft service from Penarth would be '... *a service that is going to be appreciated not only by people living in Penarth but in Cardiff and surrounding districts.'* The local newspaper went on to say that the statement brought to a head many years of rumour and conjecture regarding a new cross-channel service, as over the years several individuals had been investigating the possibilities for a ferry service, particularly for cars and freight. A gentleman named Rowland Harris had put forward a plan for a motor-vehicle ferry from Penarth to the mouth of the River Axe, which had gained the support of the Somerset local authority in providing approach roads, although the scheme was eventually acknowledged as impractical owing to the restrictions that tidal conditions would impose, and the high capital costs involved.

More insight into what the new service at Penarth might bring featured in the *Penarth Times* shortly after the initial announcements, in early July 1963. Pointing out that the SRN-2 craft had successfully made its way '... *up the Canadian rapids ...*' when on a Canadian demonstration tour, the Sales Director of Westland Aircraft Mr Hugh Gordon explained that '... *the present experimental service is not so much an experiment as far as this craft is concerned, as an opportunity for operators to find out about its capabilities*'. Revealing for the 'technically-minded' that the craft operated on a cushion of air at 65lb to the square foot, or less than half a pound to the square inch, it was stated that annoyance to beach-users would be minimal as the craft only approached the beach very slowly. Over one and a half million pounds had been committed by the manufacturers to research, in addition to further government funding, and Mr Gordon stated that ' ... *so far we haven't sold a hovercraft but at the moment there are some interesting negotiations going on ...'.* It was anticipated

that if the service was successful then the seafront terminal at Penarth would probably become inadequate as a permanent arrangement would require ancillary terminal buildings, restaurants, a car-park and hotels and the entrance to Penarth Dock was identified as a potential alternative, it being noted that that district of the town was still rail-linked at the time.

The SRN-2 craft arrived at Cardiff Docks on 21st July 1963 on board the coaster Bay Fisher, and was described as a 27t craft. An advertising postcard referred to a 66-passenger capacity and 80 mph speed capability. Shortly afterwards the tone of local newspaper reporting was notched up still further when the experimental service

John Nicholson produced a splendid drawing of the SRN-2 hovercraft, at the beach terminal at Weston super Mare, which was featured on the front cover of the Autumn 1963 edition of the quarterly journal Ship Ahoy.
Author's collection

finally commenced, with hundreds of local schoolchildren being brought down to the seafront to watch the thrilling spectacle. The late Jon Holyoak, a key mover in the resurrection of *Balmoral* in 1986, was amongst these Penarth schoolchildren and testified to the author that the report was in no way exaggerated and that history was truly then being made. Jon confirmed that being given time off school for this very special occasion was very much appreciated by himself and his classmates, and the front-page of the *Penarth Times* for Friday 26th July 1963 was almost entirely given over to this fulsome description of the first day. It is quoted here in full for its splendid imagery:

IT'S HERE: WORLD HISTORY IS MADE AT PENARTH

Monday 22nd July was a day to be remembered, for then the space-age hovercraft came first to Penarth. With a full-throated roar it thrust through it's own spray clouds at a mile a minute and zoomed onto Penarth Beach. Seaweed and sand – and little black flies - exploded frantically all round as its blast hurled them out of its path. Children jumped up and down excitedly, and some too near, foolhardy youngsters ran for shelter – too late. The bellow in the creature's throat subsided as it sank to the beach, squatting on its ample rear. The Lord Mayor, Mayoress and Chairmen gave a final polish to their chains and moved forward uncertainly over the stones to pay reverence ... History was in the making ... THE THING WAS HERE !

Public services got underway the next day, and the Mayor of Weston-super-Mare crossed on the SRN-2 to Penarth and briefly set foot on Welsh soil before being accompanied on the return flight by the Chairman of Penarth Council, William Jeffcott. Accompanied on the twelve-minute journey across the channel by a Westland helicopter just overhead, the Civic Party proceeded to a reception at the Winter Gardens on arrival at Weston-super-Mare, where speeches were made referring to a hope that the new hovercraft would bring the towns closer together. The Mayor of Weston-super-Mare, Councillor Haskins, declared that the hovercraft journey was as comfortable as a car ride. Clifton Smith-Cox had publicly thanked the Penarth authorities for their efforts and cooperation at a reception the previous day, at which the Lord Mayor of Cardiff was also present. He added that the hovercraft service was a pioneering effort and one which P. & A. Campbell Ltd were whole-heartedly behind, and that it was hoped that they would soon be able to carry cars. As a publicity stunt the venture had certainly made an impact, and much was learnt as a result of what had after all been an experiment rather than an actual new service intended to become more regular.

A somewhat more sober, contemporary account of the initial public hovercraft service across the Bristol Channel was published in the Autumn 1963 edition of *Ship Ahoy* which was the quarterly journal of the Bristol Channel Branch of the World Ship Society, published during the late 1950s and 1960s. This was written by well-known local expert Donald Anderson, an authority on White Funnel history, and conveys much of that early atmosphere of great excitement.

SRN-2, by Donald Anderson

'In the early years of the last century crowds gathered on our foreshores to watch, with some degree of trepidation and caution, the first puffing and snorting steamboat. Two generations later equally uncertain onlookers displayed scepticism, awe and wonder as peculiar, frail aircraft took to the air.

On Tuesday 23rd July 1963 the sightseers on Penarth Beach had that same sensation of wariness while they watched the SRN-2 hovercraft inaugurate her daily cross channel service to Weston. As I took my place amongst the lucky 42 passengers who were privileged to be making the first service run, I could hear the words "brave", "risk", "nervous" and "daring" on many lips although I was personally only interested in the novelty and the realisation that I was taking part in a stride forward into progress. I could not help reflecting, however, on the amazing march of science as this half ship, half plane screamed its way from the

water in a flurry of, at first, spray and later sand and seaweed as it gently lowered itself onto the beach.

Readers who know me will be aware that I am less sentimental about the passing of the paddle-boat era than many enthusiasts, for my interest lies in coastal passenger transport as such, rather than specifically in paddle-steamers. Of course, if we are ever deprived of the salty tang and open-air relaxation of the traditional cruising day, I shall be extremely sorry. For sheer efficiency, however, particularly in the field of fast, car-ferry runs over relatively short distances with difficult tidal or berthing problems, I forecast a great potential in these latest, man-made, water-bugs. Their military significance could, I imagine, be very far reaching.

The crossing to Weston, comfortably seated in a spacious cabin, tastefully fitted out, occupied only 13 minutes flying time. At our maximum speed of 70k, the view from the windows was not unduly obscured by spray and it was quite fantastic watching Monkstone and Flatholm flashing by in a few seconds. In the calm sea there was little more than a gentle bumping movement - much less than a bus - and conversation was not unduly impaired by the noise although this latter point might prove rather wearing on a longer flight.

As a restless individual I should have liked to have been allowed to wander about rather than having to remain seated. The craft is only 27 tons, however, and at this stage of development, bearing in mind its experimental nature, primarily from a mechanical point of view, it would be very wrong to take any passenger facility shortcomings too strongly to task.

When the prospects of a Bristol Channel hovercraft service were first put forward by P. & A. Campbell Ltd, the *Ship Ahoy* team reported the suggestion with tongues deeply in cheeks. I may not be expressing the views of all enthusiasts, or indeed even those of the others on "Ship Ahoy" but, personally, "Hovercraft - I like them !"'

Six months or so after the experimental service had begun the Company Chairman told shareholders that '... *much valuable experience was gained which will assist in our long-term plans to establish regular services with Hovercraft across the Bristol Channel and elsewhere*'. Ownership of the SRN-2 remained with Westland, and apparently no formal charter agreement with P. & A. Campbell Ltd was deemed necessary. Little was officially documented that throws any light on what subsequently was debated within the P. & A. Campbell Ltd headquarters offices at 4, Dock Chambers, in the Cardiff Butetown district, regarding the future of the hovercraft operation. Despite the formal statement quoted above, no more was publicly heard of possibilities for this type of service in the Bristol Channel although the experiment was said to have been successful, with 70% of advertised trips being operated. Peter Southcombe later recalled that some effort went into seeking to identify more suitable terminal facilities in the Bristol Channel, a key requirement being a relatively rock-free beach, the other problem being that of noise. In the following season a new company called Hovertransport Ltd was set up to run a new service to the Isle of Wight, which is dealt with below. It should be recorded here that there was some limited discussion within P. & A. Campbell Ltd of having another go at hovercraft operation in the Bristol Channel after the 1964 Isle of Wight season, but difficulty in finding suitable terminal locations dictated that the experiment was not repeated. The other critical difficulty was in selecting a route where it would have been possible to set fares at a level to ensure commercial success.

In addition to this the Company would naturally have had some concern about whether there might be any adverse effect on the loadings of the conventional vessels they still operated in what was still perceived to be a declining market. There had been speculation that a fast cross-channel service could offer a serious alternative to the future Severn Bridge, and Clifton Smith-Cox was on record as saying that such a service would cut hours off the long road-journey via the bridge: sadly this was not to be.

The SRN-2 hovercraft operated for a brief period of time in 1963 between Penarth and Weston super Mare. Penarth Head is to left of this picture, most of which is now inside the barrage forming Cardiff Bay. Cardiff Queen is paddling purposefully away from the Pier Head at Cardiff.

Author's collection

During the experimental use in the Bristol Channel of the SRN-2 hovercraft in 1963, promotion of single trips on board the revolutionary new craft combined with a paddle-steamer journey in the other direction between Penarth and Weston super Mare was an obvious means of making the highspeed journeys more accessible to all as seating capacity was limited. Special tickets were produced accordingly.

Author's collection

Portsmouth to the Isle of Wight, 1964

An alternative use for the SRN-2 hovercraft was found in 1964, as the short-lived Bristol Channel service between Penarth & Weston was destined not to be repeated. Hovertransport Limited was a consortium set up with four partners: these were the government-sponsored National Research and Development Corporation, Britten-Norman of the Isle of Wight in association with E. W. H. Gifford, George Nott Industries and of course P. & A. Campbell Ltd themselves.

The registered address of Hovertransport Limited was at Market Chambers, Shelton Square, Coventry and the Directors of the Company were named as S. C. Smith-Cox, R. B. Wickenden, N. D. Norman and E. W. H. Gifford. The latter was a Consulting Engineer, of Southampton. This consortium was set up in 1964 to operate what was billed as an 'Express Hovercraft Service' between Southsea and Ryde, departing from terminals at Eastney Beach on the 'mainland', and from Appley Tower at Ryde, some way to the east of Ryde Esplanade on the Isle of Wight. Peter Southcombe managed operations on the mainland, whilst Christopher Bland was his opposite number on the island. Using publicity that was clearly based on that produced for the Bristol Channel operations in the previous year, Hovertransport Ltd advertised a service at forty-minute intervals on Mondays-Fridays from mid-morning until around teatime, for the period June 17th until September 1st, 1964 at a single fare of ten shillings. The SRN-2 had, in fact, operated briefly on the same route in 1962, for about a week in the August of that year, at around the same time that the Deeside experiment had been taking place. Whether this particular operation ever, in itself, was at that point perceived to present a form of competition to the established rail-connected service of paddle-steamers and post-war motor vessels for foot-passengers that plied between Portsmouth Harbour station and Ryde Pier Head – or even acknowledged at all – is questionable.

Considerable promotional efforts were made by Peter Southcombe who had been aware (from his earlier days in naval service) of the crowds that could be expected on the front at Southsea. It was thus thought appropriate to put on a good show. The terminal consisted of a caravan booking office on the beach and a passenger shelter and thirty or so deck-chairs, all kept looking smart by copious applications of P. & A. Campbell Ltd White Funnel paint and some blue sent from Cardiff. In addition five scaffolding pole masts were erected, each fitted with a proper masthead truck and halyards, in order to fly one Westland flag and four Campbell pennants, the view of Clifton Smith-Cox evidently being that the public were always attracted by flags. An ex-Royal Navy Petty Officer was recruited as Beachmaster (who had done a similar job at the Incho landings in Korea) and who also looked after a beach crew who were all kitted out in white overalls. The Beachmaster was also provided with 'bats', aircraft carrier style, with which to signal to the hovercraft Commander, mainly for show but also to warn if children or dogs had got underneath the barriers and were in danger. Peter felt that such a show would probably have pleased Peter and Alec Campbell in the old days.

For good measure, the opportunity was also taken to promote Bristol Channel paddle-steamer services with some Cardiff-Weston advertising posters. As the crowds thinned later in the summer, one little stunt involved selecting a likely-looking family with a couple of children to be presented with a ticket for 'Passenger Number 10,000' for a photo-opportunity, even though actual numbers carried were then nearer to 8,000. Later on in the season a circus performer with a chimpanzee and photographer turned up and as nobody objected another photo-opportunity had been achieved. As Peter Southcombe put it, towards the end of the season free publicity was always welcome.

The SRN-2 craft, fitted with four Bristol Siddeley Nimbus engines, proved to be not particularly reliable but it needs to be remembered that these were pioneering years for hovercraft operation, and variations on the SRN-2 type were being developed by Westlands. The context of the Hovertransport Ltd concern at this point was still more to do with gaining experience than that of longer-term regular service provision. Other types were produced and towards the end of the Isle of Wight advertised season, one of the two just-completed SRN-5 craft gained a passenger certificate for 18 people and operated alongside the SRN-2 to offer additional capacity to cope with the great demand

Letterhead of Hovertransport Limited, the nominal company formed to operate the SRN-2 hovercraft in 1964, on the Isle of Wight route from Southsea. Author's collection

Striking artwork had graced the timetable pamphlet produced to promote the SRN-2 hovercraft sailings in the Bristol Channel in 1963, and was used again in this 1964 pamphlet which promoted the service between the beach terminals set up at Southsea and Ryde, Isle of Wight. Author's collection

being experienced. The SRN-5, and its 'stretched' version the SRN-6, were of a totally different design to the earlier SRN-2 type. For the 1964 season the 'Flexible Skirt' was developed and fitted, making for much improved performance of the SRN-2: this modification became standard on all later models.

The P. & A. Campbell Ltd interest in the Isle of Wight ceased after the 1964 experiment. Hovertravel – an entirely separate concern with an issued capital of £131,000, was owned by a number of people including Messrs Britten, Norman & Gifford and the Chairman was D. R. Robertson – and from 1965 onwards established more enduring links between Southsea and Ryde with other types. The cross-Solent route, from Clarence Pier to a modern terminal at Ryde Esplanade, still continues and prospers after its fortieth anniversary in 2005, when Christopher Bland remained with the company as its Chairman. Peter Southcombe stayed with P. & A. Campbell Ltd, and was to go on to develop other business opportunities in the south, of which more anon. Later on Seaspeed, a subsidiary of the British Railways Board, commenced operations elsewhere on the Solent, between Southampton and Cowes, in 1966. The SRN-2 was not used again in commercial service after the 1964 season, and was broken up a few years later.

There was no P. & A. Campbell Ltd involvement in any form of hovercraft operation in 1965, and the next part of this story took place towards to the end of that year when an order was placed for an SRN-6 type for operations in the south-east of England. George Nott Industries provided the capital for the purchase of this 38-seat craft, which was effectively a 'stretched' version of the SRN-5. The passenger-only SRN-6 type could be said to have gone beyond the experimental stage from a purely engineering viewpoint, although continued testing of the market to gain experience was definitely implicit in the nature of the new service to be offered. It will be recalled that P. & A. Campbell Ltd were at this point still a subsidiary company of George Nott Industries, as were Townsend Car Ferries, with whom it was arranged that P. & A. Campbell Ltd would jointly operate the next-generation craft. Having said this there was still no actual commitment from the parent company to the notion of operating car-carrying hovercraft, and it might be reiterated that car-ferry development was at an interesting and rapidly-evolving stage at this time. Thus it was still mutually convenient to both parent and subsidiary companies that the name of P. & A. Campbell Ltd was used whilst Notts considered the position, bearing in mind the way in which core business was shaping up at Dover around the distinctive Townsend car-ferry image. This was before any significant expenditure by the parent company was committed, so as to gain familiarity with the very different alternative mode of transport that hovercraft presented.

Britannia, SRN-6.024

Britannia, as the new hovercraft was named, appeared in service at Dover in 1966 jointly carrying the names of Townsend Car Ferries Ltd and P. & A. Campbell Ltd, and the first timetable published for Hovercraft Services from Dover, Hastings and Margate dated May

The shore transport used by Passenger Manager Peter Southcombe was of a modest specification, seen here outside Eastbourne Pier around 1966.
Peter Southcombe collection

15th-June 30th, 1966 offered a wide range of cross-channel and 'off-the-beach' trips on six days of the week from a number of locations. A preliminary run to Calais made on 30th April 1966 was the first-ever cross-channel hovercraft crossing. The thirty-eight seat SRN6.024 craft, named **Britannia**, operated from a base in the north-east corner of the Camber Dock at Dover, at the old Empire Shearwater ramp. (This was located adjacent to where the pontoon berth for **Autocarrier**, formerly the **Royal Sovereign**, was later provided, qv). Considerable marketing effort was directed towards encouraging schools traffic, and other publicity items pointed out that whilst the adult seating capacity would be restricted to twenty-five persons, if children were travelling then the capacity could be raised to thirty-five, plus accompanying adults who could be carried free of charge.

Britannia was scheduled to operate to the following roster in 1966, but weather and other circumstances caused frequent alterations, particularly to the cross-channel services:

Hovercraft BRITANNIA
No-passport Day-Trips to France, fare 67s/6d
(Return by ship, d.1815 from Calais)

(Saturdays Excepted)

Dover	0745
Calais	0830
Dover	0920
Calais	1005
Dover	1045
Calais	1130
Dover	1215 (arr.)

Mondays, Tuesdays & Thursdays		Sundays, Wednesdays & Fridays	
Dover	d. 1230 $	Dover	d. 1230
Hastings	a. 1345 - 1400	Margate	a. 1315-1330

Trips from the beach every 15 minutes until: (fare 12s/6d)

Hastings	1900 - 1925	Margate	1900 - 1930
Dover	2045 end	Dover	2010 end

Fares	Dover-Hastings	70/- , return by hovercraft
	Dover-Hastings $	50/- , one way by bus,
		(Dover d. 1400, or Hastings d. 1830)
	Dover-Margate	67s/6d, return by hovercraft only

This scheduling, with bus options in addition to the use of the cross-channel ferry, shows that a considerable effort was made to offer a good choice to prospective passengers. The newly-expanded south-eastern outpost of the P. & A. Campbell Ltd empire advertised a good variety of trips. This was an early manifestation of the way in which the parent Townsend ferry business could earn additional revenue on board their own vessels from passenger traffic generated by the smaller subsidiary company. It was to become a far more important feature of the latter's business turnover in the ensuing years, as the cross-channel passenger capacity offered by the growing Townsend fleet of Free Enterprise class vessels expanded.

The mechanical performance of the new hovercraft was found to be satisfactory but she did not complete the season of cross-channel trips advertised, instead reverting to just offering 'off-the-beach' trips after late-July 1966. The SRN-6 was not big enough, and it was proving to be an uncomfortable way to cross the channel in anything but the calmest weather. As there was every possibility of earning more revenue with the 'off-the-beach' trips the decision was made jointly by Messrs Smith-Cox and Wickenden to concentrate on this type of business. The other hovercraft service in 1966 across the English Channel to Calais operated by Hoverlloyd started on 6th May 1966, a few days after the P. & A. Campbell Ltd preliminary trip. One interesting aspect of this story is that the well-known Captain Jack

*The hovercraft **Britannia** SRN6-024 at Dover in April 1966 before the commencement of public services.*　　　Grahame Farr collection

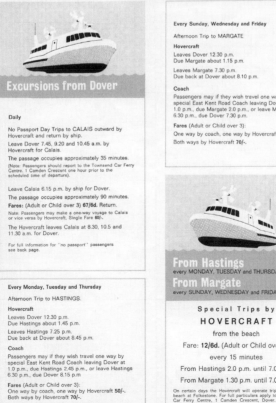

*The pamphlet which publicised most of the trips operated in the south-east by the hovercraft **Britannia** SRN6-024 in 1966.*
Peter Southcombe collection

The shore terminal premises at Margate in support of 'off the beach' trips operated by the hovercraft **Britannia** *SRN6-024 in 1966/67. This caravan was positioned on the promenade pier.*

Peter Southcombe collection

Wide, of many years experience from the Bristol Channel, was asked to go to Dover in the following year, 1967, and act as the Marine Superintendent - Hovercraft. In order to be able to do this he first went to Cowes to take the Hovercraft Drivers' course in order to qualify as a Hovercraft Captain. In so doing he became perhaps the only Captain ever to have held his Master's ticket in sail, steam and hovercraft.

In the 1967 season, the hovercraft *Britannia* offered beach trips only, but from a wider range of resorts which included Hastings, Margate, Leysdown (on Sheppey) and Greatstone near New Romney. The Margate hovercraft log from Sunday, July 2nd 1967 gives an insight into a typical day of operations, where weather conditions and visibility were recorded as good, force 2, cloudy & sunny. The craft arrived at Margate at 0930 having hovered around empty from Dover, then left for Leysdown at 0935 with 3 passengers on board. She returned from Leysdown at 1300, refuelled, and then carried out eleven 'off the beach' trips between 1325 and 1740, carrying some 323 passengers in all. The second departure to Leysdown was at 1756, this time with no passengers on board, and the hovercraft was back again at 2015, still empty. The final 'flight' to Dover, still devoid of fare-paying passengers, was at 2020, and takings that day had grossed £206. Peter Southcombe recalled one amusing occasion, late in the 1967 season, at Margate but which could however have had disastrous consequences. He and Clifton Smith-Cox were standing by the beach terminal caravan watching the hovercraft *Britannia* approaching, on an ebbing tide. The big bathing and boating pool for children just to seaward of the Marine Sun Deck, within about a hundred yards of the approach channel, was still covered in water, but only just. Somehow the hovercraft Commander got over the pool perimeter wall, having been caught by a sudden gust, and by the time he turned the craft to extricate her the tide had fallen by another few inches. He did get her out, but a dangerous and potentially damaging situation briefly existed

for those few minutes. The seriousness averted, Clifton Smith-Cox later said it would have made a good subject for a 'Giles' cartoon, with a 'big fish' in a small sea with lots of little children with toy boats looking on !

A number of resorts approached P. & A. Campbell Ltd to persuade them to try and run similar 'off-the-beach' services by hovercraft, including Bournemouth and Folkestone. Trials were carried out at Eastbourne, as the Company wanted to operate a coastal ferry service between Hastings and Eastbourne to try and make up for the revenue lost on 'off-the-beach' trips which were becoming less well-patronised. Trials were arranged which as far as the Company was concerned were quite successful, but Eastbourne Council refused to grant permission because of possible noise nuisance. A further trial was then arranged, beyond the jurisdiction of the Council, when a test was made to see if it was possible to put the craft alongside at the pier to load where speedboats normally berthed. This was not successful. The original planned terminal at Eastbourne was well east of the town at the 'Crumbles' where there is now a yacht marina. It ought also to be recorded that there had, in late-1965, been discussions between Clifton Smith-Cox and the authorities at Brighton, where there was some keenness to share in the possibilities of a cross-channel hovercraft operation, but also an awareness of potential noise problems at such a densely-developed seafront. It was subsequently concluded that Brighton was too far away from the operational base at Dover, and the Council were advised of this, it being stated that it was unlikely that the hovercraft would be able to get there in the afternoon because of its other scheduled morning cross-Channel commitments intended for 1966.

The author is indebted to Peter Southcombe for having made available most of the logs of hovercraft traffic records that were kept in the 1966 and 1967 seasons when he looked after *Britannia* operations on behalf of P. & A. Campbell Ltd and Townsends jointly. As stated,

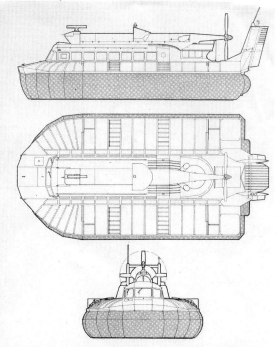

The SRN-6 hovercraft as depicted on the official British Hovercraft Corporation Limited's press release. Dimensions were: length 48ft 5in.; beam 23ft; height on landing pads 14ft 11in.; cabin size 21ft 8in. x 7ft 8in. It was powered by a 900hp Bristol Siddeley Marine Gnome engine driving a 4-blade Dowty Rotol variable pitch propellor 9ft in diameter. Top speed at operating weight was given as 60 knots over calm water at maximum power or 45-55 knots in four-five foot wave conditions. Range was 200 nautical miles. Author's collection

the interest shown by the public in these pioneering excursions was considerable although a little diminished in the second year, and when a new generation of much bigger car-carrying hovercraft did subsequently emerge the experience would be a very different one to that offered by the SRN-6 types tested out by P. & A. Campbell Ltd and by their competitors Hoverlloyd.

The operation by P. & A. Campbell Ltd and Townsend's jointly of *Britannia* ceased after 1967, and the craft was chartered to Hoverlloyd in 1968 who were then operating between Ramsgate and Calais for passengers only, before the appearance of the first generation of car-carrying hovercraft. After this she was purchased in 1969 on behalf of Hovertravel for £37,500 by Christopher Bland. During this stage of the career of the SRN6.024 it was not without a trace of irony – given that P. & A. Campbell Ltd had been a pioneering influence in the area – that she thus re-appeared on the Southsea - Ryde (Isle of Wight) route, some years after the first tentative 'Hovertransport' operation in 1964 described earlier.

Whilst unconnected with the use of the hovercraft by P. & A. Campbell Ltd in the 1966 and 1967 summer seasons, it should be mentioned for completeness that the SRN6.024 enjoyed a brief spell in early 1967 as a passenger 'wizzabout' for Cunard cruise liner passengers on board their ship *Sylvania*, being shipped on the foredeck whilst on a Mediterranean cruise.

There was said to be little enthusiasm by Townsends at Dover behind the hovercraft venture, particularly during the 1966 shipping strike when the emphasis was on getting the ferries running again and not wanting to be seen by the seafarers unions as provocative through running an alternative hovercraft service. It is recorded that the decision was taken by Townsends not to exercise an option on an SRN4 craft for 1968, and Peter Southcombe recalled that Roland Wickenden had decided firmly that his company would not be going in that direction. Fuel-prices were a factor as long ago as the 1960s, and with hindsight the hovercraft industry can be seen as not having stayed the course in the way that more conventional ro-ro shipping – for passengers and increasingly for accompanied freight – was to continue to prosper into the 70s and 80s. Perhaps these noisy craft were indeed overshadowed by the rapidly developing car-ferries which were gradually getting bigger and better, and to a degree supplanting cross-channel railway-

owned passenger steamers still largely geared to the 'classic' foot-passenger market.

To round off this brief era of involvement by P. & A. Campbell Ltd with what was undoubtedly then seen by many as an exciting way forward, one might note that the larger players Hoverlloyd and Seaspeed merged in the 1980s and the big hovercraft passed into history after their withdrawal in 2000. At the time of writing small, passenger-only hovercraft continued to cross the Solent commercially, between Southsea and the Isle of Wight, as the only such British coastal operation, but it remains the case that the P. & A. Campbell Ltd name was prominent in the development of, initially, smaller passenger-only types which progressed into the much bigger, car-carrying craft.

The next phase of P. & A. Campbell Ltd history in the south-east actually goes back to 1965, the year in which the second Townsend Free Enterprise-class vessel appeared, and with it the notably successful development of coach feeder services in the P. & A. Campbell Ltd name. However, before dealing with this we briefly revert to the home territory of the Bristol Channel to consider what was going on there in the mid-1960s after the first motor-vessel *St. Trillo* had arrived and before the second, *Vecta*, entered the fleet.

Bristol Channel traffic matters, 1963-1965

Having thus dealt with the company's attempts to expand and seek new business, and the three areas of property, new vessels and hovercraft, we must return to examine developments in the home waters of the Bristol Channel. Early in 1963 the situation was that paddle-steamer operations were about to be supplemented by the first motor-vessel for the use of the White Funnel Fleet, the venerable little *St. Trillo*. The story of this ship under her new ownership would be largely the story of her continued career on the Llandudno station, as already described. 1964 was a year not characterised by any major investment decisions as such, but a significant threshold towards further fleet expansion was crossed late in 1965 when the former Red Funnel motor-vessel *Vecta* was purchased by P. & A. Campbell Ltd for Bristol Channel use, duly renamed *Westward Ho*. The deployment of this vessel in 1966 and afterwards was to profoundly influence the fate of the two paddle-steamers and for this reason I have identified 1965 as another turning point in the company's fortunes. Thus we now return

This won a poster-design award in 1963 and was produced to promote combined steamer and coach tours, in this case from the English side of the Bristol Channel, and which had been introduced in the late 1950s. Of enduring appeal, fifty years later broadly similar trips were still being offered by Balmoral, in the service of Waverley Excursions Ltd, when schedules from Bristol or Clevedon via Penarth Pier enable suitable timings.   Peter Southcombe collection

to consider the period 1963-1965 'at home' in the Bristol Channel before turning 'away' again to business developments further afield in the south-east, which were separate and largely followed on from the experimentation with hovercraft.

A key Bristol Channel event of 1963 had been the entry into service of the motor vessel *St. Trillo*, on early-season duties, which avoided the higher operating costs of bringing out one of the two paddle-steamers. After the early season debut at Cardiff, Weston-super-Mare and elsewhere *St. Trillo* headed to north Wales to resume her place on the Llandudno station. Heralded by the *South Wales Echo* as the 'baby sister' to the Queens, *St. Trillo* was destined to feature in a modest yet significant way in Bristol Channel operations for the next few years as the White Funnel Fleet underwent the transition from steam to diesel. Not unconnected with the acquisition of this vessel was the disposal of *Glen Usk*, already then laid-up for a number of years since the decision had been taken to bring *Bristol Queen* back into use for the 1961 season. Realistically, the prolonged lay-up of *Glen Usk* since she had ended Cardiff to Weston ferry duties after the 1960 season reduced the likelihood of it ever being viable to refurbish her, had there actually then been any real need for a third paddle-steamer, whether or not continuing as a coal-burner, or converted to an oil-burner as had been envisaged. She left Cardiff for the breakers in Cork on the evening tide of Monday 29th April 1963, under tow by the Swansea tug *Talbot*, attracting a mention in the local newspaper: ' ...a Campbell's spokesman said ... she is being scrapped. She is not being renovated and put back into service. We are sorry to see her go as she is the last of the old P. & A. Campbell prewar fleet. To have modernised the old coal-fired* Glen Usk *by installing oil-fired boilers would have cost £30,000, or £45,000, if you included painting, new decks, new plates, etc,'. Her cost to the breakers ? The spokesman would only say 'We got a fair price for her – as scrap.' The article pointed out that her original cost had been around £25,000.

This left P. & A. Campbell Ltd with just the two postwar Queens for Bristol Channel duties, which in truth had been coping quite adequately during the 1961 and 1962 seasons. By this means, it was also demonstrated to the parent company that financial responsibility was being exercised by the subsidiary company, inasmuch as the disposal of the redundant *Glen Usk* meant that berthing charges at Cardiff Docks would no longer be payable for an asset which had long since ceased to have earning power, and some positive cash-flow would be generated by her scrap value. More positive for enthusiasts was the news that *Bristol Queen* would undertake her first-ever trip to the Isles of Scilly in 1963, scheduled to take place between May 17th-19th. It was to have been a charter to a Mr Huxtable of Penarth, but the company took it on directly a few weeks beforehand. This was not an entirely new venture for a Campbell paddle-steamer as *Britannia* had ventured to

Bristol Queen at rest at Lundy, probably in 1966.   Brian Owen, courtesy of Nick James

these waters as early as the turn of the century. The 'revived' style of weekend-long excursion was regarded as a considerable success, and the itinerary of **Bristol Queen** featured an 0945 departure from Cardiff on Friday May 17th with calls at Weston and Ilfracombe, arriving at Penzance at 2145 that evening. The Saturday was occupied with a 1045 departure from Penzance to St. Marys, Isles of Scilly returning from the island at 1815. The homeward schedule on the Monday involved departure from Penzance at 0930 with calls at Ilfracombe and at Barry before Clevedon was reached at 2145. Advertising for the special excursion indicated quaintly that although passengers needed to book their own hotel accommodation in Penzance, the Company would be '… *pleased to assist in this regard if desired …*', pointing out that the number of passengers carried west of Ilfracombe would be restricted to a maximum of 250.

An incident attracting major media attention on Saturday August 10th, 1963 was the reported grounding of **Cardiff Queen** in the River Avon, after having set off from Hotwells for Mumbles in the morning. Whilst this kind of incident, if it had actually occurred, would very probably have had serious consequences for the White Funnel Fleet, Chris Collard, in a review of the career of **Cardiff Queen** published in the journal *Ship Ahoy* in Autumn 1968 set the record straight: '... *The season proceeded uneventfully apart from one incident which occurred on Saturday August 10th, when the press made a great play of the fact that she ran aground in the River Avon just after leaving Hotwells landing stage. The reports were completely untrue in that she was not aground but was only delayed while mud which had been drawn into the condenser was cleared ...*'. 1963 ended fairly quietly when, as anticipated, **St. Trillo** came back round from her north Wales base to close Bristol Channel sailings, having finished at Menai Bridge in mid-September. She had made a reasonably favourable impression generally, and her presence as a versatile and compact new member of the White Funnel Fleet was to give the company confidence to try out occasional sailings to new Bristol Channel destinations in 1964. Maybe, now, things really were looking up for the business, after so many years of decline and disappointment during the previous decade.

Old ports of call revived

Whether or not Clifton Smith-Cox was a naturally good publicist for the White Funnel Fleet, the local newspapers on either side of the Bristol Channel seem to have generally been willing to carry articles on the paddle-steamers and other ventures over the years. In the depths of winter it must have been encouraging to potential customers, steamer-enthusiasts or otherwise, to read of new destinations for Campbell ships in the forthcoming season, and in February 1964 the headline 'Steamers may call at Chepstow' would have created a fair degree of interest:

' …The White Funnel Fleet may be making calls at Chepstow this summer'. Mr S. C. Smith-Cox, managing director of P. & A. Campbell Ltd, says that this season excursions are to be made up the River Severn to view the construction of the new bridge. Discussions are also taking place about the possibility of a call being made at Chepstow. "These visits would be made with the new *St. Trillo*, since the larger steamers now in operation would not be suitable for the trip" said Mr Smith-Cox.'

Chepstow calls by White Funnel Fleet steamers had not been resumed after the Great War, following the removal of the landing-stage on the River Wye. The first postwar call at Chepstow did not actually take place until the late-season, on Sunday September 20th 1964. The lack of suitability referred to was an allusion to the exceedingly tight fit of the ships masts underneath that part of the new Severn Bridge (then under construction, prior to its opening in 1966), which spanned the River Wye just above its confluence with the River Severn. She left in the morning with over 300 passengers, but delays were encountered with the trip when her anchor fouled on the evening return leg of the voyage to Chepstow, and indeed little room for error existed when turning a vessel in the tight confines of the River Wye off the historic town of Chepstow. Her planned call at Clevedon on the return to Barry had to be cancelled as a result, but the trip was nonetheless considered a great success.

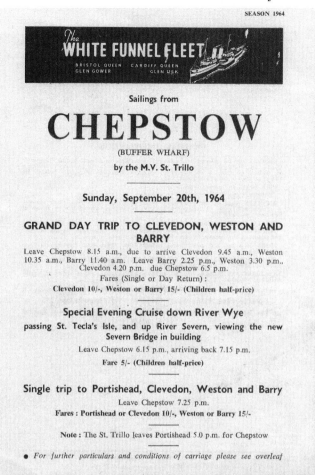

Sailing bill for the calls at Chepstow initially planned for St. Trillo *in 1964: the schedule was subsequently modified, the short cruise out of Chepstow dropped and the return departure time for Barry brought forward from 7.25pm to 7.00pm.* Author's collection

Interest was aroused a little further down the Severn estuary a couple of months after this announcement as speculation over the possibility of the construction of a new landing-stage at Newport, on the River Usk, attracted attention. Concern centred on the fact that, since the Campbell steamers had ceased to be able to depart directly from the Landing Stage at the heart of Newport after the 1956 season, an element of frustration was felt by Newport folk at having to travel by rail to Cardiff, and thence by bus to the Pier Head to join a steamer for Weston, Minehead and other destinations. Councillor Percy Jones, then due to become the next Mayor of Newport, spoke out to the press and sought to influence fellow councillors to consider the provision of a new facility at which steamers could call as there was still thought to be sufficient demand locally. Reference was made to the expanding population in the nearby Cwmbran new town at that time, as well as to the attraction of the new Butlin's Holiday Camp over the water at Minehead. A theme of Newport folk feeling resentment at being channelled through somewhere other than their own local River Usk for excursions was not a new one and a local businessman, Mr Roger Holbrook, went a little further and was quoted as saying that '... *we lost a tradition when Campbells went, and a pleasure that people of all ages could enjoy ... shortly the hovercraft will come into its own. If no interest has been shown from this part of the world in present sailing services what opportunity are we likely to have of getting a Hovercraft service*?'. Although the provisional assent of the company to the operation of a limited summer service of steamers in 1965 was said to have been secured, the response was somewhat guarded and the notion of a resurrected Newport landing-stage or some new alternative river-berth was, sadly, to remain just that.

The WHITE FUNNEL FLEET

BRISTOL QUEEN CARDIFF QUEEN GLEN USK ST. TRILLO WESTWARD HO WAVERLEY DEVONIA LUNDY QUEEN

Sailings from THE OLD HARBOUR, MINEHEAD

THE STEAMERS of the White Funnel Fleet are approximately 245 feet in length and can each carry over a thousand passengers. Each vessel has a Restaurant, also a tea room and two fully licensed Bars on Board. There are sun lounges, spacious open decks and covered accommodation is available sufficient for all passengers. The steamers are the largest, fastest and most modern of their type afloat.

SEASON 1963

CIRCULAR TOURS BY COACH AND STEAMER

These Tours, enabling visitors to Minehead and district to see some of the most beautiful scenery in the British Isles by both steamer and coach in one day, are most popular.

For full details of Tours and also of arrangements for Circular bookings in connection with steamer trips marked ★ see back of bill under the heading "Special Bus Services".

Average passage times from Minehead to: Weston (direct) 1½ hours (via Cardiff) 3 hours; Lynmouth or Barry 1 hour; Ilfracombe 1¾ hours; Cardiff (direct) 2 hours, (via Weston) 2½ hours, Clovelly, Lundy Island 3¼ hours.

SUNDAY, MAY 26th

10.45 a.m. Day trip to ★ILFRACOMBE and LUNDY ISLAND. Due to arrive Ilfracombe 1.0 p.m., Lundy 3.0 p.m. Leave Lundy 5.5 p.m., Ilfracombe 6.45 p.m.; due Minehead 8.20 p.m. Passengers for Lundy Island change steamers at Ilfracombe on the forward journey only. Steamer leaves Ilfracombe for Lundy 1.30 p.m.

10.45 a.m. Combined Steamer and Coach Tour via ILFRACOMBE to CLOVELLY and WESTWARD HO. A delightful tour **via Barnstaple, Bideford and Clovelly Cross.** Returning via **Westward Ho, Northam and Bideford**. Stops will be made at Clovelly for sightseeing and at Westward Ho for sightseeing. Leave Ilfracombe 6.45 p.m.; due Minehead 8.20 p.m. Inclusive return fare (coach and steamer) **29/6d.**, Children **16/6d.** Coach leaves Illfracombe (Pier Gates) 1.45 p.m.

8.25 p.m. Single trip to WESTON, PENARTH and CARDIFF.

Note: A steamer leaves Cardiff 8.20 a.m., Penarth 8.30 a.m., Barry 9.10 a.m. due Minehead 10.35 a.m.

WEDNESDAY, MAY 29th

11.45 a.m. Day trip to ★LYNMOUTH, ★ILFRACOMBE and CLOVELLY; due to arrive Lynmouth 12.50 p.m., Ilfracombe 1.35 p.m. and Clovelly 3.20 p.m.. Leave Clovelly 4.45 p.m., Ilfracombe 6.20 p.m., Lynmouth 6.50 p.m.; due Minehead 8.10 p.m.

Note: Passengers disembarking from the Steamer on the return journey will be landed at Minehead in Motor-boats. On the forward journey the steamer will embark passengers inside Minehead Harbour.

8.15 p.m. Single trip to BARRY, PENARTH and CARDIFF.

Note: A steamer leaves Cardiff 9.45 a.m., Penarth 9.55 a.m., Barry 10.30 a.m.; due Minehead 11.35 a.m.

THURSDAY, JUNE 6th

10.0 a.m. Special Combined Coach and Steamer Tour via ILFRACOMBE to LUNDY ISLAND. Special coaches leave Minehead Harbour at 10.0 a.m. for Ilfracombe. Steamer leaves Ilfracombe for Lundy Island at 12.15 p.m., due to arrive Lundy 1.45 p.m., returning from Lundy Island at 4.10 p.m. by steamer for Minehead; due Minehead 7.30 p.m. Tickets for this excursion should be obtained at the Company's Office on the Quay before joining the Coach, and can be purchased on the morning of the trip or in advance. Fare (Coach and Steamer) **27/6d.**, Children half-price.

Circular trip to ILFRACOMBE. (Special coaches leave Minehead Harbour at 10.0 a.m. for Ilfracombe. Passengers return by steamer from Ilfracombe at 5.50 p.m., due Minehead 7.30 p.m.)

Circular trip to LYNMOUTH. Outward by Western National bus, return by steamer from Lynmouth at 6.20 p.m.; due Minehead 7.30 p.m.

7.35 p.m. Single trip to BARRY, FENARTH and CARDIFF.

Note: A steamer leaves Lundy 4.10 p.m., Ilfracombe 5.50 p.m., Lynmouth 6.20 p.m.; due Minehead 7.30 p.m.

MONDAY, JUNE 10th

12.15 p.m. Day trip to ★ILFRACOMBE and CLOVELLY. Due to arrive Ilfracombe 1.50 p.m., Clovelly 3.20 p.m. Leave Clovelly 4.50 p.m., Ilfracombe 6.20 p.m., due Minehead 7.55 p.m.

Note: Passengers embarking on the 12.15 p.m. steamer will be conveyed from the harbour to the ship by motor boat. On the return journey the steamer will berth inside Minehead Harbour.

8.0 p.m. Single trip to WESTON, PENARTH and CARDIFF.

Note: A steamer leaves Bristol 9.0 a.m., Clevedon 10.10 a.m., Weston 10.45 a.m.; due Minehead 12 noon.

TUESDAY, JUNE 11th

10.50 a.m. Day trip to ★LYNMOUTH, ★ILFRACOMBE and LUNDY ISLAND. Due to arrive Lynmouth 11.45 a.m., Ilfracombe 12.30 p.m. Lundy 2.10 p.m. Leave Lundy 4.40 p.m., Ilfracombe 6.40 p.m., Lynmouth 7.10 p.m.; due Minehead 8.20 p.m.

8.25 p.m. Single trip to BARRY (and train to Cardiff).

Note: Steamer leaves Cardiff 9.0 a.m., Penarth 9.10 a.m., Barry 9.45 a.m., due Minehead 10.40 a.m.

THURSDAY, JUNE 20th

10.15 a.m. Special Combined Coach and Steamer Tour via Ilfracombe to LUNDY ISLAND. Special coaches leave Minehead Harbour at 10.15 a.m. for Ilfracombe. Steamer leaves Ilfracombe for Lundy Island at 12.15 p.m., due to arrive Lundy 1.45 p.m., returning from Lundy Island at 4.0 p.m. by steamer for Minehead, due Minehead 7.20 p.m. Tickets for this excursion should be obtained at the Company's Office on the Quay before joining the coach and can be purchased either on the morning of the trip or in advance. Fare (Coach and Steamer) **27/6d.**, Children half-price.

Circular trip to ILFRACOMBE. Special coaches leave Minehead Harbour at 10.15 a.m. for Ilfracombe. Passengers return by steamer from Ilfracombe at 5.35 p.m., due Minehead 7.20 p.m.

Circular trip to LYNMOUTH (outward by Western National bus), return by steamer from Lynmouth at 6.5 p.m.; due Minehead 7.20 p.m.

7.25 p.m. Single trip to BARRY, PENARTH and CARDIFF.

Note: A steamer leaves Lundy 4.0 p.m., Ilfracombe 5.35 p.m., Lynmouth 6.5 p.m.; due Minehead 7.20 p.m.

MONDAY, JUNE 24th

9.45 a.m. Day trip to CARDIFF, PENARTH and WESTON; due to arrive Cardiff 11.35 a.m., Penarth 11.55 a.m., Weston 12.45 p.m. Leave Weston 6.20 p.m., Cardiff 7.20 p.m., Penarth 7.30 p.m.; due Minehead 9.25 p.m.

9.45 a.m. Circular trip to WESTON (via Cardiff). Return from Weston by any train.

9.45 a.m. Combined Steamer and Coach tour of the WELSH MOUNTAINS. On arrival at Cardiff special coaches will meet steamer for a tour of the Welsh Mountains, via **Pontypridd, Porth, Rhigos Mountain, the Vale of Neath, Neath, Port Talbot and Bridgend,** returning to Cardiff alongside the steamer, which leaves at 7.20 p.m. for Minehead, arriving at Minehead about 9.25 p.m.

9.35 p.m. Single trip to PENARTH and CARDIFF.

Note: A steamer leaves Cardiff at 7.35 a.m.; due Minehead 9.35 a.m.

TUESDAY, JUNE 25th

10.50 a.m. Day trip to ★LYNMOUTH, ★ILFRACOMBE and LUNDY ISLAND. Due to arrive Lynmouth 11.45 a.m., Ilfracombe 12.30 p.m., Lundy 2.10 p.m. Leave Lundy 4.40 p.m., Ilfracombe 7.0 p.m., Lynmouth 7.30 p.m., due Minehead 8.40 p.m.

10.50 a.m. Combined Steamer and Coach Tour via ILFRACOMBE to CLOVELLY and WESTWARD HO. A delightful tour via **Barnstaple, Bideford and Clovelly Cross.** Returning via **Westward Ho, Northam and Bideford.** Stops will be made at Clovelly for sightseeing and at Westward Ho for sightseeing. Leave Ilfracombe 7.0 p.m.; due Minehead 8.40 p.m.

TUESDAY, JUNE 25th—continued

Inclusive return fare (coach and steamer) **29/6d.**, Children **16/6d.** Coach leaves Ilfracombe (Pier Gates) 1.45 p.m.

8.45 p.m. Single trip to BARRY (and train to CARDIFF).

Note: A steamer leaves Cardiff 9.0 a.m., Penarth 9.10 a.m., Barry 9.45 a.m.; due Minehead 10.40 a.m.

THURSDAY, JULY 4th

9.50 a.m. Special Combined Coach and Steamer Tour via ILFRACOMBE to LUNDY ISLAND. Special coaches leave Minehead Harbour at 9.50 a.m. for Ilfracombe. Steamer leaves Ilfracombe for Lundy Island at 12 noon, due to arrive Lundy 1.30 p.m., returning from Lundy Island at 3.50 p.m. for Ilfracombe, where Special Coaches will be waiting to convey passengers to Minehead, where they will arrive about 7.25 p.m. Tickets for this excursion should be obtained at the Company's office on the Quay before joining the Coach, and can be purchased either on the morning of the trip or in advance. Fare (Coach and Steamer) **27/6.**, Children half-price.

TUESDAY, JULY 9th

12.15 p.m. Day trip to ★LYNMOUTH, ★ILFRACOMBE and CLOVELLY; due to arrive Lynmouth 1.15 p.m., Ilfracombe 2.0 p.m., Clovelly 3.30 p.m. Leave Clovelly 4.55 p.m., Ilfracombe 6.25 p.m., Lynmouth 6.55 p.m.; due Minehead 8.0 p.m.

12.15 p.m. Combined Steamer and Coach Tour via ILFRACOMBE to HUNTERS INN via Two Potts and Berrydown, allowing two hours to view the inn and walk to Heddons Mouth. Homeward via **Trentishoe Common and Combe Martin.** Leave Ilfracombe 6.25 p.m.; due Minehead 8.0 p.m. Inclusive return fare **26/-**, Children **14/6d.** Coach leaves Ilfracombe (Pier Gates) 2.15 p.m.

Note: Passengers embarking on the 12.15 p.m. steamer will be conveyed from the harbour to the ship by motor-boat. On the return journey the steamer will berth inside Minehead Harbour.

8.5 p.m. Single trip to WESTON, PENARTH and CARDIFF.

Note: A steamer leaves Bristol 9.0 a.m., Clevedon 10.0 a.m., Weston 10.40 a.m., due Minehead 12 noon.

WEDNESDAY, JULY 10th

10.50 a.m. Day trip to ★LYNMOUTH, ★ILFRACOMBE and LUNDY ISLAND; due to arrive Lynmouth 11.45 a.m., Ilfracombe 12.30 p.m., Lundy Island 2.10 p.m. Leave Lundy 4.40 p.m., Ilfracombe 6.40 p.m., Lynmouth 7.10 p.m.; due Minehead 8.20 p.m.

10.50 a.m. Combined Steamer and Coach Tour via ILFRACOMBE to CLOVELLY and WESTWARD HO. A delightful tour via **Barnstaple, Bideford and Clovelly Cross.** Returning via **Westward Ho, Northam and Bideford.** Stops will be made at Clovelly for sightseeing and at Westward Ho for sightseeing. Leave Ilfracombe 6.40 p.m., due Minehead 8.20 p.m. Inclusive return fare (coach and steamer) **29/6d.**, Children **16/6d.** Coach leaves Ilfracombe (Pier Gates) 1.45 p.m.

8.25 p.m. Single trip to BARRY (and train to Cardiff).

Note: A steamer leaves Cardiff 9.0 a.m., Penarth 9.10 a.m., Barry 9.45 a.m.; due Minehead 10.40 a.m.

THURSDAY, JULY 11th

9.30 a.m. Day trip to CARDIFF, PENARTH and WESTON; due to arrive Cardiff 11.10 a.m., Penarth 11.30 a.m., Weston 12.20 p.m. Leave Weston 7.0 p.m., Cardiff 8.0 p.m., Penarth 8.10 p.m.; due Minehead 10.0 p.m.

9.30 a.m. Circular trip to WESTON (via Cardiff). Return from Weston by any train.

9.30 a.m. Combined Steamer and Coach tour of the WELSH MOUNTAINS. On arrival at Cardiff special coaches will meet steamer for a tour of the Welsh Mountains, via **Pontypridd, Porth, Rhigos Mountain, the Vale of Neath, Neath, Port Talbot and Bridgend,** returning to Cardiff alongside the steamer, which leaves at 8.0 p.m. for Minehead, arriving at Minehead about 10.0 p.m.

10.10 p.m. Single trip to PENARTH and CARDIFF.

Note: A steamer leaves Cardiff 7.20 a.m.; due Minehead 9.20 a.m.

TUESDAY, JULY 16th

9.45 a.m. Special Combined Coach and Steamer Tour via ILFRACOMBE to LUNDY ISLAND. Special coaches leave Minehead Harbour at 9.45 a.m. for Ilfracombe. Steamer leaves Ilfracombe for Lundy Island at 11.50 a.m., due to arrive Lundy 1.20 p.m., returning from Lundy Island at 4.20 p.m. for Ilfracombe, where special coaches will be waiting to convey passengers to Minehead, where they will arrive about 7.55 p.m. Tickets for this excursion should be obtained at the Company's Office on the Quay before joining the coach, and can be purchased either on the morning of the trip or in advance. Fare (Coach and Steamer) **27/6d.**, Children half-price.

TUESDAY, JULY 23rd

10.35 a.m. Day trip to ★LYNMOUTH, ★ILFRACOMBE and LUNDY ISLAND; due to arrive Lynmouth 11.30 a.m., Ilfracombe 12.15 p.m., Lundy 1.55 p.m. Leave Lundy 4.30 p.m., Ilfracombe 6.10 p.m., Lynmouth 6.40 p.m.; due Minehead 7.50 p.m.

7.55 p.m. Single trip to BARRY, PENARTH and CARDIFF.

Note: A steamer leaves Cardiff 8.40 a.m., Penarth 8.50 a.m., Barry 9.25 a.m.; due Minehead 10.25 a.m.

THURSDAY, JULY 25th

9.35 a.m. Day trip to CARDIFF, PENARTH and WESTON; due to arrive Cardiff 11.15 a.m., Penarth 11.35 a.m., Weston 12.25 p.m. Leave Weston 6.55 p.m., Cardiff 7.55 p.m., Penarth 8.5 p.m.; due Minehead 9.55 p.m.

9.35 a.m. Circular trip to WESTON (via Cardiff). Return from Weston by any train.

9.35 a.m. Combined Steamer and Coach tour of the WELSH MOUNTAINS. On arrival at Cardiff special coaches will meet steamer for a tour of the Welsh Mountains, via **Pontypridd, Porth, Rhigos Mountain, the Vale of Neath, Neath, Port Talbot and Bridgend,** returning to Cardiff alongside the steamer, which leaves at 7.55 p.m. for Minehead, arriving at Minehead about 9.55 p.m.

10.5 p.m. Single trip to PENARTH and CARDIFF.

Note: A steamer leaves Cardiff 7.25 a.m.; due Minehead 9.25 a.m.

MONDAY, JULY 29th

10.30 a.m. Special Combined Coach and Steamer tour via ILFRACOMBE to LUNDY ISLAND. Special coaches leave Minehead Harbour at 10.30 a.m. for Ilfracombe. Steamer leaves Ilfracombe for Lundy Island 12.40 p.m., due to arrive Lundy 2.10 p.m., returning from Lundy Island at 4.35 p.m. for Ilfracombe, where Special Coaches will be waiting to convey passengers to Minehead, where they will arrive about 8.10 p.m. Tickets for this excursion should be obtained at the Company's office on the Quay, before joining the Coach and can be purchased either on the morning of the trip or in advance. Fare (Coach and Steamer) **27/6d.**, Children half-fare.

THURSDAY, AUGUST 8th

10.45 a.m. Day trip to ★LYNMOUTH, ★ILFRACOMBE and LUNDY ISLAND; due to arrive Lynmouth 11.40 a.m., Ilfracombe 12.25 p.m., Lundy 2.5 p.m. Leave Lundy 4.40 p.m., Ilfracombe 6.30 p.m., Lynmouth 7.0 p.m., due Minehead 8.10 p.m.

10.45 a.m. Combined Steamer and Coach Tour via ILFRACOMBE to CLOVELLY and WESTWARD HO. A delightful tour via **Barnstaple, Bideford and Clovelly Cross.** Returning via **Westward Ho, Northam and Bideford.** Stops will be made at Clovelly for sightseeing and at Westward Ho for sightseeing. Leave Ilfracombe 6.30 p.m. Due Minehead 8.10 p.m. Inclusive return fare (coach and steamer) **29/6d.**, Children **16/6d.** Coach leaves Ilfracombe (Pier Gates) 1.45 p.m.

8.15 p.m. Single trip to BARRY, PENARTH and CARDIFF.

Note: A steamer leaves Cardiff 8.50 a.m., Penarth 9.0 a.m., Barry 9.35 a.m.; due Minehead 10.35 a.m.

SUNDAY, AUGUST 11th

11.55 a.m. Day trip to ★LYNMOUTH, ★ILFRACOMBE and LUNDY ISLAND, due to arrive Lynmouth 1.5 p.m., Ilfracombe 1.50 p.m., Lundy-

FOR FURTHER SAILINGS, FARES AND CONDITIONS—see over

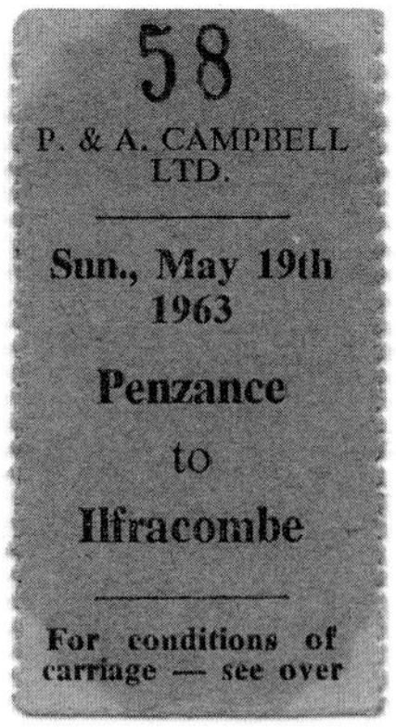

58

P. & A. CAMPBELL LTD.

Sun., May 19th 1963

Penzance

to

Ilfracombe

For conditions of carriage — see over

This 1963 specimen handbill illustrates the general style that prevailed during the 1960s and 1970s for this means of publicity. Bills were issued for each main departure point, those for Cardiff (combined with Penarth & Barry times) being the largest, and which might be issued up to five times in the season, each with a month's worth of sailings and coach excursion information. The Minehead bill was one of the smaller productions, just bigger than foolscap, double-sided and contained the whole season's details. The fleet described on the bill-head sounded very grand but by 1963 the prewar veteran Glen Usk *had gone and the last four named were launches used at Lynmouth and Lundy. The tidal pattern gave rise to non-repeating times, and was inevitably space-consuming. The obverse gave details of local bus arrangements, and of fares and conditions. These bills were distributed mainly at the piers and by agencies, to complement newspaper advertisements, and for many years were printed by T. & W. Goulding at Bristol, in a distinctive blue type, on shiny cream-coloured paper.*

Author's collection

Over on the English side of the Bristol Channel an exciting first was represented by the use of the newly-acquired *St. Trillo* to act as tender to the magnificent Swedish-American liner *Kungsholm*. This was the vessel built in 1953, which was to be followed in 1957 by *Gripsholm*, which also was to make occasional appearances in Campbell territory. The White Funnel Fleet gained some excellent publicity as the Lord Mayor of Bristol accompanied by some of the city's 'chief citizens' embarked on the tender at Avonmouth to '… *glide out to a meal on the waves* …' at Walton Bay aboard the sleek white-hulled cruise liner which '… *rode at anchor in the sunlit Bristol Channel* …' as sightseers lined the cliff-top with cameras to hand. This was just the sort of publicity that was needed, although the call had been due to take place the previous day, and the 450 American tourists who were, amongst other things, touring the stately homes of England had their tour in and around Bristol – allegedly in chauffeur-driven Princesses, with their cameras, cigars and guide-books – delayed through choppy seas on the planned day. Maybe slightly tongue in cheek, the *Bristol Evening Post* item of 5th May 1964 also noted that the crew had also gone ashore to do a spot of sightseeing – by coach.

As the season got underway a different sort of attention was aroused when *Cardiff Queen*, during a long channel cruise on 14th June, ran aground on a sandbank off Clevedon from 1515 until approximately 1900, with forty-six passengers aboard. She was undamaged, and the company Managing Director commented that '… *there had been no panic on board when she stranded, and that as far as he knew everyone got home in the normal way and there was little inconvenience*'.

Another occasional Bristol Channel destination which was to resume its place in White Funnel timetables had not been absent for quite so long as Chepstow. The little *St. Trillo* was to demonstrate her usefulness again at the Somerset port of Watchet on 19th September 1964, on a trip from Barry, described as the first call there for thirty-five years, and where it was reported that a large crowd of locals turned out to see her. Fewer arrangements were needed to organise this excursion into the neat, compact harbour at Watchet, merely the consent of the Harbour Authority and the provision of a Pilot, in order to come alongside

and berth the ship at the harbour wall. The schedule for this trip read as follows: Barry, depart 2.45 pm, Watchet dep. 4.35 pm for a 'Grand Afternoon Cruise along the Coast of Somerset passing Blue Anchor and calling at Minehead', leave Watchet 6.30 pm for Minehead & Barry.

Scrutiny of sources such as the journal *Ship Ahoy* covering this period reveals a slight paradox, where the impression of good results after the 1964 season, attributed to favourable weather and enterprising new destinations to tempt more passengers aboard, was tempered by increasingly frequent references to the paddle-wheel problems suffered by both Queens. Both were still less than twenty years old at this time and it is hard to avoid the conclusion that maintenance was in some way deficient, and it must definitely have been the case that without a backup & emergency repair facility of the type that the Underfall Yard had formerly provided, routine maintenance became more problematic to carry out. Utilisation of the vessels had become more intensive, and they had no particular home during the season where trained staff could look them over between traffic duties. Costs had been reduced to keep the company in business, and during the sixties considerable efforts had to be made when emergencies did arise, so that off-service days were kept to a minimum. The Minute Book of Directors Meetings does in fact reveal that enquiries were being made as early as during 1963 regarding the acquisition of secondhand motor-vessel tonnage, from both British Railways and the Red Funnel company on their respective Isle of Wight routes. At the Directors meeting on 20th September 1963 it was noted that no vessels were yet available, and it was not until the end of the 1965 season that these enquiries were eventually to bear fruit.

In the meantime, the management team of the White Funnel Fleet continued to demonstrate commendable enterprise by sustaining the new features of the recent seasons, such as the annual Isles of Scilly trip and the operation of odd visits to far-flung destinations like Milford Haven, as well as to the more workaday places closer to home such as Watchet & Chepstow, which had been made possible by the availability of the newly-acquired *St. Trillo*. Milford Haven represented a very full day out from Cardiff, and on Sunday 28th July 1963 the departure of *Bristol Queen* was posted at 0835 from

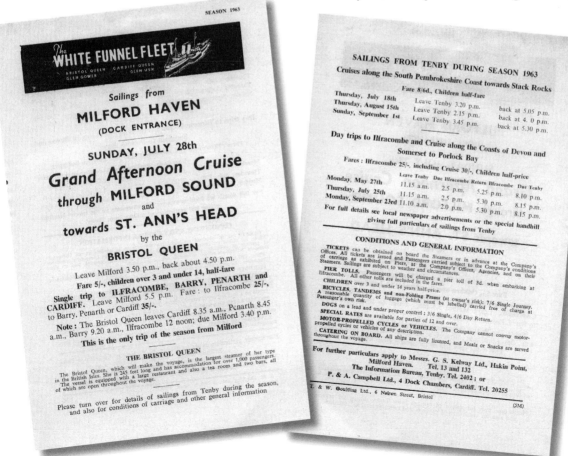

1963 Milford Haven handbill. The obverse gave details of Tenby calls.

Author's collection

The atmosphere of a quiet moment at the Pier Head, Cardiff is captured from the foredeck of the postwar paddle-steamer **Cardiff Queen.**
Brian Owen, courtesy of Nick James

Both Queens at rest, Cardiff Docks, mid-1960s
Brian Owen, courtesy of Nick James

the Pier Head, with calls at Penarth and Barry en route to Ilfracombe for a midday crossing due at Milford at 1540. It was blowing hard at Ilfracombe but Peter Southcombe recalled that after some discussion between Captain George and Clifton Smith-Cox it was decided to go ahead and cross the channel, and in fact the weather did improve by the time west Wales was reached. The special handbill stressed that this was the only trip of the season for Milford Haven, and a one-hour 'Grand Afternoon Cruise' through Milford Sound and towards St. Ann's Head was advertised from the Milford Haven Dock Entrance.

Announced at the beginning of the season, Padstow in Cornwall was to be a new port of call for 1965. This had been prompted by approaches made to the company by the Paddle Steamer Preservation Society for a partial-charter and which would necessitate the speed and capacity of one of the Queens. Both of the Queens dry-docked in the Mountstuart Dry-Dock at Cardiff, *Bristol Queen* occupying the No.2 Dock first between April 6th-13th, followed in by *Cardiff Queen* between April 13th-15th. The former laid up for a short while before re-appearing in order to tender to the Swedish-American liner *Kungsholm* on May 4th & 5th. In addition to tendering passengers on the by now annual liner-visits, cruises for the public from Avonmouth & Clevedon were also operated on those days, specifically to view the liner as the highlight of an upper Channel cruise, but also taking in the English & Welsh Grounds light-vessel on the first of the two days. As the liner was due to leave a request to the Chief Engineer of *Bristol Queen* to '*open her up and give them a run for their money*' was conveyed from Capt. Jack Wide on the bridge as the company Managing Director was with him. Emergency full speed was soon attained, with the paddle-box doors open to avoid trapping any water, and an exciting race was sustained where the speediness of the paddle-steamer evidently surprised the Swedish officers looking down from the heights of *Kungsholm* as they duly responded and gradually pulled away down-Channel – one can imagine the exuberance created on board *Bristol Queen* by this sporting indulgence, and the stories told afterwards.

The Padstow trip, from Swansea & Ilfracombe on Sunday 8th August 1965, was taken by *Bristol Queen* and was regarded as a great success as a capacity crowd of 750 passengers were carried, in glorious weather

conditions. The reception given to the paddle-steamer was described as akin to a Royal welcome, and with the presence of the Bodmin Town Band a wonderful sense of occasion was created. Limited time at Padstow on this occasion did not permit a short cruise to be offered from there, but the occasion did lead to subsequent visits. Ominously, though, *Bristol Queen* suffered paddle-wheel troubles a few days later. *Cardiff Queen* was in trouble in a rather different way when she was struck by a coastal tanker when leaving Barry Pier on 16th August. The tanker, *Wheeldale H*, had entered the Barry approaches against a signal and caused substantial damage to the port after quarter of *Cardiff Queen*, necessitating repairs at Cardiff Docks which took her off-service for two days and left her looking distinctly the worse for wear. The swift avoiding action taken by the experienced Master of *Cardiff Queen*, Captain Phil Power of Penarth, was a major factor in minimising the damage, as reported in the *Western Mail* the following day, 17th August 1965:

CAPTAIN'S ACTION AVERTS DISASTER

'Quick action by a pleasure boat crew averted disaster yesterday as a loaded 273-ton oil barge collided with the 765t steamer carrying 78 passengers. The prow of the barge *Wheeldale H* tore an 8ft gash amidships in the *Cardiff Queen* above the waterline. But the damage would have been "far worse" if Captain Philip Power had not managed to slam the steamer's engines into reverse at the last moment, the holidaymakers agreed last night. Within minutes the 250ft *Cardiff Queen* was back in the docks – she had been starting a two-hour Bristol Channel cruise – for temporary repairs. Later she was able to resume a trip to Weston-super-Mare and Cardiff.

Passengers warned

The collision happened as the steamer, owned by P. & A. Campbell Ltd was sailing stern-first into the channel 50 yards from the dock-entrance. "I caught a glimpse of a barge coming around the west breakwater towards us, and acted as fast as possible" said Captain Power of Andrew Road, Cogan. "We had started heading for the dock again and were actually picking up speed to about two knots when we collided. The 140ft. barge, owned by John Harker Ltd and loaded with 450 tons of oil, tried to swing away as the steamer passengers stayed away from the rail on the orders of the crew. "It was quite a bump, but no one even lost their balance" said Mrs. Renee James of Alexandra Road, Canton, Cardiff. " I didn't realise what a quick decision the captain had made until it was all over". The dining-room bulwark was ripped open, but the only casualty was a bottle of tomato sauce. "Not a glass moved" said a steward last night.

"Keeled over"

Some of the passengers, however, had to forego the scheduled cruise for the repairs to be made in time for the next crowd of holidaymakers bound for Weston. "But they will certainly get their money back" said a P. & A. Campbell Ltd spokesman. "The *Cardiff Queen* will not be back in service until Wednesday, so that permanent repairs can be carried out. It's fair to say that Captain Power's evasive action was quite effective". An eye-witness, Richard Harvey, a senior apprentice Cardiff pilot aboard the cutter *Lady Merret*, told me "The steamer keeled over a bit. It would certainly have been a tragedy if the skipper had not noticed the barge". The *Wheeldale H* is on charter to Shell-Mex and BP Ltd Llandarcy, and was believed to be at anchor in Barry Roads last night.'

As the 1965 season drew to a close, however, an even more significant event was about to take place. At short notice, at least as far as enthusiasts were concerned, it transpired that the Red Funnel concern at Southampton had agreed terms with P. & A. Campbell Ltd for the purchase of their 1939-vintage diesel-powered car-ferry *Vecta*. If one sets aside the limited Bristol Channel 'shoulder-season' role of the former LNWSSCo. vessel *St. Trillo*, then it was *Vecta* that was the ship which truly would become – for the White Funnel Fleet – their first motor-vessel in the Bristol Channel, and which constitutes the subject of the next phase of P. & A. Campbell Ltd history.

Before this major turning-point of further fleet-expansion is addressed we again move away from events in the Bristol Channel, as it was in 1965 that the foundations of a significant but perhaps less visible business development were laid, in the south-east of England. This was where the company adroitly sought to ensure that more diverse sources of income would support core operations through difficult times. Fundamental to this expansion was Peter Southcombe, who had now been with the company for a couple of years but was poised to spend rather more time away from the Bristol Channel to develop new business opportunities beyond the continuation of the hovercraft activities in which he had already been immersed, and which were to become rather more important as the 1960s progressed. Peter came from Ilfracombe and as a young boy growing up in the 1930s was often to be found down at the harbour watching the movements of the White Funnel Fleet. He was well acquainted with the Harbour Master and with Fred Birmingham (Senior, decd. 1942), the P. & A. Campbell Ltd Ilfracombe Agent who resided in the Quay side office from where he superintended local affairs.

The Southcombe family had a substantial bakery and restaurant business of long standing in north Devon. After being called up to naval service between late-1945 to 1948, Peter subsequently worked for the family business until 1954 and spent the next ten years working first as a Sales Representative and then in management. In 1963 he felt the urge to approach Clifton Smith-Cox directly to offer his services to take up a new commercial role which he strongly felt was then needed in P. & A. Campbell Ltd, and was initially based at Birnbeck Pier at Weston-super-Mare. In 1964 Peter transferred to George Nott Industries (later European Car Ferries) and Townsend Car Ferries before a spell back with P. & A. Campbell Ltd in 1977-1982 before finally returning to Townsend Holidays before retiring in 1987. As we shall see, he played a very significant part in the overall management of the P. & A. Campbell Ltd business throughout the 1960s and 70s, in one way or another, and we move away now from the Bristol Channel to the South Coast to examine how this developed.

Abroad

Cross-Channel Coach Excursions

By 1964 P. & A. Campbell Ltd had (for five years) been a wholly-owned subsidiary of George Nott Industries, who themselves had gained a controlling interest in Townsend Bros. Ferries Ltd after 1957. It was not surprising, therefore, that an opening was spotted at Dover to use their past experience of cross-channel excursion operations to good advantage, in order to develop additional business activities which would exploit the extensive passenger capacity offered on the new Free Enterprise class of roll-on, roll-off car-ferries being introduced by the parent company.

The original Free Enterprise car-ferry, later renamed *Free Enterprise I*, had made her maiden voyage between Dover and Calais in 1962, and *Free Enterprise II* followed her into service around three years later in May 1965. Roland Wickenden, then the Managing Director of Townsends, in discussion in late 1964 with his friend and business colleague Clifton Smith-Cox saw the potential for exploiting the fact that the new ship would often have surplus passenger capacity even when the car-decks were well-occupied.

This characteristic of the new vessel would enable its operators to tap the spending-power of day-trippers, who could be brought aboard by a coach of up to forty-one passengers capacity, which was then the maximum permissible size. Taking the space on the car deck that three or four private cars might occupy containing perhaps an average of three passengers each, the commercial advantage was thus self-evident. Dover Harbour Board insisted that all passengers passing through Eastern Docks were aboard vehicles: this literally meant that vehicles had to be used to drive foot-passengers on board via the car-decks. Most 'classic' foot-passengers for the Continent were channelled through Dover Western Docks at this time, many arriving by trains from London timed to connect with specific sailings. In this way, Townsends were happy to allocate a certain amount of space in the season for P. & A. Campbell Ltd coaches on board their car-ferry sailings from Dover Eastern Docks to Calais, with the coach then able to offer optional excursions in France to such destinations as Le Touquet, and returning in the evening from Calais to Dover. Fundamental in this proposition was the role of P. & A. Campbell Ltd to handle the additional business that was to be developed, enabling the subsidiary company to boost its own income over and above that which was being earned by conventional means in the Bristol Channel and on the north Wales coast. As an aside it is worth noting that at this point, whilst both P. & A. Campbell Ltd and Townsend Bros. Ferries were both subsidiaries of Notts, the former was the larger of the two in terms of fleet-size, if not earnings. At this time, before a town office in Dover had been opened, Townsends had very few shore staff. These consisted of traffic manager J. Briggs, his secretary, and a couple of counter staff and a handful of ticket collectors and drivers.

Some initial marketing activity in late-1964 under the Townsend Bros. Ferries banner to develop group travel had been aimed at schools and other groups, the intention being that administrative capacity within the P. & A. Campbell Ltd office facility at the Old Pier at Weston-super-Mare could be used to coordinate bookings in response to the mailshots circulated in the south-east: in practice this meant that the then recently-appointed Peter Southcombe would manage the activity.

The offer to schools essentially involved undertaking to coordinate all the necessary group travel arrangements, without any necessity for individual passports to be furnished, and in 1965 special Group Passports were organised for the first school-parties. The first party travelled under this arrangement in the early summer of 1965, before *Free Enterprise II* entered service and before much thought had been given to variations on the 'No-Passport' theme. Cross-Channel travel by P. & A. Campbell Ltd was still remembered from the time when the company had won special permission to operate the paddle-steamer *Glen Gower* direct from the three Sussex piers at Brighton, Eastbourne and Hastings to France a decade earlier.

Education with Pleasure

Dear Sir or Madam,

During the spring of 1965 we shall be offering a new type of educational day excursion for schoolchildren of all ages. Within the reach of almost every pocket, these excursions by a combination of coach and steamer will have the advantage of the coaches used to travel from your school to Dover being embarked aboard the ferry and thus made available for a coach excursion in Northern France.

The excursions will enable many children to go "abroad" for the first time; to learn a little of Northern France, the culture and customs of the people, and on the way to see the cross channel services in operation and the ease with which foreign travel is possible. Passage through customs at Dover will be experienced, and possibly the thrill of changing English "pocket money" into French Francs and spending these. To say nothing of the opportunity of practising their French on the local population!

An outing to Calais and beyond needs little special arrangement. Easily obtainable group passports are available for school parties, and this Company will be pleased to make all the necessary arrangements for travel (and catering if desired). The return cross-channel fare for children in school parties is 25/- each, to which must be added the cost for coach travel in England and France. As an example, a complete journey from Mid-Kent to St. Omer would cost about 40/- per head, or slightly less if the children are under 12 years old and choose to sit three to every two adult seats in the coaches. School staff are allowed free travel at a ratio of 1: 20 pupils.

Lastly, about the ship and safety at sea. The cross channel ships are spacious and comfortable, with accommodation for over 800 passengers as well as their cars. Special watch will be kept by the crews throughout the 90 minute sea journey when school parties are being carried. "Rough" crossings are unusual during May, June and July, and there is little risk of travel sickness, particularly bearing in mind the convenient "breaks" in the journey at Dover and Calais.

Why not complete and return the attached coupon? We will be pleased to ask one of our representatives to call and explain the details, and assist with the choice of a tour. Those listed are chosen for their particular merits, but variations can easily be made.

Yours faithfully,

TOWNSEND BROS. FERRIES LTD.

- -

CUT ALONG THE DOTTED LINE

To TOWNSEND BROS. FERRIES LTD.,
    Advance & Party Booking Office,
    The Old Pier,
    Weston-super-Mare,
    Somerset.

From (name of school).................................
(address, etc.).................................

Name of member of staff concerned

Telephone No.

Dear Sirs,

We are interested in the possibility of making a day excursion to Northern France and would like your representative to make an appointment to call.

Early promotional material for the cross-channel coach excursion business which was developed by P. & A. Campbell Ltd in conjunction with Townsend ferries. **Peter Southcombe collection**

P. & A. Campbell Ltd coach excursions, 1965

The next phase of P. & A. Campbell Ltd marketing activity in the company's own name was prompted by the thought that the old connections that the firm used to have with south coast holiday resorts might again be used to generate coach business from those places. A certain amount of subtle political pressure, mainly applied by Clifton Smith-Cox, was needed to persuade the Home Office to alter restrictions and allow P. & A. Campbell Ltd to offer 'No-Passport' excursions via Dover rather than from the previously-nominated resorts of Brighton, Eastbourne and Hastings. The Home Office eventually granted permission for 'No-Passport' day trips from Dover in 1965, provided that certain conditions were met. These were that full supervision was to be exercised by the tour-organisers, uniformed officials would be provided, and the administration and issue of the necessary paperwork and new-style Identity Cards would be tightly controlled. Possibly most importantly of all, no duty-free allowances whatsoever were to be permitted, and every passenger was interviewed by Customs and Immigration Officers on both the outward and return journeys. A particular condition was implicit in this wording, which read as follows: '... to *P. & A. Campbell Ltd in association with Townsend Car Ferries* ...', and which gave a degree of satisfaction to those that appreciated its subtle placing of the subsidiary company ahead of the parent body.

The initial coach excursions offered in 1965 were from Brighton, Eastbourne and Hastings, to the extent of one, two and three coaches per week respectively: the numbers were soon greatly increased to the limit of the shipping space available. These were the old resorts where white-funnelled paddle-steamers were still fondly remembered from a decade earlier and a small office was quickly opened under the P. & A. Campbell Ltd name in Eastbourne, with agencies at Brighton and at Hastings Pier, although formal administration was still exercised from Weston-super-Mare and Cardiff. Southdown coaches were utilised initially. Peter Southcombe successfully recruited Mr & Mrs Tanner at Eastbourne, who had worked for P. & A. Campbell Ltd in 1956 and previously, when *Glen Gower* had last offered sailings from that pier. The Brighton agency was staffed by Norman Watson, who transferred there from Weston.

After the success of the 1965 season it was suggested that demand – for cruises from the Sussex piers, without the complication of coaches – might have warranted the operation of a small motor-vessel, based on Newhaven. Peter Southcombe recalled that *Thornwick*, a Bridlington-based vessel of 300-passenger capacity not greatly dissimilar in style to *Crested Eagle*, was offered to P. & A. Campbell Ltd at a good price. Had she been purchased she would have been renamed as *Glen Thorne* – a good name for those intimate with the Bristol Channel, certainly – but Roland Wickenden vetoed the suggestion, making it clear that the role of P. & A. Campbell Ltd at that time was one which was subservient to the prosperity of Townsend Ferries. Nonetheless this idea of frustrated demand continued to exercise the minds of Messrs. Smith-Cox and Southcombe, and a few years later an additional vessel was taken on in the south-east in the belief that such a market did indeed exist.

The healthy quantity of day-trip traffic to Calais generated in 1965 led to some discussion between Messrs Wickenden and Smith-Cox of sending *Bristol Queen* round to operate as a sort of relief vessel for foot passengers, where she might have run between the Admiralty Pier at Dover and Calais or Boulogne during the week, and then offered excursions from Eastbourne and Hastings (the landing-stage at Brighton was by this time in very poor condition) at weekends. The idea was not pursued, as the Board of Trade were not prepared to grant the necessary Cl.II(a) certificate without extensive modifications to the vessel. This may have been a relief to Clifton Smith-Cox in terms of ensuring that the *Bristol Queen* remained longer in her home waters,

A Townsend Car Ferries car-sticker promoting the Free Enterprise ships on which P. & A. Campbell Ltd managed the passenger excursion activities. Peter Southcombe collection

and Canterbury using East Kent coaches and, using Maidstone & District coaches, from the Medway towns of Gravesend, Sheerness, Sittingbourne, Maidstone and mid-Kent. To serve the towns of Rye, New Romney, Hythe and the holiday-camps at Camber, Littlestone and elsewhere along the south Kent coast, East Kent coaches were hired. In addition P. & A. Campbell Ltd did good business with private coach companies carrying 'unadvertised' groups, schools and works outings. Later, some of the London coach companies such as Timpson's, Grey-Green and Surrey Motors joined in. Feeding the Townsend ferries was becoming an extensive and complicated operation carrying very large numbers of passengers.

Yet further expansion took place in 1967, soon after the demise of the Thames Eagle Steamers serving the Thanet resorts, as Peter Southcombe smartly stepped in on behalf of P. & A. Campbell Ltd to obtain the goodwill of that company, its advertising sites, and the staff and office premises in Margate, Ramsgate and Deal. More coach feeders from further afield allowed the P. & A. Campbell Ltd – generated excursion revenue to continue to grow in 1967, and in addition the former Eagle Steamers office at Southend was reopened which boosted traffic from Essex on Eastern National coaches via the Dartford Tunnel for the cross-channel excursions. Around this time thoughts turned to possibly operating one of the withdrawn GSN steamers on P. & A. Campbell Ltd account, and this is dealt with in the 1969 *Queen of the Isles* section (qv).

The climate of a heavily regulated bus & coach industry at this time was material to the way in which the P. & A. Campbell Ltd business operated, as it restricted the choice of the coach operators it was able to use to those companies which had the appropriate licences from the Traffic Commissioners for the routes involved. This meant, for example, that they had to use Southdown coaches from Brighton and Eastbourne on South Coast Express licences. In addition to this, an element of competition began to appear in the day-excursion market using capacity on the Dover and Folkestone BR car-ferries in conjunction with the nationalised bus companies, the latter being the self-same organisations that P. & A. Campbell Ltd were obliged to hire their coaches from. It was galling to the P. & A. Campbell Ltd management team on occasions to find that the ideas they had for new cross-channel excursion variants were later copied by the self-same nationalised institutions that they had just asked to quote for such new coach services. As time went by, the P. & A. Campbell Ltd initial advantage of having sole permission to use ID cards was lost, as British Railways also obtained permission to do so, firstly at Folkestone and shortly afterwards at Dover.

Traffic Manager Peter Southcombe who was in charge of the South Coast affairs of the company in the 1960s. Margate, 1966.

Peter Southcombe collection

and her operation could very well have been perceived as inflammatory at Dover given the industrial relations situation in 1966, during and after the National Seamans strike, and discrepancies between the level of wages paid to seagoing staff of Townsends and P. & A. Campbell Ltd. More to the point, the image of the paddle-steamer would almost certainly have gone down badly with passengers, particularly if the same fares were charged on both types of vessel.

Growth in 1966 & 1967

Building on the encouraging results of the 1965 season, the 1966 excursion programme was expanded in frequency and overall capacity. More offices were opened by P. & A. Campbell Ltd in Hastings and Brighton. The third Free Enterprise-class ship came into service and the new car-ferry link between Dover and Zeebrugge was opened, although it was not until 1967 that the cross-channel coach excursions started to use the Belgian route. However the season was disrupted to some extent by the National Seaman's strike, which was eventually 'broken' by Townsends although P. & A. Campbell Ltd crews in the Bristol Channel never took part.

With hindsight the strike could also be seen as the last straw for the Continental excursion sailings still offered in 1966 by the Eagle Steamers from the Thames coast and Thanet ports to Calais and Boulogne. P. & A. Campbell Ltd did operate just one coach each week from Thanet, restricting this service in order not to damage Eagle Steamers traffic from those three established traffic sources. There was also a weekly service from Herne Bay, Whitstable, Reculver

Later years

Business had continued to develop satisfactorily in 1968 and 1969. A feature of the P. & A. Campbell Ltd operation apt to be overlooked was the extent to which they also operated as agents for the cross-channel excursion business then developing in the name of other coach companies, who were content to let P. & A. Campbell Ltd see to the details of arranging advertising (to be sure of compliance with Home Office requirements), provision of couriers, franking of ID cards, and so on. P. & A. Campbell Ltd gained their revenue from the sale of ferry-tickets, providing some of their allocation of space on board the ferries made available by Townsends. In addition to this business in the south-east of England, a 'spin-off' to the conventional Bristol Channel business of the time was that such coach operators were also encouraged to organise excursions in connection with sailings from Weston-super-Mare and other piers: bus companies that developed this were, for example, Stratford Blue, Midland Red and Black & White Motorways from the a number of midlands originating points.

The range of Continental destinations grew to include Dunkirk, Ostend, Bruges, Zeebrugge, Lille, Paris, Brussels and Amsterdam, in contrast to the simple beginnings of Calais and Le Touquet. The duration of some of the trips increased to involve two nights away, being the first 'Extended Day-Excursions' which required two coach drivers. Passengers benefited from being away for over 24 hours by becoming entitled to full duty-free allowances. P. & A. Campbell Ltd managed another first in 1967 through the promotion of highly

P. & A. CAMPBELL LTD.   1970

NO PASSPORT DAY TRIPS TO THE CONTINENT

To
CALAIS - BOULOGNE - ZEEBRUGGE
OSTEND - BRUSSELS

From
BRIGHTON - EASTBOURNE
BEXHILL & HASTINGS

✱ Special Identity Cards will be provided for persons of British or Irish nationality or normal Passports may be used.

'No Passport' Day Trips to CALAIS & BOULOGNE

Allowing up to 5½ hours in France

This tour has been arranged to combine convenient departure and return times with the full afternoon ashore in Calais or the opportunity to enjoy an optional coach excursion to Boulogne.

Passengers travel by specially provided Southdown coach to the historic port of Dover, passing through the countryside and many places of interest on the way. On arrival at Eastern Docks the coach and passengers are embarked on one of the Townsend Thoresen "Free Enterprise" vessels, which are among the latest Cross-Channel ships in service. In these fast, modern ships the crossing to Calais takes only 90 minutes, during which passengers may enjoy the many facilities aboard, including restaurants, lounges, promenade decks and bars (at duty-free prices).

CALAIS. On arrival at Calais those passengers who have chosen to spend the day here, walk the short distance to the Town centre. Calais has a sandy beach, a new promenade and a Casino. Among the many places of interest to be seen are the Town Hall (Hotel de Ville), the Opera House and the Citadel. Parks include the Parc St. Pierre and the Jardin Richelieu. In the Town Hall Gardens will be seen the famous Rodin statue of the Six Burghers of Calais.

BOULOGNE. Those taking the excursion to Boulogne join their coach on board the ship and are driven ashore at Calais. The coach then proceeds to Boulogne by route N40 through Wissant and Audinghen where a stop is made for refreshments and to view the magnificent Church built with funds partly supplied by the R.A.F. Association. The journey then continues to Boulogne which is the largest fishing port in France. Boulogne is also a popular holiday resort, having a fine sandy beach and entertainments to attract the tourists. To the north of the modern shopping centre is the old walled city dating from the Middle Ages. Here may be seen the Ramparts, the Castle, the Belfry and the four old gateways, all dominated by the Cathedral of Notre Dame and surrounded by massive walls. Ample time is allowed for sightseeing at Boulogne.

Boulogne

The return journey is by a different route, passing through the market town of Marquise before reaching Calais in time to embark for the short sea crossing to Dover.

THE COACHES. For the excursions from the departure points listed in this folder, passengers normally travel upon coaches supplied by Southdown Motor Services Ltd. "Southdown" are renowned for the comfort and reliability of their coaches and the high standard of skill and courtesy shown by their drivers, which combine to ensure a relaxing and enjoyable road journey.

On certain Tuesdays and Thursdays the coaches from Bexhill and Hastings for the excursions to Calais and Boulogne are provided by the Maidstone & District Motor Services Ltd., being of a similarly high standard.

The Town Hall, Calais

These trips are organised and operated by P. & A. Campbell Ltd. (passenger ship operators) in conjunction with Townsend Thoresen Car Ferries Ltd.; Southdown Motor Services Ltd., and Maidstone & District Motor Services Ltd.

Marketing of the cross-channel coach excursions in the 1960s was in the hands of P. & A. Campbell Ltd, and passenger numbers grew each season. A range of pamphlets in the distinctive Campbell blue colour conveyed this bold image of the modern Free Enterprise class of Townsend car-ferries at Dover. Leaflets for Southampton excursions similarly portrayed the image of the latest Thoresen Viking-class ships. Numerous different excursions were offered in this particular pamphlet in 1970, with pick-ups at the various Sussex piers, including day-trips to Zeebrugge and Calais, with optional coaches to Boulogne along the coast using Southdown and Maidstone & District vehicles. Other excursions on offer included extended day-trips to Brussels via Zeebrugge, and a long day-trip to Ostend involving the Belgian RTM ferries outwards in the morning from Dover, returning in the evening via the Townsend Zeebrugge ferry. The P. & A. Campbell Ltd cross-channel coach excursions utilised space on the parent company ferries just on weekdays and not at weekends, and in 1970 emphasis was given to the then new **Free Enterprise V**. *The opportunity was also taken to advertise the 'extensive network' of Bristol Channel sailings in these pamphlets.*   Peter Southcombe collection

Cruise across the Channel in a modern Townsend Thoresen ship. Here you can enjoy the holiday atmosphere in the open plan lounges (with their duty-free bars, shops and snack bars); the restful quiet of the upper deck saloons; or the refreshing sea air on the promenade decks. A delicious meal at a reasonable price can be enjoyed in the pleasant surroundings of the ship's restaurant. In fact, there is every facility aboard to ensure a pleasant and comfortable journey across the Channel.

IMPORTANT NOTES

Customs, Currency and Immigration Information

1 All passengers other than children under 16 must be in possession of a valid Passport or supply ONE PASSPORT SIZE PHOTOGRAPH to be attached to a special Identity Card, when booking.

2 ONLY British Subjects or Citizens of the Irish Republic will be carried without passports.

3 **Currency — the maximum amount of sterling currency permitted to be taken out of the United Kingdom is £25. Amounts in excess of £25 will be seized by the Customs officer before embarkation and may not be returned.**

4 Currency exchange offices are installed aboard the ships where passengers will be able to obtain up to £25 worth of French or Belgian francs for sterling. The francs must be paid for from the sterling allowed to be brought on board. Travellers cheques cashable outside the sterling area (e.g. marked as available anywhere in the world) can be exchanged into francs for any amount. On the return journey the currency exchange officer can buy back francs from passengers.

5 There is no limit on the amount of foreign or sterling currency which may be brought into the United Kingdom.

6 Animals are not allowed on board. Passengers may not bring live birds or live plants into the United Kingdom.

7 Baggage. Passengers will be allowed only small articles (such as an attache case) as are appropriate for a day excursion.

8 Wine, Spirits, Tobacco and Cigarettes are available for consumption on board at duty free prices. Passengers who have travelled on excursions of over 24 hours duration are granted the concessions listed overleaf upon their return. NO DUTY OR TAX FREE CONCESSIONS will be allowed by H.M. Customs to day excursion passengers who have been away from the United Kingdom for less than 24 hours.

General Information

9 Tickets are available for travel only on the date stamped thereon, and include all Port charges.

Conditions of Carriage

10 All tickets are issued and passengers carried subject to the conditions of carriage of the respective companies under whose supervision or on whose coaches or ships the excursions are carried out, as exhibited at booking offices and on board the vessels.

11 The sailings are subject to weather and circumstances, and if for any reason any excursion is cancelled, any sums paid in respect thereof will be refunded in full.

TICKETS AND INFORMATION FOR THE EXCURSIONS MAY BE OBTAINED FROM THE FOLLOWING OFFICES. PASSENGERS ARE ADVISED TO BOOK EARLY TO AVOID DISAPPOINTMENT.

Book at P. & A. CAMPBELL LTD.

THE PIER HASTINGS (Tel. 3247)

THE PIER EASTBOURNE (Tel. 32578)

THE PALACE PIER BRIGHTON (Tel. 66015)

or at

... Service Travel Bureau, 23 Devonshire Road, Bexhill, or ... Motor Services Ltd., or Maidstone & District ... from which the excursions are operated.

'No Passport' Extended Excursions to BRUSSELS

THE BRUSSELS TOUR

Allowing up to 26 HOURS in Belgium

This excursion includes sightseeing tours of Bruges (or Ghent), Tervuren, the Forest of Soignes, Waterloo and of the Belgian Capital. It provides unequalled value and variety plus the benefit of duty-free concessions on return.

The journey commences by special luxury coach to Dover, where it carries the passengers aboard the ship. It is here that the courier joins the party to provide a detailed commentary and advice to passengers during the journey.

THE OUTWARD VOYAGE. The voyage is normally made by the "Free Enterprise IV" or the "Free Enterprise V", the latest and largest vessels of the Townsend Thoresen fleet. These modern ships have spacious promenade decks, attractive bars, shops and restaurants, which remain open throughout the voyage. Snacks and meals may be obtained at any time. There is comfortable seating accommodation in the saloons of the vessels and a limited number of couchettes or reclining seats are sometimes available. In these stabilised ships the voyage passes quickly and it is soon time to rejoin the coach for the journey in Belgium.

BRUGES (OR GHENT). After landing at Zeebrugge the journey commences to Brussels. In about 30 minutes the city of Bruges (known as The Venice of the North), is reached. Bruges is perhaps the best preserved medieval city in Europe and the coach is specially routed to pass the main places of interest. During the late summer, when Bruges would be reached before daylight and cannot be seen properly, a tour of Ghent is substituted. Ghent, "The City of Flowers", with its 200 bridges and 80 islands, is the home of the Counts of Flanders and is rich in history and architectural splendour.

From Bruges or Ghent the journey is via the Motorway to Brussels and the Grand Hotel Scheers, centrally situated on the Boulevard Adolphe Max. Continental breakfast may be obtained and all the toilet and other facilities of this Hotel are available.

THE TOUR TO WATERLOO. Following breakfast and perhaps a quick look around the nearby shops, passengers may rejoin the coach for the optional tour to Waterloo. The coach passes through the wide and pleasant boulevards leading from Brussels towards Tervuren where a stop is made to view the splendid French Gardens and the Royal Museum of Central Africa. The route is then through the Forest of Soignes, one of the largest forests in Europe, to Waterloo, the scene of the famous Battle where the British and Allied Forces defeated Napoleon's French Army on June 18th, 1815. After plenty of time for sightseeing, the coach returns to Brussels via the Cinquantenaire Archway and the Headquarters of the European Common Market. It arrives in time for lunch at the Hotel where a specially prepared and reasonably priced menu is available.

Brussels — The Atomium

BRUSSELS. During the afternoon passengers may choose to visit some of the many places of interest in the city. Street maps, providing details of these and how to reach them are supplied to passengers and the couriers will be pleased to advise. From the Hotel it is only a short walk to the main shopping streets.

THE EVENING TOUR OF BRUSSELS. This tour is planned to enable passengers to see most of the famous buildings and landmarks of Brussels during the short visit. These include the Botanical Gardens; the Congress Column, with its eternal flame in memory of the Unknown Soldier; the Palais de la Nation (Houses of Parliament); the Park of Brussels and the Royal Park Theatre; the King's Palace; the 15th century Ravenstein Mansion; the Albertine; St. Michael's Cathedral; the Petit Sablon Gardens; the Palais de Justice and, of course, the famous Manneken Pis statue. The highlights of the evening tour are the visits to the Atomium, which passengers may ascend in the high-speed lift to see a remarkable view of the whole city of Brussels, and the enjoyable stop made in the magnificent Grande Place, described by Victor Hugo as "The most beautiful Square in the world".

After the evening tour there is time to visit some of the many cafes or night-clubs for which Brussels is so famous. These are within easy reach of the departure point at the Grand Hotel Scheers.

THE RETURN JOURNEY. Passengers may board the coach from midnight to await departure for the return journey and the sailing from Zeebrugge. The dining saloons, bars and shops aboard the "Free Enterprise" ship remain open throughout the voyage and it is during the return journey that passengers may wish to make purchases of duty-free goods. After a sleep and a good English breakfast if desired, Dover is soon in sight and passengers rejoin their coach as the ship enters the harbour. The brief Customs formalities are soon over and the coach commences the final stage of the return journey.

Your British drivers and courier are there to guide and help you enjoy yourself. If you are in doubt about anything, ask them.

THE BELGIAN BEER FESTIVAL AT WEIZE

The Belgian Beer Festival is held annually at Weize, near Brussels. Over 12,000 people can be seated in halls where Weize Pils beer is served. There are genuine Bavarian bands and entertainment of all descriptions for young and old. Traditional style cooking of chickens and whole calves over wood fires is a feature of the Festival.

Passengers wishing to visit the Beer Festival have the choice of the following three special excursions:-

(1) Combined Brussels tour and Beer Festival excursion.
(2) Beer Festival excursion including the afternoon in Brussels.
(3) Direct excursion to the Weize Beer Festival.

The dates of these special departures are shown at the foot of the Brussels Time-table in the adjoining column.

Ask for the special leaflet and book early to avoid disappointment.

TIME-TABLE

Brussels

FROM MAY 29 UNTIL OCTOBER 23, 1970

Every Friday from May 29 until July 10 and on Sept. 11, 18, Oct. 16 & 23.
Every Wednesday from June 10 until Oct. 7.
Every Tuesday from July 14 until Sept. 1.

Depart	From	Due Back*
6.45 p.m.	**BRIGHTON** (Manchester St. Coach Stn.)	2.00 p.m.
7.35 p.m.	**EASTBOURNE** (Pier entrance)	1.10 p.m.
8.00 p.m.	**BEXHILL** (Marina)	12.50 p.m.
8.15 p.m.	**HASTINGS** (Pier entrance)	12.30 p.m.

***NOTE:** Tuesday departures return on Thursdays at the times shown. Wednesday departures return on Fridays at the times shown. Friday departures return on Sundays at the times shown.

RETURN FARES

(Including the excursions in Belgium)

Adults **130/-** Children (age 3 and under 14) **95/-**

The above fares may be subject to amendment.

NOTE: Special departures visiting the Belgian Beer Festival at Weize will operate on the following dates:- Tuesdays, September 29 and October 6; Saturdays, September 26, October 3 and 10.

See adjoining column and for full details ask for special leaflet.

DUTY FREE ALLOWANCES

(Available to Extended Excursion passengers)

It is normally permissible for persons who have been absent from the U.K. for 24 hours or more to import (for self use only) the following items free of duty and purchase tax.

One bottle of spirits (¼th of a gallon)
One bottle of wine (¼th of a gallon)
250 grams net tobacco weight i.e. 260 King size tipped cigarettes.

NOTE. The above concessions are not granted to any person under the age of 17 years

For self use or personal gifts:
Perfume ¼ pint
Toilet water ¼ pint (or ½ pint if you do not bring any perfume)
Cigarette lighter—1
Souvenirs or other articles (not mentioned above) £5 worth.

THESE ALLOWANCES ARE ONLY AVAILABLE TO PASSENGERS WHO ARE AWAY FROM THE UNITED KINGDOM FOR 24 HOURS OR LONGER.

SPECIAL NOTES

Gentlemen. Take your electric razor but note that the power supply in Brussels is 110 volts and a special adaptor is required. This may be bought aboard the ship. On the ship, 110 volts or 230 volts supply is available. Passengers should take toilet soap with them as this is not normally supplied in Belgian bathrooms.

You need not speak French or Flemish to enjoy yourself — a great many Belgians speak English, particularly in the shops, cafes etc.

Keep in mind that a Belgian franc is worth about 2d.

Ticket Offices in the south
Upper, left: *Margate (with model of former Royal Sovereign visible), 1967.*
Upper, centre: *Deal. This former Eagle Steamers building was dismantled after each season*
Upper, right: *Ramsgate*
Lower, left: *Ramsgate (this view shows a model of the former Eagle Steamers Queen of the Channel)*
Lower, centre: *Eastbourne former P. & A. Campbell Ltd office premises, latterly repainted to promote Townsend-Thoresen, mid-1970s.*
all Peter Southcombe collection

successful experimental excursions to the Weize Beer Festival (between Brussels and Ghent), the first time such trips were made available to the public. Taken together this growing range of excursions required a considerable degree of organisation in order to ensure everything ran smoothly without causing any delays to car-ferry schedules, and Peter Southcombe produced comprehensive instruction manuals for the couriers which detailed all that needed to be done to guarantee this, whilst ensuring that passengers were fully informed of what they were able to do and were given commentaries on the sights and points of interest whilst on foreign soil.

In 1965 P. & A. CAMPBELL LTD. operated their first "NO-PASSPORT" DAY TRIPS TO FRANCE in association with Townsend Car Ferries. The immediate popularity and continued success of these low budget mini tours made it essential to increase the range of excursions every year to meet public demand.

In this 1971 brochure there is an unrivalled selection of "No-passport" tours of France, Belgium, and Holland, designed to suit most individual requirements. If time or money is limited there are excursions of different durations and at various prices from which to choose. If you are travelling abroad for the first time you will be well looked after by the British coach driver or courier who travels with you on the Continental coach tours. P. & A. Campbell are confident that when you have read the contents of this brochure you will wish to join the many thousands of satisfied clients who have already travelled on these excursions. To book, or for any further information, please contact your nearest booking office (see back page) or P. & A. Campbell Ltd., The Pier, Hastings, Sussex. Telephone Hastings 3247.

NO PASSPORTS ARE REQUIRED BY PERSONS OF BRITISH OR IRISH NATIONALITY FOR ANY OF THE TOURS SHOWN IN THIS BROCHURE.

GROUP BOOKINGS FOR CONTINENTAL EXCURSIONS

All the "no-passport" tours shown in this booklet are ideally suited for private outings. Firms, clubs, schools, and other groups, are invited to apply for details of the special facilities and charges which are available. Full information is obtainable from P. & A. CAMPBELL LTD., THE PIER, HASTINGS, SUSSEX. Tel. Hastings 3247 or THE PIER, MARGATE, KENT. Tel. Thanet 21857.

THE COACH JOURNEY

Passengers travel by special coaches, supplied by leading operators, for both the English and Continental sections of the journeys. As the bookings per excursion are limited to the number of seats per coach, PASSENGERS SHOULD BOOK EARLY TO AVOID DISAPPOINTMENT.

CONTINENTAL SERVICES

P. & A. Campbell Ltd. operate the following comprehensive selection of "No-passport" day trips and extended day excursions to the Continent.

via Dover

CALAIS, BOULOGNE, DUNKIRK, LE TOUQUET, OSTEND, ZEEBRUGGE, BRUSSELS, AMSTERDAM, PARIS

via Southampton

CHERBOURG, BAYEUX, ARROMANCHES, and THE NORMANDY BEACHES, LE MONT ST. MICHEL, ST. MALO, DINARD, PARIS.

Booking facilities are available in the following areas from which there are direct departures of P. & A. Campbell Continental excursions.

BASILDON, BEXHILL, BIRMINGHAM, BOGNOR, BOURNEMOUTH, BRENTWOOD, BRIGHTON, BRISTOL, CHELMSFORD, CHELTENHAM, COLCHESTER, DEAL, DOVER, EASTBOURNE, FOLKESTONE, GLOUCESTER, GRAYS, HASTINGS, IPSWICH, ISLE OF WIGHT, LONDON, MAIDSTONE & MID-KENT AREAS, MARGATE, OXFORD, PORTSMOUTH, RAMSGATE, RYE, SOUTHAMPTON, SOUTHEND, SOUTH KENT RESORTS, SOUTH WALES, WOLVERHAMPTON and other areas.

For full details of the excursions which operate from your area please contact your nearest booking offices or P. & A. CAMPBELL LTD., THE PIER, HASTINGS, SUSSEX. Tel. Hastings 3247 or THE PIER, MARGATE, KENT. Tel. Thanet 21857.

THE BRISTOL CHANNEL SERVICES

In addition to Continental excursions, P. & A. Campbell Ltd. also operate an extensive service of passenger ship sailings between the ports and resorts of the Bristol Channel and to Lundy Island. For full information please apply to:- P. & A. CAMPBELL LTD., 4 DOCK CHAMBERS, BUTE STREET, CARDIFF. Tel. Cardiff 20255.

2

P. & A. CAMPBELL COURIERS

On all P. & A. Campbell extended day excursions and on certain day trips a courier travels with the passengers to provide advice and a detailed commentary throughout the journey on the Continent.

THE SHIPS

The Channel crossing forms an enjoyable part of the journey. The fast, modern Townsend-Thoresen "Free-Enterprise" ships are equipped with comfortable lounges, duty-free bars and shops, snack bars, and excellent restaurants where first class meals are available at reasonable prices. Open air relaxation can be enjoyed on the promenade decks and, on the latest ships, "Free Enterprise IV" and "Free Enterprise V", there are a number of adjustable reclining seats in the quiet upper deck lounges for those seeking a restful voyage.

The pamphlets advertising the cross-channel coach excursions grew in size each year and this 1971 example portrayed one of the uniformed couriers, who were then a particular feature of the foreign trips. Study of the small print illustrates how the joint operation between P. & A. Campbell Ltd and Townsend-Thoresen worked. Around thirty staff were employed to run the excursion business by this time. Peter Southcombe collection

A major step forward by the parent company Townsends was the take-over in 1968 of the Norwegian-owned Thoresen car-ferry business at Southampton and thus, in the 1969 season, P. & A. Campbell Ltd became involved in expanding the coach excursion trade on the Thoresen 'Viking' class ferries which ran between Southampton and Normandy, and offices selling excursion business were opened at Southsea, Bournemouth (and also, for one season only, at Bognor Regis). The Bournemouth one was shared with the local operator Bolsons. Operationally this activity was controlled from office premises in Southampton, with overall control and administration overseen by Peter Southcombe from his Hastings office. The continental destinations served included Cherbourg for day-trips and 'extended' day-excursions to the Normandy beaches and Bayeux, also to Mont. St-Michel, St. Malo and Paris. In 1969, an excursion from (for example) Brighton or Bournemouth to St. Malo with overnight crossings each way between Southampton to Cherbourg cost thirty-five shillings: by this time, duty-free concessions were permitted. The luxurious facilities of the 'Viking' ships were emphasised and the coach-routes used in Normandy took in historic towns such as Valognes and Dol, together with a two-hour stop at historic Mont St. Michel.

Just for good measure, a handful of coach excursions from south Wales to Normandy were also offered during July, August and September 1969 and were advertised on Bristol Channel handbills alongside the usual steamer excursions run by *Balmoral* and *Westward Ho*. A Wednesday afternoon coach departure from Llanelli, Swansea, Cardiff and Bristol via Southampton gave a Thursday in France with return back to south Wales by the Friday afternoon, with the two intervening nights at sea on one of the Viking class ferries. Whereas Dover was too far from the Bristol Channel for such coach excursions to be a practical proposition, Southampton offered scope which P. & A. Campbell Ltd were quick to exploit. These excursions were not dissimilar to the long-day, White Funnel Fleet South Coast paddle-steamer excursions which had been provided there (that is, from the Bristol Channel) at the turn of the century, with rail connections between Burnham on Sea and Bournemouth.

The principal restriction that had initially been placed by Townsends on the P. & A. Campbell Ltd operations was that the excursions offered were not to include any overnight accommodation for passengers, as it was felt that this might clash with and upset some of the big tour operator customers of Townsends themselves. From the perspective of the parent company it was perhaps inevitable that they should eventually wish to muscle in on the evident success of their subsidiary company, which by 1971 was bringing in sizeable revenues but very definitely through advertising channels that were unambiguously those of P. & A. Campbell Ltd, in association with Townsend-Thoresen Car Ferries, as the parent company had become renamed.

After P. & A. Campbell Ltd had built this business up, then, forces within the Townsend-Thoresen organisation were getting more concerned to take over the lucrative trade for themselves and centralise the administration at Dover. To all intents and purposes the P. & A. Campbell Ltd name was replaced by late 1971. 1972 publicity material for No-Passport Day Trips to the Continent was very clearly branded as being under the banner of Townsend-Thoresen, and made only a token reference to P. & A. Campbell Ltd as booking agents at their offices, which shortly after were wholly absorbed under the parent companys name. (The 'restriction' on overnight traffic was quietly dropped around this time). Accounts for P. & A. Campbell Ltd for this period did not distinguish between the revenues generated by the cross-channel coach excursion traffic as opposed to the traditional Bristol Channel business. With hindsight, it was a somewhat of a sorry coincidence that a major cutback in upper Bristol Channel operations was also effected at the end of 1971, with the withdrawal of *Westward Ho* (after serious mechanical problems) and the consequent withdrawal of 'ferry' services at Cardiff. Financially, the company affairs were now becoming even more challenging and the tax-losses situation would need to be addressed, and which is dealt with subsequently.

It would probably not have been deemed prudent by Clifton Smith-Cox (in seeking to keep things going in the Bristol Channel) to draw too much attention to the way in which a different source of income, from the South Coast business – which was cash-generative, and uninvolved with any capital cost encumbrances – assisted the core business. Here, sizeable assets dictated that provision for depreciation in more challenging market conditions had to be made. However, a good idea of the importance of the cross-channel coach excursion business can be inferred from these figures for 'Sales' from successive company reports of the period. The picture is slightly complicated by changes made in accountancy year-ends, but nonetheless enables a crude comparison can be made:

12 months ended 30th April 1969 £314k
(this period included revenue from **Queen of the Isles** *in north Wales,* **Westward Ho** *and* **St. Trillo** *in the Bristol Channel, and all cross-channel coach excursion income)*

12 months ended 30th April 1970 £331k
(this period included revenue from **Queen of the Isles** *in the south-east,* **St. Trillo** *in the final year in north Wales,* **Westward Ho** *and* **Balmoral** *in the Bristol Channel, and all cross-channel coach excursion income)*

11 months ended 31st March 1973 £272k
(this period included revenue from **Balmoral** *only in the Bristol Channel in 1972, and all cross-channel coach excursion income)*
*(*NB Previous year to 30th April 1972 figure was £309k)

9 months ended 31st December 1973 £128k
(this period included revenue from **Balmoral** *only in the Bristol Channel in 1973, all cross-channel coach excursion income now presented in Townsend-Thoresen accounts 'for administrative reasons')*

The last word on this significant yet hitherto little-documented phase of P. & A. Campbell Ltd history can be taken from a couple of contrasting paragraphs in successive Chairmans' Statements, contained within the published Annual Report & Accounts. The first refers to the 1970 season, and emphasises how a growing enterprise was seen to contribute to the larger empire:

(6th January 1971)
' ... I am pleased, however to report that during 1970 the business done in this area much increased and reached the highest level since we have operated these services ... We have given considerable attention to extending no-passport excursions giving rather longer on the Continent and embracing not only Brussels but also Paris, Amsterdam and the Normandy coastal areas. All these arrangements which were in operation in 1970 have shown a satisfactory result.

In 1969 we commenced to operate cross-channel services in connection with our sister company, Thoresen Car Ferries. To commence this service necessitated the opening of offices in Bournemouth and Southsea and the operation proved costly in the first year. In 1970 the receipts from this service were doubled, and as a result, whereas such was not the case in 1969, in 1970 a satisfactory profit resulted. It is fair to say that some of the work and effort by management and staff of this Company on the South Coast has played a small but nonetheless useful part in assisting our sister Companies in that area'.

The second was written some time after the administrative arrangements had been changed, the story was brief and to the point, and made it clear that the use of the P. & A. Campbell Ltd name would soon be dropped completely:

(20th May 1974)
'... The operations carried on under this Company's name on the South Coast in respect of cross-channel excursions are continuing to be as popular as ever. For administrative reasons it has been found more convenient for the results of these operations to be included in the accounts of our sister company, Townsend Car Ferries.'

More Fleet Expansion

The acquisition of *Vecta*

In the mid-1960s the letterheads used on P. & A. Campbell Ltd stationery still declared emphatically that the business of the company was that of Passenger Steamship Owners. Only steamships had been operated until 1963 when the little **St. Trillo** was purchased, if one overlooks the charter in 1957 of m.v. **Crested Eagle** from the General Steam Navigation Company on South Coast duties. As an experiment, this had hardly endeared the hitherto rather traditional company to diesel-propulsion. As **St. Trillo** was to find employment with the White Funnel Fleet predominantly by remaining on her north Wales station the acquisition, in September 1965, of the motor-vessel **Vecta** from the Southampton, Isle of Wight and South of England Royal Mail Steam Packet Co. Ltd (better known as Red Funnel steamers) was thus something of a first for Bristol Channel excursionists. Although she had been built as an Isle of Wight car-ferry her new owners simply purchased her for Bristol Channel excursion duties after her career between Southampton and Cowes had ended. Her purchase was something of an achievement for the company which had been seeking for some years to acquire lower-cost tonnage as a hedge against the days when either or both of their paddle-steamers might be coming to an end. **Vecta** was a distinctly hybrid diesel-powered ship when constructed in 1939, seven years before the paddle-steamer **Bristol Queen**. She was only the second British ship built to be equipped with revolutionary Voith-Schneider propulsion, after the Southern Railway had taken delivery of the car-ferry **Lymington** a year earlier, in 1938. Red Funnel Stuff, a contemporary Red Funnel publication, eulogised at length over the latest addition to the Red Funnel Fleet when still new:

M.V. VECTA
fitted with VOITH-SCHNEIDER PROPELLERS

A vessel capable of being driven with the same ease as a motor-car, of being steered with equal ease and at any speed when going either forward or astern, of turning in her own length at a rate hitherto thought impossible and of moving laterally without fore and aft motion, has unquestioned advantage on the Southampton-Cowes Motor Car Carrying Service.

So many people are familiar with the usual types of propulsion in steamships, namely, the screw propeller and paddle-wheels so frequently to be seen in these waters that they find it difficult to understand the action of the curiously-shaped Voith-Schneider propellers with which **Vecta** is equipped.

Perhaps the easiest way to visualise their action is to liken them to a man propelling a dinghy by himself with a single oar which he moves to & fro sideways in a notch in the stern transom. Although he is not rowing in the accepted manner, the lateral movement of the blade of the oar sets up a thrust which has the effect of moving the dinghy forward. When he wishes to steer, he simply moves his blade more to one side of the centre line of the boat and so the propelling movement acts as a rudder ... the Voith-Schneider method of propulsion is something entirely new in British shipping - at present there are only two vessels so equipped in service in this country – the **Vecta** being the largest mercantile ship fitted with these propellers in the world.

This promotional booklet also pointed out that **Vecta** had to be '... *a winter and a summer boat and sufficient covered accommodation for passengers was of vital importance* ...'. Covered accommodation was

An artists' impression of the new Isle of Wight Red Funnel motor-vessel **Vecta** *which was reproduced in the handbook* **Red Funnel Stuff** *in 1938.*
Author's collection

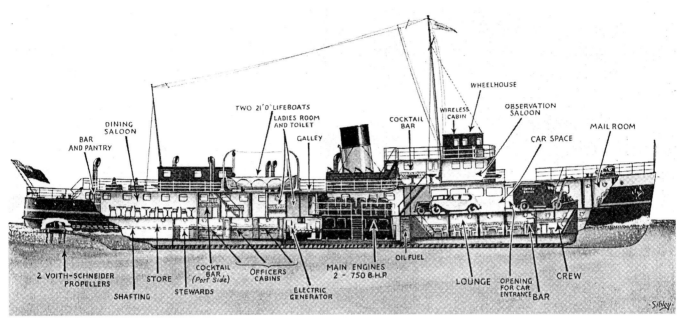

A cutaway artists' impression of Vecta *(reproduced in the handbook* Red Funnel Stuff *in 1938).*   Author's collection

provided for her full complement of motor-cars, on a deck free from obstruction, whilst a proper dining saloon was provided aft.

By the time P. & A. Campbell Ltd eventually came to acquire their first motor-vessel intended solely for the Bristol Channel, she was perhaps less manoeuvreable than when new as she was no longer fitted with the revolutionary Voith-Schneider propulsion system. Difficulty had been experienced by her owners during the Second World War in the supply of spare parts from Germany with which to effect proper maintenance. In order to address fundamental reliability problems

she underwent a major rebuild in order to replace the Voith-Schneider system with the alternative of a diesel-electric transmission and normal propeller and rudder. In *Red Funnel And Before* by Ron Adams that author succinctly described *Vecta*, in her original condition, as being '... *a navigator's dream and an engineer's nightmare* ...'. *Vecta* re-entered service in February 1946, albeit still rather a hybrid vessel with her new generators, and an article in *The Shipbuilder* magazine on 28th February of that year carried a detailed technical description of the modifications. These had been extensive:

Vecta *on her final day in service as a Red Funnel ship, at the Royal Pier at Southampton on 18th September 1965.*   Norman Bird

Vecta, off Weston-super-Mare, after she had entered P. & A. Campbell Ltd service, but still wearing her Red Funnel colours: 4th October 1965.

Norman Bird

'…to accommodate the new propellers and tail-shafts it was necessary to carry out comprehensive modifications to the after end of the hull, particularly the underwater sections. The modifications comprised the removal of the Voith-Schneider mechanism, and the casings containing it, as well as the ship's bottom in it's vicinity ... the original English Electric 6LM type diesel engines are retained except that the engine governor control gear is now adapted to give a choice of two alternative engine speeds – 375 rpm or 325 rpm. The latter speed is provided for use on day-cruises and under other similar conditions, when the power requirements of the vessel are less than on her normal fast ferry services between the mainland and the Isle of Wight…'.

Concerning speed, the article noted that whereas **Vecta** had originally achieved 15.45 knots as built, she subsequently only achieved 14.92 knots as a screw-propelled vessel, largely attributable to her increase in weight. All in all, she presented a stark contrast to the paddle-steamers **Bristol Queen** and **Cardiff Queen** when she appeared alongside them after her already lengthy Red Funnel career, which had ended on 18th September 1965. Her arrival in the Bristol Channel on 21st September

1965, at Cardiff, was marked by her almost immediate entry into service on the Cardiff-Weston 'ferry' on 24th September, still carrying her Red Funnel colours. **Bristol Queen** was stood down after sustaining damage on 24th September, leaving **Cardiff Queen** to carry on until the final Ilfracombe sailing on Sunday 3rd October. An unusual special cruise from Cardiff, Weston and Ilfracombe by **Vecta** was advertised on Monday 27th September 1965 to view the Scarweather Light Vessel, after which time she continued mostly up-channel until the time came to run the last trips of the season between Cardiff, Penarth, Weston-super-Mare and Barry on Monday 11th October. Little time was wasted, after the end of the season, in despatching her to Cosens at Weymouth for a refit which had been previously arranged within the conditions of her sale by the Red Funnel concern. This turned out to be extensive and involved the conversion of her car-deck into lounge facilities, as well as the provision of additional lavatories and officers & crew accommodation. Around £10,000 was allowed for as the cost of conversion, but the Directors Meeting Minutes do not record her purchase price, which was not disclosed. She was expected to be due back in Cardiff in January 1966, duly renamed **Westward Ho**.

*Vecta was re-named **Westward Ho** for her P. & A. Campbell Ltd service, and her forward car-deck plated in. Seen here leaving Barry Pier in the late-1960s.*

Nigel Jones

1966: three-vessel operations

However, the use that *Westward Ho* was put to in 1966 was not quite what the better-informed observers might have expected. The withdrawal of *Vecta* from Red Funnel service, and her subsequent entry into the White Funnel Fleet, followed a couple of years or so when the reliability of the two paddler-steamers had been causing concern. Any lost sailing days had a serious effect on revenue where no other vessel could be summoned to help out. The author was privileged to obtain a complete copy of an Internal Memorandum drawn up by Clifton Smith-Cox in late 1965, for the attention of the Townsend Ferries Directors, and from which it can be inferred that the purchase of *Vecta* had been intended to enable one of the two paddle-steamers to be withdrawn, and for the motor-vessel to become the 'ferry' vessel in 1966. However, things were not quite so straightforward in practice and this memorandum, which was titled 'Notes on the possible operation of three vessels in the Bristol Channel during 1966' was a lengthy document which basically argued that, having acquired a third vessel, if one assumed that overheads were broadly fixed then the marginal revenue a third vessel might earn would probably exceed marginal costs, and if that did not turn out to be the case then one of the paddle-steamers could be laid-up after having tried the three-vessel experiment. Given what did happen after 1966 it is worth considering in some detail what was being suggested and although numerous other factors were taken into account, some of the most notable were as follows:

- A belief that the market potential did actually justify the capacity that three ships could provide, particularly at the height of the season.
- The ability to run more direct sailings to Minehead (for the Butlins holiday camp traffic) would reduce the need to hire coaches, and thus lower that element of operating costs. Swansea would benefit from more sailings, as would Lundy Island, the latter then being seen as of growing significance.
- A recognition that neither paddle-steamer was due a quinquennial survey for 1966, thus reducing the financial risk of keeping them both going for another season.
- A desire to test a three-ship operation in order to assess whether the alternative combination of *Vecta*, *St. Trillo* and *Bristol Queen* might ultimately be the optimum for Bristol Channel traffic levels.

By a judicious juggling of the entry into service dates of *Vecta* and the two Queens in 1966, and the avoidance of the need to involve *St. Trillo* in Bristol Channel activities (and thus the expense of her positioning from, and return to, her north Wales base) it was calculated that the operating-costs of the two paddlers would be reduced by the equivalent of nine weeks outgoings. This calculation also allowed for the fact that with three vessels, *Bristol Queen* could be rostered to carry out the by now annual Isles of Scilly excursion at a more advantageous time, in mid-June.

Cardiff Queen loads 'luggage passengers' and excursionists at the Pier Head, Cardiff in the mid-1960s: Captain Jack Wide (partly hidden by the lifeboat) and Mate Flanagan survey the busy scene.
Brian Owen, courtesy of Nick James

In conclusion, it was estimated that additional revenue of around £36,000 might be earned with *Vecta* complementing the Queens, whilst operating costs would increase by around £29,000. The net contribution of £7,000 that was thus expected was deemed sufficient to allow the 'experiment' to proceed, and 1966 timetables were duly drawn up which revealed the improvements in service frequencies which the White Funnel Fleet would be able to offer. To complete this picture at the end of 1965 the usual reference to weather needs to be made, in the sense that the season had not been a good one, yet the results had still been satisfactory. An air of optimism that everything would work out all right in 1966 was apparent, particularly if the sun shone on the P. & A. Campbell Ltd business. Strategically, it could be argued that the purchase of *Vecta* had been the right thing to do, given that she became available at an acceptable price: tactically, the position was now more questionable as the proven two-vessel operation was to be replaced by a rather more ambitious three-vessel programme.

If this bullish view of prospects for 1966 was official P. & A. Campbell Ltd thinking, then the perception of seasoned passengers at this point makes an interesting comparison as the 1965 season ended. Norman Bird made these observations in the journal *Ship Ahoy*, having noted the retirement of the greatly respected Captain Jack George, master of *Bristol Queen* for many years:

'... Although it had been a very arduous season, with appalling weather and recurring paddle-wheel trouble, both Queens suffered few cancellations. The managing director stated that "in spite of the weather being the worst I can remember, and the actual number of passengers carried being less than last year, the upward trend in sea travel continues to a heartening degree". I returned ... to Cardiff for the last two down-channel trips of the season on October 2nd/3rd by, I had planned, *Bristol Queen*. I was slightly disappointed to learn that they would be by *Cardiff Queen*, but in the event I thoroughly enjoyed them. They were my last full day trips in her ... and I have happy memories of them: her port paddle-box lamp standards were crazily bent where she had collided with a tree on a bend in the River Avon; her after rails were twisted and two or three portholes plated over where a coastal tanker had hit her as she was coming out of Barry; her starboard bridge-wing was temporarily repaired with plywood following an attack by Weston Pier (!); there were various other scrapes and dents in addition to the usual scruffiness ; and she was running marvellously! I had not felt so fond of the *CQ* for many years. And nowhere on earth would this situation obtain, save in the Bristol Channel!'

Describing the reaction to the announcement of a proposed three-vessel operation in 1966, he continued:

'... this seemed incredible to me. To maintain existing services when every other excursion ship concern was contracting them or giving them up completely, was highly laudable, whatever faults there may have been. But to expand them was nonsense, particularly in view of the disastrous financial results of the last two seasons when three ships had been in service. The only possible merit in doing so was to test the performance in service of the new ship ... but what an expensive way to carry out such a test ! And the writing was already on the wall for the two paddlers as, in spite of their paddle-wheel troubles in 1965, it was announced that in the following winter they would undergo routine maintenance only'.

Westward Ho emerged from Cardiff Docks on Wednesday 6th April 1966 and left the Pier Head at 1805 for Weston to run an evening cruise for public relations purposes, before entering service fully on the ferry the next day when she took three round trips from Cardiff, called in occasionally at Penarth, and visited Barry Pier at low water, in the time-honoured pattern. She settled in to ferry duties over Easter, although a notable disruption occurred on Thursday 14th April 1966 when it was recorded that '*all sailings were cancelled owing to heavy snow*'. Although Cardiff to Weston ferry services were suspended for a couple of days when she acted as tender to the Swedish-American

liner *Gripsholm* in Walton Bay on Tuesday 3rd and Wednesday 4th May 1966, some excellent publicity was achieved which combined a description of the new addition to the White Funnel Fleet with a good account of the tendering activity, 1966 being the third year in which this prestigious 'Spring Adventure Cruise' charter business had been arranged, and the first to involve *Gripsholm*. It was also seen as good business for Bristol as a Corporation public relations team was taken out on the first ferry shuttle from Avonmouth at 0800 to the liner at anchor in order to set up an information bureau on board.

Then followed a busy few weeks when *Westward Ho* gradually showed herself at piers and harbours all around the Bristol Channel, on a variety of excursion sailings. First appearances were as follows:

Ilfracombe	Monday 9th May
Lynmouth	Thursday 9th June
Watchet	Saturday 18th June
Clovelly	Thursday 30th June
Mumbles	Tuesday 5th July
Lundy	Thursday 7th July
Swansea & Porthcawl	Sunday 10th July
Bideford	Friday 15th July

During this early-season period *Westward Ho* was joined by the paddle-steamers, with *Bristol Queen* entering service on Wednesday 25th May 1966 to be followed a couple of weeks or so later by *Cardiff Queen*, on Saturday 11th June 1966.

For a detailed analysis of a busy, if not necessarily typical, day in 1966 where the three ships were to be found widely scattered around the corners of the Bristol Channel Sunday 10th July has been chosen. The really long-distance trip that day, from Cardiff, Penarth and Barry via Ilfracombe to Milford Haven was taken by *Bristol Queen*. Gales delayed her arrival at Milford Haven, and the short cruise that was to have been operated from that port was cancelled, but she returned on schedule, having given Cardiff passengers something like sixteen hours of cruising. Heavy loads would still be expected on the Cardiff to Weston ferry at this time and *Cardiff Queen* that day ran a particularly intensive series of crossings which not only involved six ferry trips mostly including Penarth calls, but also an afternoon run to Ilfracombe with a Barry call for good measure. This schedule kept her occupied from before 0800 to almost 0200 the following morning! Finally, the newly acquired motor-vessel *Westward Ho* made her initial appearances at Swansea and at Porthcawl, running across to Ilfracombe and then on to a Porlock Bay cruise, ending her day by returning from Ilfracombe via Mumbles and Swansea to Porthcawl before finally pointing her bow up-channel for Barry Pier for the night. Barry Pier still represented a convenient spot for night-time layover, as P. & A. Campbell Ltd had traditionally enjoyed a degree of flexibility there as a result of paying the Docks Board an annual compounded fee for the use of the pontoon berth, accessible at all states of the tide. This gave the crew the opportunity for a little time ashore at Barry whilst *Westward Ho* lay alongside the pontoon-berth rather than being anchored out in the Channel for the night.

A full analysis of this day is given in Appendix 2, comparing scheduled and actual times taken from timetables and log-books respectively.

What of the 1966 season in general? *Westward Ho* was clearly acquitting herself satisfactorily and both Queens ran with only occasional mechanical problems. Norman Bird commented on the ability of the company to keep on top of operational difficulties with the paddle-steamers now that the newly-acquired motor-ship was largely associated with 'ferry' duties. Many regulars at the time were unimpressed with the claims to modernity and the inevitability of progress that were put forward for diesel propulsion over steam, and his comments would have reflected the view of those that had preferred the traditional paddle-steamer experience:

'... Both ships had a greater share of the more arduous, down-channel trips than *Westward Ho*, but following their "routine maintenance only" of the previous winter, both had fairly frequent

Westward Ho *berthed, unusually, on the far side of Ilfracombe harbour.*

Peter Southcombe collection

paddle-wheel troubles and some other minor boiler and mechanical troubles. **BQ** was the worse of the two and also suffered from some steering troubles right to the end. In the 1960s she seemed to have experienced frequent spasms of steering-trouble which, as is well-known, was due to her being a paddle-steamer rather than a diesel screw ship (sic). In spite of all there were only a few cancellations of sailings by both ships – a remarkable tribute to the stamina and nerve of the officers and to the ability of the Company to get repairs and patching up done so expeditiously.'

Although no official comment was made until the end of the season, many regular passengers had already deduced that 1966 was likely to be *Cardiff Queen's* final season, on economic rather than mechanical grounds. Meanwhile, a number of events throughout the summer conspired to bode ill for the White Funnel Fleet. Tragedy was narrowly avoided on Friday 24th June when, shortly after *Westward Ho* had loaded her passengers for the ferry at Cardiff Pier Head and left at 0913, the floating pontoon berth sank. Although the local newspapers pointed out that a large number of passengers had only just escaped the risk of drowning in the swirling, muddy waters of the 'drain' there was no major uproar at what could have been a potential disaster. One report specifically mentioned a group of 150 schoolchildren who had boarded the ship. All further sailings from Cardiff that day were, of course, cancelled but repairs were promptly carried out and after the steamers had used Penarth & Barry instead for two days, *Westward Ho* was back alongside the re-floated berth at 2235 on the Saturday, normal sailings from Cardiff resuming on Sunday 26th June.

1966 saw a lengthy seamans' strike, although P. & A. Campbell Ltd were able to escape the direct effects of this, because the South Wales District of the NUS accepted that as P. & A. Campbell Ltd was '... *providing an pleasure service to the community* ...' and would

therefore be exempt from strike action. The District Secretary added '... *We realise we would only be hurting people if we took action. As a result we have told our members employed by Campbells that they can remain at work. In turn, the Company have given us an assurance that they will not do anything to obstruct the union*'. It was pointed out in the journal *Ship Ahoy* that P. & A. Campbell Ltd was not a member of the Federation of British Shipowners. Other steamer companies got off less lightly, and reference is made elsewhere to the demise of the Eagle Steamers after the 1966 season.

What could have been another major incident occurred on 19th August 1966 when, in thick fog, **Bristol Queen** got stuck 'inside' Penarth Pier after missing the correct position alongside the berth. Fortunately, none of the waiting passengers were injured as she ended up at right angles alongside the length of the pier, but more damage was caused to the vessel and the pier as a tug later struggled to pull her free, dragging her along and causing plating to be dented and portholes smashed. Remarkably, passengers were dispatched on a different trip by *Westward Ho* and *Bristol Queen*, after spending the day and night under repair, was back in service the next day. Doubtless the company received a large bill from the owners of the pier for the damage sustained, which would have contributed to an increasingly fraught trading result. As if this was not enough *Cardiff Queen* had suffered a major breakdown on Saturday 30th July necessitating a night spent at Ilfracombe, the loss of her sailings on Sunday 31st July whilst she was towed to Cardiff Docks for repairs, and then three days off service before re-entering traffic on the following Thursday.

1966 was not wholly bad news for the White Funnel Fleet, however, as the opening of the Butlins Holiday Camp at Barry that year was expected to generate new business, carrying holidaymakers from the English side of the Channel to Barry, and offering campers at Barry Island a wide range of afternoon excursions from Barry Pier, which

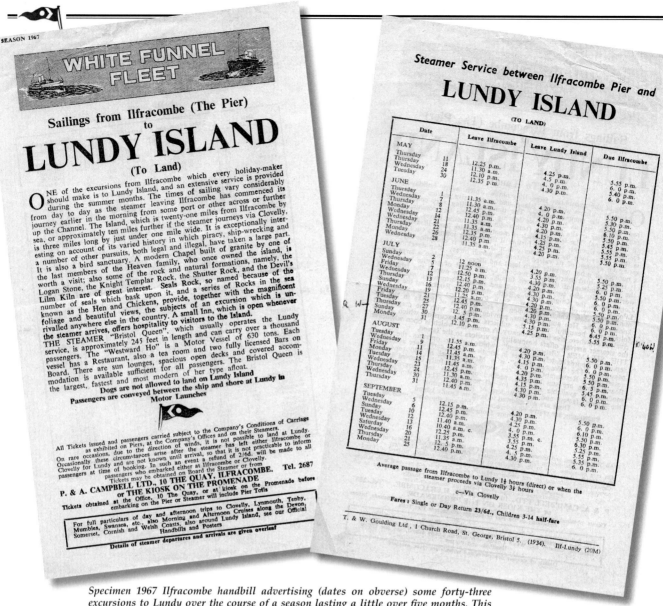

Specimen 1967 Ilfracombe handbill advertising (dates on obverse) some forty-three excursions to Lundy over the course of a season lasting a little over five months. This style of bill was in use practically throughout the 1960s and 70s. Author's collection

was located conveniently close to the new Butlins enterprise. The availability of the new *Westward Ho* had made an improved service for Barry Pier possible, and boat-trains to and from Cardiff often still ran in connection with sailings. 1966 also marked a high point for the trade to the Butlins Holiday Camp on the opposite side of the Channel at Minehead, as special coaches were provided from Ilfracombe to Minehead for Swansea steamer passengers on peak summer Saturdays, in addition to the now-established coaches running between Weston and Minehead in connection with 'ferry' sailings. However, the major event of the season occurred on Thursday 8th September 1966 when HM the Queen opened the new Severn Bridge, and it so happened that this day was *Bristol Queen's* last day in service for the 1966 season. The opening of the first new link across the estuary led to the immediate closure of the adjacent Aust-Beachley car-ferry service, and *Bristol Queen* was booked to run a special cruise to view the opening, leaving Cardiff at 0920 and calling at Penarth, Weston and Clevedon, at a fare of 20/-. Whatever her crew and passengers thought that day as they admired this massive new construction project remains questionable, but there must have been those that could already see the writing on the wall for much of the upper Bristol Channel ferry and excursion traffic.

Bristol Queen entered Cardiff Docks to lay up the following day, Friday 9th September. *Cardiff Queen* soldiered on a little longer, and prosaically made what turned out to be her final revenue-earning trip a couple of weeks later, on a 'classic' down-channel run from Cardiff,

Penarth and Barry to Ilfracombe and Lundy Island to land, calling at Minehead (in the outwards direction only) and at Lynmouth. Arriving back at Cardiff at 2140 that night, one imagines that the crew may well have toasted the paddle-steamer they had lived and worked on for those three months or so of summer. The following morning saw her preparing to make her final voyage into Cardiff Docks for lay-up, and at 1638 'Finished With Engines' was recorded, the crew were paid off, and *Cardiff Queen* was left to her slumbers alongside her older fleetmate *Bristol Queen*, her log-book for 1966 recording that she had run 10,636 miles. At that point her Chief Engineer Jack Rowles who, with the other officers, would stay on throughout the winter, proceeded to lay her up normally and it was only some weeks later that they learnt that her White Funnel Fleet service was actually over. Jack Rowles went on to become the Chief Engineer on board *Bristol Queen* in 1967, of whom we will hear more. The season continued for the solitary *Westward Ho*, whose regular ferry duties were enlivened by odd visits to Minehead, Clovelly and to Lundy Island in late-September. A cruise to view the new Severn Bridge was made on Tuesday 11th October, and after running the 'Last Trips of the Season' on Monday 17th October *Westward Ho* also proceeded to her winter lay-up.

The bitter-sweet atmosphere of those final years when the last two paddle-steamers struggled on against adverse weather and the accumulating effects of age and poor maintenance, but continued to offer peerless cruising experiences in the charismatic Bristol Channel, when changing weather, extreme tides and other circumstances combined to create an utterly unique aura. The context of this extract from the Norman Bird articles should be explained as having been written in 1969, when three years earlier it would have been thought that **Bristol Queen** was still good for another five years as she underwent her quinquennial survey and extensive repairs to her wheels in the winter of 1966/67. The trip described, advertised at 1915 from Mumbles to Barry with return to Swansea at 0015 the next day was unusual. (**Cardiff Queen** had not yet entered service that early in the season). At the time of writing the demise of both Queens was felt, by many who had followed the Company's fortunes, to have been premature but in particular the withdrawal of the one that had survived longer, **Bristol Queen**, caused great sadness:

'... I had a marvellous evening cruise in her (**BQ**) on Whit Monday May 30th, 1966. She was returning to Barry, via Mumbles, after a day trip to Ilfracombe, and then returning to Swansea for the night. There was thus an evening cruise from Mumbles to Barry, scheduled to take about four and a quarter hours - i.e. via the inshore route. But she had been having some steering trouble and the inshore route would have meant taking some risk, with low water and an ebbing tide in the narrow channel. The master, therefore, decided to take the mid-channel route, which could have added some one and a half hours to the round trip. But to obviate inconvenience to passengers and get the crew a reasonable nights rest, **BQ** was 'let rip' and made a steady 49 rpm for the whole trip in each direction – the fastest I

have ever seen those engines working (except for a brief spell on one occasion when the paddle-box doors were opened to admit more air, and she did 51 rpm). She was thus back at Mumbles early ! The return run was unforgettable. It was a marvellously clear, calm, moonlit night; very few passengers aboard; the rapid, powerful beat of the paddles giving a true impression of speed yet an air of peace; the tall raked white funnels reaching up to the sky, with the gentle hiss of a full head of steam and the shimmering of heat around those distinctive cowl tops. The sheer joy of it was almost unbearable. If I could choose only two trips as being outstanding from those I ever made in *Bristol Queen*, this would be one, and the 1962 Milford Haven trip the other, to illustrate the ship at her finest in two completely contrasted moods.

Cardiff Queen for sale

It became apparent that, rather than sending her for scrap straight after the 1966 season, the company was seeking alternative uses for **Cardiff Queen**. Rumours circulated amongst enthusiasts that a Bournemouth-based operation was under consideration for 1967, although the company made no public announcement on this matter. After the withdrawal of the last of the Cosens fleet at Weymouth at the end of the 1966 season, discussions did indeed take place in January 1967 between Clifton Smith-Cox and the Town Clerk of the County Borough of Bournemouth, on the basis that the services Cosens had formerly provided had ' ... *long represented an established and popular feature of Bournemouth's summer facilities* ...'. It had been

Bristol Queen *in dry-dock at Cardiff, April 1967, being prepared for what turned out to be her final season in service.*　　　　Nick James

Bristol Queen *at Cardiff Docks in 1967, before her final season in service.*

Brian Owen, courtesy of Nick James

put to Campbells that there was still demand there to be satisfied, but it is clear from surviving correspondence that whilst it was considered that either of the two Queens was too big and therefore too expensive to operate from Bournemouth, the possibility of a smaller motor-vessel – if one had been available – was not without interest.

Peter Southcombe recalled that in late-1966 he and Clifton Smith-Cox had indeed considered the deployment of *Cardiff Queen* at Bournemouth for the 1967 season after her withdrawal from Bristol Channel duties, and that he got as far as drawing up a provisional itinerary for her. P. & A. Campbell Ltd were in contact with the local operator Crosons as well as Cosens of Weymouth, but in January 1967 Mr Brooks of the latter company confidentially provided Clifton Smith-Cox with detailed figures of Cosens' carryings on *Embassy* in 1966, which rapidly led him to deduce that even if a P. & A. Campbell Ltd vessel carried double the volumes that the last Cosens paddle-steamer had been handling, they could not make a satisfactory return. Another alternative considered was that of switching *Cardiff Queen* with *St. Trillo*, a factor here being that the condition of Llandudno pier after the 1966 season had led the Isle of Man Steam Packet Company to decide to withdraw from the operation there of their large, turbine-steamers until repairs were effected. Thus *Cardiff Queen*, as a smaller and lighter vessel, could in theory have been deployed at Llandudno and attracted Isle of Man excursion business, which may well have been welcomed in north Wales. However, the allocation of the released *St. Trillo* to a Bournemouth station would have given that town a vessel

too slow to offer round the Isle of Wight sailings – so this notion was not progressed either, and it is on record that Roland Wickenden again quashed any such expansion into ship operation in the south-east, preferring to see P. & A. Campbell Ltd efforts continuing to focus on channelling coach-passengers towards his own Townsend ferry routes.

There were also proposals at the same time for *Cardiff Queen* to be purchased by a newly-formed company known as River Cruises (Scotland) Limited. A formal share-offer to raise £50,000 was put together and a prospectus was printed, describing how *Cardiff Queen* would be purchased for around £25,000, and a further £20,000 would be spent on refurbishment, to fit her for cruises on the Forth estuary from ports such as Leith, Burntisland, Kirkcaldy, Grangemouth & Methil, for 500 passengers. Although there was some optimism about this scheme, by the time the share offer closed only about £1,000 had been raised. In view of the running-cost projections included in the prospectus, one can only deduce that the canny Scots, and other interested parties, were unimpressed either by the running-cost projections or the claim that *Cardiff Queen* would only require a crew of eight for her new duties, comprising a Master, Chief Officer, Engineer, four deck-hands, and one assistant. It was anticipated that catering would be wholly contracted out, yet a quarter of her projected annual income was supposed to derive from profits on this catering and 'estimated winter profits' from functions when the vessel was idle.

Not surprisingly, *Cardiff Queen* continued to languish in Cardiff Docks in the hands of brokers A. M. C. McGinnity & Partners, for sale at £30,000. At the 74th Ordinary General Meeting of the Company held at 4, Dock Chambers, Cardiff on 26th January 1967 the Statement by the Chairman alluded to the situation regarding the paddle-steamers, and other salient matters:

'... The summer of 1966, if one can call it such, has now passed. Amongst other problems with which we had to contend was the effect of the seamen's strike ... prospective passengers reading about strikes and expecting that one would probably take place were loath to make party bookings, or indeed to come to the boats to travel at all, and we missed a lot of business as a result ... It is regretted that the operation of two paddle steamers as well as a screw vessel in the Bristol Channel is no longer economic and the *Cardiff Queen* has, in consequence, been withdrawn from service'.
A. R. BOUCHER, Chairman

1967: Back to two-vessel operations

The three-vessel experiment of 1966 had evidently failed, and the winter of 1966/67 presented the forlorn spectacle of both of the postwar paddle-steamers laid-up in Cardiff Docks with **Cardiff Queen**, the younger of the pair, never to sail again. Ironically, **Bristol Queen** was now approaching the first season for many years when she would be almost entirely programmed to carry out the longer distance, down-channel duties for which she had been designed as it was expected that **Westward Ho** would now dominate the Cardiff-Weston 'ferry' duties (which **Bristol Queen** had perforce had a large share of since her return to service in 1961). Considerable attention was paid to her paddle-wheels that winter, and it was made known to enthusiasts that this investment was expected to make her good for another five years. As the Severn Bridge had only opened late in 1966 there was no measure yet of how much effect this might have on ferry loadings and as Easter approached the commencement of White Funnel Fleet sailings by **Westward Ho** from Cardiff was advertised for Thursday 23rd March 1967. As in previous years the second ship was not due to come into service until a little later in May, but **Bristol Queen** unwittingly found herself nearly strikebound in the Mountstuart Dry Dock in Cardiff owing to a boilermakers dispute over a new productivity deal. Public sentiment again helped the Campbell cause, however, and the Boilermakers Union granted dispensation for work to continue so that the **Bristol Queen's** survey could be completed in time for her to undertake the annual Isles of Scilly weekend between May 13th-15th, 1967. A union official explained that the contract had been placed some time beforehand, and ponted our that the decision to allow work to continue was because: '... *we know what she means to people around here and did not want to disappoint holidaymakers, so we have let some of the men come in and work under the old agreement* ...'. Ernie Harris, then Company Secretary, stated that P. & A. Campbell Ltd were very pleased this compromise had been arrived at: '... *the vessel is undergoing a special five-yearly survey by Board of Trade officials. If the work had not been done they would not have allowed us to use the ship for passengers. This would have meant cancelling several services.*'

The Isles of Scilly cruise was regarded as a great success and took place in favourable weather. The itinerary was for **Bristol Queen** to sail from Cardiff to Penzance on Saturday 13th May 1967, calling at Penarth, Weston & Ilfracombe en-route, and lay over that night and the next at Penzance whilst running a day-trip to St. Marys in Scilly on the Sunday in between. Captain Power was in command, with Captain George also present as a sort of very welcome guest-captain – as E. C. B. Thornton put it – on the fifth such special excursion that **Bristol Queen** had undertaken. (These ventures had longer-term origins than what had in 1963 initially been a charter proposition which P. & A. Campbell Ltd subsequently had taken over themselves: occasional trips around Lands End went right back to the earliest days, and one of the very first was that undertaken by the original paddle-steamer **Westward Ho** when newly-built in 1894). The Chief Engineer of **Bristol Queen** in 1967 was Jack Rowles, who had transferred to her after the withdrawal of **Cardiff Queen** the previous year. After this promising start the season really started to get underway, and **Bristol**

Queen ran the first 1967 Swansea-Padstow trip in foggy conditions on 4th June, the journal *Ship Ahoy* noting that the despite teething troubles the newly-installed radar was proving its worth. A little later she took the annual Newport Harbour Commissioners trip, on 30th June. On 19th June her out-of-service fleet-mate *Cardiff Queen* had been towed from Cardiff where she had been lying, to Barry Dock, as the berth she had been at was required in connection with a dock modernisation scheme. In early July *Ship Ahoy* was able to report that **Bristol Queen** and **Westward Ho** were running well and that the season had thus far been '... *remarkably free from breakdowns and other incidents which were such an unfortunate feature of 1966* ...'.

P. & A. Campbell Ltd steamers were still very much apart of the way of life in South Wales in the mid-1960s, departing from the Pier Head either for the ferry run across to Weston, or further afield down-Channel. A somewhat facetious account of a trip on the ferry on board **Westward Ho** in August 1967 was given in the *South Wales Echo* under the title 'Putting to sea with gulls, girls' which portrayed the cross-channel voyage as a poor man's substitute for a deep-sea voyage on something a little larger. The following quote from the article gives a flavour of what a trip to Weston might have seemed like to Cardiff folk in those days.

INTREPID SEAMAN JON HOLLIDAY SAYS - COME WITH ME

Oh, a life on the ocean wave
A home on the rolling deep -

I couldn't quite manage this, so instead I went for a
P. & A. Campbell steamer cruise around the Bristol Channel.

The early morning sunshine had bought out a good crowd for the cruise and most people had taken their places aboard the lugger anchored at Cardiff Pier Head as I hove in sight (nautical language, you see). Up the gangplank and on to the deck already vibrating from the powerful engines, I went. On one side was a basket of racing pigeons bearing the label "To be liberated at Weston. Thank you." The pigeons squatting in the grit seemed reasonably blase about it ... The steamer swung round and headed out into the channel, the bizarre cosmopolitan townscape of Cardiff dockland receding slowly behind us ... The passengers seemed to divide fairly clearly into three groups - children, particularly boys in anoraks, older people, possibly retired, firmly rugged up against the sea winds, and courting or young married couples. Despite the weather forecast of sun and above average temperatures many people were armed with raincoats, umbrellas and even plastic rain-hats to keep off the always possible flood ... The skyline of Cardiff could now be seen as more of a piece - a tall office building or block of flats here and there, gasometers, cranes, smoke-belching chimneys, terraced houses, nests of storage tanks. Behind that was a semi-circle of hills that surround the basin on which the capital of Wales has grown.

We passed a grimy dredger slogging away at keeping the channel silt-free, then round the cliffs of Penarth to a sight of that homely little pier - its Union Jack fluttering bravely in the breeze - the ornate pavilion and the two contrasting blocks of waterfront flats. Past the pier we suddenly went into a sharp turn, kicking up white in the dull greeny-brown water as we nudged the landing stage. A contingent of Penarthians boarded us like rather refined pirates and we headed out into the channel once more ... Some people were striding about the decks with a great display of energy as though they were on a luxury cruise to the Bahamas. They took great lungfuls of the salt air, their facial expressions showing they were convinced their lives were being prolonged by at least a decade ... In the self-service cafeteria (cafe ? restaurant ? dining saloon ? galley ?) people sat and drank coffee or pop, eating crisps and cake and sausage rolls ... At Weston-super-Mare practically everyone disembarked to spend the day at Weston, take a coach-tour, or go by steamer to Minehead, Ilfracombe or Clovelly...

A different take on the theme of a quiet moment at the Pier Head, Cardiff as a handful passengers inspect **Bristol Queen**.

Brian Owen, courtesy of Nick James

Failure of Bristol Queen

As the 1967 season progressed, however, breakdowns began to plague the performance of *Bristol Queen*. The root-cause of the problems she experienced lay in the decision which had been taken to axe the company's Underfall Yard in Bristol after the 1956 season, after which date skilled craftsmen were no longer at hand to deal swiftly with running repairs to paddle-wheels and other major components, and to ensure that regular maintenance minimised the risk of long-term problems developing. The responsibility for the engines remained with the ships engineers, but it had been assumed that other maintenance would be bought in as required, to contain overheads.

When the fleet had been larger, it had been easier to juggle schedules and take a vessel out of service for mid-season maintenance. As the number of ships contracted it had become more difficult to cancel sailings for necessary repairs to be carried out. As we have seen *Bristol Queen* had been laid-up between late-1958 and early-1961, during which time the economic climate led the management to minimise any 'unnecessary' expenditure on routine attention to a laid-up ship generating no income. In 1962, after the 'lean years' had ended, she had been sent to Weymouth for specialist attention by Cosens & Co. Ltd, but critically, although her wheels received an extensive overhaul, they were not actually replaced.

Despite some £30,000 being spent on this work, some troubles with her wheels were recorded in 1963, but fewer in the two successive seasons. It should be pointed out that by their very nature paddle-wheels, with their feathering floats constantly hitting the water, require constant attention. Standard P. & A. Campbell Ltd practice had been to use two nuts to secure the floats at each point at which they were bolted to the wheels. These needed sensitive daily checking and adjustment if necessary to ensure the correct torque was applied to the securing bolts, and that nothing was working loose. The outermost acted as a

locking-nut. The covering of these assemblies in red-lead paint meant that when being checked over, a trained eye could spot if movement was happening as cracking of the read-lead coating would give a warning. Critically, in the 1966 refit this method had been changed, and a single nut with a nylon insert was used, which was intended to act as the outermost locking nut as had previously. To put the amount of this exceptional expenditure in context, the level of trading profit in 1966 that was recorded in the Company accounts was £50,000, before payment of dividends.

As the 1967 season got underway *Bristol Queen* began well enough, and she operated to a challenging schedule with a lot more time spent out of Swansea than to which she had hitherto been accustomed. The very long hours can be seen in the specimen copy (reproduced below) of a weeks' sailing instructions issued to her Master, Captain Phil Power and to Chief Engineer Jack Rowles, which involved features such as nocturnal shifts between Swansea South Dock entrance and Pocketts Wharf to take fuel after a long day as well as the odd very early start to position light from an overnight stay at Cardiff up to Bristol on the first of a morning tide. The stresses were considerable, both on the officers and crew, as well as on the fabric of the ship. If anything the engineering officers suffered more as their notional off-days increasingly became spent on dealing with emergency repairs, as Jack Rowles later recounted it. A first notable breakdown occurred on 21st July as two radius rods fractured, and another cancellation occurred very shortly afterwards, on 24th July, and repairs had to be effected firstly at Hills at Bristol and afterwards at Cardiff throughout the night. Ominous noises were reported to be heard from the paddle-wheels on 29th July, during adverse weather conditions.

Matters became more serious when, on August 3rd, another breakdown at Swansea precipated more extensive repairs which necessitated three days off service, at the Roath Basin at Cardiff,

J.H. Guy.

Cardiff.

Captain Power,
P/S "BRISTOL QUEEN"
Cardiff.

August 12th. 1967.

Dear Sir,

Kindly note the following sailings scheduled for your steamer:-

Tuesday 15th Shift from Jetty midnight to Pocketts wharf for bunkers

Wed Aug 16. Shift down to Jetty 6-0 a.m. Ssea 9-45 a.m. Mbles 10-10 a.m. Ilf 12-5 p.m. for Tenby. Tenby 2-35 p.m. c.c. back 4-10 p.m. Tenby 4-20 p.m. Ilf 7-15 p.m. for Mbles.

Thu Aug 17. Shift to Pocketts about 1-0 a.m. for Bunkers, shift down to Jetty 7-15 a.m. Ssea 8-30 a.m. Mbles 8-55 a.m. Ilf 10-45 a.m. for Padstow. due 2-55 p.m. Padstow 3-10 p.m. c.c. back 4-5 p.m. Padstow 4-20 p.m. Ilf 8-30 p.m. Mbles 10-10 p.m. for Barry due 12-40 a.m. (Fri.) one wagon of Bunkers.

Fri Aug 18. Barry 8-15 a.m. Cdff 9-15 a.m. Pen 9-25 a.m. Wes 10-25 a.m. Barry 11-20 a.m. for Lyn and Ilf. due 2-5 p.m. Ilf 2-20 p.m. Lyn 3-5 p.m. c.c. back Ilf 5-0 p.m. Ilf 5-10 p.m. Lyn 5-40 p.m. Barry 7-30 p.m. Wes 8-30 p.m. for Pen & Cdff.

Sat Aug 19. Cdff 9-30 a.m. Pen 9-40 a.m. Wes 10-40 a.m. for Lyn and Ilf 1-50 p.m. Mbles 3-45 p.m. Ilf 5-40 p.m. Lyn 6-10 p.m. for Barry, Pen & Cdff due 8-45 p.m.

Sun Aug 20. Cdff light to Bris. Bris 9-0 a.m. Clev 10-0 a.m. Cdff 11-0 a.m. Pen 11-10 a.m. Barry 11-45 a.m. for Ilf due 2-15 p.m. Ilf 2-30 p.m. c.c. Bid Bay back 4-15 p.m. Ilf 4-25 p.m. Barry 6-25 p.m. Pen 6-50 p.m. Cdff 7-15 p.m. Clev 8-10 p.m. for Bris.

Mon Aug 21. O.S. Bristol.

Tue Aug 22. Bris 8-40 a.m. Clev 9-50 a.m. Wes 10-30 a.m. Minehead 12-5 p.m. (Motor Boats.) for Lyn and Ilf 2-0 p.m. for Clov. Clov 4-40 p.m. Ilf 6-20 p.m. Lyn 6-50 p.m. Minehead 8-0 p.m. Wes 9-25 p.m. for Pen & Cdff.

Yours faithfully,

Sailing instructions issued to Captain Power for Bristol Queen *late on in the 1967 season.*

Late Roy Barclay / Authors collection

until 6th August. Jack Rowles had expressed his serious misgivings to George James, the Marine Superintendent, on the suitability of the work done to her wheels the previous winter, and could see that a major breakdown was now highly likely. He therefore tendered his resignation and gave the necessary notice that he would leave the ship. This was more than worrying at such a crucial stage of the season, but a few days of calm prevailed, before the next breakdown on 20th August which led to '*BQ*' being docked for yet more repairs. These foreshadowed the fateful day, which was to lead to the end of the commercial paddle-steamer era in the Bristol Channel, and after her experienced Chief Engineer had left the vessel. Replacement engine-room personnel had been found, but by the mid-1960s it would have been near-impossible to recruit engineers familiar with the quirks of paddle-steamers, their fragile paddle-wheels and comparatively antiquated triple-expansion steam engine technology. Some of the regular passengers from that time have since described an atmosphere of doom, perhaps prompted by an awareness of the instruction that was evidently given in early July, according to *Ship Ahoy*, for *Bristol Queen* to run with a 10% reduction to her normal speed, to eases stresses generally.

The late August Bank Holiday Saturday, 26th August 1967, should have seen *Bristol Queen* depart from Cardiff at 0915 and call at Barry at 1000, before crossing the Channel to make further calls at Minehead, Lynmouth and Ilfracombe. Then should have followed a crossing to Mumbles Pier, an afternoon Gower Coast cruise of 90 minutes duration, and then the return crossing from Mumbles to Ilfracombe before *Bristol Queen* retraced her steps up-Channel to Lynmouth, Barry, Penarth and Cardiff. Minehead passengers were due to return to Cardiff by means of a bus to Weston, thence per the 1915 'ferry' sailing by *Westward Ho* to Cardiff. Nick James, in recent years the Chairman of the Paddle Steamer Preservation Society, was on board that day, and recalled that shortly after *Bristol Queen* left Barry it became apparent that something was seriously wrong. Whilst the official version of events was that *Bristol Queen* sustained damage to her paddle-wheels off Barry as a result of encountering floating debris, it seems more likely that the state of her wheels was such that a float broke loose, and rapidly caused much damage in the confines of the starboard paddle-box. The order to shut off power was not immediate and there were some anxious moments as ruptures appeared in the paddle-boxes before the order to stop the engines was given. Contact with floating debris would have been all the more serious with fragile floats and wheels: the damage was extremely serious, the sailing was terminated, and *Bristol Queen* later limped back, under her own power but at restricted speed, to Cardiff.

Her 1967 season prematurely ended, she later moved under her own power to the safety of the Queen's Dock at Cardiff on 29th September, whilst the management frantically re-arranged the disposition of the rest of the fleet to fill the gap as best they could. It seems certain that the revised method of using the nylon-insert nuts to secure the floats to the wheels had been a major contributory factor to the breakdown but there was no doubt that this failure was a major blow, from which it was unlikely that the twenty-year old Campbell flagship *Bristol Queen* would be able to recover.

End-1967: fleet manoeuvrings

The sudden withdrawal of *Bristol Queen* at the critical peak of the Bristol Channel season was clearly going to cause catastrophic financial problems if no action was taken. An immediate decision was made to bring *St. Trillo* round from her north Wales duties, which were temporarily abandoned, to take over the Cardiff-Weston ferry while *Westward Ho* was switched to cover most of the paddlers' duties. Not too much damage was done to receipts in the August Bank Holiday week as *St. Trillo* was able to commence Bristol Channel operations on the Bank Holiday Sunday, 27th August, only one day after the accident to *Bristol Queen*, having sailed overnight across Cardigan Bay and around the tip of west Wales to arrive at Cardiff at 0700. Timetable alterations were necessitated to reflect the slower speeds of the two motor vessels, and passengers were turned away on occasions when their capacity was inadequate for the big loads that *Bristol*

Queen would still then have been carrying on certain key days at that point of the holiday season.

Fortunately Clifton Smith-Cox knew of a suitable vessel which was lying idle, and a charter agreement was very hastily put together with the Isles of Scilly Steamship Company (IoSSCo.) for their almost new relief vessel, the 1965-built *Queen of the Isles*, to proceed to north Wales to deputise for *St. Trillo* which had departed from the Llandudno station so hastily. This ship had seen relatively little use for her intended purpose since construction, and the rapidity with which *Queen of the Isles* was crewed and stationed at Menai Bridge was commendable, and she was able to re-open the north Wales excursion programme on September 4th, just over a week after *St. Trillo* had been summoned to the Bristol Channel. Her activities on this service have already been documented, but it is appropriate to mention here that the failure of *Bristol Queen* triggered what was to become a rather longer relationship between the IoSSCo. relief vessel and the White Funnel Fleet than might have initially been envisaged, involving spells of duty in the Bristol Channel and subsequently in the south-east of England in addition to north Wales.

Altered timetable publicity was produced shortly after the change of vessels, and the introduction to the principal handbill entitled Amendments to Sailings – September 1967 confined itself to the curt statement that '*For reasons beyond their control Messrs. P. & A. Campbell Ltd regret that certain amendments to the sailings previously advertised for September 1967 have to be made*'. Then followed a summary of alterations to timings which, whilst in itself very carefully worded, nevertheless only fully made sense if read wholly in conjunction with all other bills. Alterations had had to be made on twenty days during the month of September. Although a complete reprint would have been a much better way to communicate the differences in times on certain days to the travelling public, a potentially confusing situation was created by skimping on printing costs, although the supplementary bill cheerfully concluded that '... *apart from the foregoing amendments all sailings are as advertised on posters and handbills. Where short cruises have been substituted for longer ones fares will be suitably adjusted ...*' (*St. Trillo* thus carried out most of the Bristol Channel duties that *Westward Ho* would have undertaken, and was even recorded as having 'raced' her on one occasion). *St. Trillo* set off back to Menai Bridge on 27th September, and was thus home in time to close her own season at Llandudno on 1st October, releasing *Queen of the Isles* to return to her IoSSCo. owners.

At the end of the 1967 season, then, paddle-steamer enthusiasts were obliged to conclude that an era had ended, and that a turning-point in the fortunes of the White Funnel Fleet had truly been reached. Having been earlier shifted from Cardiff to Barry prior to her eventual disposal, *Cardiff Queen* had already gone from the scene and, while the motor vessels soldiered on, only the most ardent optimist could imagine any possibility of either of the paddle-steamers returning to active service. As the realisation set in that there was no operational future for the flagship *Bristol Queen* speculation started as to whether an alternative, non-operational future for her lay in some form of static preservation. The eminent local maritime historian Grahame Farr added his weight to the lobby that advocated retention of *Bristol Queen* as an asset for Bristol, in the form of a floating maritime museum, as her hull was thought to still be sound, even if she was beyond restoration to seagoing condition. An editorial article in the *Bristol Evening Post* on Thursday 7th December likened her role to that of Brunel's *Great Britain* as a potential candidate for restoration, as a potent symbol of Bristolian ship-building prowess.

The piece was entitled:

WORTH SAVING ?

'Bristolians have a built-in love of the sea and ships ... we have sparked off an ambitious, almost romantic campaign to save Brunel's mighty Great Britain steamship, sadly abandoned and aground in the distant Falkland Islands. The suggestion is to patch her up, bring her back across the Atlantic with a volunteer crew, and convert her into a floating museum in the heart of the city's waterways.

*The scene from the pier at Penarth as **Bristol Queen** pulled away on what turned out to be her final day in service, 26th August 1967.*

Brian Owen, courtesy of Nick James

The idea of a maritime symbol of Bristol's seafaring is indeed appealing – and could prove a major tourist attraction. But estimates of the cost of restoring the **Great Britain** are put at over £1 million. We cannot see approval for this sort of expenditure, but there is a very worthwhile preservation scheme much nearer home. This is the saving of **Bristol Queen**, last of the distinguished line of Bristol Channel paddle steamers. Her scrap value is put at only £18,000 and for between £30,000 and £40,000 she could be returned to full working order and kept here. The **Bristol Queen** – proudly bearing the City's name – would make an ideal companion for the tug **Bristolian**, already under negotiation, for a waterfront reminder of our maritime links.'

In the event Bristol City Council found itself unable to justify purchase of **Bristol Queen**. P. & A. Campbell Ltd would not allow her to be sold for use which might conflict with their own business interests. They perhaps feared that if rescued initially for static use she might later be restored and steamed again, and compete directly with the surviving members of the White Funnel Fleet, thereby hastening their demise. The future for **Bristol Queen** looked even more bleak when in early 1968 news broke that a cargo ship had collided with her at the berth where she was then laid-up. The errant ship, when going out of control in severe weather conditions in Cardiff Docks, caused considerable damage and reduced still further the chances of her sale in operational condition. The inevitable happened, and by February it became apparent that the representatives of a Belgian breakers yard were going to secure her for scrap, and that the appeal to raise funds to keep her in Bristol had failed.

Both Queens go to scrap

In the early part of 1968, then, both of the once majestic postwar paddle-steamers of the White Funnel Fleet were to be found languishing in quiet corners of the south Wales docks at Barry and at Cardiff. The younger **Cardiff Queen**, then lying in Barry Dock, appeared to have some hope of salvation dangled before her as her sale to a Mr Critchley for use as a floating nightclub in Newport, on a tidal river-berth, was announced on 24th January. Ambitious plans for her conversion were revealed to the local press, involving a proposed expenditure of about £50,000 to create a nightclub with a 'top-class' cabaret and dancing, and a dining-room to seat 200, as well as the alternative option of turning the vessel into a floating retail-outlet selling cut-price goods and jewellery, together with a 'mod boutique' and a record bar if the nightclub plan and associated licensing was rejected. There was even talk of the addition of a swimming-pool. Mr Critchley, a director of Critchcraft (Newport) Limited, stated that he was also mindful of the vintage paddle-steamer character of the boat, and that he would '*open up the engines and polish them up*'.

Cardiff Queen duly left Barry Docks under tow for her new home on the River Usk in Newport on 29th February 1968. What happened next, however, was not exactly what had been intended. Her new berth was located just below the Transporter Bridge, and the White Funnel News section in the Spring 1968 edition of *Ship Ahoy* recorded that:

'... this berth consisted of a sloping mud-bank, and when the tide ebbed the steamer pulled out 13 hawsers and slid almost broadside across the river with four men stranded aboard. Tugs retrieved her on the afternoon tide (the next day, Thursday 1st March) and she was towed into Newport South Dock where she remained until Tuesday 9th April. She was then towed to Cashmore's shipbreaking yard in the Usk for breaking-up, her new owner having decided that it was not practical to continue with his nightclub plans ...'.

This was clearly a big disappointment for Mr Critchley, who had told the *South Wales Argus* before having made the decision to sell **Cardiff Queen** for breaking that '... *it would cost up to £10,000 to put the Mill Parade berth right. The **Cardiff Queen** slipped out because of the mud and this would have to be dredged away, and other improvements made, for the berth to be safe. In the meantime she is costing us money every day. Just getting her off the mud cost us £2,500 and taking her*

back to Barry will probably cost us another £1,000. We are getting very short of money and it looks as though we shall have to scrap her – there has already been an offer from a Belgian firm. We have breathing space of about a fortnight before making up our minds'. He added: '*We talked to the experts before deciding on the Mill Parade berth. They thought there was a fairly good chance she would be all right. She wasn't, and it has been a bad blow to us*'.

A correspondent from *Ship Ahoy* described a final visit to **Bristol Queen** in Cardiff Docks while **Cardiff Queen** lay licking her wounds in Newport Docks:

'... **Bristol Queen** was berthed in the top corner of the Queen Alexandra Dock, and seemed quite alive for a winter Sunday afternoon. A word to the friendly watchman soon had us aboard. We were surprised to find the diesel generator running, but the reason soon became evident. Going below, we found that work was proceeding on fitting deadlights to all the portholes, thus the lights were needed to see one's way around. In the sun-lounges the familiar 'coffins' (lifebelt boxes) were being sawn up to make boards for securing over the windows to guard against seas breaking in on the tow across the North Sea to Belgium. A visit to the dining-saloon and tea-bar revealed all the tables and chairs being removed, and the lifejackets piled up ready for removal. (These have since been advertised by Critchcraft Ltd of Chepstow, at ten shillings each, or £4 per dozen). On deck, most of the cowl ventilators had been removed, and their stumps covered over to prevent any sea flooding down them on the journey. A visit up to the bridge, with its twisted starboard wing and view of the damaged foredeck was equally depressing, when one remembers so many happy summers days spent on the ship in the last few years. We then had a look in the bar on deck which was such a friendly meeting place for so many years, and which will never serve another drink. A few empty beer-cans were all that was left here. Our tour ended in the engine-room, and shortly after we came ashore for the last time, and were soon on our way home'.

Bristol Queen was spared the public ignominy that her younger fleetmate had suffered in her final weeks, and went to her end rather more quietly, albeit in a sorry-looking state after the collision in Cardiff Docks. Norman Bird briefly described the weeks preceding her last voyage: '... *on January 14th, she was struck by the Liberian tanker **Geodor** which was attempting to berth at Queens Dock, Cardiff in high winds. **Bristol Queen** suffered extensive damage to her bulwarks, starboard bow and bridge-wing, and her foremast was snapped off, falling into the dock. She was subsequently sold to a Belgian firm, believed to be Scrappingco. S.R.L., and after delays because of gales, left Cardiff on 21st March in tow of the German tug **Fairplay XI**. She passed Antwerp, bound for Willebroek, on the 26th. Her dining-room tables – stout, good-quality furniture – were used to board her up for the voyage*'. Inevitably, this was a time when one would reflect on the end of an era, as the last paddle-steamers physically disappeared from the Bristol Channel scene, thus leaving excursion services solely in the hands of motor-vessels.

Litigation: Bristol Queen postscript

The author is indebted to Tony McGinnity, the Joint Managing Director of P. & A. Campbell Ltd in latter years, for this anecdote concerning litigation over the damage suffered by **Bristol Queen** when **Geodor** collided with her. The case did not come to Court until 1972, after another insurance claim in respect of the written-off **Westward Ho** had eventually been settled after the motor-vessel's withdrawal in 1971. Although out of strict chronological sequence here, it nicely closes this chapter in the history of the P. & A. Campbell Ltd paddle-steamer era, in Tony McGinnity's own words:

'... the further claim on the **Bristol Queen** concerning the damage caused by the tanker **Geodor** whilst the latter vessel was manoeuvring actually did come to Court at the District Registrar's in Cardiff. The actual sum claimed was modest at £5,000 - but a point of principle was involved and Clifton Smith-Cox was not going to give way. **Bristol Queen** had been damaged in lay-up, never to sail again. At that juncture efforts were being made to arrange the vessel's preservation in Bristol although the prospects of a sale for scrap were beginning to loom large on the horizon.

The *Geodor*, a Liberian flag tanker, whilst under tow and pilot's orders, took a lurch to port and severely damaged the **Bristol Queen's** starboard bridge, deck edge and handrails in way. As is the custom in these matters a complaint was lodged by Campbell's with the *Geodor's* port agent and her owners agreed through their third-party insurers or Protection & Indemnity Club that they were liable for repairs. A bond was duly posted. However, as time progressed, the claims adjusters sitting in London and whose probable youth meant a damaged paddle-steamer was to them like an extinct dinosaur, instructed Cardiff solicitors to make enquiries. Their subsequent report brought a letter from *Geodor's* P&I Club that, whilst they accepted liability for the damage to **Bristol Queen**, what did it matter anyway? The **Bristol Queen** was going for scrap so repairs were not important. They would pay nothing. It was a valid argument and probably not unreasonable, but their letter was written in a rather cavalier manner which infuriated Clifton Smith-Cox. He decided he would not let the matter rest.

It is perhaps appropriate to mention at this time that Mr Smith-Cox relished a good scrap. For many years a vigorous chairman of the Long Ashton Magistrate's Court, his frequently unorthodox but common-sense pronouncements attracted publicity in the local and occasionally the national press. He was not going to be put off with a little local difficulty. In addition, the planning permission for a new hotel overlooking the Avon Gorge granted by Bristol City Council to Mount Charlotte Investments (his principal business interest) had led to him being lampooned by the satirical magazine *Private Eye*. This episode, by the way, cost Bristol City Council more than £1m in compensation. I gave evidence as an expert, supported by Captain George Gunn. The other side produced a retired shipbroker

who simply stated that **Bristol Queen** only represented scrap value.

Clifton Smith-Cox, in a move typical of his tactics to go out and win, had employed an experienced but very elderly solicitor to represent P. & A. Campbell Ltd in Court. The solicitor, nearing eighty, was rather deaf. This meant that Clifton & I in standing behind him in Court were frequently bawling instructions into his ear, often facts that could or should not have been aired in Court. This brought frequent rebukes to the Campbell camp from the Judge, but at the same time the Judge was getting a far better side of the argument from Campbell's than normal Court procedure allowed. It was clear from the expressions on the other side's Counsel that they were aware of this as well.

It was then that Campbell's produced the knockout blow in the shape of a prize witness, none other than Mr John Critchley, whose company had bought Birnbeck Pier some years after their ill-fated purchase of *Cardiff Queen*. John Critchley gave evidence to the effect that he had been interested in buying **Bristol Queen** for an unstated role but had been put off by the damage caused by *Geodor*. Pressed by the Defendant's Counsel, Critchley said that if he had bought **Bristol Queen** then he would have offered a price reduced by the amount of the repairs i.e. £5,000. After this the District Judge hinted that as the case had already run into two days, it might be an idea if the parties came to a settlement to avoid the costs of a third day in Court. This hint was so phrased as to suggest that it was the Defendant who should make the offer. In fact, this is what occurred at a pavement meeting outside the Court when the Defendants offered to settle the claim in full, plus costs. The effect of this was that the P&I Club probably paid out in total more than three times what they would have had to pay to meet the original claim! Clifton Smith-Cox and his team later that evening enjoyed a celebratory dinner with a good deal of wine at the Central Hotel, Cardiff, incidentally operated by the Mount Charlotte Group so that the cost was kept in house, so to speak.'

At Cardiff Docks after withdrawal: **Bristol Queen** *after the premature end of her 1967 season.*   Brian Owen, courtesy of Nick James

Although billed as the final departure of **Balmoral** *from the pontoon at Hotwells, Bristol on 1st October 1971, with Captain Wide saying farewell, sailings from Bristol (from the lock entrance to the Floating Harbour, in the centre distance) occasionally took place in the 1970s.*

Author's collection

Chapter 3
AFTER THE PADDLERS
Consolidation then retrenchment

The 1968 season – *Westward Ho* partners *St. Trillo*

There are various ways in which one can look back at the 1967 season and the unhappy end of the last paddle-steamer, ***Bristol Queen***, and her withdrawal after barely twenty-one years of operation. From a traditionalist viewpoint the demise of the last P. & A. Campbell Ltd steamship in the Bristol Channel truly marked the end of an era stretching back to 1887, eighty years before, when ***Waverley*** had come south from the Clyde and established a presence at Bristol. Doubtless there were passengers whose custom would now be lost, through their lack of enthusiasm for sailing on new-fangled motor-vessels, despite the paradoxical fact that both prewar specimens that were now to keep the Campbell flag flying were significantly older than the two postwar steamers they had displaced. Equally, a percentage of passengers would be indifferent to the means of propulsion offered – or even perhaps completely oblivious, if one believes contemporary accounts of the feisty atmosphere on board the Cardiff-Weston ferry on Sundays, when much of Wales was then 'dry' and a cross-channel trip could offer the considerable attraction of unrestricted access to a drink or two, in convivial company.

But from a managerial viewpoint, the motor-vessels offered a slightly more economic means of operation, in terms of fuel costs, even if crew numbers were little different to the paddle-steamers they had replaced. Both ***St. Trillo*** and ***Westward Ho*** were significantly smaller than the Queens, but offset against this was a need to trim capacity anyway as demand had reduced on upper Bristol Channel sailings after the Severn Bridge opened. It was also hoped in 1968 that a third motor-vessel – ***Balmoral***, then in Red Funnel Isle of Wight service – might be acquired when replaced by one of the new car-ferries planned for the Cowes crossing. It seems that ***Queen of the Isles*** was never seen as a permanent fleet member by Clifton Smith-Cox, although he was sufficiently pleased with her service at the end of 1967 to agree

a further charter-period for her in 1968, so as to keep open the north Wales station now that ***St. Trillo*** had become the secondary Bristol Channel ship.

The retirement of Mr A. R. (Arthur Roy) Boucher as Chairman of P. & A. Campbell Ltd was announced at the 75th Ordinary General Meeting at Cardiff on 30th January 1968, with Clifton Smith-Cox assuming the role of Chairman accordingly. He paid tribute to the long service – practically a quarter of a century – of his predecessor in these terms: '... *your Directors are extremely sorry that after many years association with the Company, Mr Arthur Roy Boucher, who, until the end of October was the Chairman, has retired. I have no doubt that shareholders would wish to extend to him their thanks for all the work which he has done. His colleagues will certainly miss him ... your Board invited me to become Chairman of the Company on Mr Boucher's retirement.*' The rest of the new Chairman's statement contained a number of messages, some optimistic and others less so. On a positive note, reference was made to the success in 1967 of the rapidly-developing cross-channel coach excursion business to France carried out in the P. & A. Campbell Ltd name in the south-east, and to the planned introduction in 1968 of 'No-Passport' day-trips to Belgium, in association with Townsend Bros. Ferries as well as to the retention of a north Wales operation as a result of the decision to again charter the Isles of Scilly vessel ***Queen of the Isles***. Less pleasant matters were references to losses made by ***Bristol Queen***, and her withdrawal following her wheel damage. It is worth mentioning here that George Nott Industries became European Ferries Ltd in 1968, which organisation went on to acquire Thoresen Car Ferries Ltd in that same year. Despite this change to the parent company structure the Annual Report and Accounts of the subsidiary company P. & A. Campbell Ltd continued to be published and presented wholly separately.

St. Trillo is well laden with passengers in this official P. & A. Campbell Ltd postcard view. Together with Westward Ho, the two motor-vessels maintained Bristol Channel services in 1968.
Author's collection

A sanguine look ahead was provided in the Winter 1967 edition of *Ship Ahoy*, which balanced regret at the loss of the paddle-steamers with a recognition that the less attractive motor-vessels were at least a lot better than nothing:

'... The final decision to withdraw both paddle-steamers from service has been taken, and although far from unexpected, their loss, to those of us for whom so long paddle steamers have been a refuge, relaxation and a "way of life", will leave a deep sense of grief and nostalgic memories. But this should not prevent us from being grateful to the Company for having retained these relics of a more gracious era thus far into the jet age. Now that "progress" in the form of two pre-war diesels has come to stay, let us hope that these little ships will bring happiness to many and prosperity to the White Funnel Fleet – but may we also hope that a fair proportion of the profits accruing from these comparatively economical vessels will be used to improve the standard of passenger amenities. For instance, while we can never again expect the gleaming silver and snowy linen of the paddle-steamer heyday, surely we can now anticipate something better than squashy cardboard cups, dreary pork-pies and soggy sugar! Also, could not some reasonable degree of shelter be provided at Barry Pier, where a long wait on a wet, windy and seat-less platform can mar the memory of an otherwise happy day?'

Further White Funnel Fleet manoeuvrings, 1968

St. Trillo stayed in north Wales after wintering at her Port Dinorwic base, to operate early-season sailings between May 5th-24th, including tendering to the now annual Swedish-American liner visit which was undertaken that year by the new *Kungsholm*. *Westward Ho* opened Bristol Channel sailings at Easter, to be joined by *St. Trillo* towards the end of May. Perhaps the most enterprising manoeuvre, after *Queen of the Isles* had taken the annual Isles of Scilly trip between May 25th-27th, was her positioning voyage to Menai Bridge which was advertised to carry passengers from Cardiff and Mumbles on Wednesday 29th May, scheduled to reach the island of Anglesey at 2330 that evening. It was recorded that twenty passengers availed themselves of this most unusual 'round trip' on *Queen of the Isles*, whose funnel had been painted white.

Whilst the established pattern of two-vessel operation was broadly followed in the Bristol Channel by *St. Trillo* mainly on the ferry and *Westward Ho* going further afield, there were instances of swapping of duties and on a couple of occasions *St. Trillo* made it as far as Bideford and Lundy. Capt. Philip Power had command of *St. Trillo*, and Capt. Hardcastle took *Westward Ho*. In north Wales, the long-serving Capt.

O. Williams remained on board *Queen of the Isles* as Pilot to her Scillonian master, Capt. Davies. A final manoeuvre of interest in 1968 was the so-called 'proving run' of *Queen of the Isles* from Cardiff round to the south-east, a two day voyage on 14th-15th September, in anticipation of her 1969 season in those waters.

Shortly after this on 2nd October, *St. Trillo* left for home at Port Dinorwic, leaving *Westward Ho* to close the Bristol Channel season on 8th October on a charter after ferry sailings ceased on 7th October. As the 1968 season ended the situation regarding the following year was somewhat unclear. It appeared unlikely that *Balmoral* would be available as hoped to join the White Funnel Fleet for 1969, and that *St. Trillo* would therefore again be needed for Bristol Channel duties in partnership with *Westward Ho*. This meant that no vessel was then earmarked for north Wales duties in 1969, as by this point plans for the deployment of *Queen of the Isles* in the south-east were being finalised. Fortunately however, things did not quite turn out in this way and the fortunes of Bristol Channel cruising were to take a very positive swing in March 1969, when the announcement was made that *Balmoral* – with her superior accommodation and speed – would after all be joining the White Funnel Fleet to offer an improved Bristol Channel service. This acquisition was to prove to be significant for a number of reasons. It allowed the immediate reinstatement of the north Wales station and, more importantly, it enabled stronger foundations for longer-term business to be laid down in the Lundy excursion trade as interest grew in the 'Atlantic Island'.

Acquisition of *Balmoral*

In retrospect the story of *Balmoral* is, to a great extent, the basis of the story of the last decade or so of the White Funnel Fleet in the Bristol Channel. Although rumours of her probable acquisition from the Red Funnel concern had circulated in 1968, her arrival in the Bristol Channel in May 1969 actually came as something of a surprise as schedules for the season had been drawn up on the basis that *Westward Ho* and *St. Trillo* were to maintain Bristol Channel operations. The eventual release of *Balmoral* from her Southampton-Cowes ferry and cruising duties was made possible by the introduction of another Red Funnel purpose-built car-ferry, *Norris Castle*, which joined the earlier *Carisbrooke Castle*, *Osborne Castle* and *Cowes Castle* on their cross-Solent duties. With the passing of *Balmoral* from Southampton, the era of Red Funnel Solent cruising thus came to an end, with no ceremony, after 15th September 1968. These cruises had served the Isle of Wight pleasure-piers of Ryde, Sandown, Shanklin and Ventnor (and of course Cowes) whilst going round the Island, as well as other south coast piers further afield. In moving to the Bristol Channel, *Balmoral* was reunited with her old running-mate *Westward*

St. Trillo wintering at Port Dinorwic.
Richard Danielson collection

Ho (formerly *Vecta*). Retaining her name was a nice if somewhat ironic touch, if one looked back to the heady days at the turn of the century when the P. & A. Campbell Ltd 'flyer' *Cambria* battled it out with the Southampton company's paddle-steamer *Balmoral* when she, too, had a white funnel. When the motor-vessel *Balmoral* entered service in 1949 she was in effect a replacement for her 1900-built namesake, which had been broken up after her arduous Second World War duties.

Why was the acquisition of *Balmoral* such a sound move for P. & A. Campbell Ltd? After two decades of active Red Funnel service, when she had been very well maintained, she certainly still had plenty of life left in her. Her employment on the Southampton-Cowes ferry and local excursions had been less punishing than the livelier conditions and longer hours she was to encounter in the Bristol Channel. On summer Saturdays she had worked a round trip between Southampton and West Cowes at three-hourly intervals, and during her final season her regular sailings had been enlivened, on 16th June, by a notable CCA charter proceeding eastwards from the Solent to Littlehampton, Worthing, and off Brighton, and had run a number of excursions to view the last traditional Cunarder *Queen Elizabeth*, then in her final year. Her fate was sealed by the launch of the new larger-capacity car-ferry *Norris Castle* at the Vosper-Thornycroft Woolston yard on 8th August 1968, and she had been advertised for sale shortly afterwards. It was said that British Railways (Southern Region) had expressed interest in *Balmoral* as a possible substitute for their paddle-steamer *Ryde*. It was, perhaps, a sign of the times that *Norris Castle* was notable compared to her predecessors by having greater heavy-vehicle capacity and commensurately less passenger accommodation.

Maybe one could at this stage advance the view that it was the essentially functional nature of *Balmoral* – her size, facilities, economy, speed, reliability and general suitability for the Bristol Channel – that was to underpin the future of the White Funnel Fleet at the time she joined it. These same characteristics were to ensure her own longevity within the Campbell fleet, as well as afterwards. A south of England newspaper described her characteristics in concise form when launched at Southampton twenty years earlier and when it was stated that her role would be for use on the Southampton-Cowes passenger service, or for excursion trips, or tender work to liners.

JOHN I. THORNYCROFT & CO., LTD.

BALMORAL: The motor passenger vessel *Balmoral*, building to the order of the Southampton, Isle of Wight, and South of England Royal Mail Steam Packet Co. Ltd more popularly known as the Red Funnel Line, was launched on June 27th by John I. Thornycroft & Co. Ltd, at their Woolston works. Ordered to replace the vessel of the same name rendered unserviceable through war duties, the *Balmoral* will have an overall length of 203ft 7ins., and a breadth on deck of 30ft, with a loaded displacement of 530 tons. She will be classed by Lloyds Register, and will have Ministry of Transport certificates for the carriage of passengers.

The *Balmoral* is a twin-screw vessel, and will be driven by two Sirron oil-engines, built at Thornycroft's Woolston works, each of 600 b.h.p., at 300 r.p.m. It is estimated that the speed of the vessel will be 15 knots. The lines and general layout are based on those of the Isle of Wight Company's *Vecta*, built by Messrs. Thornycroft and Co. Ltd in 1938. On the promenade deck forward there will be an observation saloon with bar, and aft an entrance house. The dining-room, forward on the main deck, will have seating accommodation for 66 persons. The pantry and galley are at the forward end of the dining-room, and at the after end an up-to-date cocktail bar is being installed. The windows to these compartments are large and rectangular, giving good range of view. The car-space at the aft end of the main deck is partly sheltered by the promenade deck, and has an area of 1,060 square ft. Large double-doors will be fitted in the bulwarks to enable easy loading and discharging of cars. The *Balmoral* was named by Mrs C. B. Pinnock, wife of the Chairman of Red Funnel Line.

Balmoral would prove to be relatively economic to operate, and essentially reliable. She was capable of slightly higher speeds than *St. Trillo*, and better equipped for catering, having originally been fitted with a waiter-service restaurant. In fact she was generally regarded as highly suitable for her new duties, and the deal struck with the Southampton company for a ten-year demise charter reflected a lesson learned after *Vecta* had been purchased outright in 1965. By leaving her ownership with Red Funnel any need to update her to meet Board

Early in her new White Funnel Fleet career, **Balmoral** *has arrived at an uncharacteristically deserted Ilfracombe Pier.*   Ilfracombe Museum

of Trade requirements was avoided. The terms of the demise-charter were that after ten years *Balmoral* would finally change ownership for a nominal £1.00, but in the meantime her passenger certificate duly announced that she had been chartered by Townsend/European Ferries. The scene was thus set for *Balmoral* to make her Bristol Channel debut on Friday 23rd May 1969, on Cardiff-Weston ferry duties, having received her new White Funnel Fleet funnel colours at Cosen's Weymouth yard a few days earlier. Her Red Funnel career had thus lasted less than twenty years, between 1950 and 1968, and after spending the winter of 68/69 at Southampton she left Weymouth at 1300 on 16th May 1969 and arrived at Barry at 1130 the following day. She did not have a high-profile 'launch' into P. & A. Campbell Ltd service, doubtless due to the relatively late stage at which the deal had been confirmed. The media did however make it clear that benefits to passengers would result from her greater speed, which would allow slightly more trips to be run from Bristol and Weston.

A modest 'column-inch' type-advertisement was placed in the south Wales newspapers to announce the debut of *Balmoral*, and a rather complicated promotional pricing structure which (if one sat down with a calculator, and a few spare minutes) seemed to suggest a tapering rate of discount applied to the well-established advance-purchase coupon offer used for many years:

NEW ADDITION TO WHITE FUNNEL FLEET

Able to carry well over 800 passengers at 15 knots - and offering spacious accommodation with excellent catering facilities - the mv *Balmoral* will join *Westward Ho* in the Bristol Channel to provide a faster, more extensive service than was originally planned. With this in mind the Company have decided to make a further issue of:

COUPON BOOKS ALLOWING REDUCED RATES FOR
STEAMER TRAVEL
FOR SEASON 1969

Book One costs £2.15s 0d, and buys steamer tickets worth £4.
Book Two costs £2.5s 0d, and buys steamer tickets worth £3.
Book Three costs £1.10s 0d and buys steamer tickets worth £2.
Each book contains coupons which are exchangeable for steamer tickets during the season and may be used by the holder to buy tickets for other members of his family including children.

She ventured further west on her second day in service, showing herself at Mumbles after having run down from Cardiff, Penarth and Barry to Ilfracombe on Saturday May 24th, 1969 before crossing to Wales in the pattern established some ten years earlier (after the demise in 1958 of the 'Swansea steamer') to cater for south Wales holidaymakers seeking a week in Ilfracombe by means of weekly Saturday crossings as distinct from just day-trippers. Very soon she had become a regular sight all round the Bristol Channel ports still used by the White Funnel Fleet, and one notable further-flung outing on Sunday 24th August 1969 was to Tenby, prior to running a cruise round Caldey Island, and along that exceptionally scenic part of the Pembrokeshire coast.

Features of the 1969 season from bills

A good idea of the range of trips that could now be offered by the two former Red Funnel ferries can be gained from looking at what was able to be advertised from the elegant pier at Clevedon. There was no longer a regular 'Bristol boat' as there had been in the early-1950s, which then enabled practically daily departures from the pier at Hotwells, and so the well-located pier at the north Somerset town of Clevedon was an important source of traffic on the English side of the Bristol Channel. Clevedon Pier still received a remarkably good service which perhaps reflected its long-standing and loyal customer base as well as the fact that Clevedon was the home of Clifton Smith-Cox himself, and where one might expect a close personal interest in keeping business buoyant there. The good tidal range at Clevedon Pier meant that calls could often be fitted in to whatever schedule the tides imposed on the Cardiff-Weston ferry vessel. Occasionally

there would be days when a departure might be made from Bristol to a down-Channel destination, and this would embrace a Clevedon call. Thus the handbill for the period July 6th to October 4th 1969 showed that over a roughly ninety-day period, departures were offered from Clevedon Pier by boat on twenty-eight days. In addition to this, there were a further twenty-one days when a bus would run from the Pier Gates at Clevedon to connect with a sailing from Birnbeck Pier at Weston super Mare, so that on average there was an excursion of some sort on offer every other day throughout the summer. The tides imposed subtle variations in cruises where a few minutes extra, on a bigger tide, could be exploited to advertise a different cruise. An example of this could be seen in the occasional offering of a cruise up the Severn, such that on Saturday 26th July one of these was advertised to view the 'new' Severn Bridge, taking two hours and five minutes, without calling anywhere. A couple of weeks later that advertised for Sunday 10th August was booked to call at nearby Portishead (which was quite unusual by this time) after departure from Clevedon and take two hours and twenty minutes for the round trip. As an alternative to staying aboard for the whole up-river trip, this cruise permitted around one and a half hours of time ashore at Portishead. This option would of course be of more interest to those who had come across the Channel beforehand than the Clevedon faction. Older regulars at Clevedon could recall that before the Second World War such a trip along the coast from Clevedon to Portishead might have been coordinated with an excursion on the remarkable Weston, Clevedon and Portishead Light Railway, long since sadly vanished.

Rather more esoteric on Clevedon handbills was the mention of inclusive three-day trips by coach from Bristol, via the Townsend-Thoresen ferry between Southampton and Cherbourg in order to visit Brittany: these were advertised to leave on four Wednesdays during the season with return by Friday afternoon. More mention of this other P. & A. Campbell Ltd activity was made in the section on the cross-channel coach excursion business.

1969 bills for Weston super Mare were marginally bigger, reflecting the more or less daily Cardiff & Penarth ferry crossings from Birnbeck Pier, as well as occasional down-Channel options. Some of these might be arranged on a day where, after a single morning ferry crossing from Wales, the steamer would then proceed from Weston directly to Ilfracombe, and occasionally offer a cruise beyond. Unlike the Clevedon bills, Weston bills placed some emphasis on the attraction of the newly-opened Butlins Holiday Camp at Barry Island, by

Westward Ho sustained serious collision damage at Weston super Mare in June 1969 and is seen here in Cardiff's Roath Dock undergoing repairs.
Richard Clammer collection

offering an inclusive ticket to cover travel across the Channel and day-admission to the camp, entitling them to all its amenities until 1830 hours. If the steamer happened to be sailing from Weston to Cardiff, this would involve a train between Cardiff and Barry Island, or vice-versa, depending on the tides. Through booking arrangements with British Railways were in place locally, and the ships' Purser carried a stock of train-tickets to issue to steamer passengers when necessary.

A traditional feature of P. & A. Campbell Ltd handbills was reference to sporting fixtures when these tied in with sailings. One such example in 1969 was on Saturday 13th September when football at Cardiff – Cardiff City versus Leicester City, or Cardiff RFC versus London Welsh – could be enjoyed by Westonians leaving their pier at 1010 for Cardiff. Barry Pier again featured in such arrangements, and return from Cardiff was offered at either 1554, by way of a boat-train from Cardiff General to Barry Pier for a 1630 sailing, or directly from the Pier Head at 1840. Cardiff bills were very substantial affairs, and included Penarth and Barry timings, with three or four successive issues being needed to deal with the whole season between Easter and October. The other main bills published were for Minehead, Lynmouth, Ilfracombe and Swansea & Mumbles Pier jointly.

Development of the Lundy trade in 1969

The entry of **Balmoral** into White Funnel Fleet service in 1969 coincided with interesting times on the Atlantic island of Lundy. Having been in private ownership for many generations, 1969 marked a significant turning point in the fortunes of the island, following the death on June 23rd 1968 of Albion Harman, the son of Martin Coles Harman, and in whose ownership Lundy had been vested since the 1920s. The death of Albion Harman saw his one-third ownership of the island (his two sisters each owned the other thirds) initially transferred to his widow. The three lady-owners decided to sell the island in 1969, and the property was duly valued and an auction arranged to take place on Friday 18th July, at Barnstaple. Throughout this time day-to-day affairs on the island remained in the hands of Felix Gade, the long-serving Lundy 'Agent' who had overseen the postwar resumption of steamer calls at Lundy in 1949.

Clifton Smith-Cox had enjoyed harmonious relations with the Harmans, and had been a frequent visitor to Lundy during the 1950s and 60s. He was acutely aware of the potential implications of the impending change of ownership, and worked closely with Felix Gade. There was mutual benefit to the island and to P. & A. Campbell Ltd through sailings at twice-weekly or occasionally thrice-weekly intervals which were the main means of transporting visitors. By the time of the auction sale of Lundy it was made clear to prospective purchasers that an agreement was in place for P. & A. Campbell Ltd to be the sole operator of excursion sailings to the island, for a period of ten years from January 1st 1969. As the P. & A. Campbell Ltd business to Lundy necessitated the retention on the island of launches for landing passengers, this arrangement was clearly reasonable given the commitment to the ten-year charter of **Balmoral** from the Red Funnel concern. Landing Fees of two shillings per adult and one shilling per child payable for passengers landing from P. & A. Campbell Ltd ('the Licensee') steamers were quoted in the new Agreement, and elsewhere reference was made to the provision of housing accommodation for their personnel on the island, as well as equipment and moorings for the boats, all of which was to be honoured by the purchasers. The island ('the Licensor') was, in return, to be responsible for the provision and maintenance of a suitable landing stage on the island.

As it turned out the island changed hands for £150,000 and became the property of the National Trust which in turn leased it to the Landmark Trust. Greater public awareness of the existence of Lundy was generated by the circumstances leading up to this transaction, which involved a donation by millionaire 'Union' Jack Hayward to ensure Lundy was kept for the nation. This heightened awareness was good for the White Funnel Fleet's business and record levels of traffic to Lundy were recorded in 1969. The by-now established pattern of two-vessel Bristol Channel operation continued with **Westward Ho** and the 'new' **Balmoral**, as **St. Trillo** saw out her last season in north Wales and **Queen of the Isles** was engaged in the south-east of England.

A major event for Lundy was the Dedication ceremony on Sunday September 28th, 1969 involving **Westward Ho** making a special sailing to the island from Ilfracombe. She was supported by **St. Trillo**, as relief vessel, together carrying over 1,100 passengers on what turned out to be the last day of service for the latter ship. The Ilfracombe handbill described the special trip thus:

NATIONAL TRUST DEDICATION CEREMONY at LUNDY

11.00 am Special Excursion to LUNDY ISLAND (to land) and also a Grand Cruise around the Island.

After leaving Ilfracombe at 11.00 am the *Westward Ho* will proceed to Lundy, thence Cruising around the Island, before landing passengers at about 1.30 pm. During the cruise passengers will have an opportunity of viewing from the steamer – the Island, Church of St. Helena, Knight Templar Rock, Lighthouses, Tibbett's Point, Gannets Bay, North Light, St. James Stone, Jenny's Cove, Shutter Point, The Rattles, Rat Island, etc.

Leave Lundy for the return journey, 5.30 pm, arriving back at Ilfracombe about 7.10 pm, Special Cheap Return Fare to include the Cruise, also landing on the Island, 26/6d.

Writing in the *Illustrated Lundy News & Landmark Journal* in the summer of 1970, John Smith (the Chairman of the Landmark Trust) made a number of points regarding the policy that was to be adopted by the new owners of Lundy, and which was to have a bearing on the fortunes of the White Funnel Fleet's excursion sailings to the island in the ensuing decade. Defining Lundy as 'a world apart', he laid down certain policies: '*Lundy – thanks to the Harman family – offers simplicity and tranquillity, which are now rare elsewhere. Therefore Lundy should not try to offer things which can be got elsewhere, if that would endanger these qualities. The motto should be: "Lundy offers you nothing but itself"*'. He continued: '*... Getting to Lundy should not be too easy. It should be a bit of an adventure, to sort out a little those who try, and so that those who have been there are a little different from those who have not ... However, the island must be kept supplied and visitors must not suffer needless inconvenience or disappointment. Therefore our policy over landing should be not to make it easier but to reduce the number of occasions on which it is impossible*'.

The immediate developments on Lundy that followed the change of ownership were more to do with improving the infrastructure, principally in the shape of accommodation for visitors, rather than anything that impinged on the running of steamer services. When the island acquired a larger ferry of its own shortly afterwards, the coaster **Polar Bear**, this vessel had far greater cargo capacity than her fishing-boat predecessor **Lundy Gannet** but she still only carried twelve passengers and therefore had no appreciable effect on P. & A. Campbell Ltd passenger figures. These continued to show gradual increases over the next few years as more folk discovered the unique charms of the unspoilt and still – occasionally – inaccessible island out in the Channel, frequently invisible from the Devon & Cornwall coast, yet often standing sentinel on the horizon.

Other aspects of the 1969 season

After her first season of 1969 **Balmoral** continued to run in tandem with **Westward Ho** in the 1970 and 1971 seasons, but the breakdown of the latter led to its demise after 1971 and the withdrawal by P. & A. Campbell Ltd from much of their upper Bristol Channel business. This in turn led to the Lundy trade becoming a greater proportion of the business left in the 1972 season and afterwards as **Balmoral** continued on her own. However, we are jumping ahead here, and now look at a more anecdotal account of what Bristol Channel cruising appeared like to a non-enthusiast in 1969. After then considering how the former Red Funnel duo were deployed in 1970/71, the story then turns to the next major step in the Company's fortunes, the demise of the 'ferry'.

The company also continued to promote a wide variety of coach-excursions in connection with the sailings and one odd one that seems to have been tried in 1970 was for Cardiff & Penarth passengers who were given the option, on the second of four 'ferry' departures on Sunday August 23rd (at 0930, 1145, 1425 and 1900 (ex-Barry Pier) from Cardiff to Weston) to proceed to Longleat House in order to view the lions, then a novel attraction as an excursion. The other vessel was advertised at 0830 from Cardiff (via Weston) to proceed to Ilfracombe before then cruising to off Clovelly and around Lundy: this was a CCA charter for which it was subsequently reported that numbers and weather were disappointing.

The new **Balmoral** did not attract all of the attention in 1969, however, and some delightful quotes can be found in this newspaper report which documented an unusual trip carried out on Sunday June 1st, 1969 by *Westward Ho* from Weston-super-Mare to Mumbles and Tenby, when the Paddle Steamer Preservation Society arranged a special charter sailing. A correspondent of the *Bristol Evening Post* by the name of Ray Dafter penned this account. Pat Murrell, then involved in the organization of the special sailing, went on to become one of the prime movers, in 1986, in the **Balmoral** Restoration Fund, as well as spending a number of seasons on board her as Purser in Waverley Excursions Ltd days in the 1990s and subsequently:

RAY DAFTER ON A VOYAGE OF REDISCOVERY...
and the woman on the beach didn't even care
'With our ship safely anchored in the bay we went ashore ... "And where have you come from?" asked a woman on the beach. "Weston super Mare" I replied, trying to sound nonchalant. "Very nice too" she said, and walked off uninterested. I felt she had not grasped the importance of our visit; the pioneering spirit which had swept us on to this shore. After all, the Welsh resort of Tenby has not been visited by a ship from Weston for more than 30 years. I suppose we should have taken something to mark the occasion: a message of greetings to Tenby's leading citzens perhaps. Or a stick of Weston rock. The tide was out when we arrived but the organisers had planned for this. The *Tenby Queen* and other pleasure craft came out to meet us and ferried us ashore. It would not have been more impressive if natives in canoes had come out to greet us. Suddenly the resort was bustling with 350 visitors who had ventured on the special long day cruise on the mv *Westward Ho*.

"You could call this a voyage of rediscovery" said Mr Patrick Murrell, secretary of the Bristol Channel branch of the Paddle Steamer Preservation Society. "It was because no one has made this journey for such a long time that we decided to do it for our annual outing. We like to do something different" he said. "I am sure there are many people in and around Bristol who do not realise how beautiful the coastline of Wales is". The outing scored another first. "Up to now we have always gone on steamships but this year we are using a motor-vessel. We are going modern." said Mr Murrell.

The *Westward Ho*, built in the late-1930s is modern to paddle-steamer preservationists, I suppose.

Up on the bridge I found another paddle-steamer fan, Capt. Cyril Smith. "There never was a prettier ship to sail the Bristol Channel than the paddle-steamer", he said. "It is a pity we don't have the means to keep them going. They just were not economical." Capt. Smith spent 20 years at sea with the Royal Mail line before joining P. & A. Campbell. Wasn't his present consignment tame compared with his days on the high seas ? "Never", he said. "This is far more exciting. Here we go rock hopping. There is always something going on here but on the big craft you are always at sea". Capt. Smith said he could foresee the heyday of the pleasure-craft returning. "People are beginning to realise that sailing takes the strain off driving. A cruise can drain away the aggression which builds up in motoring".

With the Society's red, white & yellow flag flying from the mast we headed home again on the second leg of the 175 mile cruise. The trip started at Cardiff at 0815, ending at 2330. That is what they called a long day cruise. Most of the passengers travelled from Weston-super-Mare although Penarth & Mumbles were also

Westward Ho at Tenby, 1st June 1969, on charter to the P.S.P.S.
I. Ireland, Pat Murrell collection

ports of call. Most of the shipping enthusiasts boarded at Weston - members of the P.S.P.S., the Coastal Cruising Association and the Bristol Shiplovers Society. None of them was more enthusiastic than Mr Ernest Dumbleton, chairman of the P.S.P.S. Bristol Channel branch and vice-chairman of the Shiplovers. "I have seen some very interesting ships in the Barry Roads" he said. "But my main purpose has been to enjoy myself. Now isn't this so much more peaceful, tranquil than travelling on the roads?"'

Swansea: the move to the ferryport, 1970
The slightly greater turn of speed that **Balmoral** had over the older *Westward Ho* enabled a little more flexibility in planning the timetable, and made it that bit easier to reach some of the more far-flung destinations of the Bristol Channel which had been visited regularly by the paddlers in the earlier part of the 1960s. Another factor that influenced overall passenger carryings – and to an extent fitted in well with the increased emphasis now being put on Lundy sailings – was the decision made late in 1969 to invest in improved passenger facilities at Swansea. Behind the scenes, Captain George Gunn (who had been the master of Cardiff Queen during the 1950s when she had been the regular Swansea steamer, and still acted on Clifton Smith-Cox's behalf in certain matters affecting the continuing Swansea & Mumbles business) had been concerned at the deteriorating condition of Campbell's traditional berth at Pockett's Wharf, on the west bank of the river Tawe. Handbills referred to this berth as being at Swansea (South Dock Entrance), the term Pockett's Wharf being colloquial. He believed that, if better facilities could be created, Swansea passenger figures were still capable of growth if properly nurtured. This initial view was taken whilst two ships were still in operation and the Cardiff-Weston ferry was being sustained and, in the event, developments led by another shipping company provided the solution.

For many years the old City of Cork Steam Packet Company, latterly as the B&I Line, had run their traditional overnight 'classic' passenger service from Fishguard Harbour (in west Wales) to Cork in the south-west of Ireland. As car-ferries evolved in the 1960s the decision was made to abandon Fishguard in favour of Swansea, where a brand-new terminal and linkspan on the east side of the River Tawe would be known as the B&I Ferryport. This new terminal's proximity

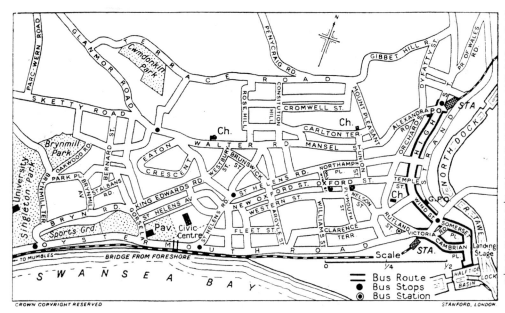

Town map of Swansea, from the 1939 edition of the Bristol Channel District Guide, showing the location of the one-time Pocketts Wharf hard by the South Dock half-tide basin at Swansea, described as the Landing Stage. This map illustrates the proximity of the berth to Swansea Victoria station, itself practically adjacent to the Rutland Street terminus of the Swansea and Mumbles Railway. Until its closure the services of this railway linked Mumbles Pier and Swansea, particularly useful if the steamer was only calling at one or the other for reasons of time or tide. After 1969 Pocketts Wharf (referred to on bills as South Dock entrance) ceased to be used by the White Funnel Fleet steamers, which instead made use of a berth on the opposite side of the River Tawe, further downstream and less tidally restricted.

Author's collection

to the motorway network was heavily promoted and a fast new multi-purpose ship was ordered, which could sustain the rather longer Swansea-Cork nine/ten-hour passage on a daily basis. Offering day and night sailings *Innisfallen* – as the new B&I Line ship was duly christened – took up the station in May 1969. An area of harbour wall to seaward of the car-ferry linkspan appeared, to Captain Gunn, to offer an ideal alternative to persevering with the traditional Pocketts Wharf berth, which was more tidally-limited and had very little car-parking. For a modest investment in car-park facilities on the other

side of the river, he argued, much new business would be attracted as passengers from all parts of south and west Wales could easily get to the new terminal by car through the Kings Dock entrance. In addition handling the vessel would be easier than turning off the South Dock entrance, or on occasions being limited by adverse tides to only being able to call at Mumbles Pier.

During the latter part of 1969 Captain Gunn entered into detailed negotiations with the local British Transport Docks Board (BTBD) management to develop a combined proposal for additional car-

After car-ferry services to Cork started running from the Ferryport (which had opened in 1969) **Balmoral** *and* **Westward Ho** *from 1970 made use of a berth immediately to seaward of where B+I Line's* **Innisfallen** *is seen moored at the linkspan. Being much further out of town, it was less accessible to foot passengers, but quite an improvement for those arriving by car.*

Author's collection

parking space for about 35-40 cars adjacent to the Ferryport to be laid out together with modified pedestrian arrangements, hand-rails, etc. Publicity for 1970 mentioned that the fee for the use of this new private car-park by excursionists would be two shillings and sixpence. In addition he arranged for the local bus-operator South Wales Transport to lay on connecting buses from the David Evans store, Princess Way (not far from the Quadrant bus-station) to the new White Funnel Fleet Swansea Ferryport terminal, which eased access from the town-centre for those on foot. A few years later the starting point of the connecting bus was extended back to Swansea High Street railway station.

The final BTDB estimate for the works was £1100, and it was assumed – at least by Traffic Manager Jack Guy at the Cardiff office, who was responsible for producing the detailed timetables of the White Funnel Fleet vessels – that they could be completed in time for the 1970 season. Swansea & Mumbles ship timings that year reflected both the new location and the reduced tidal constraints of the new berth. However, the parent company, in the person of Company Secretary Ernie Harris, took some persuading that capital investment of this nature was justified. As late as February 1970, Captain Gunn was still arguing forcefully (despite originally having had the approval of Group Company Chairman Roland Wickenden, and of Clifton Smith-Cox who had delegated to him the negotiating responsibility), that the investment would be repaid by the additional business gained within two to three years. It was also argued that additional rental costs (payable to the BTDB) of £120 p.a. would be recouped by the car-parking charges raised. It was feared that without the new berth the remaining Swansea traffic would diminish further. As things turned out the work was completed on time, Captain Gunn was proved right, and Swansea enjoyed better services for much of the 1970s than had been the case during the 1960s.

Westward Ho broadly tended to sustain Cardiff-Weston ferry and other up-Channel services during the 1970 season whilst **Balmoral** was utilised mainly on longer down-Channel runs. In simple terms 'big' tides enabled more ambitious schedules to be offered as a vessel could proceed further down the Channel in the morning and still be able to return in the evening. An example of such longer duration trips from Swansea was that offered on Thursday July 16th, 1970 to Padstow in Cornwall. This was billed as a 'Grand Day Excursion', the critical factor being the time of the tide on the River Camel. An 0800 departure from Swansea Ferryport to Ilfracombe, calling en-route at Mumbles Pier, preceded departure from the premier north Devon resort to Padstow for arrival at 1435, whilst there was still sufficient tide there to enable a short cruise to be offered from Padstow, passing Polzeath, Pentire Point and proceeding towards Port Isaac. The return departure time from Padstow was advertised at 1615, arriving back at Swansea at 2250, a particularly full days work for **Balmoral**. The previous day had similarly made the most of the tides when a slightly more leisurely departure at 0905 from Swansea to Mumbles and Ilfracombe preceded departure from that port to Tenby, in distant Pembrokeshire, with an advertised arrival at 1425. The opportunity was taken to offer a short cruise from Tenby around Caldey Island before **Balmoral** retraced her steps at 1600 for Swansea, arrival back being advertised at 2125.

A look back at the 1960s

Huge changes had been made during the decade of the 1960s, and what looked like a new, stable fleet position at the end of 1969 with two motor-vessels on Bristol Channel duties made an interesting comparison with the deployment of two paddle-steamers at the commencement of the decade. In the intervening years there had been experiments involving new technology and in different trading areas, but now it appeared that a

Visits by White Funnel Fleet steamers to Padstow Harbour, in north Cornwall, were only of an occasional nature owing to its distance beyond the natural outermost limits of the Bristol Channel. Calls were revived in 1963 by Bristol Queen, *after a lapse since prewar times. After the paddlers had gone, the slightly greater speed of the newly-acquired* Balmoral *over* Westward Ho *made it possible to offer trips on suitable tides, one such being advertised on Monday 25th August 1969 when departure was from Swansea (South Dock) at 0740 calling at Mumbles Pier and Ilfracombe. The return, to Mumbles Pier only, was scheduled for 2240, something of an epic day-out for south Walians.*   Author's collection

Westward Ho *about to arrive at Minehead Harbour around 1970/71. Her similarity to the later* **Balmoral** *is distinctly evident in this view.*
Author's collection

period of calm had arrived. Yet truly all was not well with the company finances, as the 1969 season had been exceptionally difficult. At the 78th Ordinary General Meeting of the Company, which was held at Cardiff on 29th January 1971 a detailed Statement by the Chairman was delivered which explained the rather poor results for the 1969 season. Referring to the losses incurred on the **Queen of the Isles** operation in the south-east, qv, and the closedown of the north Wales operation, it was pointed out that this would have happened after 1968 on the basis that **St. Trillo** was to have been needed in the Bristol Channel in 1969. As the acquisition of **Balmoral** had happened rather late in the planning-cycle money had already been committed to the overhaul of **St. Trillo** for 1969 Bristol Channel operations and, rather than pension off **St. Trillo** there and then her life was prolonged by a further, final season at Llandudno. Her breakdown at a critical time in 1969 had thus sealed her fate, and that of the north Wales station too. All these factors had had an adverse effect on trading results.

However, a brighter future was seen for core Bristol Channel operations and 1970 could be seen as the start of a new phase, with the two well-matched former Red Funnel motor-vessels settling down together in a slim-line company, shorn of all other operations apart from the relatively lucrative cross-channel coach excursion business being conducted in the Campbell name in the south-east on Townsend-Thoresen vessels. As the 1971 season approached, a note of caution was expressed regarding operating costs:

'... The cost of operating vessels has gone up very considerably in recent years and outstripped by far any comparatively small increases in fares which have taken place. The price of fuel oil in 1971 will be much greater: wage rates have increased as shareholders will know from reading the newspapers, the cost of repairs continues to go up and up and so, of course, does the cost of everything else upon

which our service relies; either by way of facilities which it uses, goods which it purchases, or labour which it employs. There have to be, as a consequence, sizeable increases in fares for the summer of 1971 such as will produce increased revenue to the order of some twenty-five per cent. Notwithstanding this, however, fares are cheap compared to most other forms of transport and certainly are cheap compared to what they were in pre-War days.'

The statement finished on a bullish note by making a confident prediction of restored profitability for the 1971 season, and also referred to the feasibility study of a car-ferry service between Swansea & Ilfracombe that was then underway. Clifton Smith-Cox had been interested in the potential for the deployment of a vessel from elsewhere in the European Ferries group which possibly would soon be available. He secured the agreement of Roland Wickenden, then Managing Director of Townsend Car Ferries Ltd, to commission a Scandinavian consultancy Aukner & Neuman A/S to carry out the economic feasibility study. Captain Gunn, then a Swansea Pilot but also the local P. & A. Campbell Ltd Agent and relief Master, was closely involved in this initiative to look at whether a viable car and commercial vehicle ferry operation might be established, having ascertained that the Swansea City Council was sufficiently enthusiastic to part-fund such a study, and that the Oceanography Department at Swansea University were prepared to become involved in hydrographic survey work at Ilfracombe Harbour. The study was to determine whether the anticipated traffic levels that an all-year round ferry service would generate would be sufficient to make an adequate financial return on the operating costs involved, based on a twice-daily service in the off-season, possibly increasing to three or four times daily in the high season, utilising a vessel for about 300 passengers which was estimated then to cost around £1.8m.

The main prompt for this study was of course the existence of the lightly-utilised new linkspan provided at Swansea Docks for the benefit of the new B&I Line ferry route to Cork which had commenced in 1969. For much of the day this facility lay idle as *Innisfallen* tended to just carry out one round trip between Wales and Ireland each day, usually turning round at Swansea in the early evening before returning overnight to Cork. Another factor, though less overt, was the potential to find employment for one of the early vessels from the Townsend cross-channel business which had been built up at Dover during the 1960s, and generate new income for P. & A. Campbell Ltd. Newer, progressively larger vessels of the 'Free Enterprise' class had been introduced, primarily designed for car-carrying, and these had been supplemented from 1968 by *Autocarrier* (of which more anon) as a commercial vehicle ferry. In the summer of 1970 the first four Townsend car-ferries (of which two ran from Dover to Calais, and two to Zeebrugge) were about to be joined by *Free Enterprise V*, with significantly greater commercial vehicle capacity and which, it was reasoned by P. & A. Campbell Ltd, would render *Autocarrier* surplus to requirements in the south-east. There was a rumour that *Free Enterprise II* might be a candidate for transfer, as Townsends had put her up for sale in 1969, but her tonnage was far in excess of that thought necessary for a Wales-Devon link, and she had a car-deck height which was insufficient for the commercial vehicles that such a route targeted.

The challenge was the absence of a comparable terminal facility or suitable road system in north Devon, together with the need to create new harbour access in Ilfracombe itself, in the Larkstone area. The findings of both the hydrographic study and the Norwegian consultancy report were encouraging, although the latter based its optimism on the assumption that an unidentified third party would meet the costs of constructing the terminal at Ilfracombe. Assuming that this occurred then the ferry operator would simply pay an annual user fee rather than take on the capital cost of building work as well. Captain Cyril Smith (who had had command of both *Westward Ho* and *Balmoral*) was involved in discussions with the Ilfracombe council, and used his knowledge and experience to produce drawings of the harbour works envisaged to address the conditions there. Questionnaires and surveys suggested that the substantial mileages saved by motorists between south Wales and Devon and Cornwall would make the route a popular one, based on anticipated fares of £3.00 per car and £1.00 per adult, and profitability was predicted.

Despite this confidence nothing actually materialised after the completed study was submitted, in July 1970, to P. & A. Campbell Ltd and to European Ferries, the owning group for Townsend Car Ferries Ltd. With hindsight it is hard to imagine how road access from a car-ferry terminal more or less adjacent to Larkstone at Ilfracombe could have

been achieved without considerable upheaval, or what scale of defensive breakwater construction might have been needed to prevent a linkspan from being damaged in heavy seas. The idea was not entirely forgotten, however, and surfaced again in the very last years of the life of the company, as close-down seemed imminent. The concept then was for a linkspan (available from elsewhere) to be attached from just inside of the pier gates leading to fingers parallel to but just short of the Stonebench at Ilfracombe, for a shallow-draughted vessel, despite the risk of disruption in adverse weather conditions. After the firm of P. & A. Campbell Ltd had ceased operations, as late as 1983 a Parliamentary debate was stimulated by the Member for North Devon on the matter. Whilst the transcript of this session in Hansard makes fascinating reading the proposal for a south Wales to Devon ferry link again came to naught.

Another idea considered in 1970 as a P. & A. Campbell Ltd initiative was for a ferry link between Avonmouth and Waterford, but this met with some resistance in Ireland from crane-operators whose jobs were thus threatened. Whilst Clifton Smith-Cox and James Ayres of Townsends investigated this, the former lost interest once it became apparent that, had it been pursued further, any new business would have been in the Townsend-Thoresen name.

St. Trillo finale

Despite the withdrawal of *St. Trillo* at the end of 1969, and with it the closure of the north Wales station, it was thought within the company that she might yet be used again somewhere if an appropriate commercial opportunity arose, or where another party could be persuaded to shoulder the burden of financial risk through a charter agreement. Evidence of this situation can be found in the response from P. & A. Campbell Ltd to the County Borough of Southend on Sea which had, in October 1970, written to Peter Southcombe noting that *St. Trillo* was laid up through lack of work, and queried whether there was any prospect that a steamer service could be laid on between Southend and either Margate or Ramsgate in 1971. The almost inevitable response from the company was that it was felt that the increasing operating costs for a vessel of the size of St. Trillo would, combined with a relatively short season, outweigh any likelihood of such a venture being profitable. In addition the difficulty of berthing at Margate Pier was seen as a strong reason not to attempt such a service. The polite counter-suggestion that Southend Council might wish to contemplate a charter met with an equally predictable response, and thus the old north Wales vessel slumbered a little longer before her eventual trip to the breakers. Before moving on to consider the 1971 season itself, we now turn our attention to the experiment which was undertaken by P. & A. Campbell Ltd with an extra vessel in the south-east during 1969.

Following the closure of the north Wales operation after the 1969 season and withdrawal of St. Trillo, Balmoral still occasionally ventured around to the Irish Sea to act as tender for the Swedish America Line visits by Kungsholm. She is seen here off Douglas, Isle of Man going out to the liner on 17th May 1970.
Stan Basnett

Queen of the Isles in the south-east

Background

A number of factors are relevant when considering the operation, in the 1969 season, of the 1965-built chartered motor vessel *Queen of the Isles* by P. & A. Campbell Ltd on excursion work in the south-east of England, quite apart from the continued availability of the 300 passenger-capacity vessel herself. Firstly, based on the evident success of their Continental coach-excursions in conjunction with the Townsend 'Free Enterprise' car-ferries, P. & A. Campbell Ltd believed that a market could exist for one of their own vessels to operate coastal and cross-channel cruises from resorts in south-east England. This view was encouraged by approaches from local authorities and pier companies seeking to revive excursion opportunities for passengers directly through the use of those piers in the area still extant. Three such bodies were the Hastings Pier Company, the Margate Pier & Harbour Company, and the Eastbourne Pier Company.

A second factor was the withdrawal of the 'Eagle Steamers' of the General Steam Navigation Company (hereafter referred to as GSN) who had, during their last season in 1966, operated an attractive trio of substantial, well-appointed motor vessels on various coastal and cross-channel excursion services from various Thames coast ports. There was a long tradition behind these. One of the trio of GSN motor-vessels was a survivor of WW2, namely *Royal Daffodil* (2) built in 1939. The other two replaced wartime losses and these were *Queen of the Channel* (2) dating from 1948, and *Royal Sovereign* (4) dating from 1949. Like Campbells GSN had faced difficulties after the war when seeking to reintroduce 'No-Passport' trips to the Continent from English piers, and had only succeeded in doing so in 1954 following successful lobbying by P. & A. Campbell Ltd. Whereas P. & A. Campbell Ltd had given up on the Sussex station after 1956, in the 1960s GSN continental excursions had continued and the company was still carrying good numbers to Boulogne, Calais and Ostend. GSN finally withdrew after the 1966 season: it was stated that as a result of the seamans' strike and the experiment of operating from Great Yarmouth, only 100,000 passengers were carried in 1966, compared to over 230,000 in 1965. All three vessels were put up for sale.

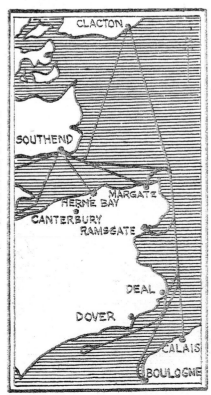

ROUTES OF EAGLE STEAMERS

A map of Eagle Steamers Thames & coastal routes taken from a 1960 Southend timetable booklet, which illustrates much of the area in which P. & A. Campbell Ltd operated cross-channel coach excursions from 1965 onwards, and themselves operated Queen of the Isles *in the 1969 season*

Author's collection

P. & A. Campbell Ltd were interested in filling the gap left by the withdrawal of GSN. By 1967 the cross-channel coach excursion traffic was developing nicely, and a plan emerged to acquire *Royal Sovereign* and convert her into a dual-purpose vessel which could have operated as an excursion vessel by day for P. & A. Campbell Ltd, and by night as a commercial vehicle carrier. The first negotiations for the purchase of *Royal Sovereign* were carried out by P. & A. Campbell Ltd, but she was eventually registered in the name of the Stanhope Steamship Company for tax purposes. When she became operational in her new guise in 1968 she was managed and run entirely by Townsend Car Ferries Ltd, within the European Ferries group, and in the event the vessel ran as *Autocarrier* carrying only commercial vehicles, on a very limited passenger certificate for drivers only, and so P. & A. Campbell Ltd excursions by this vessel never actually materialised. Planning for excursion use of this vessel had reached a fairly advanced stage for the 1968 season, and her ports of call would certainly have involved Margate (where the local authorities were keen to see a replacement to fill the gap left by the demise of the Eagle Steamers) and Hastings, where day-trips to the Isle of Wight were a possibility. A new edition of the White Funnel Handbook was produced for the 1968 season, which included a photograph of *Autocarrier* alongside those of fleetmates *Westward Ho*, *St. Trillo* and the chartered *Queen of the Isles*. Although no timetable bills for the prospective south-east excursions were distributed, the broad aims of P. & A. Campbell Ltd were known about by means of what would now be called 'leaks'. It must be questioned whether the style of accommodation achieved by the conversion of what had been an impressive excursion ship into a particularly functional-looking commercial vehicle carrier lacking open-deck space would have been a success traffic-wise. The practicality of loading on board temporary seating for daytime use on the vehicle-deck, and then removing it again before night-time freight duties, was thus never put to the test. The purchase of *Queen of the Channel* was also considered, in that case for exclusive use by P. & A. Campbell Ltd, but although the vessel was inspected this scheme never got off the ground.

The speculation surrounding this expansionist move by P. & A. Campbell Ltd took place during 1967. During this period the demise also occurred of the short-lived operations of the 'Coastal Steam Packet Company' in the Thames Estuary, using the former Clyde paddle-steamer *Jeanie Deans* renamed as *Queen of the South* (II). This had possibly suggested to P. & A. Campbell Ltd that where others had failed with costlier vessels of higher capacity, there might be a niche for them to exploit with a more economic motor vessel. They would have hoped that the public had forgotten the unreliability of that ill-fated paddle-steamer operation – and so it came about that in late-1968 plans were finalised for a 1969 season venture into excursion ship operation in the south-east using *Queen of the Isles*. The cross-channel coach excursion traffic continued in the P. & A. Campbell Ltd name, but was marketed separately.

An alternative view, however, was that P. & A. Campbell Ltd were rash to contemplate this south-east experiment at all given the prevailing general background of falling demand and failed businesses, not to mention the particularly restricted passenger capacity of the vessel they had selected. This brief episode of P. & A. Campbell Ltd history in the south-east is considered here at some length as it perhaps reflects the thinking of the company at the time in trying to build new sources of traffic, and use was judiciously made of available chartered tonnage to do so. That the episode was to prove financially unsatisfactory was regrettable, involving an element of bad luck, but it was nonetheless a bold attempt to diversify at a time of changing market circumstances.

Initial plans

The Chairmans' Statement of 30th January 1968 accompanying the company accounts for the twelve-month period ended April 1967 had touched on the demise of both Bristol Channel 'Queens' by late-August 1967, referring to the '… *thoroughly uneconomic* …' operation of older paddle-steamers. As well as mentioning the continued hovercraft operations in the south-east in order to gain experience of running that

*Townsend Ferries operated **Autocarrier** as a commercial vehicle ferry, and it is highly doubtful whether the plan to also use her for coastal excursion duties would have succeeded. Nevertheless she was illustrated as a member of the White Funnel Fleet in the 1968 White Funnel Handbook.*

Ian Boyle collection

type of craft, the increased success of the cross-channel coach-excursion traffic in conjunction with the Townsend car-ferries was recorded. In his first statement as Chairman, Clifton Smith-Cox (who had assumed the Chairmanship from Arthur Roy Boucher following his retirement in October 1967) went on to say that '... *investigations are being made into the possibility of operating a passenger service in the south-east.*'

It should be remembered that P. & A. Campbell Ltd had officially said, after the 1968 north Wales season with **Queen of the Isles**, that they were withdrawing from that station. The chartered Isles of Scilly vessel had on occasions been too small to cope with the high-summer levels of demand still sometimes being experienced, which limited her usefulness. **Queen of the Isles** was not at any stage intended for use either in the Bristol Channel or at Llandudno in 1969, and so by late-1968 became committed to the south-east experiment.

Proving Trials, late-1968

In anticipation of this venture, **Queen of the Isles** had made a 'proving run' to the south-east from the Bristol Channel at the end of the 1968 season, after she had returned from north Wales to Barry, leaving Menai Bridge overnight on 12th September. This trip was advertised to the public, with these timings:

Saturday 14th September
Barry dep. 0845, Ilfracombe dep. 1200, Penzance arr. 2100, dep. 2120, overnight passage
Sunday 15th September
Weymouth dep. 0830, Bournemouth dep. 1100, Eastbourne dep. 1830, Hastings dep. 1945, Dover arr. 2300.

Various connections were laid on for passengers to be able to join this trip at different ports: a boat-train ran from Cardiff to Barry Pier, a bus was laid on for Bristol passengers to join at Ilfracombe, and **Westward Ho** conveniently ran across from Swansea and Mumbles to arrive at Ilfracombe ten minutes before the **Queen of the Isles** was due away so as to offer a sea connection as well. South Coast passengers were also provided for, with a bus provided on the Sunday night back from Eastbourne to Bournemouth for those who had joined there. (Quite coincidentally, Sunday 15th September 1968 should have been the day on which **Balmoral** ran her final Red Funnel excursion prior to her withdrawal by the Southampton company, but adverse weather led to the cancellation of this trip).

Although it had been planned that **Queen of the Isles** would call at Margate Jetty for 'berthing trials' on Monday 16th September 1968, this call did not take place because of a heavy swell at the time. The vessel stood off and the Company representatives boarded her from a pilot launch. The omission of the Margate call was to prove disastrous for it was discovered later that the high superstructure of the vessel caught on and was easily damaged against the perpendicular piles of the jetty. (This had not been a problem for paddle-steamers with their wide sponsons nor for the screw-driven Eagle Steamers with their very wide belting, but the belting on **Queen of the Isles** was not wide enough to hold her off and the use of various types of fender failed to overcome the problem). Thus, in 1969 many calls at Margate were cancelled when it proved impossible to berth the vessel

Queen of the Isles proceeded around to the Thames coast on this 'proving run' but was unable to berth at Margate. Peter Southcombe and Clifton Smith-Cox (with trilby) can be seen boarding her, in the swell, from the pilot launch on 16th September 1968. The unsuitability of this vessel for berthing at Margate was to prove regrettable.

Peter Southcombe collection

At the end of the 1968 season **Queen of the Isles** *ran around from the Bristol Channel to the south-east on a 'proving run' to test her suitability for use in that region in the following year. She is seen here disembarking passengers at Eastbourne on 15th September 1968. Peter Southcombe (coat in hand) is on the pier. Compared to the paddle-steamers deck-space on board this little motor-vessel was somewhat limited.*

Peter Southcombe collection

without damage. From Margate **Queen of the Isles** proceeded to off Southend, towards Clacton, then to off Calais and back to Ramsgate where Messrs Gilbeys Floating Gin-Palace – namely the chartered ps *Ryde* – was encountered off Margate. **Queen of the Isles** then sailed for Penzance on Tuesday 17th September 1968.

The 1969 programme for **Queen of the Isles** was contrived to provide a commendably diverse range of coastal cruises and cross-channel excursion opportunities, from Sussex coast piers as well as serving London Tower Pier, Essex and various Kent coast and continental ports. Both Brighton piers were unavailable for use at this time. Of modest, trim appearance she was in truth a passenger/cargo vessel, with a substantial cargo-hold forward and her speed, when newly built by the celebrated Charles Hill shipyard in Bristol, was thirteen knots. Much behind-the-scenes activity was necessary to plan the details of the 1969 operation, and Captain George Gunn undertook condition surveys of the ports that **Queen of the Isles** would be using. Together with Passenger Manager Peter Southcombe he made the necessary arrangements for berthing with all the relevant Pier Companies and Harbour Authorities in England and on the Continent including: Sussex – Eastbourne, Hastings ; Kent – Deal, Margate, Ramsgate; Essex – Southend, Clacton; Continent, Ostend. Bunkering would take place abroad to exploit the lower fuel prices then on offer across the English Channel. Unfortunately Captain Gunn did not make independent inspections of Boulogne and Calais, since Clifton Smith-Cox was able to recall the arrangements that had applied for paddle-steamers in earlier years at the French ports, and had assumed that everything would still be in place for an excursion vessel. In reality, the rather different dimensions of **Queen of the Isles** were to prove problematic, especially when she berthed at Boulogne at low water on a big spring-tide, requiring passengers to negotiate an almost vertical gangway. In addition to this wide variety of calling-points, it was intended that **Queen of the Isles** would also serve Shanklin on the Isle of Wight, and London Tower Pier. Berthing overnight at Newhaven and at Dover would also occasionally be necessary.

By the early part of the year, then, the arrangements were in place for the planned commencement of the new venture in May 1969. Before this, use was made by P. & A. Campbell Ltd of **Queen of the Isles** and she found herself in familiar waters when programmed to run the now-annual Isles of Scilly mini-cruise. This was scheduled from Cardiff and Weston super Mare to Penzance on Easter Saturday April 5th, 1969, running over to St. Marys on Easter Sunday for a long day

trip, and then returning on Easter Monday to Cardiff. **Queen of the Isles** was then briefly used by the Isles of Scilly Steamship Company themselves for 'Flower Season' sailings in April 1969. The south-east programme was due to commence on Saturday 24th May 1969 with an inaugural cruise from London Tower Pier to Southend and Margate, but before this **Queen of the Isles** was also programmed to perform a Cardiff-Lundy day excursion on May 18th 1969 before taking up her new duties. Circumstances at Ilfracombe and a difference of opinion between Agent Fred Birmingham (who was for going) and Captain Evans about a viable level of passenger numbers prevented what would have been her only Lundy call from taking place that day. A nicely coloured special handbill was produced to advertise the positioning run from the Bristol Channel to the south coast.

A characteristic of the 1969 south-east programme was thus the wide variety of ports served and the diversity of different cruises offered. The season was planned to run for a little under four months, until Tuesday 16th September. The combination of Thames estuary and south coast sailings entailed an element of light running to position the vessel on some days. To illustrate the complexity of her roster an outline is given here of a typical extended weeks' operational cycle. It is worth recalling, by way of comparison, that after the Second World War with two vessels on the south coast in certain years, the P. & A. Campbell Ltd territory only ranged between Folkestone and the Isle of Wight, and did not include Belgium. It might also be observed, by a glance at an Eagle Steamers route-map from a few years earlier, that there was a notable correlation between the Thames estuary and Kentish locations once served by the GSN fleet and what P. & A. Campbell Ltd were now about to offer. Thus **Queen of the Isles** in 1969 was really attempting to serve two distinct territories, one of which had been familiar to P. & A. Campbell Ltd themselves up until the late-1950s and which featured Eastbourne, Hastings and Shanklin on the Isle of Wight, and Brighton (by coach connections as the landing-stages at both piers there were no longer available). The other was basically that of the old Eagle Steamers which comprised London Tower Pier, Southend, Clacton, Margate, Ramsgate and Deal, plus the continental ports: it will be recalled that the former booking-office premises at certain of these places had been acquired and were already in use for sales of the various cross-channel coach excursions. An inevitable result of attempting to serve these two territories with one ship was of course that the excursions on offer to the public would be spread rather thinly.

P. & A. Campbell Ltd.
Queen of the Isles schedules, 1969

Friday 27th June
From Hastings & Eastbourne   to Shanklin, IoW,
                                      (plus short coastal cruise)
(Return to Hastings at night by bus from Eastbourne)

Saturday 28th June   *off-service at Newhaven*

Sunday 29th June
From Eastbourne & Hastings   to Boulogne
(Bus connections from Brighton)

Monday 30th June
From Deal & Ramsgate   to Margate
                                       (+2hr Thames Estuary cruise)

Tuesday July 1st
From Ramsgate   to Ostend
(Bus connections from Margate)

Wednesday July 2nd
From Ramsgate & Deal   to Boulogne
(Bus connection outwards from Margate, steamer returned at night to
Margate thence bus connection for Ramsgate passengers)

Thursday July 3rd
From Margate   to Clacton
                                       (plus pm cruise towards Felixstowe)
(Bus connection from Ramsgate in morning, steamer returned at night
to Margate and Ramsgate)

Friday July 4th   *off-service at London*

Saturday July 5th
From London Tower Pier   to Southend & Margate
                                       (plus short coastal cruise)

Sunday July 6th
From Southend   to Calais

The period illustrated was broadly typical of the season, albeit with certain important variations to accommodate the Isle of Wight. Shanklin calls took place on a number of Fridays, and Tower Pier was served approximately fortnightly. To carry out this trip involved considerable light running, often overnight around the Kent coast in both directions, in order to start from and finish at London. The range of supporting bus journeys was noteworthy, and a number of round trips using bus/steamer options were offered in addition to the direct steamer trips evident from the above. Although neither of the piers at Brighton were in use for steamer calls at the time, a number of bus connections ran from Brighton to Eastbourne on days when there was a 'No-Passport' day trip from Eastbourne & Hastings to Boulogne.

Poor results

An account of her initial voyage on 24th May from London Tower Pier referred to the impressive ability of *Queen of the Isles* to turn her bows down-river without assistance from a tug, with around 130 passengers on board, some of whom were members of the Coastal Cruising Association on a nominated excursion. The weather was misty, about eighty passengers joined at Southend, and difficulties were later experienced in putting gangways ashore at the awkwardly-shaped pier at Margate (known locally as the jetty, but referred to by P. & A. Campbell Ltd personnel as the pier). Some late running was experienced, but *Queen of the Isles* nevertheless arrived back at Tower Pier twenty minutes early. Her first cross-channel trip was run on 25th May 1969 from Southend to Calais. Local trips from Margate were advertised the next day, and followed by a Ramsgate-Ostend run on 27th May. Her first cross-channel excursion on 29th May at 0945 from Hastings to Boulogne (with bus connections at 0745 from Brighton, and at 0830 from Eastbourne to Hastings) took modest numbers and was met by the Mayor and various dignitaries and girls in local costume. On the following day the first Shanklin cruise took about sixty passengers. These were not promising carryings initially, and the overall results from the season were to prove patchy – good in some places but poor in others.

The operation of *Queen of the Isles* was not without operational difficulties at the beginning of the season and her successive Scilly masters (initially Captain Evans, who was briefly replaced by Captain Ashford, and subsequently Captain Davies) kept the owners advised of a series of scrapes involving damage to piers at Ramsgate and at Eastbourne in early June, plus a collision with a motor-barge at Ostend. *Queen of the Isles* grounded on a sandbank at Boulogne on 15th June,

Queen of the Isles about to call at Hastings Pier during 1969. She offered a varied schedule of excursions along the Sussex coast as well as from the Thames estuary ports, with crossings to the continent as well.
Peter Southcombe collection

The condition of the landing-stages at both of Brighton's piers deteriorated after the cessation of White Funnel Fleet excursions after 1957, and **Queen of the Isles** *was unable to call during her 1969 season in the south-east. A ticket-office was maintained at Brighton Palace Pier to sell cross-channel coach excursions during the late-1960s, which departed from the nearby Southdown coach station. This postwar view illustrates the substantial landing-stage extension at the Palace Pier.*
Author's collection

The landing-stage at Brighton West Pier was an altogether more substantial affair, and this aerial view illustrates the large catchment area that the pier once served, as well as emphasizing the maintenance liability involved in keeping such a structure in good order, to suitable safety standards.
Author's collection

which caused propeller damage leading to excessive vibration. There was anguished correspondence between owner and charter-party, and repairs were effected when she was deliberately beached at Ramsgate, on 19th June when it was possible to attend to her safely at low-water. Considerable discussion ensued regarding insurance claims. Obviously incidents such as these, combined with poor figures on some sailings, contributed to a less than satisfactory financial performance.

One unsatisfactory aspect was the inability to offer adequate catering for all-day long trips. *Queen of the Isles*, when initially placed in service by P. & A. Campbell Ltd could basically only offer sandwiches, crisps and drinks and Peter Southcombe resorted to 'borrowing' stewards from Townsends in order to be able to offer something more substantial such as salads with cold meat or fish –although better than snacks, this was still not altogether what people expected on full-day trips. One particular positive feature however was that whilst the Townsend organisation had never been able to get access to the berthing facilities for their car-ferries at Ostend used by the Belgian state operator RTM, a smaller passenger-only vessel was able to dock unhindered within the commercial harbour area there. It was said that Townsends were distinctly surprised at the

prospect of this feature of the 1969 plan to deploy *Queen of the Isles*. Another feature of her cross-channel trips was the necessity to carry a wireless operator in order to comply with BoT requirements, which stretched the generosity of Townsends that bit further when Peter Southcombe arranged through the Senior Officer to 'borrow' these personnel, so that they could join the outwards sailing of *Queen of the Isles* at Eastbourne, Southend Deal or Ramsgate as required: he could have done the job himself.

The final results for the 1969 *Queen of the Isles* season when drawn up showed a substantial loss: income of around £25,000 was exceeded by costs of approximately £32,000. Charter fees accounted for about £12,000 of these costs. Perhaps *Queen of the Isles* was an unsuitable vessel for such operations, and did not attract passengers with her limited deck-space and catering facilities, restricted capacity and rather slow speed of around 12 knots. Furthermore the inability of the company to call at Brighton would have reduced earnings potential. The Statement by the Chairman accompanying the accounts for the twelve month period ended 31st April 1970 succinctly described the withdrawal of the vessel from the south-east:

'… During the summer of 1969 we operated a service in the South East of England … the operation of this service was of necessity expensive and had to be planned over the whole summer months. In the event the traffic in the early and late parts of the season proved extremely unsatisfactory and while in the peak weeks the vessel on journeying to the Continent did so fully booked on most occasions the revenue derived in this short period in no way compensated for the losses incurred during the other months. In addition, the coastal services … proved completely unsuccessful. The experiment was carried out with a view to seeing whether a cross-Channel service of this nature might have proved satisfactory and enabled us to build up a new source of revenue in the future. The experiment was not continued in the year 1970.'

The statement went on to acknowledge that as well as **Queen of the Isles** having to some extent reduced carryings on the P. & A. Campbell Ltd coach excursions using the Townsend Dover car-ferry services, '… *a very considerable stepping-up of competition* …' had occurred in the trade generally, with an awareness that the railway boats were now being better marketed for excursion opportunities. So ended another phase of P. & A. Campbell Ltd history: although **Queen of the Isles** was deployed again by her owners the Isles of Scilly Steamship Company on their main Penzance to St. Marys run during the summer of 1970, a short while later she was recorded as having been sold to the Tongan Government. As we have already seen, the cross-channel coach excursion business in the south-east of England would continue for a few more years in the Campbell name. After this interlude of P. & A. Campbell Ltd operation of a chartered vessel on its own account in the south-east, we now revert to the scene in the home waters of the Bristol Channel as the decade of the 1970s got underway, and where business efforts would now be mostly focussed.

The next turning point

Ignominy at the 1971 season-end

Westward Ho and **Balmoral** had run reasonably well in tandem during 1970, although both were now clocking up much higher daily mileages than those to which they might have been accustomed to in their more leisurely Solent days in Red Funnel service. Between them Cardiff-Weston ferry services were still maintained on a daily basis, in a time-honoured tradition which dated back to 1893. This was when the chartered paddle-steamer **Sea Breeze** had established the P. & A. Campbell Ltd presence, but time was running out now for the upper Channel services, both as a result of the opening of the Severn Bridge, and on account of the deteriorating condition of the ageing pontoon-berth structure at Cardiff Pier Head. The similar structure at Barry Pier, dating from Barry Railway Company days and only slightly younger than the Cardiff facility, was also facing increasing maintenance costs, which the company was having difficulty in justifying in relation to passenger earnings. As if this was not enough a third pontoon structure, that at Hotwells in the River Avon which enabled steamer calls to be made on the tidal River Avon at Bristol, was also giving increasing cause for concern, largely on cost-grounds in relation to diminishing passenger numbers. At Bristol and at Cardiff the days had long gone where the port authorities would automatically carry out routine maintenance in the certain knowledge of a healthy income from steamer operators as passenger numbers remained steady. Now, any necessity for capital expenditure inevitably led to the port authority seeking to reimburse themselves directly. We have already seen how the Newport landing-stage facility had reached the point where its continuation could no longer be economically justified after 1956, and so again in 1971 P. & A. Campbell Ltd were reaching the time where hard decisions would have to be made, particularly at the Pier Head at Cardiff.

Queen of the Isles *arriving at Shanklin Pier, Isle of Wight, on 11th July 1969. On most Fridays when she ran to the island, short coastal cruises (of about 90 minutes duration) were offered for the sum of ten shillings from Shanklin Pier before the return to Sussex.* Eric Payne collection

As if this was not enough, the partial collapse of Clevedon Pier the previous year had reduced the commercial potential of the upper Bristol Channel for the steamers still further. A final call by *Balmoral* had taken place on 11th October 1970, and the collapse occurred a few days afterwards when the structure underwent load-testing for insurance purposes. Thus another source of income for the White Funnel Fleet was in jeopardy as there was no immediate prospect of repairs being carried out. However, the clientele in that area were not overlooked in the 1971 season, as an arrangement was entered into with WEMS Coaches to run connecting buses from Clevedon (picking up at the sea-front Glass Pavilion at the Green Beach) to Weston for most sailings from Birnbeck Pier. A little extra enterprise was also shown, as the coach was used on a number of days to offer a link for Portishead customers as well.

What was to become one of the biggest sources of worry to the harried P. & A. Campbell Ltd management in 1971 turned out to be mechanical rather than structural in nature. The condition of *Westward Ho's* engines got steadily worse during 1970 and towards the end of the season the problems had become so serious that she was withdrawn from traffic prematurely, after problems on a return voyage up-Channel from Lundy on 18th September. Although she received a considerable amount of attention during the ensuing winter, it was known at the commencement of the 1971 season that all was not well down below on the former *Vecta*. As the commentary in *Harbour Light* (successor journal to *Ship Ahoy*) put it in June 1971: '... *it is hoped that the fine weather of both Easter and Whitsun, with its consequent good payloads, together with many regular and some new charters, may have contributed to the financial success of early season '71, and that the engine troubles plaguing* Westward Ho *will not have had a too deleterious effect'*.

The 1971 season got underway normally enough, with *Balmoral* opening sailings on Thursday 8th April and running over Easter, until Sunday 18th April when she retired for a few days to Barry Dock. Early May was to see her first brief sortie away from the Bristol Channel that season, to the Isle of Wight, and the full summer season started on 6th May with *Balmoral* running in the upper Channel on a cruise from Cardiff & Weston around the islands of Flat Holm & Steep Holm. *Westward Ho* made her first public appearance of 1971 a few days later, on Wednesday 12th May, and both vessels were thereafter scheduled to swap around between upper Channel and down-Channel duties quite frequently. Some intricate planning was necessitated by the visit of *Kungsholm* a few days later, which saw *Westward Ho* tendering at Avonmouth on Saturday 15th May for virtually the whole day, as well as running an evening cruise from Weston '... *through Walton Bay and around the luxury Swedish-American liner* Kungsholm ...' between 2015-2230. *Balmoral* had already then set off for a second White Funnel Fleet sortie away from the Bristol Channel in 1971, this time to north Wales and the Isle of Man where tendering to *Kungsholm* took place at Llandudno and at Port St. Mary on Monday & Tuesday 17th /18th May respectively. (This was to the 'new' i.e. 1967-built *Kungsholm*.)

At this stage, *Westward Ho* had only lost one day in service as a result of mechanical troubles, on Friday 14th May. Worse was to come on Saturday 29th May, and another whole days' worth of trips had to be abandoned as she broke down again. A more serious spell of breakdowns set in a week later when troubles started on the evening of Saturday 5th June, and led to her being out of service completely between Sunday 6th and Saturday 12th June, and running fewer services than scheduled on Sunday 13th June. *Balmoral* covered as much of the timetable as she could during this time, mainly down-channel at the expense of ferry and other up-channel sailings. Friday 11th June was an exception, as *Balmoral* took ferry sailings and abandoned a Lundy trip as the ailing *Westward Ho* lay in the Queens Dock at Cardiff receiving attention.

Demise of *Westward Ho*

A more settled spell of sailings running broadly to plan through July and August now gave the P. & A. Campbell Ltd management some respite. *Westward Ho* was seen at Lundy on Tuesday 31st August, but this turned out to be her final appearance there. As the 1971 season-end approached the situation became confused as a particularly serious breakdown on 2nd September led to the final withdrawal from service of *Westward Ho*, and an announcement that services would in future

be cut in order that only one vessel would be needed in service. A completely revised one-vessel timetable was issued for the period September 9th to October 12th 1971 after a few days where *Balmoral* again struggled heroically to cover as much as possible of the workload that had been planned for two vessels. This was headed:

> *Sailings from CARDIFF (Pier Head), PENARTH & BARRY PIERS*
> *by the Motor Vessel* **BALMORAL**
> **LAST TRIPS OF THE SEASON**
> *The following are our sailings for the remainder of the season.*
> *All previously issued timetables are cancelled.*

The breakdown was noted in the magazine *Cruising Monthly* for October 1971: '... *Westward Ho's port engine snapped two connecting rods while tied up at Bristol Hotwells: the engine was wrecked and the deckhead above damaged. The vessel returned to Cardiff, with her passengers, on one engine – the previously more troublesome starboard one. She has made no further sailings this season ... and it is most unlikely that she will resume service next year.*' This final deterioration in the mechanical condition of *Westward Ho* forced a decision which triggered the announcement of major service cutbacks, and it is known that the company had in fact already considered her disposal as well as the necessity for cutbacks in upper Channel services, and the withdrawal from the use of the pontoon-berth facilities at Cardiff, Barry & Hotwells.

The fate of *Westward Ho* was now sealed. A newspaper report on 22nd September 1971 was prompted by a statement that consideration was being given to the closure of ferry operations:

Bridge blamed as channel steamer services face axe
'Cross-channel passenger services out of Cardiff and Barry could be stopped next year because of competition from the Severn Bridge. P. & A. Campbell Ltd are considering withdrawing the 84-year old link because of a sharp fall in passenger traffic. This summer they have operated two passenger steamers – *Westward Ho* and *Balmoral*.

Limited use
The company's chairman and managing director Mr Sidney Smith-Cox, said last night, "The services have certainly run at a loss for the past two years. This is due almost entirely to the Severn Bridge. But there is no question of the company going out of business". He said limited use of the two ports, although not from the same pontoons, was being considered. Penarth might be used to some extent. "There will be no interference with the services from Swansea which, if anything, might be improved" he said. "Nor will there be any interference with other services in the lower end of the channel." The company, which belongs to the European Ferries organisation based in Dover, will issue a statement about next summer's services before the end of the month. Use of services from Cardiff and Barry this season are said to be similar to last year, when there were 52,000 boardings. This compares with 114,000 in 1964, before the Severn Bridge was opened. Yet at Swansea there were 9,000 boardings last year compared with 3,000 in 1964.'

The reference to Swansea in this statement was not entirely straightforward as minimal services were provided there in 1964, whereas by 1970 the development of Lundy trade had, together with other factors, led to more down-channel sailings being offered by what was still a two-vessel fleet. A few weeks later the promised statement regarding the future was made, and it is reproduced here in full:

'As a result of ever-increasing costs, the impact of the Severn Bridge and the high cost of maintaining facilities at Cardiff and Barry it has been decided to discontinue regular steamship (sic) sailings in the upper reaches of the Bristol Channel at the end of the 1971 season. A regular daily service between Swansea and Ilfracombe will be operated and a service from Ilfracombe to Lundy Island will be maintained on Sundays, Tuesdays and Thursdays. Other excursions from Ilfracombe will take place on the other days of the week. Certain calls will be made at Tenby and a number of journeys from Porthcawl to Ilfracombe will also take place. Full details of the foregoing services will be made available as early as possible. A number of connecting coach services from Minehead and elsewhere to Ilfracombe in connection with sailings to Lundy will be operated and it is hoped that arrangements can be made for through bookings to Ilfracombe by train and steamer from Cardiff and district. Birnbeck Pier at Weston-super-Mare will continue to be operated as a Pleasure Pier.'

It was also intimated that company hoped to secure an alternative embarkation point in Cardiff Docks for sailings, but this was not to materialise. No explicit mention was made of the withdrawal of *Westward Ho* in this statement, but the thinking was clear and the better-informed regulars knew at this point that she had now reached the end of her long career. However, there was some minor good news as well as it was announced that due to the fine weather it had been decided to continue channel steamer excursions until October 18th, 1971 and another, small bill later appeared to cover the very end-of-season trips, headed 'Extension of sailings: Last Trips of the Season'. The story of *Westward Ho* as an active P. & A. Campbell Ltd vessel effectively ends here, and at the end of October she left the Bristol Channel – with both shafts geared to one engine, and running at about 10 knots – for Hayle Wharf, in Cornwall, to lay-up.

However, the machinery damage she had sustained proved to have other complications for her owners, in terms of subsequent insurance claims with significant financial implications. The author is again indebted to Tony McGinnity for the explanation: with only one operational engine, which was itself in poor condition, her sale value was very much in question. The damaged English Electric diesel engine dated from the immediate postwar years and was long out of production. The only practical solution was to replace the damaged engine with another of similar horsepower although a good deal of adaptation would have been necessary to do this, and the cost of stripping out the old engine would be considerable. Then there would be the question of matching the engines to provide similar consistent output on both propeller shafts. On the advice of their consultant marine superintendents, West Marine Surveyors & Consultants Ltd., P. & A. Campbell Ltd submitted a claim to their insurers for two replacement engines, the cost of which by far exceeded the insured value of the vessel and thereby suggested she was a 'Constructive Total Loss'. Underwriters threw this claim out and a battle then ensued which became quite acrimonious. The underwriters, whilst conceding the proposed solution was the only practical one, sought to suggest that the vessel's value for insurance had been placed at too high a level.

To support this argument they obtained a valuation of the vessel from shipbrokers, which purported to show that had the vessel had been offered for sale prior to the accident its value would have been little more than scrap.

But, not for nothing had Clifton Smith-Cox fought so hard to keep P. & A. Campbell Ltd afloat, and a friendly expert was engaged who had acted as broker for the sale of other coastal passenger vessels and who agreed to write a contrary opinion on the vessel's valuation in the open market. This stated that with both the original engines assumed to be intact, the vessel would have sold for a figure closer to the insured value. At first there was talk of arbitration, and even a High Court action, but in the end the insurers backed down mindful of the considerable costs involved if they should lose. Rather like the litigation following the damage that was sustained by *Bristol Queen* after her withdrawal, this bout of P. & A. Campbell Ltd brinkmanship won the day and the company settled for a significantly higher cash sum than they had at first been offered, on the basis of un-repaired damage, and the resultant cheque helped considerably to improve the depleted cash resources of the company.

As she lay at Hayle, advertised for sale, a possible future for *Westward Ho* as a nightclub was anticipated. About a year after she had forlornly arrived in Cornwall a tug arrived to take her, on 7th October 1972, to Manchester where she did indeed she did spend a few years in this role, at Salford Docks, as the *North Westward Ho*.

The 'last' Bristol call

More publicity was obtained on the occasion of the 'last' Bristol departure of *Balmoral* on Friday 1st October 1971. Just as symbolic as the imminent withdrawal of the White Funnel Fleet from the long-established Cardiff-Weston ferry, the sailings from the Hotwells pontoon berth on the River Avon at Bristol in the shadow of the celebrated Clifton Suspension Bridge were a poignant reminder of the very earliest days of Campbell sailings from the original home port which had begun back in the 1880s. The last sailing advertised to call at Bristol was an afternoon excursion from Barry and Cardiff, leaving the latter at 1350. Departure from Bristol was scheduled at 1655, for Weston, Penarth, Cardiff and Barry. It was doubtless believed at this time that regular sailings from Bristol were to be severed for good, although happily a solution was found in subsequent years whereby *Balmoral* made occasional calls in the lock-entrance to Cumberland Basin, or just inside the basin or further up the 'floating harbour' after the pontoon-berth on the river itself had passed out of use and gradually lapsed into dereliction.

John Coe, writing in the *Bristol Evening Post* of Saturday 2nd October 1971, described the event thus:

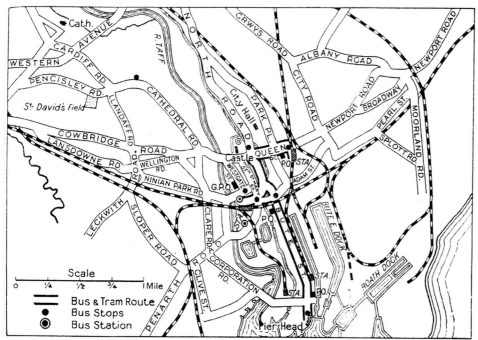

Town map of Cardiff, from the 1939 edition of the Bristol Channel District Guide, showing the location of the Pier Head at the bottom of Bute Street, accessible in the 1960s by trolleybus as well as by train to Bute Road station. Clarence Road station (to the left of the Pier Head) closed in the early-1960s. Once steamer calls at Cardiff had ceased after 1971 the nearest available pier was at Penarth. Construction of the Cardiff Bay barrage has meant that the Pier Head is no longer open to the sea, the mudflats that once characterised the area being permanently submerged.
Author's collection

**The White Funnel Fleet steam into the sunset..............
Bristol sea link ends**

I said farewell to the White Funnel Fleet with a sharp pang of regret, for it was half a century almost to the day that I first sailed down the Avon in the old **Britannia**. In future the company will operate in the Severn Estuary and elsewhere after flying its familiar ensign in Bristol waters for 83 years. Like the railways it is a victim of private motoring. Captain John Wide, of Bristol, who skippered the mv **Balmoral** on her last trip down the Avon yesterday evening, told me: "I am very sad. I have been with Campbell's for 42 years, and now this is the end of the attractive Bristol run. Campbell's was like a well-knit family. Everyone knew each other. I remember the period when we used to leave Hotwells packed, whether early morning or late in the evening. Bristolians used to love their paddle-steamers. Now we do well to collect a few dozen people for a trip." In a tribute to Mr Clifton Smith-Cox of Clevedon, the firm's Chairman and Managing Director, Capt. Wide said: "But for his hard work, dedication and enthusiasm, the Bristol run would have ended long ago".

Campbell's long association with Bristol ended without fuss or ceremonial. There were no farewell speeches or funeral orations. But many private regrets. The majority feeling among the older and more devoted passengers – some of whom asked for their tickets to keep as souvenirs – was that now a link with childhood had gone they would transfer their allegiance to Campbell's at Weston-super-Mare. Fewer than 150 joined the **Balmoral** at Hotwells for the last regular trip down the Avon ... The last word this sad Saturday is spoken by Mr Smith-Cox: "We kept going as long as we could, but it is my duty to show a profit, and the Avon operation has been losing money. I love ships, and particularly the Campbell ships, and like everyone else I feel sad. But one has to face the facts of life. I certainly hope we shall see a Campbell steamer at Bristol Docks in the future, but it definitely won't be on a regular run - perhaps a chartered cruise or something like that".

As the sun went down in full splendour on a perfect autumn evening over Weston Old Pier, Mr Smith-Cox shook hands with his old friend Capt. Wide and left for home a few miles away. And a few of the elderly passengers with long memories of the upper reaches of the Bristol Channel went to their local near the pier-head to talk about old ships and old times over a glass of ale.

Four hundred or so passengers were on board **Balmoral** that day, and elsewhere purser Neil O'Brien was quoted as saying that '... *for the past few years we have made this particular run every three weeks. Usually we have had not more than 200 people on board*'. Captain John Wide was at this point within days of his retirement from a long and distinguished career with P. & A. Campbell Ltd. However, rather like the fact that the termination of Bristol calls by the White Funnel Fleet at the end of 1971 turned out not to be final, neither was his retirement, and he continued to be seen on board in later years in an occasional relief capacity, even coming out of retirement for long enough to take command of **Devonia** for a period later in the 1970s.

Another nail in the coffin - the last 'ferry'

Monday 18th October 1971 was the day when Cardiff-Weston 'ferry' services finally ended. To older observers of the White Funnel Fleet the end of this particular season must have seemed terrible, with such drastic cutbacks coming so close together - firstly, the withdrawal of one of the two motor-vessels which one might have hoped would have gone on sailing together for a few more years and, secondly, the closure of the route at the very heart of the P. & A. Campbell Ltd territory – from Cardiff's historic Pier Head, no less – after the knife had already been taken to Bristol calls and was poised to cut out Barry Pier out as well. What was to be left for the regulars, many of who lived 'up-channel', and who would have little, if any, interest in supporting the expected Swansea-based 1972 season ? Newport services had been axed way back in 1956 and now Cardiff was to be chopped out. Penarth would only receive very occasional calls. Likewise, Weston would be left with only a few, irregular

sailings. The tragic sight of the forlorn remains of the severed Clevedon Pier was probably sufficient to diminish the loyalty of many for the greatly reduced White Funnel Fleet steamers of yore. Reports in Wales of the last day of "ferry" operations recorded the poignancy of the occasion. The last sailing from Cardiff Pier Head was at 1815, with the traditional call at Penarth Pier ten minutes later en-route across the Bristol Channel to Birnbeck Pier. The *South Wales Echo* carried an article describing the first ferry crossing at 0930 that day, headed Farewell To An Era: alliteratively subtitled Sentimental Trip for Sad Seven:

'… With her brass bell shining and her crew of 12 busy either on deck or on the bridge mv *Balmoral* nudged off from Pier Head today for her last day of scheduled runs from Cardiff. After her winter refit and Board of Trade survey she will be berthed at Swansea and continue to run across the Channel to Ilfracombe and will only pay the occasional visit to Cardiff and to other ports where she has been a "regular" for three years. For several years her owners P. & A. Campbell Ltd have been losing money on the regular ferry and cruise services run by the *Balmoral* and her two sister ships m.v. *Westward Ho* and m.v. *St. Trillo*. They decided to cut down the number of ports served by their ships and now Cardiff, like Bristol, Weston and Penarth will no longer have timetable services to take them across the water. Today was a sad day for the seven passengers and for the crew as the *Balmoral* cast off for the first of her two final runs to Weston. One of the two women on board, Miss Joan Howard of Plasturton Avenue, Cardiff sat down in her favourite spot near the aft end of the upper passenger deck and recalled the days of the paddlers " ... it was wonderful to watch the big wheel going round and round ... even with a diesel engine it gives such a tranquil feeling to sit facing the stern and watch the water slip away. You don't have to worry about not getting a place to sit now but when I was young all the ships were really packed.'

Over on the other side of the Bristol Channel the *Weston Mercury & Somerset Herald* on 22nd October 1971 gave vent to a slightly more emotional farewell to the ferry link between Weston and Cardiff, and reflected on some of the reasons which unaccounted for this sad day:

The Last Steamer

'Final is final, but somehow there has always been a rather special finality about the departure of the last steamer of the year from Weston's Birnbeck Pier. As the usual ceremony takes place with the mingling of the ships siren, pier fog hooter, and fireworks, one feels that another season in the history of the seaside resort of Weston is really at an end. In this week of heavy rain and gale-force wind we have been especially reminded that more than the breath of Autumn's being is upon us. Wintry days are here, the shutters are up.

As the *Balmoral* moved away from the Pier on Monday night the feeling of finality and indeed of regret must have been very much in the thoughts of some of the onlookers, because it was a special moment in the history of the Bristol Channel pleasure steamers. The *Balmoral* was making the last of the regular steamship sailings from the Pier.

A short while ago Messrs. P. & A. Campbell, whose name has so long and with such distinction been linked with pleasure steamer services in the Channel, announced that because of ever increasing general costs, the outlay involved in maintaining facilities in Cardiff and Barry, and the cross-channel link created by the Severn Bridge, regular steamship (sic) sailings in the upper reaches of the Channel would be discontinued at the end of this season.

Next year the service in the upper reaches will be limited to some charter trips and a very limited number of public excursions from Weston, Penarth and possibly Cardiff. There will be connecting coaches from Bristol whenever services operate from Weston, and it is hoped that there will be one or two weekends when excursions from Penarth and possibly Cardiff to Weston and Ilfracombe can be made. A vessel is to be made available during the greater part of May for charter excursions, and at the end of the season. Further down the Channel the regular daily service between Swansea

The final departure of **Balmoral** *from the Pier Head, Cardiff on 18th October 1971.*

Author's collection

and Ilfracombe will be operated, and there will be a service from Ilfracombe to Lundy three days a week … although we may never see the return of the White Funnel Fleet as we knew it of yore, we must hope that even as there is a revival of interest in reopening long closed railway lines and bringing back steam trains, so also enthusiasm for steamer travel about the Bristol Channel may not only be sufficient to make the restricted services planned for next season worth while, but justify an improvement on them in the years ahead.'

With hindsight the reference to '*reopening long-closed railway lines*' was prophetic. Although the railway preservation scene had barely taken off then, the following couple of decades would see significant developments around the Bristol Channel. Most notably these would be at Minehead with the gradual build-up of the West Somerset Railway undertaking, and further west in north Devon as a part of the old Lynton and Barnstaple narrow-gauge line eventually came back to life at Wooda Bay. On the other side of the channel great efforts were made at Barry Island to create a new heritage railway and, further up-Channel, the Dean Forest Railway was to build up its operations from Lydney.

The demise of the Cardiff-Weston ferry thus marked the retirement at the age of 68 of Captain John Wide, a remarkably long-serving employee of P. & A. Campbell Ltd. He expressed his feelings more strongly, describing the closure of ferry services as '… *a real tragedy* …'. One could wholly understand this view, from a loyal officer who had had command of P. & A. Campbell Ltd ships, such as **Glen Avon**, in the years before the Second World War. At the closing of this particular chapter of the history of the company little more can be said: there had been a huge scale of cutbacks compared to when the reach of the White Funnel Fleet was at its heyday before the Great War, and this now brought operations right down to just one, go-anywhere vessel. The reasons for the falling numbers and rising costs were understood, but as things turned out the future for upper Bristol Channel sailings was not to be quite as dire as

then predicted. The important point was that the company would carry on – and still with one or two surprises in store!

1971 in retrospect

The end of the 1971 season marked another step-change for the White Funnel Fleet, as the operation of two vessels gave way to just one. This was, perhaps, a development that was comparable to the earlier step-change at the end of the 1958 season when the Swansea station had been shut down, and left a reduced traffic requirement for only two paddle-steamers in the Bristol Channel, where previously three had found work. The pattern of two-vessel operations implemented in 1959 – when the company had been in receivership - had then endured for a good many seasons, with ups and downs, and with flurries of activity elsewhere. Essentially, the services which had been operated during 1971 by the two motor-vessels were not greatly different to those which two paddle-steamers – initially the postwar **Cardiff Queen** and the older **Glen Usk**, and later both Queens – had offered from 1959 onwards, as the company had tried to put a period of sustained financial difficulties behind it. Once the 'Lean Years' had ended the company, shorn of any substantial burden of equity, could carry on its existence as a subsidiary of George Nott Industries (and their successors) provided that trading results each year were satisfactory to the parent company, who had provided what effectively amounted to a large loan to enable P. & A. Campbell Ltd to continue trading, and that the personalities involved were content with this arrangement during the 1960s.

The financial background to the situation which obtained in 1972 can be put in context by looking at how many years the company had actually made a profit. In the early 1960s, for the first few seasons after the period in receivership had ended, modest profits were recorded in the published P. & A. Campbell Ltd accounts, and dividends were paid out to Ordinary Shareholders – who were relatively few in number – in respect of each season from 1959 to 1965. Things got more difficult after the 1966 season, after which Ordinary shareholders never received any dividends again. Thereafter losses were declared in respect of the 1967 and 1969 seasons, and the trend would be that profit levels continued to fall during the early 1970s. It was thus inevitable that the 'large loan' to P. & A. Campbell Ltd would come under increased scrutiny.

Losses had been incurred by the three-vessel experiment in 1966, and by the substantial expenditure on **Bristol Queen** and then the effect of her subsequent catastrophic breakdown in 1967. More cumulative losses were racked up in north Wales in 1967-69, which led to the withdrawal from the Llandudno station as **St. Trillo** ended her days. On top of this, **Queen of the Isles** had lost money in the south-east in 1969, and in 1971 **Westward Ho** had expired. As if this was not enough now came the decision of the parent company to 'tidy up' the management of the P. & A. Campbell Ltd business in the south-east of England after the 1971 season, namely the operation (in the name of the subsidiary company) of the cross-channel coach excursion business on the Townsend-Thoresen car ferries. Mention was made earlier (in Chapter 2) of the P. & A. Campbell Ltd annual Report and Accounts, to explain the loss of cross-channel coach excursion income from the Bristol Channel trading results, but it is worth reiterating here that it had produced much revenue for both the parent and subsidiary companies since its successful development in the mid-1960s. The re-organisation of finances was not carried out overnight, but after 1971 the separation of activity had been made final and in 1972 the advertising changed to stress the primary Townsend-Thoresen image. No more earnings from the cross-channel coach excursion business were attributed to P. & A. Campbell Ltd thereafter: this revenue had effectively bolstered earnings from Bristol Channel passenger services during difficult times, but it was to become increasingly clear that in the 1973 and ensuing seasons the operation of **Balmoral** would have to pay its own way if she was to survive as the sole P. & A. Campbell Ltd business activity.

Whilst the annual accounts for the trading activities of P. & A. Campbell Ltd were presented quite separately from those of European Ferries, there was mention of the very substantial adverse balance carried forward, and thus the link to the parent company. The White Funnel Fleet business had been carried on throughout the 1960s, as a subsidiary activity as far as the parent group was concerned, and one could argue that without the cross-channel coach excursion income it would have probably ceased trading much earlier than it did. The point here is that the parent group tolerated the delicate finances of its subsidiary whilst it was deemed useful, and this was in no small way linked to personalities and the good relationship that existed between Clifton Smith-Cox and Roland Wickenden, and whose untimely death in 1972 would have yet more impact on what the former was trying to hold together.

Mention was made under 'Financial Reconstruction' that tax-law was a factor in the takeover by George Nott Industries of P. & A. Campbell Ltd in 1960. By means of what was known as 'Group Relief' the losses of a subsidiary could be offset against the profits earned by a parent company, and the legislation passed in 1970 (the Income & Corporation Taxes Act 1970) did not materially alter the situation under which Townsends, latterly European Ferries, were able to benefit through what appeared in the accounts of the subsidiary as an 'adverse balance' which was carried forward each year. From the beginning of the 1960s through until the early-1970s the building programme of the Free Enterprise ships had been progressing, and the introduction of eight of these vessels necessitated a very substantial capital funding requirement. In this regard the ability of the parent group to offset the 'adverse balance carried forward' in the accounts of its subsidiary against its own balance-sheet had been an important reason for Townsends to regard their ownership of P. & A. Campbell Ltd as useful in the fiscal sense.

In addition to the effects of this on the balance sheet, the profit & loss account of the parent company had also benefited from the income which was generated on board the car-ferries from the foot-passengers handled by the subsidiary. But this factor had now started to run its course and, setting personalities aside, it was perhaps inevitable that tensions would grow. From a Dover perspective it was possible to see, on the one hand, a burgeoning fleet of smart new Free Enterprise car-ferries gaining market share on the English Channel. On the other, it was possible to pick up a little blue leaflet in a different corporate style advertising day-trips to the Continent marketed by a company with a different name, but which nonetheless referred to the Free Enterprise fleet, and so there would be some individuals in the parent organization who would naturally ask the question – why this was not all being conducted in a single, unified manner? The Bristol Channel was a long way from Dover, and only known to a few personnel in the expanding European Ferries undertaking. Whatever the capital accounts showed however, European Ferries could still reasonably expect Clifton Smith-Cox to turn in an annual trading profit rather than losses that caused negative cashflow, and this was becoming increasingly challenging.

A couple of extracts from the Annual Report and Accounts of European Ferries Limited from this time illustrate here the change in the way the Campbell subsidiary came to be viewed. Whilst Roland Wickenden had been the Chairman of European Ferries in the late 1960s and into the early 1970s he could say, in his Statement in December 1969, that '… *the reorganisation of the Campbell fleet to which I referred last year has, as anticipated, produced much improved results in the Bristol Channel and that company is now making a satisfactory profit contribution …*'. This reflected a view of the affairs of the subsidiary after the demise of the Bristol Channel paddle-steamers and the consolidation of activities with the motor vessels **Westward Ho** and **Balmoral**. Three years later, in the December 1972 Statement by the Chairman which accompanied the Accounts for the twelve months ended 30th April 1972, when Keith Wickenden had just succeeded his brother (who died in October 1972) this view was given: '… *the Bristol Channel operations of P. & A. Campbell Ltd have returned to profitability although the company's activities are not at present of material significance in the context of the Group …*' which was scarcely a ringing endorsement of the worth of the subsidiary. Jumping ahead momentarily, whilst one year later on the Accounts of European Ferries Limited (for the eleven months ended 31st March 1973) could state that '… *P. & A. Campbell Ltd continues to make a useful, albeit modest, contribution to our profit …*', this was in fact to be the last reference made by the parent group to the subsidiary.

Compared to the 1958 step-change in the Bristol Channel though, the 1971 cutbacks were perhaps more drastic, with seemingly very little left out of which to fashion a profitable survival. Fears were expressed that one vessel could not operate economically on its own, as overheads would remain but with substantially reduced earnings potential. How was this dilemma to be tackled? As 1971 passed into 1972 and **Balmoral** rested between the seasons, it became apparent that overheads would be reduced as much as possible, and the sale of Birnbeck Pier has already been recorded, the proceeds from which would have eased the cashflow situation at this difficult time. **Westward Ho** was to be sold, and it was rumoured that **St. Trillo** had also been sold, evidently for use by a yacht-club, for an undisclosed sum, although this particular transaction later fell through. These capital transactions would clearly have helped but in themselves were not the answer to the underlying problem. Of less impact was the news that, in a modest way, the territory of the White Funnel Fleet would not be quite as extensively trimmed as feared, and it became known that Barry Pier had received sufficient maintenance from its owners, the British Transport Docks Board, to keep on going for a few more seasons, and would thus generate a little extra, much-needed revenue.

Yet despite these changes after the 1971 season and the difficulties seen to lie ahead, the White Funnel Fleet had survived and, as **Balmoral** set off from Barry for overhaul at Penzance late in January 1972 to be prepared for her first year of single-vessel operations, advance sailing information was promulgated as it always had been well before the season in order to boost sales of coupon-books and season-tickets to a still loyal hard-core of regulars. The pattern was to be as promised after the cutback of upper Bristol Channel services, namely an emphasis on Swansea-based sailings with very little on offer for Penarth or Weston residents compared to past years. The established destinations further west – Minehead, Lynmouth, Ilfracombe, Clovelly, Porthcawl, Mumbles, Tenby and Lundy – still featured, and a touch of enterprise was demonstrated by the opportunist promotion of a few publicly-advertised north Wales sailings as a consequence of the annual Swedish-American Line calls at Llandudno and at Douglas by **Kungsholm**, with **Balmoral** booked to perform the now customary tendering duties. She would have to stand very much on her own during the ensuing decade.

From the waterline when approaching on the launch from the beach landing-stage, **Balmoral** *seemed huge as one came alongside the steps suspended from the 'Lundy door'. Re-embarcation of two or three hundred passengers might easily take well over an hour depending on how many launches had been mustered at Lundy. First off, first back on was the customary means of trying to ensure everybody had a similar length of time ashore, which would go all too quickly, especially on a sunny summers day. 15th September 1979*

Author

Chapter 4
THE FINAL DECADE
The 1970s to the end of the White Funnel Fleet

Single-vessel operations, 1972-1976

As the 1972 season approached *Balmoral* was now very much on her own, both in terms of her solitary role as the upholder of the proud White Funnel Fleet tradition in the Bristol Channel, and as one of a very small and diminishing number of excursion steamers in British waters generally. It has already been demonstrated that Lundy had become relatively more important to the business of P. & A. Campbell Ltd since the change of ownership of the island late in the 1960s. From being a privately-owned island with unique charm for day-visitors, the new owners gradually set about the restoration of old buildings for holiday lettings and Lundy became better known as a National Trust owned property, steadily attracted more visitors and started to take on its present appearance. In 1972 the significance of earnings derived from the Lundy excursion trade was heightened as *Balmoral*, on her own, was to run something approximating to a regular timetable in the Bristol Channel. This was largely based around providing the principal link between Ilfracombe and the twenty-four miles distant island of Lundy, usually thrice-weekly in the high season, for day-trippers and staying passengers alike. These would generally commence elsewhere in the morning, mainly at Swansea or further up-Channel as tidal patterns permitted, returning from Lundy and Ilfracombe in the evening. To a large extent Swansea now became the operational base for *Balmoral*, where fuelling and victualling were generally arranged, with Cardiff now out of the picture and Bristol visits very rare.

Some brief explanation is relevant here regarding other passenger links to Lundy: during the 1960s the converted fishing boat *Lundy Gannet* had provided an all-year round facility for the mails, cargo and a limited number of passengers. This service ran from Bideford, but had been switched to Ilfracombe in April 1970. In no way could the activities of *Lundy Gannet* be said to have been in competition with the White Funnel Fleet steamers for Lundy excursionists, and indeed the island economy rather depended on the capacity of the much larger excursion vessels to cater for summer visitors. A replacement for *Lundy Gannet* with greater cargo capacity was sought by the Landmark Trust for Lundy duties, and the former coaster from Greenland known as *Aqdleg* which was renamed *Polar Bear* entered service between Ilfracombe and Lundy in May 1972. She did not carry passengers at first, and both vessels ran alongside one another for a couple of years until eventually the older ship was laid up and disposed of. By that time *Polar Bear* had acquired a certificate for twelve passengers, and the fares structure that applied was based on passages in the Lundy-owned vessel being charged at the same rate as P. & A. Campbell Ltd

fares. A degree of interchangeability operated in practice, to the benefit of those wanting to stay on the island for a few days in summer and use either vessel to and fro between Ilfracombe and Lundy. At that time a hotel facility existed on the island, initially the 'Manor Farm' but after 1971 visitors not wanting self-catering were accommodated at Millcombe, the one-time owners residence.

The basic handbill issued at Ilfracombe by P. & A. Campbell Ltd to advertise Lundy excursions in 1972 had not altered its format for many years, but now grew a little larger with the text having been brought up to date after the change of ownership. To put the expansion of the Lundy sailings programme into perspective, there had been forty-three sailings advertised in 1967 but by 1970 this figure had increased to seventy, within a season of similar duration. A somewhat diffident prose style, possibly that of Clifton Smith-Cox himself from when this style of advertising was initiated in the early-1960s, can just be detected here:

Sailings from Ilfracombe (The Pier)
to
LUNDY ISLAND
(To Land)
By the Motor Vessel Balmoral

... for many years the island was the property of the Harman family, having been purchased by Martin Coles Harman, the financier. In 1969 the ownership of the island passed to the National Trust who are preserving it for use by the public. It is undoubtedly different to any other area owned by the Trust and its beauty, seclusion and peace will now remain unspoiled. It is, perhaps, as good an example as is to be found anywhere of the value of the National Trust to the Nation.

The *Balmoral*, which operates the Lundy service, is a Motor Ship of 688 tons with accommodation for over 700 passengers. The vessel has a restaurant and a tea room and two fully-licensed Bars on Board. There are sun lounges, spacious open decks and covered accommodation is available sufficient for all passengers.

This explanation of the role of Lundy in the P. & A. Campbell Ltd business sets the scene for the way in which a typical week in the summer of 1972 for *Balmoral* featured trips from Swansea and Mumbles to Ilfracombe & Lundy Island (to land) running on Tuesdays, Thursdays and Sundays. At Lundy, the launch *Lady Moyra* maintained

WHITE FUNNEL FLEET
Sailings from PENARTH & BARRY PIERS
by the Motor Vessel BALMORAL

THE VESSEL is a large sea-going ship capable of accommodating over 800 passengers. The vessel has a restaurant and tea bar where meals and snacks can be obtained, also fully licensed bars. There are sun lounges, spacious open decks and covered accommodation is available sufficient for all passengers.

SEASON 1972

Minor details: the vessel on this billhead is not Balmoral, as passengers might reasonably have inferred, but St. Trillo, minus her second funnel. The phrase 'a large seagoing ship' was particularly memorable back in the 1970s.

Author's collection

Lundy became an increasingly important source of revenue to P. & A. Campbell Ltd during the 1970s as **Balmoral** *provided the principal seasonal link with the mainland. The coaster* **Polar Bear** *(centre) is seen here at anchor off Lundy, to the right is* **Lundy Gannet**, *and the old landing-stage has been positioned on the beach to handle passengers from all three vessels. 28th September 1972.*   Miss Gwyneth White

the link between ship and shore in succession to **Lundy Queen** which had been lost in October 1971. Further regularity was achieved by a pattern of the basic Swansea-Ilfracombe crossing extending to Clovelly on Mondays and to Lynmouth on Wednesdays. At both of these locations landing took place by launch. Saturdays were more varied, with Fridays often tending to be off-service days. If Lundy sailings featured prominently in the existence of **Balmoral** in this first year of single-vessel operations in 1972, a wide variety of other destinations featured as well, a few of which were on a very occasional basis. Bristol saw a visit from **Balmoral** as early as 29th April whilst on charter, berthing being arranged at the entrance to Cumberland Basin. Cardiff had disappeared for good from the territory of the White Funnel Fleet, however, and passengers in south-east Wales had to be content with a few days worth of sailings from Penarth on an approximately fortnightly basis, on a few days of which Barry Pier would also receive a visit. Boat-trains to Barry Pier had ceased operating after October 1971, and bills referred to buses from Barry Town Hall for Penarth passengers that might have boarded, say, a Penarth-Weston sailing and which had returned across the channel to Barry. The proximity of Barry Island station was seemingly overlooked, perhaps not surprisingly as the train-service from Barry to Penarth (that is, via Lavernock) had vanished many years earlier, but the unsuspecting might have had an unpleasant surprise at the length of the journey if attempting to make their own way from Barry Pier to Barry Town Hall on foot.

The regular Cardiff-Weston ferry might have closed down, yet there were still days when **Balmoral** would perform two or three return Penarth-Weston crossings, giving some semblance of the former facility. Other ports still somehow managed to retain the appearance of a White Funnel Fleet presence, according to the multiplicity of handbills of varying sizes and format that were still printed in the time-honoured style. Watchet was bestowed with a weekly coach-link, on Thursdays, to Ilfracombe, in connection with Lundy excursions. Minehead was served by the same coach, which offset to some extent the restricted number of calls which could be provided at the extremely attractive and historic tidal harbour. Further along the coast, Lynmouth still had trips from the resort as well as to it, with **Balmoral** carrying out a typical Wednesday schedule involving a 'double-run' from Ilfracombe to Lynmouth in the afternoon, so as to take passengers to Lynmouth to be landed by launch after others had boarded the vessel there from the same launch coming out to rendezvous with **Balmoral**. This 'double-run' had the obvious merit of maximising the potential for seeing the outstanding north Devon coastline from the sea for holidaymakers

at either end. Further west, Clovelly still saw occasional calls but Bideford received only a very few visits by this time.

Over in Wales, Porthcawl still generated reasonable numbers, and tended to be served on Swansea days whenever tides permitted. Mumbles Pier would generally receive a call after **Balmoral** had left Swansea for Ilfracombe, and on her return across the Channel later in the day. In addition, evening cruises to view the Gower coast were offered from Mumbles Pier, often on Sundays and Wednesdays. Bus connections were still offered to give better opportunities for intending passengers when the limitations of the tides might otherwise have been a deterrent to custom: for example, a 'Grand Evening Cruise' from Porthcawl to Ilfracombe was offered on Saturday 22nd July 1972 at 5.30 pm, the handbill explaining that on arrival back at Swansea at 9.40 pm '... *special coaches will be waiting to convey passengers to Porthcawl, where they will arrive about 10.15 pm*', at an inclusive fare of £1.00. In 1972 the principle had been established that if the ship could only practically berth once in the day at a tidally-restricted location such as Porthcawl, then this was generally on the outward part of the journey, with buses proving acceptable to passengers only on the return leg. Further west, Tenby Harbour received the occasional visit by **Balmoral**, with that on 3rd September offering the opportunity to take a cruise 'passing Saundersfoot and towards Pendine'.

As had been the case for many years a number of cruises continued to be promoted with onwards coach tours, a long-standing feature of the Bristol Channel cruising operation. Aside from the feeders mentioned, a programme of excursions ran from Ilfracombe after the steamer had arrived on its cross-channel run. These ranged from the old favourite destinations of Clovelly & Westward Ho!, or Lynton and the Valley of the Rocks, as well as mystery tours. On odd days, Welsh Mountain tours were still offered when sailings from the English side permitted. It should also be mentioned that although the White Funnel Fleet north Wales business had closed down after 1969, **Balmoral** still journeyed around Wales to tender to the annual Swedish American Line visits of **Kungsholm** in the early 1970s.

Behind all this bustle of summer activity, the rest of the White Funnel Fleet could only contemplate a future of decay in their enforced idleness. **St. Trillo** lay in Barry Dock awaiting sale, and was initially sold through West Marine Surveyors for £15,000 to a Mr Nigel Wait of Reigate, Surrey for conversion to a floating restaurant. At the time of purchase he had no specific idea of where he would locate this venture, and it was understood that his imagination had been captured by the successful sale and conversion of the former Clyde paddle-steamer

Caledonia for use as a floating pub on the Thames Embankment around that time. Whilst *St. Trillo* continued to lie at Barry Dock the purchaser took on the dock dues payable but eventually his plans collapsed, and *St. Trillo* was sold on to Liverpool scrap merchants Oldham Bros., who subsequently resold the vessel to Dublin breakers in 1975, with the proviso that the Crossley engines be stripped for spares. *Westward Ho* lay for sale at Hayle, and was eventually recorded as having been sold to Compass Caterers for use as a floating restaurant and discotheque at the Docks in Manchester. She left Hayle under tow on 7th October 1972, arriving at Eastham on the 14th to traverse the Ship Canal. Neither vessel, then, was ever to sail again commercially, although the larger *Westward Ho* was renamed *North Westward Ho*, and was officially opened in her new role at Salfords's Pomona Dock in October 1973. She survived there for a good many years before the attraction waned and she too was disposed of, being eventually broken up at Torcross. Before this she had for a while been reunited on the River Thames with her former Red Funnel fleet-mate *Medina*.

Towards the end of 1972 Clifton Smith-Cox let it be known that the new style of single-vessel White Funnel Fleet operation was to be regarded as a commercial success. Speaking to a *Bristol Evening Post* reporter on 10th December 1972 he stated that Bristol Channel operations had returned to profitability, due to '... *changes made last year when the company gave up a lot of their operations in the upper part of the Bristol Channel ... they had got rid of a lot of the cost and kept a greater part of the revenue*'. He went on to say that '... *in this coming summer we shall have much the same sort of of service but there will be rather more calls at Weston*'. This 'success' was however thought in certain quarters to be a matter of opinion, or at least a relative matter: it appeared to others that there was still untapped commercial potential at the surviving up-Channel locations, and indeed a frustration amongst loyal passengers who would still wish to sail directly from Bristol, Weston & Penarth but who were not particularly attracted to excursions from Swansea and Mumbles, whatever the claimed benefits of regular-interval sailings from those ports across to Ilfracombe. Clevedon Pier

itself might have dropped out of the range of ports of call hereabouts but this view applied just as pertinently to charter sources of traffic from Bristol and the surrounding area, and the development of this business as well as the continuation of the annual Isles of Scilly mini-cruise was very much to be nurtured by Commander Tom Foden to the benefit of the Company and became a significant source of income. Around this time Cdr. Foden, who was known in the early-1970s to Clifton Smith-Cox through their being neighbours in Clevedon, became involved in this aspect of the business. Cdr. Foden had taken an early role in the formation of the Clevedon Pier Restoration Trust, which eventually led to the successful re-opening of the pier in the 1990s, and he became a well-known part of the scene thereafter.

Balmoral keeps the business going

A slightly earlier statement made to the same newspaper, on 10th October 1972, was just as interesting in that an upbeat note was struck by Tony McGinnity, one of the directors of West Marine Surveyors & Consultants Ltd, which company was then acting as Marine Superintendents for P. & A. Campbell Ltd, when describing the imminent sales of the motor-vessels *St. Trillo* and *Westward Ho*. He emphasised that these disposals '... *did not mean that Campbells were closing down the Severn estuary services ...*' and went on to explain that '... *there are thoughts of acquiring another ship of much the same size for the Bristol Channel services*'. No further details were given, but the statement provided an intriguing insight into White Funnel Fleet forward thinking and this was a fascinating revelation, even if nothing actually happened in this direction for another four years. More directly, the reference that had been made by Clifton Smith-Cox to more calls at Weston amounted to an admission of an over-emphasis on the Swansea trade in 1972, and in 1973 and thereafter the focus of Bristol Channel traffic gradually moved back up-Channel somewhat.

This brief look at the White Funnel Fleet in 1972 can be neatly rounded off by quoting from the Statement by the Chairman which accompanied the Accounts for the eleven months ended 31st March 1973:

The withdrawn **St. Trillo** *drifts around aimlessly in the Graving Dock at Cadoxton, within the Barry Docks complex, shortly before being towed away to the breakers in 1975.*

Author

'... I referred last year to changes that would be made in the operation of the Bristol Channel services during the summer of 1972, which is the one whose results are covered by this report. An endeavour was made to make the services far more regular and on a regular timetable, in particular between Swansea and Ilfracombe and Ilfracombe and Lundy Island. This pattern yielded results and with the considerable increase in the number of charters obtained, the Bristol Channel operations proved profitable.'

If a new pattern had indeed successfully been established in 1972, it clearly made sense to build on it, and a relatively stable period now followed. Although upper Channel sailings had been restricted in 1972, slightly more were offered to satisfy demand at Penarth and at Weston in 1973, and a simple indication of this shift was that the single sailing-bill that had sufficed for all Penarth and Barry calls in 1972 gave way to two separate bills in the following year, for the early and later parts of the steamer season. The tidal pattern meant that Penarth/Weston sailing weekends could be advertised roughly at fortnightly intervals, and when this happened on consecutive Saturdays & Sundays the opportunity was often taken to offer inclusive weekend-trips to Ilfracombe with Dinner, Bed and Breakfast at an inclusive rate at the Carlton Hotel. Initiated in 1972 (or perhaps 're-launched' after similar initiatives in the early-60s to other Ilfracombe hotels), this facility was offered on about half a dozen suitable weekends in 1973, and demonstrated that a worthwhile new effort was being made to offer a wider range of services tailored more closely to changing patterns of demand.

Charters featured a little more frequently, due in no small way to the efforts of Cdr. Foden in his role as the latter-day 'Clevedon Agent'. A brief quote from the 1974 Statement by the Chairman nicely sums up the view of the company towards this traffic, and which was promulgated to shareholders: '... *The introduction of rather more regular services proved beneficial and in particular the number of charters and private parties showed an increase.*' These were often open to the public, such as on Saturday & Sunday 18th/19th May when **Balmoral** was advertised to run direct to Lundy from up Channel (Barry, Penarth & Weston one day, Portishead and Weston the other) in aid of the Clevedon Pier Restoration Fund. Special handbills were produced, which sternly implored prospective passengers to ensure that their enjoyment of the day was not compromised: '... *Do not ruin a wonderful day with seasickness. It is quite unnecessary in this age. "Dramamin" or similar tablets should be taken one hour before embarking if you think you will need them ...*'. A couple of direct Swansea-Lundy sailings on behalf of the National Trust were advertised in April, claiming that the direct passage was a 'first time ever' experience. On both sets of charter days special arrangements were made for the reception of passengers at Lundy, and novelties like postal First-Day Covers arranged.

Despite the relative success of **Balmoral's** first few years of Bristol Channel service the standard of on-board catering attracted severe criticism from some passengers, and was felt to compare unfavourably with the facilities that the paddle-steamers had offered in earlier years. Even if one accepted that silver service had vanished for good on the motor-vessels which had replaced them, the variety and quality

WHITE FUNNEL FLEET

One of the most popular and reasonable Charter Cruises
The now famous

Clevedon Pier Restoration Fund Cruises

to

LUNDY ISLAND direct
Two special Spring sailings

on

SATURDAY and SUNDAY, 19 and 20 MAY 1973

SATURDAY 19 MAY. Leaving BARRY at 8.30 a.m., PENARTH at 9.10 a.m., WESTON-super-MARE at 10 a.m. for LUNDY direct, arriving about 2.45 p.m. Returning from LUNDY at 5.45 p.m. Due WESTON about 10.20 p.m. and PENARTH 11.05 p.m. Passengers for BARRY disembark at PENARTH.

SUNDAY 20 MAY. Leaving PORTISHEAD at 8.30 a.m. and WESTON-super-MARE at 10 a.m. for LUNDY direct, arriving about 2.45 p.m. Leaving LUNDY at 6 p.m. and arriving WESTON about 10.30 p.m. and PORTISHEAD about 11.45 p.m.

COACHES to connect with these sailings leave BRISTOL (Canon's Marsh Coach Park) at 8.40 a.m. and CLEVEDON (Glass Pavilion Green Beach) at 9 a.m. on BOTH DAYS. Coaches will be waiting for passengers on the ship's return to WESTON on both days. A coach will also be run from BATH at a cost of 25p each. **Passengers are requested to state when booking if tickets are required for any of the above coach services.** Ample car parking is available adjacent to The Royal Hotel, Portishead and The Old Pier, Weston.

SPECIAL BASIC FARE from Weston, Penarth, Portishead
or Barry (returning to Penarth) £2.70
Less a reduction for Advance Bookings before 15 April .... .35
Less a further reduction for block booking of 12 or more
before 15 April .... .35

MINIMUM FARE   £2.00

Coach supplement from Clevedon or Bristol – 15p Bath 25p – payable at the same time as steamer ticket.

The above basic fares have not been increased since the first Clevedon Pier Restoration Fund Cruise in 1970. They include all pier tolls and landing and embarkation dues at Lundy Island.

Children under 12 half-price

THE CRUISES will take place in the recently refitted MV BALMORAL, the largest and fastest coastal passenger ship in the Bristol Channel.

In order to ensure maximum comfort, the passenger list will be restricted. Less than two-thirds of the normal complement only will be carried. Public rooms on board are centrally heated in cold weather.

These DAY CRUISES will enable passengers to visit this beautiful unspoilt Island out of the main season, at a time when it is considered to look its best. No cars are allowed on the Island, and it is one of the most unpolluted parts of the British Isles. It is a BIRD SANCTUARY.

A SHORT TOUR OF LUNDY will be specially organised for this visit, by the Curator of the Lundy Museum.

A SPECIAL LUNDY POSTMARK will commemorate this visit. EXHIBITS DESTINED FOR THE NEW LUNDY MUSEUM will be on show in the Church.

ENTERTAINMENT ON BOARD WILL INCLUDE:-
* Entertainment, music and dancing on the return voyage
* Tombola
* A Clevedon Pier Preservation Fund stall where Guide Books to Lundy and other items can be obtained, including literature about the progress of the restoration of the Pier
* A visit to the bridge for children when the Captain will autograph photographs of MV Balmoral

MEALS ON BOARD. Light snacks are served from the snack bar throughout the voyage. A limited number of luncheons and suppers will be available in the restaurant. In view of past experience, ADVANCE BOOKING is advised from Messrs P. & A. Campbell Ltd., 4 Dock Chambers, Bute Street, Cardiff. The price of meals is £1 for luncheon and 80p for a simple supper. You will be very hungry on the return voyage after the fresh air and exercise on Lundy. There are two bars on board.

Do not ruin a wonderful day with seasickness. It is quite unnecessary in this age. 'Dramamin' or similar tablets should be taken one hour before embarking if you think you will need them.

EARLY APPLICATION for advance steamer and coach tickets is essential and should be made without delay, either personally, or sent with a remittance, enclosing a stamped addressed envelope to any one of the addresses below:-

The Bristol Omnibus Co. Ltd. Travel Centre, St. Augustine's Parade, Bristol 1.

The Bath Bus Station Travel Centre, Bath.

Messrs Bowyers World Travel Bureau, 67 Hill Road, Clevedon, and Branches.

Phoenicia Travel Ltd., The Precinct, Portishead, and Branches.

WEMS Luxury Coaches, 2 Regent St., Weston-super-Mare.

Messrs P. & A. Campbell Ltd., 4 Dock Chambers, Bute Street, Cardiff. (Telephone Cardiff 20255) or The Old Pier, Weston-super-Mare. (Telephone 21068).

Or any member of the Clevedon Pier Supporters' Club.

Notes 1   Provided the excursion takes place, it will not be possible to refund any ticket money.

2   On rare occasions, due to the direction of the wind, it may not be possible to land on Lundy. In these circumstances, a Cruise around Lundy, thence across Bideford Bay and to off Clovelly, will be substituted.

3   In the event of insufficient funds being collected to repair the Pier, the Clevedon Pier Supporters' Club reserves the right to donate monies received to such other causes as they may think fit.

SUPPORT CLEVEDON PIER RESTORATION FUND BY ENJOYING AN EXHILARATING DAY AT SEA AND ON LUNDY ISLAND REMEMBER — CLEVEDON PIER IS THE ONLY REMAINING EXAMPLE OF THIS PRICELESS TYPE OF VICTORIAN MARINE ARCHITECTURE

Coupons, Passes and Season Tickets are not available for these Excursions.

Conditions of carriage are in accordance with Messrs P. & A. Campbell's normal conditions exhibited at their offices and on board their ships.

A TICKET FOR THIS POPULAR CRUISE MAKES A MOST ATTRACTIVE GIFT

Special Note. Passengers requiring overnight accommodation in WESTON will be offered special terms at the Royal Pier Hotel, adjoining the Old Pier, if they mention this Special Cruise when booking.

Printed by the Clevedon Printing Co. Ltd., Six Ways, Clevedon, Somerset. Tel. 4224

The loss of Clevedon Pier after its collapse in 1970 caused a loss of revenue to the company, and a Restoration Fund was started in 1972. This was enthusiastically supported by Commander Foden who arranged charters which were beneficial to both the pier cause and to the White Funnel Fleet. The obverse of this bill carried the instructions on how to reduce the risk of seasickness, in firm tones.   Author's collection

M.V. BALMORAL, M.V. KUNGSHOLM AND S.S. KING ORRY AT DOUGLAS, ISLE OF MAN

Many British coastal excursion vessels are still remembered through the beautiful artistry of the late John Nicholson. This Isle of Man scene from the early-1970s captured **Balmoral** *tendering* **Kungsholm,** *with the Manx classic turbine-steamer* **King Orry** *in view. The latter was withdrawn after the 1975 season.* Author's collection

of the fare offered fell far short of what was required by passengers on long day trips. In contracting out the catering arrangements on board *Balmoral* to a Mr Jones, who employed a number of former P. & A. Campbell Ltd personnel and appeared determined to supply the least and charge the most, P. & A. Campbell Ltd had effectively abdicated responsibility, and standards continued to slide below those encountered on other coastal and short sea vessels. In July 1973 the deficiencies of selling '*instant tea – a powder derived from tea and milk*' in cardboard cups were accurately pointed out in the editorial in *Cruising Monthly* and it was observed that *Balmoral* was a serious offender in this direction – such standards would not have been tolerated on, for example, the IoMSPCo. steamers in the north Wales and Isle of Man excursion trade. This attack drew a spirited response from P. & A. Campbell Ltd who explained that cardboard cups were used because plastic ones caused a nuisance when thrown overboard. Instant tea was served '... *to avoid stale tea in teapots and so speed up service ...*', and was apparently used by '... *thousands of caterers throughout the country*'. If this point seems a small one, it nevertheless understates the true extent of the failure of the operator to realise that what was actually being sold was rather more than basic sea-transport, and that their thinking should have moved forwards to a recognition of the broader leisure needs of passengers. Eventually people did take their trade elsewhere, as had been foreseen in *Cruising Monthly*.

Equally one must recognise the genuine difficulties that faced the P. & A. Campbell Ltd management in providing any excursion services at all in the varied waters of the Bristol Channel, where *Balmoral* lacked any kind of 'home port' to facilitate victualling and worked such long hours with poorly-paid crews, who were obliged to sleep on board in cramped conditions, in all kind of weathers, and frequently out in the Channel at anchor, night after night. The increasingly wide gap forming between the survival of P. & A. Campbell Ltd at all and the demands of the travelling public was accentuated on sailings which sometimes became a feat of endurance rather than a pleasure cruise. Poor on-board conditions and adverse weather evidently combined on 3rd June 1973 when the Coastal Cruising Association jointly promoted with P. & A. Campbell Ltd a novel excursion to Newquay in Cornwall, billed as the first landing trip since 1930. W. P. Clegg reported the days events in the July 1973 edition of *Cruising Monthly*:

' ... A dry and potentially sunny day saw nearly 200 people embark on *Balmoral* at Swansea and Mumbles for the trip to Ilfracombe on the first leg ... the ship rolled across to Ilfracombe, arriving some twenty minutes late. The cross-currents gave her passengers some bad moments, and it is possible that this caused more people to disembark at 'Combe than had originally intended.

Warm sunshine greeted her arrival here, where a crowd of hardy Devonians embarked for the 4-hour trip to Newquay. The run of bad luck experienced this year by most enthusiast charters – notably bad weather – continued. At times, conditions were bad and the ship rolled and pitched violently, while the Atlantic swell made landing at Newquay impossible. In spite of this, the generally unkempt condition of the ship and, for a time, the complete absence of light refreshment facilities (caused, we understand, by lack of gas), morale generally remained high. Most people, however, were glad to get ashore when the ship arrived back in 'Combe at about 1945.

By and large, it was a socially successful day. The venture did not have the enthusiast support it should have done, and conditions on board left much to be desired, but the Captain is to be thanked for handling his ship so well in the difficult conditions and swell.'

Joint ticketing arrangements with British Rail were still in force, and special handbills were produced annually to promote the fairly regular steamer excursion opportunities from Swansea in conjunction with rail-tickets from Newport, Cardiff and Bridgend, with a bus connection from Swansea High Street station to the B&I Ferryport from which all Swansea sailings departed. Weekly tickets were available at a cost of £5.00 per adult for any seven days to suit the purchaser, and if used fully represented very good value, and which could be maximised by staying away a few nights depending on the precise sailing pattern. Connoisseurs might still go out of their way for unusual trips, such as that offered on Saturday 28th July 1973 from Swansea and Ilfracombe to Bideford when the tide also permitted the operation of a short cruise for passengers from Bideford down-river to view the Bell Buoy, giving Swansea & Ilfracombe passengers the rare alternative of a brief spell ashore at Bideford.

Remarkably, fifteen years or so after the demise of the 'Swansea steamer', handbills in 1973 still advertised a Period Fare ticket of £4.00 from Swansea to Ilfracombe which could be used to return via steamer to Penarth and thence by train to Swansea if a passenger so wished, on payment of a supplement of 50p. Ever thoughtful, the text went on to explain that this facility could also be applied in the reverse direction for passengers wishing to travel outwards by train from Swansea, Neath or Port Talbot stations via the steamer from Penarth to Ilfracombe. All pier tolls were included in fares by this time, except oddly at Mumbles where a toll of 3p was charged on embarkation.

A disappointing feature of the late part of the 1973 season was that weather disrupted the annual Isles of Scilly mini-cruise scheduled for the weekend of 28th-30th September. Gales prevented *Balmoral* from proceeding beyond Ilfracombe on the outwards voyage on Friday 28th September, passengers being transported by bus onwards to St. Ives.

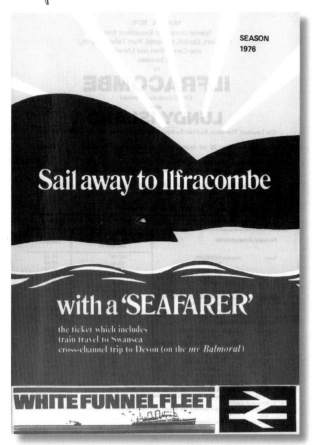

SEASON 1976

Sail away to Ilfracombe

with a 'SEAFARER'

the ticket which includes
train travel to Swansea
cross-channel trip to Devon (on the *mv Balmoral*)

WHITE FUNNEL FLEET

FARES and CONDITIONS

Tickets can be obtained at the Railway Stations Ticket Offices and are issued subject to the Conditions of Carriage of British Rail and P. & A. Campbell Ltd., which latter conditions are exhibited at the embarkation office at the Ferryport Terminal at Swansea.

To Ilfracombe (Rail and Steamer)

	Single or Day Return £	Period Return (Valid 3 months) £
Newport)		
Cardiff)		
Bridgend)	4.50	8.25
Port Talbot)		
Neath)		
Carmarthen)	4.10	7.50
Llanelli)		

NOTE: On Saturdays and Sundays (June 12th until September 11th inclusive) when no steamer returns from Ilfracombe to Swansea there is a service to Penarth and passengers holding return halves of tourists tickets may return to Penarth without extra charge.

Fares to LUNDY ISLAND

Passengers wishing to travel beyond Ilfracombe to Lundy Island book tickets to Ilfracombe at the Railway Station and pay an extra fare of 60 pence to the Purser on board the steamer to cover the single or day return passage between Ilfracombe and Lundy. Period tickets are not issued to Lundy Island.

Children 3-14 half price.

LUNDY ISLAND. On rare occasions, due to the direction of the winds it is not possible to land at Lundy. These circumstances occasionally arise after the steamer has left Ilfracombe. In such an event a Cruise to Lundy Island will be substituted.

PIER TOLLS and Landing Charges are included in the fares except at Mumbles (5p embarking).

SPECIAL RATES are available for parties of 12 and over travelling Monday to Friday, and 25 and over travelling on Saturday or Sunday.

PORTABLE RADIOS. The Steamship Company reserves the right to prohibit the use of these instruments on their steamers should circumstances demand.

DOGS are charged at the usual rate for the railway journey and on the steamer the charge is 50p single or day return. Dogs cannot be landed at Lundy.

MOTOR PROPELLED CYCLES AND VEHICLES cannot be conveyed on this service.

CATERING ON BOARD. All ships are fully licensed, and Meals or Snacks can be served throughout the voyage.

BOARD OF TRADE. Regulations concerning the number of passengers the vessel is permitted to carry are strictly observed.

For further particulars apply to BRITISH RAIL at the stations mentioned above; CLAY TRAVEL LTD., Dunraven Place, Bridgend. Tel. 2531; W.B.TRICK, SON & LLOYD, Borough Chambers, Neath (& Port Talbot). Tel. 3504; OWEN TRAVEL LTD., 6 The Arcade, Llanelli. Tel 4778. Carmarthen. Tel. 7044 or P. & A. CAMPBELL LTD., at 4 Dock Chambers, Cardiff. Tel. 20255.

In addition to the range of publicity produced by the company to promote excursions from each Bristol Channel pier, the well-established through booking arrangement with the railways brought in modest additional business from stations in south Wales, this pamphlet regularly being seen each season in ticket offices. This one gave connecting train times from main line stations between Newport and Carmarthen in conjunction with sailings from Swansea to Ilfracombe, which ran to a broadly regular pattern.

Author's collection

SEASON 1976
Special Combined Excursions from
Newport, Cardiff, Bridgend, Port Talbot, Neath,
also Carmarthen and Llanelli
via Swansea
to

ILFRACOMBE

(On all dates shown below)
and

LUNDY ISLAND

(On Tuesdays, Thursdays, & certain Sundays, also Saturdays May 22, June 26 and July 10.)

Every Tuesday, May 25 till September 21 inclusive (June 15, August 3, 17, 31 and September 14 excepted).

Every Wednesday, May 26 till September 15 inclusive

Every Thursday, June 10 till September 16 inclusive (July 1, 15, 29 and August 12 excepted).

Saturdays May 22, June 26 and July 10 from all stations, also July 24, August 7, 21, September 4 and 18 from Llanelli and Carmarthen.
and

Sundays, June 20, July 25, August 8, 22 and September 5.

From NEWPORT, CARDIFF, BRIDGEND, PORT TALBOT and NEATH

Forward Arrangements		Tuesdays, Wednesdays, Thursdays and Saturdays May 22, June 26, and July 10	Sundays
Train	Departs: NEWPORT	*07.16	07.30
	CARDIFF	07.45	07.48
	BRIDGEND	08.07	08.10
	PORT TALBOT	08.22	08.26
	NEATH	08.32	08.38
Steamer	Arrives: SWANSEA (High Street)	†08.48	†08.58
	Departs: SWANSEA (Ferry Terminal)	09.15 S	09.20
	Arrives: ILFRACOMBE	11.35	11.40
	LUNDY ISLAND	13.25 L	13.25
Return Arrangements:			
Steamer	Departs: LUNDY ISLAND	16.35 L Y	16.30
	ILFRACOMBE	18.45 (18.20 Weds.)	18.20
	Arrives: SWANSEA (Ferry Terminal)	†21.05(†20.40 Weds.)	†20.40
Train	Departs SWANSEA (High Street)	21.25	21.35
	Arrives NEATH	21.38	21.48
	PORT TALBOT	21.49	21.59
	BRIDGEND	22.08	22.17
	CARDIFF	22.36	22.45
	NEWPORT	*23.13	*23.13

L Steamer does not proceed to and from Lundy Island on Wednesdays.
Y 16.50 on July 27, August 5, 10, 19, 24 and September 2.
* Change at Cardiff.
† Buses convey passengers between the station and the ferryport at an additional charge of 16p each way.
S 9.20 on Saturdays due Ilfracombe 11.40.

From CARMARTHEN and LLANELLI

Forward Arrangements		Tuesdays, Wednesdays & Thursdays	Saturdays, July 24, August 7,21, September 4 and 18
Train	Departs: CARMARTHEN	07.40	07.40
	LLANELLI	08.14	08.14
	Arrives: SWANSEA (High Street)	†08.38	†08.38
Steamer	Departs: SWANSEA (Ferry Terminal)	09.15	09.20
	Arrives: ILFRACOMBE	11.35	11.40
	LUNDY ISLAND	13.25 L	—
Return Arrangements			
Steamer	Departs: LUNDY ISLAND	16.35 L Y	
	ILFRACOMBE	18.45 (Weds. 18.20)	19.45 A
	Arrives: SWANSEA (Ferry Terminal)	†21.05 (Weds. †20.40)	†22.05
	Departs: SWANSEA (High Street)	23.00	23.00
	Arrives: LLANELLI	23.20	23.20
	CARMARTHEN	23.57	23.57

A 19.15 on September 18th.
B 21.35 on September 18th.
† Buses convey passengers between the station and the ferryport at an additional charge of 16p each way.
L Steamer does not proceed to and from Lundy Island on Wednesdays.
Y 16.50 on July 27, August 5, 10, 19, 24 and September 2.

Additional Saturday Sailings between SWANSEA and ILFRACOMBE
(Calling at Mumbles in each direction)

On certain **Saturdays** when no day-return tickets are issued from Newport, Cardiff, Bridgend, Neath and Port Talbot to Ilfracombe, and no sailings operate between Penarth and Ilfracombe, sailings between Swansea and Ilfracombe or vice versa are as follows:

SATURDAY	Depart SWANSEA	Depart ILFRACOMBE
July 24, August 7, 21, and September 4	09.20 17.40 M	12.00 M 19.45
September 18	09.20 16.45	12.00 19.15

M indicates to or from Mumbles only.

Passengers returning from Ilfracombe on any of the above days should ensure that a satisfactory rail connection is available.

Steamer Services
For full particulars of steamer services from Penarth, Barry, Porthcawl, Mumbles and Swansea, please ask for special leaflets.

Aside from these outward appearances of normality, season by season, the finances of P. & A. Campbell Ltd were following an unhealthy trend. Many years had passed since any dividends had been paid to Ordinary shareholders, and it was perhaps partly momentum that had kept things going rather than dynamism. Even then some commentators realised that the business was running on borrowed time, as it were, and that it could not be assumed that Bristol Channel excursions would continue for ever unless something was done to turn things around.

1974: first impressions

The author's first encounter with *Balmoral* took place in the early season of 1974, and so this account now moves to a first-hand but perhaps slightly more subjective view of P. & A. Campbell Ltd history. As *Balmoral* arrived off Penarth Pier on a low-tide one could look down into the murky brown waters of the Bristol Channel as this '... *large sea-going ship capable of accommodating over 800 passengers*' approached cautiously, to embark a few dozen hardy souls for a return trip to Weston super Mare and up to Bristol. Perhaps something larger had been imagined, but the illustration on the top of the handbill which proudly advertised 'Sailings from PENARTH & BARRY PIERS' had suggested a somewhat grander vessel: it was a little while before it became clear that the block used under the bold title WHITE FUNNEL FLEET was actually a rendering of the even smaller *St. Trillo*, with one of her two funnels smudged out so as to create a slightly misleading image of the sole representative of this grand-sounding fleet. This first voyage obviously made some impression, however, and a disappointment shortly afterwards was to discover how many places this fleet no longer sailed to, notably Cardiff itself.

The situation regarding Barry Pier was a little confused at this time, as the combined bill for Penarth & Barry sailings clearly indicated days through until August on which occasional Barry calls would take place as well as at Penarth, except that they were obviously not happening. Another disappointment, whilst on a sortie around the extensive Barry Docks system a few weeks later, was the sight of a very forlorn-looking *St. Trillo*, then laid up in the Graving Dock at Cadoxton, deserted and drifting around aimlessly whilst secured by a couple of slack ropes. It was obvious to an onlooker that her career had ended, and indeed she was towed to the breakers about twelve months later after the only glimpse of her. All of this was sufficient to engender some kind of basic gratitude that the lone *Balmoral* was still operational from the rather fine surviving pier at genteel Penarth, and interest in her diverse activities proceeded to gradually develop.

Later it was discovered that the pontoon-berth at Barry Pier had been severely damaged by gales the previous winter, although as timetable bills had already been printed it had clearly been assumed that repairs would have been effected. The company was doubtless unable to justify making any contribution to the cost of repairs, and thus another White Funnel Fleet 'port' disappeared. Otherwise, the 1974 season proceeded in a manner similar to 1973, with Lundy sailings from Swansea dominating the broad midweek pattern, although occasional Lundy landing trips from up-Channel were being offered. These struck one then as being of a rather marathon character: the normal pattern (when tides were favourable) was for *Balmoral* to commence at Penarth then proceed via Weston to Ilfracombe and Lundy. This, as later discovered, was not of course how it had been done in previous times, and with rather speedier vessels to boot: the schedule on Sunday 26th May 1974 was typical, with *Balmoral* booked to depart from Penarth at 0910 and not return until 2300, having run via Weston in the outwards and return directions, to give passengers a couple of hours ashore on Lundy if they were lucky. Whilst this arrangement was fine for Weston passengers, and doubtless optimal for P. & A. Campbell Ltd to earn some token 'ferry' revenue, it was less good for the south Wales contingent whose numbers then seemed to outweigh those from the English side. These sorts of journey times, combined with the distinctly unappealing catering already alluded to, suggested that White Funnel Fleet sailings were operating on borrowed time, and it was resolved to enjoy what was left while it was still possible, picking and choosing the more unusual trips to places like Minehead or Lynmouth, in order to explore further afield whilst exploiting the ship as my own, personal ferry across the Bristol Channel.

Other matters of note concerning 1974 more generally were of less immediate relevance to daily operations. It was known that the Isles of Scilly Steamship Company (hereafter termed IoSSCo.) had placed an order in 1972 for a ship to replace their 1956-built *Scillonian* (II), a vessel of broadly comparable dimensions to *Balmoral*. She was relatively unusual by 1974 as one of a very small number of passenger & cargo ships still trading in UK waters not to have been purpose-built as a car-ferry, the only others then being *Orcadia* trading out of Kirkwall to the north isles of Orkney, and *Naomh Eanna* trading from Galway in the west of Ireland to the Aran islands. The type was distinguished by a sizeable cargo-hold forward, and the relevant derricks and cargo-handling-equipment for dealing with modest loads, plus limited passenger accommodation. Of the three, *Scillonian* had by far the greatest amount of passenger accommodation and clearly represented a strategic possibility for Bristol Channel excursion use.

Early in 1974 it became apparent that Ryton Marine of Wallsend, with whom the order for a replacement *Scillonian* had been made, had gone into liquidation. The immediate effect of the Ryton Marine liquidation announcement, however, was to cause the IoSSCo. to rethink their plans, having thus written-off an extensive sum of their shareholders money as a result, and towards the end of 1974 it was announced that the 1956-built vessel would receive an 'extended refit' to keep her in service for another five years. The full significance of this chain of events on the fortunes of P. & A. Campbell Ltd, as things turned out, was not to become publicly apparent until 1977. Before this, though, a meeting had taken place in 1973 between Messrs. Smith-Cox & McGinnity and the full thirteen-strong IoSSCo. Board of Directors, and over lunch at St. Marys on the Isles of Scilly an agreement was reached that P. & A. Campbell Ltd would have 'first refusal' when *Scillonian* was released, at a price '*over which we will not fall out*', as Tony McGinnity later recalled the discussion. As an aside, the comparison between the minimal management that then went into the running of the White Funnel Fleet – 'one man and a boy' as Clifton Smith-Cox mockingly described himself and long-serving Traffic Manager Jack Guy at Cardiff – and the full IoSSCo. Board gave him much cause for merriment in subsequent years.

Tony McGinnity (1937-2008) had been involved with P. & A. Campbell Ltd affairs through his own ship-broking agency in the 1960s. He became a non-executive Director in 1976, and Joint Managing Director with Clifton Smith-Cox from 1977, with a brief to diversify the interests of the company. Author's collection

Balmoral *awaits tide time at Sharpness Dock on 18th April 1978, before sailing down the Severn Estuary to Avonmouth Dock.* Author

1975-1976: More of the same

The general pattern of single-vessel operations now established for the past three seasons, 1972-1974, continued with slight modifications. Whilst **Balmoral** wintered in the River Dart after the end of the 1975 season, negotiations for the sale of *St. Trillo* were concluded after it was reported that the project to sell her for use on the River Thames as a floating restaurant had collapsed. She left Barry in mid-April on a one-way voyage to Dublin and the breakers, after an active career that had spanned well over three decades before her withdrawal in 1969.

A notable feature of 1975 was that this season was the last which still featured the tendering activities in support of the annual visit to the Bristol Channel and North Wales by the Swedish-American liner **Kungsholm**. If one looked carefully at the 1975 season handbill for sailings from Penarth on Friday 13th June an extra sailing was offered after **Balmoral** had returned from a day of Weston ferry crossings and an Ilfracombe run, and a few diehards turned out for the 7.35 pm departure that evening advertised as a 'Single Trip to Menai Bridge (Isle of Anglesea)' due at Menai Bridge the following day at 3.45 pm, at a special fare of £10. A round-Anglesey charter to the Coastal Cruising Association was due to be performed by **Balmoral** on the Sunday, 15th June, from Llandudno and Menai Bridge, prior to tendering duties at Fleetwood on 16th June and at Douglas, Isle of Man on the 17th. Bristol Channel services resumed as normal on Thursday 19th June at Swansea after **Balmoral** had returned overnight from the Irish Sea and given her crew a short break for the remaining part of Wednesday 18th June. It must be said that this represented neat scheduling by tying together the charter and tendering duties, and a few folk at £10 a head could only boost the bottom line as the ship was going around Wales anyway. Sadly this turned out to be the last year that the services of the White Funnel Fleet for tendering duties were needed as the Swedish American Line ceased to operate after August 1975. Thus ended a tradition going back to the early years of the century when P. & A. Campbell Ltd paddle-steamers, such as **Bonnie Doon**, had tendered to the Canadian liners arriving off Avonmouth Docks for a period prior to the Great War.

One minor change in 1975 was that the inclusive weekend trips advertised from up-Channel to Ilfracombe now featured accommodation at the Gilbert Hotel. Another feature of 1975 was that no Clovelly calls from up-Channel featured in the schedule, although these had not been particularly frequent in the previous few years, and were now basically restricted to Swansea days. Otherwise the range of trips offered was broadly consistent, and a frequently advertised facility for Penarth passengers was the combination of an evening cruise to Birnbeck Pier combined with a Victorian Evening on Birnbeck Island when tides permitted. Offered since about 1972, the inclusive cost of steamer travel and a Victorian Banquet was £5.50, and special publicity was produced to market these which described the occasion as '… *a night out for the adventurous* …' and explained that on Birnbeck Island '*... time has stood still since the reign of Queen Victoria who, in 1862, decreed that the pier and Pavilion should be built for the entertainment of her loyal subjects. Now you may also indulge in the elegant luxury and the gastronomic and musical delights from the age of Mrs. Beeton, Strauss and the Music Hall*'. Whether or not these occasions represented a particularly alcoholic form of indulgence the author cannot say, but the handbills alluded to a lavish feast with wine, mead and Somerset cider, entertainment and dancing and also referred helpfully to the fact that '*Bar facilities aboard ship will be specially arranged for Cruise/Banquet ticket holders*' as proprietors Eifion & Betti Owen looked forward to '… *meeting their old friends from across the water* …'. Certainly the experience of waiting on the then already increasingly dilapidated Birnbeck Pier after such a splendidly bibulous evening for the ferry crossing back to Penarth Pier would have been a most memorable one.

A few variations on the main Ilfracombe runs and occasional up-Channel days could still be found when, for example, on Friday 29th August 1975 **Balmoral** ran a morning Penarth-Weston return ferry crossing followed by a sailing to Mumbles, and a Gower coast cruise, before returning to Weston and Penarth and a final crossing back to Weston. Thus **Balmoral** continued to earn what she could by versatile scheduling and her own inherently economical operating costs, until the 1975 season finally closed on Sunday 19th October after the Isles of Scilly weekend had taken place over the previous weekend. The weather had been generally favourable and Cruising Monthly was able to report that *Balmoral* appeared to have enjoyed a highly successful season, especially with Lundy excursion passengers, without speculating on the parlous company finances.

In 1976 a few subtle changes were discernible compared with 1975, whilst many of the regular features of the well-established single-vessel pattern were sensibly perpetuated. *Balmoral* made a trip south in order to undertake a Coastal Cruising Association charter around the Isle of Wight in April, prior to commencement of regular Bristol Channel sailings from Penarth on Saturday 17th April 1976. Penarth handbills dropped any mention of Victorian Evenings at Birnbeck Island, and it was reported that the owners were seeking to sell their property, only four years after having purchased it from P. & A. Campbell Ltd. Excursions from both Penarth & Weston to Minehead for a day at Butlins Holiday Camp were still a significant feature when tides permitted a call at Minehead Harbour on the way down-channel in the morning, with a return by bus in the evening from Minehead to Weston, and thence by steamer for passengers originating at Penarth. By exploiting steamer/bus combinations, it was still found possible to market what as billed as 'A New Excursion' from Weston on Monday 26th July 1976, when *Balmoral* sailed to Mumbles in order to connect with coaches to Porthcawl, with a direct steamer return from Porthcawl Harbour. This was after passengers had enjoyed a couple of hours ashore after their bus journey largely through industrial South Wales, during which time a little extra income had been earned by the vessel making a short Gower Coast cruise from Mumbles.

Lynmouth still generally received weekly calls, on Wednesdays, when it was possible to either sail on *Balmoral* at 12.35 pm to Ilfracombe and return by sea '... *passing the Foreland Point and Lighthouse, Glenthorne, etc. and towards Porlock Bay*', with arrival home by about 1700, or proceed by Western National bus at various times on a 'Circular Trip' – the parlance used was still that which dated from prewar days. Additionally a reasonably regular Lundy service, on Thursdays, using a bus link to Ilfracombe, was still provided for

holidaymakers in Lynmouth. If one looked carefully at Ilfracombe handbills, a reasonable variety of short coastal cruise alternatives was still offered, such as to Wooda Bay, or to Morte Point, off Woolacombe, or along the North Devon Coast to off Heddonsmouth. There was even an experimental attempt to offer a few trips down the Cornish coast, with an impressive and evocative description of the sights to be passed en-route, such as that on Friday 3rd September, advertised as a '*Long Day Cruise along the coasts of Devon and Cornwall, passing Capstone Hill, The Tunnels, Lee Bay, Bull Point and Lighthouse, Morte, Baggy and Downend Points, Woolacombe, Croyde and Saunton Sands, Westward Ho!, Bucks Mill, Clovelly, Gallantry Bower, Hartland Point and Lighthouse, Bude and towards Tintagel*'. Regrettably, it was subsequently reported in *Cruising Monthly* that the three Friday cruises were all dogged by delays at Clovelly, which prevented them from progressing even as far as Bude. No public trips ran to Bideford in 1976, but the same journal was able to confidently report that overall '... *prolonged perfect cruising weather this summer has resulted in* **Balmoral** *having a very successful season indeed. This has been boosted by a large number of charters in the early part of the season and others have been accomplished in the height of the season, after a day's public trips, the latter usually extending* **Balmoral's** *schedule till the early hours of the next day ...*' and that '...*on public trips passengers have regularly been turned away at Ilfracombe and Weston and occasionally at Penarth and Porthcawl*'. Towards the end of the season, however, disruption due to poor weather featured on a number of days. The Lundy launch *Ravenswood* sank at her moorings (but was subsequently raised) leaving Lundy landings in the hands of *Lady Moyra* alone for the remainder of the season.

An unusual excursion was a sailing on 28th September 1976 from Swansea and Mumbles to Tenby, and thence direct to Lundy Island to land. Having sailed at 0800 with only half a dozen passengers for the first leg of the voyage across Carmarthen Bay and collected another 100 or so at Tenby, in a memorably heavy swell *Balmoral* eventually made it to Lundy where a number of her passengers could recover ashore in the warm afternoon sunshine. For the author this was an exceptionally memorable first trip to Lundy. Apparently P. & A.

During the summer of 1975, **Balmoral** *is seen alongside the breakwater at Porthcawl, having arrived from up-Channel. After a brief call she resumed her cruise along the south Wales coast, past Sker Point, to the Mumbles.*

Author

141

*A different atmosphere existed on Lundy before the construction of the new pier in 1999, and rather less certainty attached to landings on the beach if weather conditions were variable. In the summer of 1976 **Polar Bear** had become the Lundy packet after withdrawal of **Lundy Gannet**, and **Balmoral** often crossed thrice-weekly to the island from Ilfracombe, most commonly from Swansea and Mumbles but also less frequently from Penarth and Weston super Mare, dependent on tidal patterns.*   Author

Campbell Ltd had traditionally tended to run an annual long-day trip out of Tenby around this time of year, which was aimed at the farmers in Pembrokeshire who might squeeze a day-off from their toils ashore. An account of this epic trip in *Cruising Monthly* politely referred to difficulties encountered in approaching Tenby's small harbour after dark on the return voyage, which was to result in a final arrival back at Swansea at 0110, over one and a half hours late: the relatively close-up view that passengers had of Saundersfoot beach after **Balmoral** overshot Tenby by a few miles and had to put herself about to call at the little jetty there was not recorded. There was no-one to take a rope at Mumbles Pier at this late hour and in order to allow one passenger to disembark a deckhand leapt on to the pier after the ship nosed in close enough after another had lassooed a bollard, and a gangplank was very quickly slid on and off the pier: it was assumed the passenger would be able to extricate himself at the other end of the pier. This was not far short of being literally a full day out after an 0500 start from Cardiff the previous day, and the character of Lundy together with this means of getting there was now, for the author, indelibly etched.

The conclusion reached by the journal of the Coastal Cruising Association was that, mechanically, **Balmoral** had behaved very well in 1976 and had coped admirably with crowds and an ambitious programme of sailings in the Bristol Channel and occasionally elsewhere. The picture behind the scenes, however, was not so straightforward, and it was now the case that the P. & A. Campbell Ltd business was again coming under closer scrutiny from the parent company. The continued existence of the subsidiary was being increasingly seen as an irrelevance by certain factions in the parent European Ferries group, and demands for change were becoming apparent to an embattled Clifton Smith-Cox and his future co-Director Tony McGinnity.

Scillonian – a final flourish

The early part of the decade had started with the unhappy experience of the forced contraction of the fleet to a single ship after 1971, but a degree of stability had followed as **Balmoral** sailed on alone for a few summers and established a new pattern of single-vessel operations. Her sometimes shabby appearance perhaps belied a basic resilience, that of survival itself, when a number of other British shipping companies

had given up passenger excursion operations with dedicated vessels by that time. 1976 was a variable summer, and although it may not have been outwardly apparent as business seemingly continued as normal, there was now increasing pressure on Clifton Smith-Cox from the parent company to give up the business of the subsidiary company altogether as profits dwindled. The early-1970s had been something of a survival operation, and it will be remembered that a number of attempts to diversify had been made in the 1960s, so as to put P. & A. Campbell Ltd on a firmer footing. The strategic intention had been to secure some degree of year-round stability instead of staying with just a riskier, seasonal dependence. A longer-term survival of the business was the key motive, provided that this could be built on a reasonably stable footing. By the mid-1970s turnover was now significantly less after the cross-channel coach excursion activities had been transferred to the parent company, even if things in the Bristol Channel seemed little changed and – in short – had become more exposed.

Some of the old fighting spirit was still left in the company though, and the injection of fresh capital would enable another ship to be acquired in 1977. The sturdy former Isles of Scilly ferry **Scillonian** (II) marked a visible and definite attempt to turn the ailing company around as Mr A. M. C. McGinnity was invited to join a strengthened P. & A. Campbell Ltd Board first as a non-executive director and then as full-time Joint Managing Director. The second ship was in reality only part of the plan though, and his brief was to develop new spheres of activity, which were less tangible to followers of **Balmoral** alone as the new vision was for diversification into ship-broking, with the expectation that this might represent a more sustainable future than seeking to persevere solely with the excursion ship business and its challenging economics. The thinking behind the acquisition of an appropriately-sized and somewhat younger vessel, capable of economic all-year round operation in Bristol Channel conditions, could scarcely be faulted in the desire to keep the P. & A. Campbell Ltd flag flying in a practical manner. A bid would thus be made by the company to become the dedicated provider of a combined Lundy cargo and passenger service, tailored to combining the modest but steady freight requirements of the island community with the need to provide sufficient seasonal capacity for increasing numbers of summer visitors.

Shortly before her release from the Penzance to Isles of Scilly service, **Scillonian** *is seen at St. Marys handling vehicular traffic in the traditional manner over the side. April 1977.*   Author

That all was not well was not necessarily apparent to observers. Occasionally a mention might be made of the continuing tenuous profitability of the company, and the image of P. & A. Campbell Ltd operations then was one of frugality as the hardworking and occasionally unkempt *Balmoral* clocked up long days in service to try and capture as much revenue as possible in a changing leisure economy. However, if one looked closely enough, study of P. & A. Campbell Ltd Annual Reports & Accounts during the early 1970s revealed a deteriorating trend in financial performance. Annual Statements by the Chairman became more brief as the seasons went by, and gave fewer clues each year as to the official outlook of the Company, but the stated position for the 1976 season, which turned in a £15k profit, scarcely revealed the pressure being applied on Clifton Smith-Cox from European Ferries to 'do something' about P. & A. Campbell Ltd as the financial contribution being made by the subsidiary to the parent group was increasingly being regarded as unsatisfactory. This might have not been so much of a worry if the personalities had not changed, but the close friendship that had existed between Clifton Smith-Cox and Roland Wickenden until the latter's death in October 1972 was gradually turning into something more pecuniary. Keith Wickenden took over the role of Chairman of European Ferries shortly after the death of his brother, and Ken Siddle became Managing Director and, as such, the nominee representative of the European Ferries group on the P. & A. Campbell Ltd board which Clifton Smith-Cox continued to chair. Ernie Harris had retired as Secretary, and his place had been taken by E. C. Overington. As the seventies progressed less worth was seen by a new, harder-headed European Ferries headquarters staff – involved, after all, in a very substantial and rapidly expanding commercial ferry company – to be derived from something so comparatively trivial as the operation of one rather ageing pleasure steamer in an entirely different area, with its own set of overheads, quite away from any obvious form of central control or discipline, and with its own arguably old-fashioned, pleasure-steamer image.

One terse paragraph entitled 'Activities' summed up the declared position of P. & A. Campbell Ltd in the Annual Report & Accounts for the year ended 31st December 1976: *'There has been no change in the activities of the Company during the period. The whole of the turnover and trading profit arose from the Company's principal activities. These are the operation of passenger vessels and the carriage of passengers'.*

In round figures, the accounts revealed that income of £219,000 during 1976 had generated a trading profit of a mere £13,000, which after various adjustments became a profit of £15,000 after taxation. This ratio of profit to turnover clearly did not satisfy forces within European Ferries and when put under continuing pressure, Clifton Smith-Cox decided to turn to Tony McGinnity – privately, at this point – for help as his professional involvement with the company was long-standing. As the two men saw it there were two choices: either to yield to the pressure from the parent company to close the whole operation down, or to react positively and find a means of diversification for P. & A. Campbell Ltd in order to improve profitability. The latter course was chosen, and heralded the start of what was hoped might be a new era for the company. The remainder of this story, then, stems from the consequences of the decisions taken after a position had been agreed with the parent company and which would allow a new direction to be pursued by the subsidiary.

Although the company owned by Tony McGinnity, West Marine Surveyors, had continued to act for P. & A. Campbell Ltd it was with some reluctance that this new approach was considered. The deteriorating mechanical performance of *Balmoral* was causing increasing calls on their time, and the annual fee paid had not changed for some time and was now a good deal lower than that received by West Marine for a number of other vessels they were then handling. Apart from this, Tony McGinnity had given up an active role in West Marine the previous year, having earlier become Divisional Director (Marine) with the Barrow in Furness ship-owners James Fisher & Sons plc, and moved to the Windermere area where he had overall responsibility for some twenty-six ships. However, he had remained firm friends with Clifton Smith-Cox since they had met during his involvement with the paddle steamer *Consul* as managing owner. Although of different ages, both men got on well and shared a common approach to getting things done together with a somewhat iconoclastic attitude to officialdom. Clifton Smith-Cox was not only an accountant by profession but an outspoken businessman and magistrate, whilst Tony McGinnity was a surveyor and ship-manager with technical knowledge and who also had the strength of character to oppose the stubborn streak of the older man, leading to occasional arguments between them, but not over policy.

When their discussions opened, Clifton Smith-Cox confided to Tony McGinnity that the European Ferries Group no longer wished to continue with the P. & A. Campbell Ltd business after 1976, and that either a buyer be found or it would be closed down. Whilst efforts to find a buyer continued, to no avail, European Ferries conceded that *Balmoral* could be commissioned for 1977 as a final gesture, but after that there would be no further reprieve. Interest had been expressed by a London firm called John Williams Sons & Sharp, but this came to nought when they discovered that the minimal profits now being earned were at the cost of what they perceived as a 'clapped-out' ship in need of either extensive refurbishment or replacement, with elderly sea staff and little or no shore organisation. When they asked why EFL were not prepared to invest in the business themselves there was no answer other than the obvious one. It was shortly after this that the Lundy situation became a key issue.

These discussions had obviously taken place behind the scenes, and the awareness amongst the clientele of the White Funnel Fleet as to the future direction the company might seek to take was minimal, with just the odd rumour combined with supposition regarding the affairs of the Isles of Scilly Steamship Company (IoSSCo.). Delivery in early-1977 of the new *Scillonian* (III) from the Appledore shipbuilder's yard for the Penzance - St. Marys run finally took place, and shortly afterwards the tangible evidence of a new direction for the White Funnel Fleet became apparent as a second ship was acquired. The ship was, of course, the former 1956-built Scilly ferry *Scillonian* (II) regarding which the earlier agreement had been reached with the island-owned shipping company (cf).

The other direction in which P. & A. Campbell Ltd was to embark was less visible, that of a new venture into ship-broking and ship-management activity, which was to be carried out from the Bristol office, at Alliance House in Baldwin Street. These premises, close to the Floating Harbour, now became the registered offices of P. & A. Campbell Ltd despite the continuing use of the Cardiff premises in Bute Town which had been retained for day-to-day passenger enquiries and sales purposes. By this time only a small upstairs room at 4, Dock Chambers was used by P. & A. Campbell Ltd as the scale of operations, which had earlier necessitated the use of a larger ground-floor, had contracted and economies had been effected. It was hoped and expected that the new direction to be taken at the Bristol office might even outgrow the core excursion ship operation, and prove more profitable.

A course towards diversification had thus been laid, and the Directors Report for 1977 was now able to state under the heading 'Activities' the following: '*During the year the company added the management of ships to its activities. The principal activity, however, was the operation of passenger vessels and the carriage of passengers.*'

The Lundy question

Clifton Smith-Cox had been closely watching how Lundy managed its own shipping service provided by the coaster *Polar Bear*. The good relationship that had existed with Lundy's owners – the Harman family, in the 1960s – was largely perpetuated in the 1970s through John Smith, the Chairman of the Landmark Trust. The thinking that emerged as P. & A. Campbell Ltd came under pressure to improve its financial performance was that mutual advantage ought to accrue if the White Funnel Fleet could take on a year-round role based on serving Lundy, saving the Landmark Trust the expense of running its own vessel. It was not necessarily envisaged that the former *Scillonian* would take on this role in her P. & A. Campbell Ltd guise straightaway. The decision to purchase her from the IoSSCo. reflected her status as an essentially sturdy vessel, with plenty of years of service still in her. Critically, she was available at the relatively low price of £150,000, in fully operational condition. Therefore, whilst *Balmoral* still had life

in her, then *Scillonian* – if purchased – could be put to use elsewhere whilst representing a longer-term replacement for *Balmoral* when her time came. Alternatively, she was identified as readily saleable – potentially at a profit to P. & A. Campbell Ltd – should circumstances necessitate that course of action.

Such was the strategic thinking at the end of 1976 when Clifton Smith-Cox had presented his plan to European Ferries Chairman Keith Wickenden, prior to seeking funding for the purchase. A provisional understanding – but critically no more than that - had been reached with the Landmark Trust as regards the possible takeover of the loss-making *Polar Bear* by P. & A. Campbell Ltd and, as it had been phrased in the proposition to the parent company: '*... If the Balmoral operated the Bristol Channel summer service, the Polar Bear operated the winter service one day a week or possibly two between Ilfracombe and Lundy Island, and the Scillonian were chartered probably for work in the North during the whole year and the Polar Bear similarly during the summer, a very interesting and highly profitable venture results.*' In the meantime, Lundy operations by the Landmark Trust with their own coaster *Polar Bear* carried on as normal.

The ability of *Balmoral* to successfully undergo a quinquennial survey in 1977 was cited, and Clifton Smith-Cox opined that both *Polar Bear* and *Scillonian* were vessels that '*... at the moment are in great demand for charter in connection with North Sea Work.*' Also identified was the further charter business potential for *Scillonian* (II) to relieve her successor *Scillonian* (III) for a month each year on the Penzance - Isles of Scilly run whilst the latter was undergoing annual winter refit. Looking ahead to the day when *Balmoral* might be withdrawn the proposition continued: '*... Referring to services in the Bristol Channel, when it was decided to abandon operation of Balmoral, Scillonian could operate in the Bristol Channel for a considerably shortened summer period and thus provide the services during the period that they are really profitable. She could then go on charter during the winter. I am referring to services from the Spring Bank Holiday to mid-September, that is about three and a half to four months.*'

In conclusion Clifton Smith-Cox boldly put it to Keith Wickenden that this scenario carried '*... no risk whatever*' for European Ferries, and predicted that it would indeed result in a substantial profit. It was stated that *Polar Bear* was then incurring losses of about £45,000 per annum, and that if *Balmoral* were to be sold then she might command a price of around £30,000 and he pointed out that this was something like that which she had originally cost. A clever proposition had thus been put to European Ferries, and in view of his own advancing years he openly stated that he would be very happy to step aside (whether or not he actually intended this) to let somebody else run the operation, but that his underlying motive was to see the P. & A. Campbell Ltd activity survive even if it were to be sold as a going concern should European Ferries choose to dispose of the business once profitability was restored. The future of the company now partly lay in the way in which the extra ship would actually be deployed, and upon the outcome of the negotiations with the Landmark Trust regarding the servicing of Lundy. Just as importantly, it would also depend upon the success of the new venture into ship-broking, ship management and other associated activities that Tony McGinnity was to pursue in the P. & A. Campbell Ltd name. Once the assent of European Ferries to this scheme was secured, it remained for P. & A. Campbell Ltd to confirm with the full IoSSCo. board the price to be paid for the purchase of *Scillonian* (II), and for Peter Southcombe to be 'recalled' (from European Ferries at Dover, where he had been since 1971/2 after cessation of the cross-channel excursion activities) to assume the day-to-day management responsibility for excursion operations for the 1977 season.

Scillonian becomes *Devonia* – Bristol Channel & elsewhere, 1977

The new Isles of Scilly ferry *Scillonian* (III) ran her maiden voyage on 25th May 1977. *Scillonian* (II) was retained for a little while until her successor fully settled down at Penzance, and was then dispatched to her new home in the Bristol Channel. Arriving with minimal advance warning to the 'regulars', the management had to act rapidly to turn their new acquisition into something useful, as there had been a degree of uncertainty throughout the negotiations

As yet un-renamed, **Scillonian** *is seen here arriving at Mumbles Pier on 25th June 1977. Her schedule that day was for an 0920 departure from Swansea, calling at Mumbles at 0940 for Ilfracombe, returning to Mumbles only, for an afternoon Gower Coast cruise at 1430, leaving Mumbles a second time at 1735 for Ilfracombe, returning from there at 1945 for Mumbles and Swansea, arriving at 2205.* Nigel Jones

for her purchase, and therefore no final plans had been drawn up for her deployment. The IoSSCo. had hung on to her for longer than the purchasers would have wished, and a degree of nervousness would have existed within P. & A. Campbell Ltd. At this point, it was hoped that **Balmoral** would be able to attend the Jubilee Year Fleet Review at Spithead, if **Scillonian** (II) was released in time to take over the Bristol Channel commitments of **Balmoral** around mid-June accordingly. Her entry into Bristol Channel passenger-carrying service, still named **Scillonian** but sporting a hastily-repainted white funnel, duly took place on Midsummer Day itself. Running late, her very first revenue-earning Bristol Channel voyage was to take the evening return trip from Ilfracombe to Swansea on Tuesday 21st June, after **Balmoral** had brought passengers from Swansea & Mumbles across to Ilfracombe and Lundy that morning. **Balmoral** had then been programmed to leave the Bristol Channel directly from Lundy, via St. Ives and Penzance for Fleet Review duties at Southampton. The plan was that the changeover of vessels should have taken place at Lundy Roads – a delightful touch – but delays incurred by **Scillonian** in getting away from Swansea Docks where she had been preparing for duty meant that **Balmoral** had to be ordered to return her Lundy passengers to Ilfracombe. She then made her delayed departure south whilst passengers waiting to return from Ilfracombe to Swansea enjoyed the novelty of being conveyed by **Scillonian** after she had arrived light from Swansea.

Scillonian then spent the next few days on Bristol Channel duties, carrying out the timetable that had been planned for **Balmoral** before the Fleet Review attendance was confirmed. After this brief period of finding the way around her new territory, the opportunity was taken on an off-service day at Swansea, Monday 27th June, to rename **Scillonian** as **Devonia**. This was generally regarded as a very satisfactory revival of a name of a much-loved paddle-steamer from the past, when the Barry Railway Company had taken delivery of the prestigious Clyde-

built pair **Gwalia** and **Devonia** into their red-funnelled fleet in 1905. The latter was to become a member of the White Funnel Fleet in the 1912 season and thereafter, but was not to survive WW2.

One particularly noteworthy voyage carried out by the newly-christened **Devonia** was a special day-return sailing from Pembroke Dock direct to Lundy Island on Wednesday 6th July 1977 which offered something of an endurance test even to White Funnel Fleet stalwarts, being advertised to leave Hobbs Point at 0930 and arrive at Lundy at 1340. She had not offered any form of cooked meal service in her Isles of Scilly days, and compared with **Balmoral** this was a particular weakness. However, it was still not clear to the seagoing public just what P. & A. Campbell Ltd proposed to actually do with their new acquisition after she had appeared on Bristol Channel duties, even if there was a consensus that she appeared to be a sensible purchase on account of her size, seaworthiness and potential versatility. But such sentiments would not pay the bills, and the initial impression put about was that the new home for **Devonia** in 1977 would be on South Coast duties, the essential point about her being that she was still 'in class' when acquired from the Scilly company; in other words, and could therefore be operated straightaway by P. & A. Campbell Ltd, without any preliminary expenditure on dry-docking, repairs or other modifications.

A press release which was reproduced in the *South Avon Mercury* on 24th June 1977 stated that after July when Bristol Channel charter work had been complete **Devonia** would '*... proceed to the South Coast and continue operation from one of a number of resorts which are presently under consideration by the Company.*' A tentative schedule for South Coast operation had been drawn up, and it was notable that Clifton Smith-Cox had called on the expertise of his former South Coast Area Manager Peter Southcombe to help him manage the new activities of **Devonia**, as full-time Passenger Traffic Manager on secondment from European Ferries at Dover. This schedule would have involved

Devonia being based at Brighton Marina and running westwards six days a week, either to Shanklin or Ryde and for round Isle of Wight trips, or to Portsmouth, Southampton and occasionally Yarmouth, or variations thereon.

In the event neither Brighton Marina nor Bournemouth Pier became available to *Devonia*, and the plans had to be abandoned. Instead *Devonia* appeared at very short notice on a new Thames coast service, based at London's Tower Pier. In view of the unsatisfactory results of the operation of *Queen of the Isles* in the south-east during 1969, this perhaps seemed a surprising development, but the details of the new operation were rather different in that *Devonia* was to adhere to a much simpler, more regular pattern of sailings without the extensive light running which had characterised the earlier experiment in the south-east of England.

The new service was advertised to commence on 14th July 1977, with *Devonia* leaving Tower Pier daily (except Mondays) at 1000 and proceeding to Southend with a call at Greenwich, a voyage timed to take just under four hours. For these duties she had a Class IV certificate enabling her to carry 614 passengers. On three days a week – Wednesdays, Saturdays & Sundays – a cruise from Southend was advertised at 1415, returning by about 1600 so that a regular departure time of 1615 back up-river could be adhered to each day, whether or not *Devonia* had lain at anchor or cruised around the Thames estuary in no particular direction for 90-minutes. The Thames operation of *Devonia* was not trouble-free – she experienced engine trouble on 18th August, and was holed the next day, albeit not terribly seriously.

A few of the Bristol Channel regulars who patronised *Balmoral* were sufficiently curious to venture to London to sample what *Devonia* had

Handbill advertising the summer 1977 services operated by **Devonia**.
Peter Southcombe collection

London's Tower Pier ticket office, used for the cruises operated in 1977 by **Devonia**. Martin Oatway

to offer, and one reporter noted that on her trip on 20th August 1977 she had only around 100 passengers on board departing from Tower Pier, and ascribed this to her having a few days previously been off-service whilst undergoing repairs. In addition to this immediate uncertainty about her programme, she had received little prior publicity for the new venture. Around twenty more passengers boarded at Greenwich, and thus there was plenty of room even though much of her forward deck remained roped off throughout the voyage. She seemed well-kept, and drew around seven foot which, it was noted, would restrict her Bristol

During the summer of 1977 the former Isles of Scilly ferry **Scillonian**, *duly renamed* **Devonia**, *was deployed on a regular schedule linking London Tower Pier with Southend. Carrying a white funnel but still in her old hull colours, a good number are seen on board her pulling away from Southend Pier for the short afternoon cruise.*

Peter Southcombe collection

Channel use somewhat. Plentiful shipping was encountered, and the extensive damage at Southend Pier was noted following a serious fire earlier. Yet more shipping in the roads off Southend was spotted during the short cruise from Southend Pier, and although the return journey to London was against the tide good time was made, and *Devonia* had to wait until her booked arrival time until other vessels cleared the berth. Although *Devonia* usually berthed in the Pool overnight, a visit by Russian naval vessels was expected and so she anchored downstream that night.

Later on in the season, a fouled propeller on 18th September caused a very late arrival back at Tower Pier in the evening, and the subsequent cancellation of trips on 19th-23rd September whilst *Devonia* was hastily dry-docked in the Royal group of docks by Green, Silley Weir for underwater attention. Rather late in the day, the initiative was taken to include trial calls at Gravesend in both directions on the sailings from and to Tower Pier on Saturday & Sunday 24th/25th September, the latter being the day when the Thames service ceased for the season. This marked the end of the initial phase of the deployment by P. & A. Campbell Ltd of *Devonia* as a passenger-carrying excursion vessel. There was no news of any agreement yet being reached with the Landmark Trust regarding the hoped-for Lundy contract, and the future prospects for the additional vessel in the White Funnel Fleet seemed unclear.

It was said that one factor which may have impinged on the profitability of this venture in the south-east in the 1977 season by *Devonia* (and, to a degree, that undertaken by *Queen of the Isles* some years beforehand, in 1969) was the cost of pilotage on the River Thames. For a voyage commencing at Tower Pier, a river Pilot was needed as far as Gravesend, after which a Channel pilot was required. However, the full costs of pilotage were allowed for when the programmes were

planned, so the suggestion that such costs caught operators by surprise is untrue, even if three different pilots coming aboard might have been observed during a return excursion from London.

Balmoral had carried on as normal in the Bristol Channel during the 1977 season, noteworthy features being the reinstatement of occasional calls (i.e. by launch) at Lynmouth on sailings from up-channel. These had not taken place since 1971. A couple of odd cruises towards Bude had been offered, on Fridays July 8th and 15th, as extensions of straightforward Swansea/Mumbles to Ilfracombe & Clovelly sailings. On the other side of the Bristol Channel, occasional longer Gower Coast cruises were still offered and one such was that early in the season, on Saturday 25th June, leaving Mumbles at 1400 for a cruise passing Worms Head and towards Rhosilli, due back at Mumbles at about 1730. Another 'experiment' to which Penarth handbills drew special attention was the running of a few trips from Penarth to Ilfracombe and Lundy Island (to land) without a call en-route at Weston, thus considerably speeding up the passage from south Wales and enabling a more worthwhile amount of time for passengers to enjoy ashore on Lundy.

As the 1977 season drew to a close, *Devonia* was the first vessel to lay up whilst *Balmoral* continued in service. She operated the now established annual Isles of Scilly mini-cruise under the guidance of Tom Foden (now named as the Cruise Director) in early October, prior to heading south for a charter to Waverley Travel on 21st October consisting of a cruise from Southampton & Cowes to Bournemouth, for a further non-landing cruise to Portland Harbour. There was to have been a trip the following day to Eastbourne, but this was cancelled owing to a lack of passengers. *Balmoral* thus headed for the River Dart, and winter lay-up, on 23rd October, where she joined her fleetmate *Devonia*. However, the latter did not enjoy a lengthy sojourn

The view from Southend Pier before **Devonia** *departed on one of her Thames Estuary cruises. Note the furniture acquired to supplement the cargo-hold hatches.* Martin Oatway

there and a new phase in her White Funnel Fleet career beckoned as the first fruits of attempts at diversification became apparent.

The new regime also started to take a hard look at conditions on board **Balmoral** around this time, and Rod Staker (brought in by Tony McGinnity as Operations Manager) interviewed crew members and reported at length on what he judged to be the deficiencies of the style of on-board operations and morale. It was beginning to be more of a recognised fact that things could not continue unchanged: P. & A. Campbell Ltd in 1977 were still operating outside any kind of Trade Union framework, paying low wages and experiencing high turnover of personnel accordingly. Living conditions on board the ship were poor, and the practice of overnight berthing alongside a recognised place (even if only occasionally between her complex schedules) where the crew could get ashore or go home had ceased a few years earlier, as both Cardiff Pier Head and Barry Pier had become unavailable. Nearly all of the old White Funnel Fleet hands had gone now, and this problem was not simply going to solve itself.

At this point it was assumed that in 1978 **Balmoral** and **Devonia** would switch places. In the absence of any specific alternative work for the former Scilly vessel, **Balmoral** was now thought more to be more appropriate for a Thames coast season (this situation was soon was to change, qv). The report concluded that proper recruitment campaigns ought to be started at the end of the 1977 season, on the assumption that 'day-men' would suffice (and for whom proper overnight accommodation on-board would not then be needed) for **Balmoral** on the Thames, but that for **Devonia** the provision of good on-board overnight and messing facilities was recommended as being of the

utmost importance, both to reflect the lack of any routine night-time berthing during the Bristol Channel summer season and prospective oil-rig supply charter use. Seamen were to be engaged in accordance with clear standard contract terms which respected NUS convention, and a disputes procedure implemented. Plans for the conversion of **Devonia** were duly drawn up, but a lack of certainty on the future disposition of the ships then meant that they were not implemented immediately.

Before going on to consider this next phase of the career of **Devonia** in Scottish waters as an oil-rig support vessel – a novel task for a P. & A. Campbell Ltd ship – it is appropriate to jump ahead a little to the publication of the Annual Report and Accounts for the twelve month period ended 31st December 1977, which revealed an alarming position. Whilst 1976 had yielded a slight trading profit before adjustments, which indicated a positive cashflow, the extra expense in 1977 associated with the crewing of two vessels was considerable and the extra revenue earned insufficient to have improved profitability in the manner that had been hoped for. The Profit & Loss Account attached to the 1977 results showed the comparative position:

y/e	31.12.1977	31.12.1976
Gross Receipts	£235,494	£195,692
Expenses	£285,346	£180,878
Net (Loss)/Profit	£(49,852)	£ 14,814

This was a very worrying result, although with hindsight it was not too surprising in view of the fact that the 1977 Thames programme had been launched with so little advance notice, and that the company had been deprived of anything much in the way of advance or party bookings from tour operators. However, it had been felt that the only alternative would have been to lay up **Devonia** during 1977 in the hope that charter work would have been secured, and that as the passenger certificate and dry-docking had been already paid for (that is, by the IoSSCo., when she was still with them) then that benefit could not be wasted. There was still no sign of any new Lundy agreement yet, and so **Devonia** continued to incur expenses whilst idle after the initial 1977 passenger activity, to add to the significant costs of emergency repairs during her brief Thames operation. Hopefully, all this was about to change as 1978 approached, and the hoped-for charter of **Devonia** was secured.

The sequence of events becomes complicated here, as the expectation in late-1977 was that the charter for **Devonia** would run until early summer in 1978. Therefore, Peter Southcombe went ahead with detailed planning for an expanded 1978 programme of Thames coast services to be undertaken by **Balmoral**, on the basis that the main 1978 Bristol Channel summer sailings would be handled by **Devonia**. His brief therefore was quite simply to operate **Devonia** (that is, after her return from the winter charter) where the financial downside would be minimised. As will be seen, this was not quite how things actually worked out.

Devonia goes north

Positive news at the beginning of 1978 was that work in Scottish waters had been secured for **Devonia**, and she started work at Loch Kishorn on 9th January. This charter with Chevron had been obtained in late 1977 after intensive negotiations by Tony McGinnity, and was for an initial four months with options for two further, successive four month periods. At that stage it was hoped that the whole twelve month option would be taken up but as events turned out this proved not to be the case. (Had the charter been perpetuated, of course, then the Thames plan would have been cancelled in order to keep Bristol Channel sailings going with **Balmoral**). A scratch crew had been put together at short notice and the vessel taken to Falmouth instead of the more usual visit to Holmans at Penzance who were then fully booked. **Devonia** received a thorough overhaul with repairs to all derricks and wires as it was anticipated these would be needed in the north.

At this juncture, the Marine Survey Office of the Department of Transport sprung an unpleasant surprise on P. & A. Campbell Ltd: hitherto, the vessel on its Class IIa certificate (an essential for charter in the north or elsewhere) had operated in the cargo/passenger role with two holds. Before now granting the necessary certificate they insisted on the fitting of an additional steel watertight bulkhead in No. 2 hold which added an additional and unexpected £20,000 to the Falmouth refit costs. The argument put forward by the D.o.T. for the permission to operate without the bulkhead was that for the purposes of floodability it was assumed both holds in the vessel would normally be full of cargo. This unfortunate piece of officialdom meant that the vessel could not be used in the future as a relief vessel on the Isles of Scilly run. (As an aside, some years later after the vessel had been acquired by Torbay Seaways, that company asked for and obtained permission from the DoT to remove this bulkhead).

Bad news followed almost immediately as she received damage on her second day in service on charter to Chevron, and had to be sent to Lamonts yard on the Clyde on 16th January 1978 for repairs which took until the end of the month. The damage had been extensive, and amongst other things *Devonia* required to be fitted with a new rudder as well as having her keel repaired. A little later it was reported that she was based at Kyle of Lochalsh and usually made three trips daily to the oil-rig lying in the Sound of Raasay. Nevertheless, at this point it was assumed that the charter would continue indefinitely, and thus plans were finalised for *Balmoral* to undertake her normal Bristol Channel duties in the 1978 season, and the proposed 1978 Thames operations dropped as the company would not now have the additional

ship available as had been intended. The damage sustained by *Devonia* led to considerable loss of revenue and the cause was never fully established: one theory was that the vessel had struck a dummy torpedo as the area in which she was operating had been extensively used for torpedo trials by the MoD. Her crew consisted mainly of people recruited in Scotland although Campbell mate Flanagan was an exception. The master was a retired CalMac employee employed on account of his extensive knowledge of those waters. Oddly, two crew members disappeared never to be seen alive again, and the body of one was found floating near the berth at Kyle of Lochalsh. A third casualty was a watchman at Bristol, which as Peter Southcombe later recalled, represented more losses than on any previous Campbell ship.

The charter duties were, however, to terminate prematurely and on the return of *Devonia* to Bristol early in May 1978 it was discovered that both engines had sustained damage through crew negligence and extensive repairs were required before any thoughts of her operation in 1978 could be entertained. A highly undesirable business situation now existed, as it was felt (by Clifton Smith-Cox) to be too late to reverse the decision to scrap the Thames programme, despite the extensive preparations that had been made, even though – perversely – the White Funnel Fleet was back up to strength with two passenger ships. *Devonia* thus lay idle for the moment but in the meantime discussions with naval architects had been entered into regarding

After the 1977 summer season **Devonia** *was chartered for oil-rig supply work in Scotland.*
Peter Southcombe collection

A White Funnel Fleet 1970s scene: Lundy boatman Albert Fisher awaits to board **Balmoral** *at Ilfracombe Pier.* Betty Saunders

drawing up plans for her conversion into a more suitable configuration for passenger cruising, as well as addressing the fundamental need to provide adequate crew accommodation, which she had never needed as an Isles of Scilly day-boat. When that time came though, nothing was actually done as the cost was felt by Tony McGinnity to be too high, and not to be contemplated until further long term charter work could be secured for *Devonia* outside her passenger commitments. This was to prove regrettable, although hardly surprising in view of the lack of progress so far in reversing the company fortunes, and it had been acknowledged that this would take some time.

In the meantime, efforts to find out of season work for her were intensified. One possible charter might have been to the then growing Virgin music business developed by Richard Branson, for *Devonia* to sail around the coast of Britain to various ports whereupon she would provider a stage for the Sex Pistols to perform upon. The band aroused a degree of controversy in the seventies, and the charter proposition was vetoed by Clifton Smith-Cox on the grounds that the band had insulted the Queen. A little later, whilst lying in the centre of Bristol, she was briefly used as a set for filming the comedy series It Ain't Half Hot Mum, which brought in a small amount of income.

Overall though, the business situation which P. & A. Campbell Ltd faced in late 1978 was distinctly uncertain.

Diversification commences

A critical time had now arrived for the future of P. & A. Campbell Ltd. After fighting off pressures from hostile factions within European Ferries Clifton Smith-Cox had carried his argument in favour of diversification of the company yet despite having experimented in new territories in 1977 with the additional vessel, the financial performance had deteriorated. However, he still had a breathing space and at the beginning of January 1978 Ken Siddle, the Managing Director of European Ferries, gave his blessing to the launch of the prospective ship-broking and ship management business to be undertaken in the P. & A. Campbell Ltd name by Tony McGinnity, who also recruited

Richard Coupland to create a 'presence' in the chartering market. In an Internal Memorandum to European Ferries directors dated 10th January 1978, Tony McGinnity had been given the equivalent of a letter of introduction within the parent company as his appointment as Joint Managing Director of P. & A. Campbell Ltd was announced:

The European Ferries

Internal Memorandum
from Mr K. Siddle

P. & A. Campbell Ltd

P. & A. Campbell Ltd since its incorporation in 1891 has concentrated on one principal activity, i.e. the operation of Excursion vessels.

It has been decided to enlarge the scope of this Company's operations by entering into the field of Ship-Management, Chartering, Ship and Insurance Broking, and related fields. As a first step Campbell's motor vessel *Devonia* has been chartered to the Chevron Oil Company and is now engaged on ferrying oil workers to oil-rigs under construction at Kishorn in Scotland. Active negotiations are also in progress to acquire the management of a seismographic survey vessel which will work mainly in West African waters.

P. & A. Campbell Ltd has acquired West Marine Surveyors and Consultants Ltd, a company of which Mr McGinnity is Chairman and Managing Director. Mr W. J. Ayers and Mr S. C. Smith-Cox, the Chairman & Managing Director of P. & A. Campbell Ltd will be joining the Board of that company.

Mr McGinnity will be actively engaged in the new field of operations of P. & A. Campbell Ltd and to this end will become Joint Managing Director with Mr Smith-Cox.

Mr McGinnity will welcome an opportunity to meet you and get to know the various company operations. He will take steps to initiate such meetings. Should you receive any approaches regarding possible ship management, chartering, brokerage or other allied matters I would be grateful if you would direct these enquiries to Mr McGinnity at P. & A. Campbell Ltd 4 Dock Chambers, Bute Steet, Cardiff, or the Company's new Head Office which will shortly be fully operational at Alliance House, Baldwin Street, Bristol.

Ship-broking and related activities were very much a behind-the-scenes matter as far as the everyday passengers were concerned, yet of considerable significance as part of the diversification programme to be spearheaded by Tony McGinnity and intended to restore viability to the P. & A. Campbell Ltd business. The idea put to European Ferries was that *Devonia* would be 'the ship of the future' although it could not be denied that the parent company continued to be lukewarm on passenger services in the Bristol Channel. P. & A. Campbell Ltd would develop two areas outside this mainstream activity, firstly ship management whereby for a fee they would employ crew, arrange insurance, deal with claims, supervise repairs and generally act as ships husbands with West Marine Surveyors providing technical back-up and, secondly, where EFL had frequent need to employ outside professional and commercial services for ship sale and chartering through brokers, this activity too could be channelled through the Campbell subsidiary.

Amongst the first sale of vessels negotiated by P. & A. Campbell Ltd was that of the former Atlantic Steam Navigation pair **Baltic Ferry** and **Cerdic Ferry**, to Greek buyers. To put this transaction into context, the commission of £40,000 earned from the sale was a sum considerably in excess of a season's profit from the operation of **Balmoral**.

Coming back to everyday matters things were little changed in the Bristol Channel in early 1978 as far as the enthusiasts were concerned, as *Balmoral* underwent her survey at Penzance prior to commencing the Bristol Channel season as normal at Easter. *Devonia* was still away in Scotland, seemingly until further notice. Rumours amongst the enthusiasts of an expanded Thames coastal cruising programme in 1978 performed by *Balmoral* receded, as it seemed less likely that *Devonia* was not now likely to be released in time to take over the Bristol Channel excursion vessel role. The pivotal element of the Lundy trade being the primary economic rationale for the continuing survival of the White Funnel Fleet meant that the Bristol Channel would have first call on the one vessel if only one was to be available that year. Around the beginning of 1978, then, an 'ordinary' season for *Balmoral* beckoned.

Revival of two-vessel operations in the Bristol Channel, 1978

Yet even at this twilight hour in the life of P. & A. Campbell Ltd there was still some spark of the old enterprise left which meant that 'new' ports of call could still be found to offer variety in the coastal cruising scene, in this case tied into a new educational trips market. There was novelty in booking an individual passage on the first postwar White Funnel Fleet sailing from Sharpness Docks, on Tuesday 18th April 1978. *Balmoral* was scheduled to undertake an educational trip for schoolchildren up to the Gloucestershire port of Sharpness the previous day, and berth there overnight prior to returning the following afternoon to Avonmouth Docks on a public sailing. After *Balmoral* locked out from the basin into a murky River Severn, she remained astern of a Swansea-bound Harkers coastal tanker; and the brief run downstream under the Severn Bridge and into the lock at Avonmouth Docks was in contrast to the more common experience of cruising along the north Devon coast to Ilfracombe in the summer, and left a lasting impression of the sheer diversity and size of what the early Campbell territory must have seemed like. All that was lacking when *Balmoral* arrived at Avonmouth was a boat-train to Bristol to bring back how it really used to be.

Slightly later on in this early part of the season it was possible to visit Bideford by sea as *Balmoral* revived cruising on the River Torridge – albeit with a brief stop of only a few minutes – which had not been offered from up-channel since 1969. This excursion took place on Saturday 6th May 1978 with departure from Penarth Pier at 0900, and an outwards call at Weston super Mare at 0950. The trip had been organised by the Missions to Seamen, and after a couple of hours pause at Ilfracombe to await the tide, taking the Pilot aboard from the pilot-cutter in a modest swell off the Bideford Bar made for a fascinating trip. Having gone up the River Torridge on the afternoon tide *Balmoral* was only able to return that evening to Ilfracombe and Penarth, the Weston contingent being catered for by a special coach home from Penarth after the ship had ended her day there at 2215. This enabled a scheduled arrival back at Weston at about 0015 on the Sunday morning. As the early season progressed it appeared that it would become a distinctly interesting one as the news broke locally that *Devonia* had arrived back in Bristol from Scotland on 8th May 1978, her charter work over for the time being, and that she was likely to be used to supplement Bristol Channel sailings by *Balmoral* in the main summer season. This was indeed a startling piece of news, and the enthusiast fraternity eagerly awaited the release of amended timetables which revealed how, from mid-July, additional trips would be offered both from up-channel – mainly by *Balmoral* – and from Swansea & Mumbles, mainly by *Devonia*, in the first season of two-vessel operations since 1971.

The loss of the rumoured Thames excursion programme could be seen as the price for the doubling-up of the Bristol Channel programme, although no reasons were given publicly to explain the thinking behind the change of plan. This represented a disappointment for enthusiasts in the south-east as the 1978 Thames programme would have been much more varied and interesting than that offered the previous year, with Ramsgate included in the ports of call. But realistically, one knew that there was a good degree of risk in the course that had been chosen, and whilst the occasional opportunity to 'change steamers at Ilfracombe' like in the old paddle-steamer days might now be taken, it seemed far from certain that there was really enough trade to justify the extra costs. A further item of news was that a 'new' launch had been acquired for use at Lundy, in order to make ferrying arrangements

easier. This launch was purchased from the Watts family at Weston, and after arrival at Ilfracombe was duly renamed *Westward Ho*, and took up station at Lundy shortly afterwards under the capable supervision of the long-serving P. & A. Campbell Ltd Lundy boatman Albert Fisher.

As the early season progressed *Devonia* received a repaint into full P. & A. Campbell Ltd colours, and her entry into regular Bristol Channel service alongside *Balmoral* took place on 21st July 1978. Her first few days had been spent on charter duties, and an initial glimpse of *Devonia* in her very smart new colours was had at Penarth Pier that Friday, as she came alongside from Bristol in the capable hands of Captain Jack Wide, recalled from retirement to take charge of the new member of the White Funnel Fleet, assisted by Mate Flanagan, another Campbell stalwart. One had doubts even then about whether she would succeed as a Bristol Channel excursion vessel, as she offered less deck-space and fewer facilities than *Balmoral*, and the fact that she clearly had a tough seagoing reputation from her Isle of Scilly days was barely offset by the inherent commercial disadvantage of being less likely to attract new business, particularly on account of her lack of suitable catering facilities. Although in addition it was difficult then to attract suitable staff to provide consistent standards of catering this seemed to be a serious omission. Coastal cruising was, after all, meant to be a business that aimed to provide an enjoyable leisure experience rather than one that tested the stamina of passengers, and the lesson appeared not to have been learned that if first-time passengers suffered a bad trip it would almost certainly be their last one. Nonetheless revised timetable bills were duly issued for the high-season two-vessel period of operation, whereby a schedule that had been intended for *Balmoral* alone was augmented by the range of the additional trips which *Devonia* was to offer. This took place, broadly, without any withdrawal of those sailings which had already been advertised by the handbills released earlier, or re-timings.

The novelty of two steamers at large in the Channel was certainly considerable, although in practical terms up-channel passengers only really got more of the same, by way of virtually daily sailings from *Balmoral* from Penarth whilst *Devonia* carried out her duties at Swansea, largely unseen by the up-channel clientele. This arrangement had the merit of matching the lower passenger capacity of *Devonia* to the slightly lower demand from Swansea compared to the numbers Penarth could still generate, and was more than adequate for Ilfracombe-Lundy numbers which might range from 150 or so to 200 or 300 per day depending on weather. One particular plus for the Penarth trade was that on many of the additional sailing days it was possible to offer a revived 'ferry'-type service of two or three round trips to Weston super Mare by *Balmoral* as *Devonia* was covering what would have been her down-channel commitments. The lively Somerset resort still had plenty to offer passengers from south Wales for either half- or whole days, as folk so chose. Through fares for rail & steamer journeys from South Wales stations between Newport and Carmarthen continued to be offered by either steamer.

Whilst the author mostly remained loyal to *Balmoral* during this season, largely on account of her allocation to mainly up-channel duties, the novelty of sailing on both steamers in one day was not to be missed, and this was possible by an early start by train to Swansea on Saturday 5th August 1978 in order to board *Devonia* for one of the 'Augmented' but regrettably lightly patronised extra crossings to Ilfracombe, in this case departing at 0920 and calling at Mumbles at 0940. No cruise out of Ilfracombe was initially offered by *Devonia* that day, but a later bill had revised this situation. Such a crossing was reminiscent of the way in which the Swansea steamer in the old days used to cross to Ilfracombe, although it might have made three return trips carrying holidaymakers and day-trippers alike on a summer Saturday before 1939, or two round trips in postwar days until the practice of stationing a vessel at Swansea had ended after 1958. Arrival at Ilfracombe was around midday on the 'new' steamer, and *Devonia* proceeded to vacate the berth and anchor off.

On this particular Saturday, the original schedule had been for *Balmoral* to run from Penarth & Weston to Lynmouth and Ilfracombe, arriving at 1310 and thence offering a cruise to Lundy Island Roads at 1320, for the price of £3.50. It should be clarified here that on this tide,

Devonia *off Penarth Pier at the start of her 1978 season: her career as a White Funnel Fleet steamer was shortlived.*   Author

Devonia *is seen here on her first visit to Lundy in that guise in her new colours, on 22nd July 1978.*   Nigel Jones

and having run down from Weston as well as from Penarth, in the era before the new pier was built there were days when time only existed to handle 'singles' at Lundy in the half-hour or so that was available off the island landing-beach. An 'anti-clockwise' circuit around the Bristol Channel was thus possible and matters were made more interesting by the somewhat impromptu decision that had been made shortly before to programme **Devonia** for a second, shorter coastal cruise from Ilfracombe that afternoon towards the Foreland, price £2.00. This meant that a 'clockwise' circuit around the Bristol Channel from Penarth that day on the two steamers was also possible by using the train between Swansea and Cardiff. **Balmoral** came in to Ilfracombe and quickly left for Lundy Roads, and **Devonia** duly berthed again at the pier to take this trip at 1500 which was not programmed to arrive back until 1730. Later, **Balmoral** reappeared on the horizon from Lundy and quickly called at Ilfracombe prior to setting off back up-channel in order to catch the tide. As **Balmoral** sailed out of Ilfracombe harbour at 1715 for Penarth and home, an extremely lightly-laden **Devonia** was making ready to come on to the berth for her own 1830 return to Mumbles and Swansea. This was a relatively rare glimpse of the two vessels together that year, seeming to be a real novelty but probably unsustainable, and that summer passed all too quickly with **Devonia** running her last trip on 3rd September 1978 from Swansea to Lundy and return before going to lay up in Bristol on the following day, there to face an uncertain future after a short experimental Bristol Channel season in which the elements had not been particularly kind.

The financial results for the 1978 season, which included charter income from the Scottish work, now showed a seriously worsening trend compared to 1977 when **Devonia** had operated briefly on the Thames:

y/e	31.12.1978	31.12.1977
Gross Receipts	£322,523	£235, 494
Expenses	£425,776	£285,346
Net (Loss)/Profit	£(103,253)	£(49,852)

Such financial results exacerbated the difficult relationship which P. & A. Campbell Ltd now had with those running the parent company, the European Ferries group, and there was still no sign of the hoped-for agreement with the Landmark Trust regarding a mutually advantageous means of servicing Lundy Island, and on which premise assent had been given to the acquisition of the second ship. Neither was the sought-after further charter work forthcoming, and after the 1978 season ended it was not yet apparent that **Devonia** would in fact never again sail in revenue-earning White Funnel Fleet service, as she lay alongside **Balmoral** in Bristol that winter. Eventually, at the end of 1978, it was decided that **Devonia** would not be used for day passengers again unless support for the Lundy option was forthcoming, and that all effort would be directed towards finding her all-year round employment, being then placed in care & maintenance with a watchmen on board and her engines regularly turned over.

A missed opportunity

A brief explanation of what might have happened had the original 1978 ship deployment plan been implemented is appropriate at this juncture, given the critical state that the finances of P. & A. Campbell Ltd had now reached. Had plans to improve facilities on board **Devonia** gone ahead and she had become the Bristol Channel vessel that season, then one might conjecture that the sought-after Lundy agreement might have been achieved thereafter and **Polar Bear** withdrawn, so that P. & A. Campbell Ltd could manage the all year round passenger & cargo trade in 'home waters' with just one vessel for the Lundy traffic, thus achieving some overall economy of scale where two had previously traded in the summer. Moreover, there were reasons to believe that **Balmoral** could well have been successful in the Thames trade in 1978 where the reaction to **Devonia** in 1977 was lukewarm at best.

Peter Southcombe later recalled that numerous charter enquiries received from prospective customers in the Thames estuary area could have been handled by **Balmoral** as she had a dining saloon and

*For the 1978 summer season **Devonia** was deployed as a second vessel in the Bristol Channel, mostly carrying out the sailings from Swansea. The traditional P. & A. Campbell Ltd colour scheme appeared to rather suit her hull form, with its pronounced flaired bow. Seen here at Ilfracombe after arrival from Swansea on 5th August 1978.*
Author

an area suitable for dancing and other functions, in the below-deck bar aft (but could not have been undertaken by the poorly-equipped *Devonia*). Calls at Ramsgate, where an old Eagle Steamers office also used by Campbells many years before was still in situ, would have featured regularly. These would have been instead of calls at Margate, and would have been less susceptible to tidal constraints on a simple, regular weekly timetable cycle. Cooperation from Tower Pier had been agreed, and assistance had also been promised by the railway authorities in charge of Gravesend Pier. Southend Corporation was keen to see steamer traffic passing through its pier, and much help was promised by the owners of Clacton Pier. The outline 1978 Thames programme, then, would have looked like this:

Sats, Sunday, Monday and Tuesdays	Tower Pier-Southend, + cruise,
Wednesdays	Gravesend-Southend-Ramsgate + English Channel Cruise
Thursdays	Gravesend-Southend-Clacton + North Sea Cruise
Fridays	(off-service)

The comparative economics of *Devonia* and *Balmoral* in the Bristol Channel and Thames areas respectively remain a matter for debate, although on the debit side the deeper-draughted former Isles of Scilly vessel – even if eminently suitable for Lundy sailings – would have been more restricted on upper Bristol Channel duties for calls at Penarth, Weston & Portishead, leading to potential revenue losses there. However the fateful decision to run two ships in the Bristol Channel in 1978 was taken and in Peter Southcombe's own words '... *in the end the company did the worst possible thing and lost a good deal of money as a result ... the whole course of events might have been very different if the original plan had been carried out but we shall never know for sure. I think it was just another lost opportunity, in latter days Campbells were so good at that ...'.*

1979-retrenchment

A recurring theme during much of the final decade of the White Funnel Fleet had been the delicate balance essential to the scheduling of just one intensively-utilised vessel in order to tap as many markets as possible around the Bristol Channel. This task was made more difficult as the number of available calling places had declined, and opinions varied as to the relative merits of the up-channel traffic versus the passenger volumes that could be picked up at Swansea & Mumbles. To capture both meant that some positioning runs were needed, often at anti-social hours for the crew, and to make it all even more difficult was the necessity for fuelling and victualling *Balmoral*. Road-access for these activities was easy at Swansea Ferryport but much less so up-Channel, and in retrospect it is hard to avoid concluding that the operating losses that had been sustained each season since 1975 were perhaps exacerbated by an undue emphasis on the provision of Swansea-based, down-Channel sailings. There may have been the praiseworthy objective of providing an easier, regular-interval type timetable but this appeared to have been at the expense of neglecting potential demand from the more populous upper-Channel catchment area. On the credit side, the shorter Swansea-Ilfracombe passage times meant that more time ashore on Lundy could be offered. For the 1979 season it appeared that this imbalance was to happen again, largely because the deteriorating condition of Birnbeck Pier meant that fewer calls could now be scheduled, restricted to at or near high water there. Some attempts to improve catering were made: this had been in the hands of a Welshman, Mr Jones, up until 1977 and in 1978 R. L. Stephens of Brixham had taken over, but only lasted for one season. Silence prevailed as regards any public pronouncement on the results of the two-vessel operation in 1978, and observers were left to draw the obvious conclusion as *Devonia* remained laid up.

Although *Balmoral* reappeared at Easter in 1979, as normal, and worked her way through the summer as if nothing was wrong, the financial situation was becoming more serious and Ken Siddle had

After the 1978 summer season **Devonia** *was laid up, in the centre of Bristol, in sight of the spire of the beautiful church of St. Mary Redcliffe.*

Martin Oatway

FOLLOWING RECENTLY INCREASED COSTS, PARTICULARLY OF FUEL, A SURCHARGE OF 30p PER ADULT AND 15p PER CHILD WILL BE IMPOSED FROM JULY 1st, 1979.

WHITE FUNNEL FLEET

P. & A. CAMPBELL LTD.

SAILINGS FROM PENARTH (THE PIER)

By the Motor Vessels BALMORAL and DEVONIA

BALMORAL which performs most of these journeys is a large sea-going ship capable of accommodating over 800 passengers. The vessel has a restaurant and tea bar also where meals and snacks can be obtained, fully licensed bars. There are sun lounges, spacious open decks and covered accommodation is available, sufficient for all passengers.

SEASON 1979

(For details of Easter and other early season sailings please see special leaflet)

SUNDAY, MAY 27th

9.30 a.m. Day Trip to ILFRACOMBE and LUNDY ISLAND (to land). The steamer sails direct to Ilfracombe, due 12.25 p.m. and Lundy, due 2.15 p.m. Leave Lundy Island 4.40 p.m., Ilfracombe 6.30 p.m. direct for Penarth, due 9.35.

SPRING BANK HOLIDAY MONDAY, MAY 28th

A steamer leaves Swansea (Ferry Port Terminal) at 9.15 a.m. for Ilfracombe Leave Ilfracombe 7.15 p.m. for Swansea (due 9.35 p.m.)

THURSDAY, MAY 31st

9.00 a.m. Day Trip to ILFRACOMBE and LUNDY ISLAND (to land). The steamer sails direct to Ilfracombe due 12.10 p.m. and Lundy Island due 2.00 p.m. Leave Lundy Island 4.50 p.m., Ilfracombe 6.40 p.m. direct for Penarth due 9.35 p.m.

FRIDAY, JUNE 1st

WESTON. Leave Penarth 10.00 a.m., leave Weston 8.15 p.m.

10.00 a.m. Day Trip to ILFRACOMBE and Cruise to Baggy Point, due Ilfracombe 2.00 p.m. Leave Ilfracombe 5.10 p.m. for Penarth (due 9.05 p.m.)

By arrangement with the Waverley Steam Navigation Company Limited

Visit to Penarth of the World's only remaining sea-going Paddle Steamer "WAVERLEY"

THURSDAY, MAY 31st

8.00 p.m. Evening Cruise in the Channel towards Watchet and Minehead, back about 11.00 p.m. **Fare £2.95.** Children half price.

SUNDAY, JUNE 3rd

10.15 a.m. Day Trip to ILFRACOMBE and Cruise around Lundy Island, due Ilfracombe 1.30 p.m. Leave Ilfracombe 6.15 p.m. for Penarth (due 9.30 p.m.). **Fare Ilfracombe £6.95** or including cruise around Lundy **£9.95.** Children half price.

MONDAY, JUNE 11th

WESTON. Leave Penarth 9.30 a.m. Leave Weston 7.30 p.m.

9.30 a.m. Day Trip to ILFRACOMBE and Cruise to off Woolacombe, due Ilfracombe 1.30 p.m. Leave Ilfracombe 4.20 p.m. for Penarth, due 8.20 p.m.

TUESDAY, JUNE 12th

9.20 a.m. Long Day Trip to ILFRACOMBE and LUNDY ISLAND (to land). The steamer sails direct to Ilfracombe due 12.10 p.m. and Lundy Island due 2.00 p.m. Leave Lundy Island 4.50 p.m., Ilfracombe 6.40 p.m. direct for Penarth, due 9.35 p.m.

FRIDAY, JUNE 15th

WESTON. Leave Penarth 9.30 a.m., 11.30 a.m. Leave Weston 10.30 a.m., 8.15 p.m.

9.30 a.m. Cruise across the CHANNEL. Back 11.20 a.m.

SUNDAY, JUNE 24th

9.45 a.m. Day Trip to LYNMOUTH, ILFRACOMBE and Cruise to Bideford Bay, due Lynmouth 12.15 p.m., Ilfracombe 1.0 p.m. Leave Ilfracombe 5.15 p.m., Lynmouth 6.30 p.m. for Penarth, due 9.05 p.m.

Note: Steamer leaves Ilfracombe 2.30 p.m. for the cruise.

9.45 a.m. Day Trip to MINEHEAD and to Butlin's Holiday Camp at Minehead. Passengers leave Penarth 9.45 a.m. by steamer for Lynmouth when special coaches will be waiting to convey them to Minehead, due 1.30 p.m. and Butlin's due 1.35 p.m. Leave Minehead Harbour by direct steamer at 7.10 p.m., due Penarth 9.05 p.m. Admission to the Holiday Camp extra, payable on entry.

Note: Steamer leaves Minehead 7.10 p.m. for Penarth.

MONDAY, JUNE 25th

WESTON. Leave Penarth 9.30 a.m. Leave Weston 7.30 p.m.

9.30 a.m. Day Trip to ILFRACOMBE and Cruise to off Woolacombe, due Ilfracombe 1.30 p.m. Leave Ilfracombe 4.20 p.m. for Penarth, due 8.20 p.m.

Note: Steamer leaves Ilfracombe 2.30 p.m. for the Cruise.

9.30 a.m. Combined Steamer and Coach Tour via WESTON to CHEDDAR GORGE. Leave Weston 7.30 p.m. for Penarth. Coach leaves Knightstone Garage (opposite Marine Lake) 2.00 p.m.

TUESDAY, JUNE 26th

9.20 a.m. Day Trip to ILFRACOMBE and LUNDY ISLAND (to land). The steamer sails direct to Ilfracombe due 12.10 p.m. and Lundy Island due 2.00 p.m. Leave Lundy Island 4.50 p.m., Ilfracombe 6.40 p.m. direct for Penarth due 9.40 p.m.

SATURDAY, JUNE 30th

9.15 a.m. Day Trip to LYNMOUTH, ILFRACOMBE and LUNDY ISLAND (to land), due Lynmouth 11.55 a.m., Ilfracombe 12.40 p.m. and Lundy 2.30 p.m. Leave Lundy Island 4.50 p.m., Ilfracombe 6.40 p.m., Lynmouth 7.25 p.m. for Penarth due 9.45 p.m.

9.15 a.m. Day Trip to MINEHEAD and to Butlin's Holiday Camp at Minehead. Steamer due Minehead 10.40 a.m. Coach will return from Butlin's Camp at 4.25 p.m. Minehead Bus Station at 4.30 p.m. and bring passengers to Ilfracombe to connect with the steamer leaving there at 6.40 p.m. for Penarth. Admission to the Holiday Camp payable on entry.

9.15 a.m. Single Trip to MINEHEAD, due Minehead 10.40 a.m.

SUNDAY, JULY 1st

9.45 a.m. Day Trip to LYNMOUTH and ILFRACOMBE, due Lynmouth 12.50 p.m. Ilfracombe 1.35 p.m. Leave Ilfracombe 5.45 p.m., Lynmouth 6.30 p.m. for Penarth due 8.50 p.m.

9.45 a.m. Day Trip to MINEHEAD. Steamer due Minehead 11.30 a.m. Coach will return from Minehead Bus Station at 3.15 p.m. and bring passengers to Ilfracombe to connect with the steamer there at 5.45 p.m. for Penarth.

9.45 a.m. Single Trip to MINEHEAD, due Minehead, 11.30 a.m.

MONDAY, JULY 9th

9.05 a.m. Day Trip to ILFRACOMBE and CLOVELLY (to land). The steamer sails direct to Ilfracombe, due 12 noon, and Clovelly, due 1.55 p.m. Leave Clovelly 4.00 p.m., Ilfracombe 5.50 p.m. direct for Penarth, due 9.10 a.m.

TUESDAY, JULY 10th

8.50 a.m. Day Trip to ILFRACOMBE and LUNDY ISLAND (to land). The steamer sails direct to Ilfracombe due 11.35 a.m. and Lundy Island due 1.25 p.m. Leave Lundy Island 4.50 p.m., Ilfracombe 6.25 p.m. direct for Penarth, due 9.30 p.m.

8.50 a.m. Combined Steamer and Coach Tour via Ilfracombe to Exmoor arriving back at Penarth 9.30 p.m. Coach leaves Ilfracombe (Coach Station) at 2.15 p.m.

FRIDAY, JULY 13th

WESTON. Leave Penarth 9.15 a.m., 11.15 a.m., 7.45 p.m. Leave Weston 10.10 a.m. 12.15 p.m., 6.45 p.m., 8.45 p.m.

9.15 a.m., 11.15 a.m. and 7.45 p.m. Cruises across the Channel, back 11.00 a.m., 1.05 p.m. and 9.35 p.m. respectively.

SATURDAY, JULY 14th

11.40 a.m. Day Trip to ILFRACOMBE, due Ilfracombe 2.30 p.m. Leave Ilfracombe 4.30 p.m. for Penarth, due 7.20 p.m.

7.25 p.m. Evening trip to PORTISHEAD and Cruise up the Avon Gorge calling at Bristol, due Portishead 8.50 p.m., Bristol 9.45 p.m. Leave Bristol 10.00 p.m., Portishead 10.50 p.m., due Penarth 12.25 a.m. (Sunday).

7.25 p.m. Single Trip to BRISTOL.

Note: Steamer leaves Bristol 9.30 a.m., Portishead 10.20 a.m. for Penarth.

SUNDAY, JULY 15th

9.20 a.m. Day Trip to ILFRACOMBE and LUNDY ISLAND (to land). The steamer sails direct to Ilfracombe, due 12.40 p.m. and Lundy, due 2.30 p.m. Leave Lundy Island 4.50 p.m., Ilfracombe 6.40 p.m. direct for Penarth, due 9.30 p.m.

9.20 a.m. Combined Steamer and Coach Tour via Ilfracombe to Exmoor arriving back at Penarth 9.30 p.m. Coach leaves Ilfracombe (Coach Station) at 2.15 p.m.

MONDAY, JULY 23rd

9.15 a.m. Day Trip to ILFRACOMBE and CLOVELLY (to land). The steamer sails direct to Ilfracombe, due 12 noon and Clovelly, due 1.55 p.m. Leave Clovelly 4.00 p.m., Ilfracombe 5.50 p.m. direct for Penarth, due 9.10 p.m.

9.15 a.m. Combined Steamer and Mystery Tour of North Devon via Ilfracombe, arriving back at Penarth 9.00 p.m. Coach leaves Ilfracombe (Coach Station) at 2.15 p.m.

TUESDAY, JULY 24th

8.50 a.m. Day Trip to ILFRACOMBE and LUNDY ISLAND (to land). The steamer sails direct to Ilfracombe, due 11.35 p.m. and Lundy, due 1.25 p.m. Leave Lundy Island 4.35 p.m., Ilfracombe 6.25 p.m. direct for Penarth, due 9.45 p.m.

8.50 a.m. Combined Steamer and Coach Tour via ILFRACOMBE to EXMOOR arriving back 9.35 p.m. Coach leaves Ilfracombe (Coach Station) at 1.45 p.m.

FRIDAY, JULY 27th

WESTON. Leave Penarth 9.45 a.m. Leave Weston 8.00 p.m.

9.45 a.m. Day Trip to MUMBLES and Cruise along the GOWER COAST via Weston due Mumbles 1.45 p.m. Leave Mumbles 4.50 p.m. for Penarth, due 8.50 p.m.

9.45 a.m. Combined Steamer and Coach Tour via WESTON to CHEDDAR GORGE. Leave Weston 8.00 p.m. for Penarth. Coach leaves Knightstone Garage (opposite Marine Lake) 2.00 p.m.

SATURDAY, JULY 28th
Special Attraction

9.15 a.m. Day Trip to MINEHEAD, LYNMOUTH, ILFRACOMBE and LUNDY ISLAND (to land), due Minehead 10.40 a.m., Lynmouth 11.55 a.m., Ilfracombe 12.40 p.m. and Lundy 2.30 p.m. Leave Lundy Island 4.50 p.m., Ilfracombe 6.40 p.m., Lynmouth 7.25 p.m., Minehead 8.35 p.m., Penarth 10.00 p.m.

SUNDAY, JULY 29th

WESTON. Leave Penarth 9.00 a.m. Leave Weston 9.50 p.m.

9.00 a.m. Day Trip to ILFRACOMBE and LUNDY ISLAND (to land), due Ilfracombe 12.40 p.m., Lundy Island 2.30 p.m. Leave Lundy Island 4.50 p.m., Ilfracombe 6.45 p.m. for Penarth, due 10.40 p.m.

9.00 a.m. Combined Steamer and Coach Tour via WESTON to LYME REGIS, SEATON, BEER and SIDMOUTH. Leave Weston 9.50 p.m. Coach leaves Weston Pier Gates immediately on arrival of steamer.

9.00 a.m. Combined Steamer and Coach Tour via ILFRACOMBE to EXMOOR, arriving back at Penarth 10.40 p.m. Coach leaves Ilfracombe (Coach Station) at 2.15 p.m.

MONDAY, JULY 30th

9.30 a.m. Day Trip to LYNMOUTH and ILFRACOMBE and Cruise to Baggy Point, due Lynmouth 12.35 p.m., Ilfracombe 1.20 p.m. Leave Ilfracombe 5.00 p.m., Lynmouth 5.45 p.m. for Penarth due 8.10 p.m.

Note: Steamer leaves Ilfracombe 2.30 p.m. for the cruise.

9.30 a.m. Day Trip to MINEHEAD. Steamer due Minehead 11.10 a.m. Coach will return from Minehead Bus Station at 2.45 p.m. and bring passengers to Ilfracombe to connect with the steamer leaving there at 5.00 p.m. for Penarth.

9.30 a.m. Single Trip to MINEHEAD, due Minehead 11.10 a.m.

FRIDAY, AUGUST 10th

WESTON. Leave Penarth 9.45 a.m. Leave Weston 8.00 p.m.

9.45 a.m. Day Trip to ILFRACOMBE and CRUISE to BAGGY POINT, due Ilfracombe 1.45 p.m. Leave Ilfracombe 4.45 p.m. for Penarth, due 8.50 p.m.

Note: Steamer leaves Ilfracombe 2.30 p.m. for the cruise.

9.45 a.m. Combined Steamer and Coach Tour via WESTON to CHEDDAR GORGE. Leave Weston 8.00 p.m. for Penarth. Coach leaves Knightstone Garage (opposite Marine Lake) 2.00 p.m.

SATURDAY, AUGUST 11th
Special Attraction

9.10 a.m. Day Trip to MINEHEAD, LYNMOUTH, ILFRACOMBE and LUNDY ISLAND (to land), due Minehead 10.40 a.m., Lynmouth 11.55 a.m., Ilfracombe 12.40 p.m. and Lundy 2.30 p.m. Leave Lundy Island 4.50 p.m., Ilfracombe 6.40 p.m., Lynmouth 7.25 p.m., Minehead 8.35 p.m., Penarth 10.00 p.m.

SUNDAY, AUGUST 12th

WESTON. Leave Penarth 9.00 a.m. Leave Weston 9.50 p.m.

9.00 a.m. Day Trip to ILFRACOMBE and LUNDY ISLAND (to land), due Ilfracombe 12.40 p.m., Lundy Island 2.30 p.m. Leave Lundy Island 4.50 p.m., Ilfracombe 6.45 p.m. for Penarth, due 10.40 p.m.

9.00 a.m. Combined Steamer and Coach Tour via WESTON to LYME REGIS, SEATON, BEER and SIDMOUTH. Leave Weston 9.50 p.m. Coach leaves Weston Pier Gates immediately on arrival of steamer.

9.00 a.m. Combined Steamer and Coach Tour via ILFRACOMBE to EXMOOR, arriving back at Penarth 10.40 p.m. Coach leaves Ilfracombe (Coach Station) at 2.15 p.m.

MONDAY, AUGUST 13th

9.05 a.m. Day Trip to ILFRACOMBE and CLOVELLY (to land). The steamer sails direct to Ilfracombe, due 12.10 p.m. and Clovelly, due 2.00 p.m. Leave Clovelly 4.15 p.m., Ilfracombe 6.20 p.m. direct for Penarth, due 9.15 p.m.

9.15 a.m. Combined Steamer and Mystery Tour of North Devon via Ilfracombe, arriving back at Penarth 9.15 p.m. Coach leaves Ilfracombe (Coach Station) at 2.15 p.m.

FRIDAY, AUGUST 24th

WESTON. Leave Penarth 9.45 a.m. Leave Weston 8.00 p.m.

9.45 a.m. Day Trip to ILFRACOMBE and Cruise to BAGGY POINT, due Ilfracombe 1.45 p.m. Leave Ilfracombe 4.45 p.m. for Penarth, due 8.50 p.m.

Note: Steamer leaves Ilfracombe 2.30 p.m. for the Cruise.

9.45 a.m. Combined Steamer and Coach Tour via WESTON to CHEDDAR GORGE. Leave Weston 8.00 p.m. for Penarth. Coach leaves Knightstone Garage (opposite Marine Lake) 2.00 p.m.

SATURDAY, AUGUST 25th

11.40 a.m. Day Trip to LYNMOUTH and ILFRACOMBE, due Lynmouth 1.45 p.m., Ilfracombe 2.30 p.m. Leave Ilfracombe 4.30 p.m., Lynmouth 5.15 p.m. for Penarth (due 7.20 p.m.)

7.25 p.m. Evening trip to PORTISHEAD and Cruise up the Avon Gorge calling at Bristol, due Portishead 8.50 p.m., Bristol 9.45 p.m. Leave Bristol 10.00 p.m., Portishead 10.50 p.m., due Penarth 12.25 a.m. (Sunday).

7.25 p.m. Single Trip to BRISTOL.

Note: Steamer leaves Bristol 9.15 a.m., Portishead 10.05 a.m. for Penarth.

Despite what was stated at the top of this bill **Devonia** *was withdrawn after 1978 and it was* **Balmoral** *which maintained Bristol Channel sailings, albeit augmented by a first appearance of the operationally preserved paddle-steamer* **Waverley** *in 1979.*
Author

written to Clifton Smith-Cox in December 1978 demanding to know why the entire P. & A. Campbell Ltd passenger operation had not yet been closed down. The issue was ducked and Mr Siddle had backed off temporarily as he was persuaded that commitments (i.e. with Lundy) had been entered into for the 1979 season. Even at this late stage the occasional surprises could be mustered, and unusual calls in 1979 included an odd charter out of Newport, reinstatement of a few calls at Watchet (not visited since 1971) and even a surprise call at the Royal Portbury Dock at Bristol. Late in the season an opportunity to sample an unusual cruise, on Saturday 22nd September 1979, when a convenient big daytime tide enabled *Balmoral* to be scheduled to leave Bristol at 0900 and Penarth at 1110 for a 'Long Sea Cruise' passing Barry, Nash Point, Porthcawl and Mumbles and thence along the Gower coast returning to Mumbles Pier to land at 1445. An hour ashore there was sufficient to buy an ice-cream and do very little else apart from enjoy a nice view of Swansea Bay and contemplate the return up-Channel in pleasant weather back to Penarth for 1830, whereupon the ship would proceed to Bristol. Just to maximise earnings that day this was in fact a return evening trip from Penarth to Bristol, due back at Penarth at 2300, thus giving the crew something like a sixteen-hour day. As the next day involved departure at 0900 from Penarth to Lundy, there was little opportunity for a lie-in for the particularly hard-worked crew whilst such tides were there to be exploited to the full.

An Isles of Scilly mini-cruise was again offered, between Friday 5th and Monday 8th October 1979, although the weather was very unkind. For Penarth passengers, the 'Last Trip of the Season' was billed for Sunday 14th October 1979, at 1015 to Portishead and Bristol, back at 1700. However, this was not the very last *Balmoral* trip of 1979 for Penarth folk, as things turned out. What would have been her last sailing on Sunday 21st October, very late into the season, from Bristol and Portishead to Ilfracombe, and short cruise to off Woolacombe, had a Penarth call added in part-compensation for an earlier missed call. *Balmoral* thus ceased operations after returning that evening to Portishead, whence her Bristol passengers proceeded home by coach, the vessel following on the next tide.

A significant feature of the 1979 Bristol Channel season was a brief, first appearance of the preserved paddle-steamer *Waverley*, by agreement with P. & A. Campbell Ltd, in late-May and early-June. Yet still there was no resolution – at least for the company – of the sought-after Lundy issue, nor any public admission that the days of the company might now be numbered. As poor weather during the 1979 season suggested that trading results were going to leave much to be desired, Clifton Smith-Cox had to come to terms with the ultimatum that Ken Siddle had issued. The European Ferries parent-body was definitely going to insist on action for 1980, and its Managing Director saw no future whatever for the survival of the P. & A. Campbell Ltd activity within his Group. His view was that the excursion business should be disposed of – if a purchaser could be found – and that the other activities, i.e. ship-broking and ship-management, if they ever got off the ground and started to show potential, could simply be absorbed into his own Marine Division at Dover.

Perhaps Clifton Smith-Cox was starting to become weary of attacks on his personal fiefdom, and after some soul-searching about the form of an 'ideal' Bristol Channel operation based primarily on the needs of Lundy and regular services from Swansea, he made an approach to John Smith of the Landmark Trust. This was without reference to his co-Director Tony McGinnity, but something approaching brinksmanship was now involved. P. & A. Campbell Ltd was to offer to let the Trust take the company over, with no charge for goodwill, and in a letter written in July 1979 he stated that '... *I have with regret to inform you that European Ferries will not be through their subsidiary P. & A. Campbell Ltd operating passenger ferries in the Bristol Channel after 31st October 1979.*' He added that it was his intention to retire but went on to make certain suggestions, which he invited the Trust to consider. These amounted to an offer to charter *Devonia* to the Trust for all-year round operation and which would thus enable them to dispose of *Polar Bear*, together with the recommendation that the overall mix of Lundy crossings and general Bristol Channel excursion sailings should basically remain unchanged in order to keep as much revenue as possible.

Balmoral was advertised to run from Penarth at 0910 on Friday 7th September 1979 to Lynmouth, Ilfracombe and Clovelly. A coach excursion was offered on the outwards journey from Lynmouth, to Minehead, for the Butlins Holiday Camp. The return journey back up the Bristol Channel was at 1750 from Ilfracombe, with a call at Minehead Harbour on the rising evening tide. The steamer calls were advertised in the time-honoured fashion as passengers descended to the low-water stage of Ilfracombe pier to embark.　　　　　Author

A little later in the year they met to discuss the proposition in more detail, and by October 1979 it was agreed that the Landmark Trust would charter a ship rather than acquire the goodwill and assets of P. & A. Campbell Ltd. After a certain amount of to-ing & fro-ing, it was eventually decided that whilst *Balmoral* seemed the best bet to operate in 1980, still being in possession of the necessary certification, thereafter *Devonia* would be preferable. From company documents that have survived from this critical period in the death throes of the White Funnel Fleet one could quite easily infer that the Landmark Trust remained not wholly convinced that *Devonia* – still un-rebuilt, and languishing – represented an ideal solution from the Lundy perspective. Thus she was not regarded as being a better bet than *Balmoral*, for all of the obvious reasons concerning the better facilities for day-excursionists on board the established vessel, which had now served the island excursion market for over ten years.

It was on this basis, therefore, that a new joint venture company was to be formed to operate *Balmoral* in 1980. Thus, without anyone recognising it at the time, the era of P. & A. Campbell Ltd as both passenger excursion ship owners and operators in their own right was, strictly speaking, at an end.

The era of Birnbeck Pier as a steamer embarkation point was also now about to end, but this sad occasion was more in the public domain as the final day of sailings from Weston super Mare drew close, on 19th October 1979. The Weston newspaper quoted a statement by Traffic Manager Peter Southcombe that '... *The company very much regrets having to take the decision but we have to concentrate on the more profitable routes*'. For the final cruise departing at 1800 from Penarth Pier and at 1915 from Birnbeck Pier *Balmoral*, with Captain Cyril Smith in command, was scheduled to take an evening cruise around Steepholm, which she did as hundreds of well-wishers waved farewell. Returning at 2030, she lay alongside whilst a spectacular firework display lasting ten minutes was presented from the top of the landing-stage, and responded by firing rockets from her bridge. The last departure of all was her final return trip at 2100 that evening from Birnbeck Pier to Penarth, with six long blasts on her siren, as many streamers were thrown on to her starboard side as she swung away from Weston for the last time. Back at Penarth at about 2200 all passengers came ashore and, as *Balmoral* set off into the night, one could now reflect that P. & A. Campbell Ltd had finally been forced to turn their back on what had once been one of the major Bristol Channel destinations and which was still the biggest resort in

The condition of Birnbeck Pier at Weston super Mare deteriorated considerably during the 1970s, and calls ceased after the 1979 season. This depicts the condition of one of the piles during that final year.

Tom Clift

White Funnel Steamers Ltd, 1980

Here also was to be another parallel with past years, when a fundamental business change occurred to the company structure behind the White Funnel Fleet, but which had little or no visible effect as far as the travelling public were concerned. In 1960, when sailings had resumed under the P. & A. Campbell Ltd banner – but after the company had been taken over by George Nott Industries following the prolonged period in Receivership – no-one seemed to notice the difference, and there was scarcely any actual change of image. In 1980 *Balmoral* sailed on as a P. & A. Campbell Ltd-owned and managed ship, but on charter and marketed in the name of the new joint-venture company White Funnel Steamers Ltd. Possibly only of academic interest to many passengers, this change of business terms was intended to herald a new era and was based around the needs of Lundy with the intention of securing a longer-term future for the Bristol Channel excursion business. Attention was barely drawn to the name of the new organisation on publicity, although a new pamphlet style was introduced to cover the bulk of the season rather than just relying on varying sizes of handbill as in the past. The regulars were pleased to see that the well-known P. & A. Campbell Ltd logo, the blue pennant with chevron and white ball, had been retained, which doubtless aided a sense of continuity.

The transfer of risk to the new organisation was more than just a gesture towards the continued pressure from European Ferries on Clifton Smith-Cox to get rid of the P. & A. Campbell Ltd concern, the intention being that sailings would be put on a sounder financial footing with more emphasis on regularity. The charter period was for five years, with a clause permitting the charterer the option to terminate annually if they so wished. The charterer was to be responsible for refit costs after the first year, and the charter fee was £2,500 per annum, and a separate management agreement was drawn up in place alongside the formal charter document. The terms of the charter were such that the Campbell management could demonstrate to the parent group that they had removed risk in that the charterer was to take revenue risk as well as pay the management fee. Tony McGinnity was no longer involved

the area – yet with no chance of justifying repairs to its historic pier through lack of funds. Whilst there had been due ceremony at Weston super Mare, the cessation of 'own account' sailings was not a certainty, nor was the knowledge of this likelihood yet in the public domain. Here was a parallel – if one were needed – with so many previous occasions in the history of the closing years of the White Funnel Fleet when cutbacks had occurred without ceremony and without anyone being aware of it at the time: the demise of *Cardiff Queen* after 1966, the breakdown of *Westward Ho* and her subsequent withdrawal in 1971, the last Bristol Channel trip taken by *Devonia* in 1978, and now the last proper P. & A. Campbell Ltd sailing. Surely, now, the end was nigh for the whole operation?

Balmoral at Watchet after having crossed the Channel on an afternoon excursion from Penarth on Saturday 10th May 1980. Watchet Docks still then handled cargo ships, but none was present that day which left plenty of harbour wall available for this relatively rare visit by an excursion ship.

Author

in the daily affairs of the new operation but remained as Joint MD. Weston calls had now gone for good, and the White Funnel Steamers timetable for the 1980 season presented a new image of slightly more consistent timings of basic Swansea-Ilfracombe-Lundy sailings on three or four days a week, supplemented by the well-established Lynmouth Wednesday trips and a good number of Monday Clovelly trips. Penarth-based weekends (on those occasions where tides permitted Friday, Saturday, Sunday and Monday sailings at reasonable hours) were still offered at roughly fortnightly intervals.

The P. & A. Campbell Ltd offices at Bristol and Cardiff were retained but most administrative expenses were to be attributed to White Funnel Steamers Ltd. Peter Southcombe continued to manage the day to day business of the new venture in 1980, with Rod Staker looking after operations and technical matters, whilst West Marine Surveyors provided their professional services. Tony McGinnity continued to oversee the other side of the business. It was hoped and expected that the new arrangements would be part of a transitional step towards the long-sought agreement to consolidate Lundy services, that *Polar Bear* would eventually be displaced by the new order, and that the P. & A. Campbell Ltd proposal to the Landmark Trust to transfer Lundy cargo handling to Swansea would be eventually adopted. A press release issued by European Ferries in March 1980 announced the new arrangements for the season, and gave just a hint of the debate that had taken place to create the new compromise structure, but which still stopped short of being the demise of P. & A. Campbell Ltd as a going concern that Mr Siddle had been seeking:

NEWS FROM P. & A. CAMPBELL LTD
FUTURE OF WHITE FUNNEL STEAMERS

Summer passenger shipping services to the Isle of Lundy are being transferred from P. & A. Campbell Ltd to the Landmark Trust which administers the island, and any profits will in future be devoted to maintaining its amenities. Sailings will be operated by the vessel *Balmoral*. P. & A. Campbell's other vessel, *Devonia*, is to be sold or chartered.

A spokesman for the European Ferries Group, of which P. & A. Campbell Ltd is a member, said the company had been trying for sometime to rationalise this smaller area of its operation and was reluctant to deprive the Bristol Channel of a major tourist attraction and the island of a vital link. "This has proved to be a most acceptable solution for all concerned" he said. "At the same time P. & A. Campbell Ltd will be able to concentrate on its more profitable activities of ship management, chartering and broking".

Little, if any, difference will be noted by the general public under the terms of the new arrangement. The *Balmoral* will be chartered to a new company, White Funnel Steamers Limited, which will be wholly owned by the Landmark Trust. However, P. & A. Campbell Ltd will continue to manage the passenger services and all arrangements for booking, chartering, and any other matters will be dealt with at their various offices.

P. & A. Campbell's other vessel *Devonia*, a combined passenger/cargo vessel, is now on the market for sale or charter. In recent years *Devonia* has carried out relief work on the Bristol Channel passenger service and has also been on charter in the north of Scotland with the oil-supply industry. Directors of the new company will be Mr S. C. Smith-Cox, who will act as Chairman and Managing Director - he is also Chairman of P. & A. Campbell Ltd - and Mr J. L. E. Smith of the Landmark Trust. P. & A. Campbell Ltd have operated vessels in the Bristol Channel since 1887 and annually carry some 20,000 passengers to the island, which came under the administration of the Landmark Trust in 1969.

Commenting on the prospects for 1980 Mr Smith-Cox said that he looked forward to a good year. "Passenger services in the Bristol Channel are only viable because of the large public demand for travel to Lundy Island and because, coupled with this, many people wishing to travel from Penarth, Swansea and elsewhere to North Devon can be conveyed by a vessel which is also serving Lundy. In these circumstances the shipping service is dependent on the island and the island is dependent on the shipping service."

"Progressively through the years due to the advent of the motor car, coastal passenger shipping services all around the British Isles have greatly diminished" he added. "In fact in 1979 P. & A. Campbell Ltd was the only company operating a shipping service similar to that provided in the Bristol Channel on an economic basis. However, this activity is outside the normal scope of European Ferries and we are very pleased that they have agreed to this most amicable solution.

20th March 1980 European Ferries HQ, London

The vulnerability of a seasonally-based shipping operation to the vicissitudes of the weather again became apparent during the 1980 season and as *Devonia* lay idle in Bristol the failure of the company to have secured any work for this vessel only served to emphasise the difficulties that were to be faced. The sailings that *Balmoral* continued to offer were still there to be enjoyed, though, and perhaps sensing that this might very well be her last year in operation, it seemed a good idea in June to take the plunge and devote a few days to Bristol Channel cruising irrespective of whatever the weather might throw up. A typical full day-excursion fare such as Penarth to Ilfracombe was then £6.50 and so a weekly sailing ticket, offered for any seven consecutive days at a price of £15.00, represented a remarkable bargain even if only used for three or four days. *Waverley* was scheduled to be in the Bristol Channel between 30th May and 8th June in 1980, a longer period than the previous year, and as her programme was carefully planned so as not to clash with that of *Balmoral* some interesting options were possible. On Sunday 1st June *Balmoral* had been booked to sail from Penarth to Ilfracombe and Lundy (to land) whilst the paddle-steamer was to run from Swansea and Mumbles to Ilfracombe and then cruise around Lundy – conveniently, interchange between the two was possible, and so one could do what one would not have expected to do again after 1978, which was to change steamers and circumnavigate Lundy by paddle-steamer. Monday 2nd June 1980 was a 'regular' Clovelly day from Ilfracombe and on this day *Balmoral* started from Penarth, thus enabling a mere half-dozen passengers to go ashore for a sunny afternoon at Clovelly. It must be said that a number of would-be White Funnel Steamers passengers from Wales that day had opted to sample *Waverley* instead as she ran out of Swansea and Mumbles to give morning and afternoon Gower coast cruises.

The weather held, and on Tuesday 3rd June 1980 the early start by *Balmoral* at 0845 from Swansea had prompted a stay on the Monday night at Ilfracombe, so as to join the ship there at the more leisurely time of 1205 for her 'regular' afternoon Lundy excursion, due back at Ilfracombe at 1830. On this day *Waverley* sailed out of Minehead and unusually offered an up-Channel cruise around the Holms. After a second night at Ilfracombe, a fourth and final day's use of the weekly ticket was on the 'regular' Wednesday afternoon run to land at Lynmouth, and then it was back via the 1830 crossing from Ilfracombe to Swansea, and train. The weather had been excellent, as had been the value of the weekly ticket, and as this point there still seemed some hope that Bristol Channel cruising, by a 'full-time' vessel, had a future even if *Balmoral* looked shabby and *Waverley* was in demand in Scotland and elsewhere around Britain.

Later in 1980 the journal *Cruising Monthly* reported on the poor early season carryings: '... *the dreadful weather of the early part of the main season gave way to weather little worse than average during the school holiday period. However, the weather, combined with some aspects of the 1980 schedule, has led to* Balmoral *continuing to have a poor season.*' The report noted the cancellation of a number of Clovelly Monday calls, and the poor patronage of the Saturday double Swansea-Ilfracombe runs, and continued: '... *overall the lesson does not seem to have been learnt that at weekends in particular the best trade is to be found up-channel. Perhaps in view of the recession that seems to have hit particularly hard in South Wales, more short cruises (e.g. Gower Coast, Penarth-Minehead) may also be the answer.*'

One can only speculate as to what the fate of the White Funnel Steamers Ltd undertaking might have been after the 1980 season had the weather instead been more favourable. Traffic levels were poor, and things were not looking good as the season-end approached. As

*Calls at Clovelly still featured in the 1980 season timetable of the White Funnel Steamers Ltd undertaking. There were however very few passengers on this occasion on 2nd June 1980, and one launch sufficed to ferry less than a dozen folk ashore from **Balmoral** anchored close to this unusual destination with its single, car-free street stretching steeply upwards from the substantial breakwater.*

Author

*A new style of publicity was employed in 1980 by White Funnel Steamers Ltd. The public would not have thought that a great deal had really changed though: **Balmoral** still looked much the same as during the preceding decade.*

Author's collection

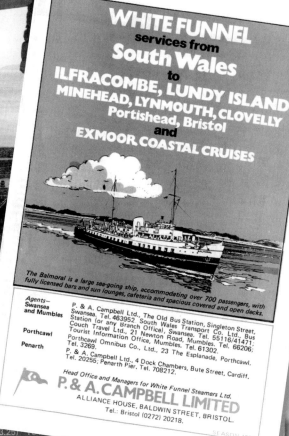
From Penarth Pier

To Ilfracombe (£6.50, Child £3.25)
To Lundy (£7.95, Child £4.00)   To Clovelly (£7.95, Child £4.00)

		LEAVE Penarth	DUE Minehead	DUE Ilfracombe		LEAVE Ilfracombe	LEAVE Minehead	DUE Penarth
May	Sun. 18	...	9.40 a.m.	—	12.30 p.m.	L	6.30 p.m.	—	9.15 p.m.
June	Sun. 1	...	9.40 a.m.	—	12.30 p.m.	L	6.30 p.m.	—	9.15 p.m.
	Mon. 2	...	9.00 a.m.	10.30 a.m.	12.30 p.m.	C	6.30 p.m.	8.30 p.m.	9.50 p.m.
	Mon. 9	...	12.55 p.m.	2.40 p.m.	—	—	—	5.15 p.m.	7.10 p.m.
	Sun. 15	...	9.40 a.m.	—	12.30 p.m.	L	6.30 p.m.	—	9.15 p.m.
	Mon. 16	...	9.00 a.m.	10.30 a.m.	12.30 p.m.	C	6.30 p.m.	8.30 p.m.	9.50 p.m.
	Sun. 29	...	9.40 a.m.	—	12.30 p.m.	L	6.30 p.m.	—	9.45 p.m.
	Mon. 30	...	9.00 a.m.	B10.30 a.m.	12.40 p.m.	C	6.20 p.m.	8.20 p.m.	9.50 p.m.
July	Sun. 13	...	9.40 a.m.	—	12.30 p.m.	L	6.30 p.m.	—	9.45 p.m.
	Mon. 14	...	9.00 a.m.	B10.30 a.m.	12.40 p.m.	C	6.20 p.m.	8.20 p.m.	9.50 p.m.
	Sun. 27	...	9.40 a.m.	—	12.30 p.m.	L	6.30 p.m.	—	10.15 p.m.
	Mon. 28	...	9.00 a.m.	★	12.05 p.m.	C	6.10 p.m.	8.10 p.m.	9.50 p.m.
Aug.	Sun. 10	...	9.40 a.m.	—	12.30 p.m.	L	6.30 p.m.	—	10.15 p.m.
	Mon. 11	...	9-15 a.m.	—	12.05 p.m.	C	6.10 p.m.	8.10 p.m.	9.50 p.m.
	Sun. 17	...	9.50 a.m.	—	12.55 p.m.	L	6.50 p.m.	—	9.35 p.m.
	Mon. 18	...	9.00 a.m.	10.30 a.m.	12.30 p.m.	C	6.30 p.m.	—	9.30 p.m.
	Sun. 31	...	9.50 a.m.	—	12.55 p.m.	L	6.50 p.m.	—	9.35 p.m.
Sept.	Mon. 1	...	9.00 a.m.	B10.30 a.m.	12.30 p.m.	C	6.30 p.m.	—	9.30 p.m.
	Sun. 14	...	9.50 a.m..	—	12.55 p.m.	L	6.50 p.m.	—	9.35 p.m.
	Mon. 15	...	9.00 a.m.	10.30 a.m.	12.30 p.m.	C	6.10 p.m.	B8.10 p.m.	9.50 p.m.
	Sun. 28	...	9.50 a.m.	—	12.55 p.m.	L	6.50 p.m.	—	9.35 p.m.
	Mon. 29	...	9.00 a.m.	—	12.20 p.m.	C	6.10 p.m.	—	9.00 p.m.
Oct.	Sat. 4	...	7.25 p.m.	—	10.30 p.m.	—	9.40 a.m.	—	12.05 p.m.
	Tues. 7	...	8.40 a.m.	—	11.30 a.m.	L	5.45 p.m.	—	9.30 p.m.
	Wed. 8	...	9.30 a.m.	—	12.30 p.m.	PB	5.30 p.m.	—	8.45 p.m.
	Tues. 14	...	9.00 a.m.	—	12.10 p.m.	L	6.30 p.m.	—	9.20 p.m.

B—Landing or embarking at Minehead by motorboat. L—Lundy (to land) see Page 6 for details. PB—Porlock Bay.
C—Clovelly—see note Page 3 for details. *Calls Lynmouth (weather permitting) 11.15 a.m. and 6.40 p.m.

COMBINED RAIL AND SEA SERVICES (Via Swansea Ferryport) TO ILFRACOMBE
(also to Lundy and Lynmouth on the days stated in the Notes on Page 6)

Mondays —Bank Holidays, May 26 and Aug. 25.
Tuesdays —May 20, 27. June 10, 24. July 8, 22, 29. Aug. 5, 12, 26. Sept. 9, 23, 30.
Wednesdays —Every Wednesday from May 21 until Sept. 24.
Thursdays —May 22, 29. June 5, 12, 19, 26. July 3, 10, 17, 24. Aug. 7, 21. Sept. 4, 18.
Fridays —Every Friday from July 4 until Sept. 12.
Saturdays —Every Saturday from June 21 until Sept. 20.

RAIL TIMES		Forward		Return	
		All Dates	Sats. only	Weekdays	Sats. only
Newport	...	0717 B	1239	▲2314 B	2314
Cardiff	...	0740	1301	2235	2250
Bridgend	...	0802	1320	2205	2226
Port Talbot	...	0817	1332	2151	2211
Neath	...	0826	1339	2141	2202
Swansea	...	▼0841	1354	2125	2148
Carmarthen	...	0740	1240	▲2208	2208
Llanelli	...	0813	1313	2134	2134
Swansea	...	▼0835	1335	2115	2115
B—Change at Cardiff.					

DEPART:
Weekdays: Leave Swansea 9.10 a.m. due Ilfracombe 11.30 a.m. **Saturdays:** leave Swansea 9.10 a.m. and 2.15 p.m. due Ilfracombe 11.30 a.m. and 4.35 p.m.
RETURN:
Leave Ilfracombe 6.30 p.m. due Swansea 8.50 p.m. **Free Bus between Swansea Station and Ferryport.** Fares from any listed station: Ilfracombe £6.50, Lundy or Lynmouth £1.50 extra payable on board. Children 5–14 years half fare.

CLOVELLY
Monday sailings from Penarth to Ilfracombe are extended to Clovelly where landing is by motorboat (weather permitting). Passage time between Ilfracombe and Clovelly is about 1¾ hours. Return sailings leave Clovelly 4.30 p.m. —except July 28 (4.10 p.m.), Aug. 11 and Sept. 15 (4.15 p.m.).

SPECIAL SAILINGS

Monday, June 9—12.55 p.m.
Cruise calling at Minehead and along the coast towards Porlock Bay. Due back Penarth 7.10 p.m. Fare £4.95, Child £2.50.

Monday, June 23—11.50 a.m.
To Portishead and Bristol. Due Portishead 1.10 p.m., Bristol 2.15 p.m. Leave Bristol 4.25 p.m., Portishead 5.30 p.m. due back Penarth 6.55 p.m. Fare £3.95, Child £2.00.
Note: **From Bristol 2.15 p.m.** The vessel returns down the Avon Gorge for a short cruise, then back to Bristol at 4.00 p.m. Additional Fare £1.00, Child 50p.

Monday, July 28—9.00 a.m. Monday, Aug. 11—9.15 a.m.
Combined Coach and Sea Trips. By sea to Ilfracombe due 12.05 p.m. Coach leaves Bus Station 2.15 p.m. and takes the coast road over Exmoor to Minehead due 4.30 p.m. Leave Minehead Harbour 8.10 p.m. direct for Penarth due back 9.50 p.m. Fare £6.50, Child £3.25.

Saturday, Oct. 4—12.55 p.m.
To Portishead and Bristol. Due Portishead 1.50 p.m., Bristol 2.50 p.m. Leave Bristol 5.10 p.m., Portishead 6.00 p.m. Due back Penarth 7.15 p.m. Fare £3.95, Child £2.00.

THROUGH BOOKINGS (RAIL & STEAMER)
Now available from Stations on the Rhymney Valley Line. For full particulars ask for Special Leaflet at the railway stations concerned.

BUS SERVICE BETWEEN CARDIFF BUS STATION AND PENARTH PIER
Buses now operate a regular daily service on this route. On Sunday mornings a Special Bus leaves Cardiff Bus Station 40 minutes prior to the Steamer Sailing Times. Full details from City of Cardiff Transport Dept., or P. & A. Campbell Ltd.

2

3

if in a final, defiant flourish one novel new excursion was operated, successfully, on 27th September 1980, when a landing excursion from Penarth to Steep Holm was operated and around 200 passengers went ashore by tender, the launch used being the Weston-based *Ivanhoe*.

Shortly after this the annual Isles of Scilly trip, based this year on St. Ives for overnight accommodation for three nights, was again affected by poor weather. Apart from being unable to actually get beyond Ilfracombe to St. Ives on Friday 10th October 1980, necessitating a lengthy coach journey to West Cornwall from Ilfracombe, conditions were such that *Balmoral* again failed to reach St. Ives the next day, and passengers were obliged to content themselves with the alternative of a trip from Penzance on *Scillonian* (III) if they wished instead. A road-connection for a River Fal cruise was also arranged for those passengers that required it, but the disappointment was obviously considerable. *Balmoral* struggled down to St. Ives but only so as to bring her mini-cruise passengers back up-Channel to Ilfracombe, Penarth and Portishead (as Weston was no longer an option) on the last day of what should have been the Isles of Scilly weekend, on Monday 13th October 1980.

And so the end of season came and with it inevitably the last trip from Penarth to Ilfracombe and Lundy on Tuesday 14th October 1980. This in itself was a rather different way to end the season compared to so many decades previously when the 'Last Trip of the Season' had generally been on the 'ferry' from Weston back to Penarth and Cardiff. Poor weather again intervened, and the Lundy leg had to be cancelled. Those that turned out to see *Balmoral* on her final arrival back at Penarth Pier that evening on what actually proved to be her final sailing as a P. & A. Campbell Ltd-owned ship did not then know

that the end had now been reached, even if the poor season had made it obvious that an even more intractable financial result had ensued for White Funnel Steamers Ltd. However, the official position at this point was that there would still be sailings in 1981. It was not until shortly before the 1981 season was due to get underway that more startling announcements were made, and the awful truth dawned: although the famous P. & A. Campbell Ltd name would live on a little longer, the days of the White Funnel Fleet had truly ended after *Balmoral* finished her duties that autumn night in 1980.

The end of P. & A. Campbell Ltd

For some observers 1967 had represented the end of the traditional White Funnel Fleet when the career of *Bristol Queen*, the last paddle-steamer, had abruptly ceased. But the long-established Bristol Channel excursion business tradition had continued, as well as activities elsewhere, although it might have been said that the company was on borrowed time throughout the 1970s. This study has sought to describe the means by which Clifton Smith-Cox and others exercised a determination to maintain the continuity of Bristol Channel excursions during this period, and indeed the survival of *Balmoral* herself was very much a factor in events after 1981. These are rightly the subject of separate studies, notably as documented by Alan Brown in *Shanklin: Ill-Fated Prince* in describing the career of *Prince Ivanhoe*, the vessel that in 1981 was in direct succession to the long line of P. & A. Campbell Ltd steamers. The purpose here in closing the story of P. & A. Campbell Ltd, Passenger Steamship Owners is to document the final activities of the Limited Company, which had been formed back in 1893.

Although it was not known at the time, this was practically the end for **Balmoral**, *as the last P. & A. Campbell Ltd ship, in October 1980. She had arrived in the River Avon from Penarth, swung at the Tongue Head, gone astern into the Cumberland Basin entrance-lock and was awaiting her return departure time on the same tide.*

Author

Right up until the end, an office was maintained at the Quay by the Ilfracombe Agent. Bookings were handled by Fred Birmingham. He was a third-generation member of the family which had served P. & A. Campbell Ltd right back into the 1890s, when the Ilfracombe Agency had first been established in the early years of the Limited Company.
Author

The situation at the end of the 1980 season was that **Devonia** had remained idle throughout, unreconstructed, and with diminishing prospects of ever finding gainful employment again with P. & A. Campbell Ltd. When the White Funnel Steamers Ltd accounts were drawn up, based on the chartered-out **Balmoral** operation, it was clear that the Landmark Trust – having taken most of the risk on the season's operations whilst P. & A. Campbell Ltd acted as managers – would not be repeating the exercise, having sustained significant financial loss, and the then Lundy Agent stated that the 1980 steamer season had from his perspective been 'a financial disaster.' The loss quoted in subsequent P. & A. Campbell Ltd accounts for the year ending 31st December 1980, published in May 1981, was put at £177,630, but revealed little of the exact joint venture position. Modest levels of ship-broking and ancillary business had been transacted through the Bristol office, but the commercial value of the once famous Campbell name was now perceived as extremely limited. What was to be done? The European Ferries group had made it quite clear that P. & A. Campbell Ltd activities must be cut away from main Group business. Discussions took place in late-1980 between Clifton Smith-Cox, John Smith of the Landmark Trust and Terry Sylvester representing the interests of Waverley Steam Navigation Ltd, whose presence in the Bristol Channel with the preserved paddle-steamer **Waverley** had recently become established. In a nutshell, the fortuitous acquisition of former Isle of Wight ferry **Shanklin**, renamed **Prince Ivanhoe**, was in due course to facilitate what amounted to a handover of interests where excursion sailings would be maintained but operated by a different body, with a new remit and – more to the point – an attractive and seemingly suitable vessel. Clifton Smith-Cox could now relax, as it were, content that a future still beckoned for Bristol Channel excursion sailings, in new hands.

Whilst the initial public message at the end of the 1980 season had been that it would be business as usual again in 1981, a follow-up statement with the annual pre-season mailing-list letter to season-ticket & coupon-holders set out the new arrangements:

The brief reign of Prince Ivanhoe

Balmoral, the last operational ship owned by P. & A. Campbell Ltd, had ended her active career sailing on charter for White Funnel Steamers Ltd in 1980. In 1981 the role of P. & A. Campbell Ltd in Bristol Channel excursion sailings was to be as managers of **Prince Ivanhoe**, itself owned and operated by the Firth of Clyde Steam Packet Company. The letter-heading to be found on P. & A. Campbell Ltd notepaper now defined the final role of the company as Ship Owners, Ship Managers, Ship & Insurance Brokers, although the first element only alluded to the two laid-up vessels – **Balmoral** and **Devonia** – awaiting disposal. The other elements were exemplified by fees earned from a number of diverse activities, and from a contract to supervise the maintenance of the local Bristol sewage disposal vessel m.v. *Glen Avon*, owned by the Wessex Water Authority. P. & A. Campbell Ltd acted as the chartering brokers for the employment of the commercial vehicle ferry **Viking Trader**, and efforts were being made by Tony McGinnity to negotiate the sale of **Free Enterprise II** on behalf of the European Ferries group.

To conclude the P. & A. Campbell Ltd story properly requires that we go back a little, to the beginning of the 1980 season, to consider the circumstances of a third Isle of Wight vessel which had entered service as **Shanklin** in 1951. This was for the Southern Region of British Railways, linking Portsmouth and Southsea with Ryde on the Isle of Wight. (The first and second ex-Isle of Wight vessels had, of course, been **Vecta** and **Balmoral** from the Southampton company). By the 1970s railway shipping activities were collectively branded under the 'Sealink' name, and its Isle of Wight division then included car-ferries for the Portsmouth to Fishbourne and Lymington to Yarmouth routes as well as a 'classic' trio of elderly motor-vessels for foot-passengers, then still plentiful in numbers. **Shanklin** was the third of this trio, which had been ordered after the Second World War to replace older paddle-steamers which basically operated between Portsmouth Harbour station and Ryde Pier, from whence the railway network to much of the Isle of Wight radiated.

Shanklin was notably Denny-built, to a high-standard. Her withdrawal by Sealink in March 1980 was partly attributable to the failure of one of her two diesel-engines, as well as to falling demand for 'classic' foot-passenger crossings to the Isle of Wight as the number of car-ferries in service grew, and fast-craft prospects developed. Although **Shanklin** had supposedly been 'mothballed' after withdrawal, and might have been reactivated had this been necessary,

The new order in the Bristol Channel for the 1981 season was represented by the smart, former Isle of Wight ferry **Shanklin**. *Renamed* **Prince Ivanhoe**, *she was owned by the Firth of Clyde Steam Packet Company, and was operated by Waverley Excursions Ltd in association with the paddle-steamer* **Waverley**. *She is seen here approaching Minehead Harbour on 16th May 1981.*   Author

the surviving sisters **Brading** and **Southsea** coped on their own during the summer of 1980 and so it became known that the younger ship was available for sale by the autumn of that year. Those involved with the Clyde-based operation of the paddle-steamer **Waverley** had good reason to be interested in the possibility of acquiring **Shanklin** as a second vessel which could generally support the continued operation of the operationally-preserved paddle-steamer. At this point it seemed that her destiny, once restored to health, would mostly involve Scotland whilst **Waverley** was elsewhere, particularly as the then diminishing Firth of Clyde cruise operations of Caledonian MacBrayne – who in 1980 had continued to deploy the former car-ferry **Glen Sannox** in such a role – might well have been terminated for 1981.

After an inspection in October 1980, an offer by Waverley Steam Navigation Ltd to purchase **Shanklin** was successfully made. By November 1980 she had returned to her birthplace, or at least to the Clyde, where a refit at Govan took place in early-1981. During this time the debate about the future of Bristol Channel cruising – and the servicing of Lundy – had been taking place and soon enough it seemed inevitable that **Prince Ivanhoe**, as **Shanklin** had been renamed, was lined up to take on her new role as the successor to **Balmoral** for the main summer season. This would involve an early start, triggered by the fact that despite the lack of certainty in late-1980 that a White Funnel vessel would resume operations in 1981, P. & A. Campbell Ltd had taken on early-season commitments which warranted **Prince Ivanhoe** being brought into Bristol Channel service as early as April 1981 to honour these. In Scotland it had been decided that **Glen Sannox** would again be operated by Caledonian MacBrayne, for cruising on the Firth of Clyde in the summer of 1981, and this appeared to leave less potential there for **Prince Ivanhoe**.

And so the dilemma with which Clifton Smith-Cox had struggled now appeared to have been solved, and the couple of brief forays which **Waverley** had enjoyed in the Bristol Channel in 1979 and 1980 could perhaps be seen as a good omen for the new order which now beckoned, thus providing the continuity which he had sought. That it was expedient

for P. & A. Campbell Ltd to stay in business to act as ship-managers and commercial agents for **Prince Ivanhoe** was wholly appropriate under the circumstances as the business could change hands amicably, so to speak. This was largely to do with a framework, albeit a slender one, still being in place to handle publicity, marketing and sales. A part of this was the existence of the Ilfracombe Agency, in the hands of the stalwart Fred Birmingham, whose family had been loyal to the Campbell cause since the 1890s. The outlook of the company for 1981 was therefore one of a very much slimmed-down activity, but with revenue flowing from the management activities associated with the entry into Bristol Channel service of **Prince Ivanhoe**, which fully took place on Saturday 16th May 1981 at Penarth, although some charter and other minor work had already been carried out in early-May.

At this point, insofar as European Ferries as the parent company was concerned, the P. & A. Campbell Ltd shipping subsidiary business had now ceased, and it was expected that the ships would be sold without further ado. An Internal Memorandum from Ken Siddle to Tony McGinnity, dated 24th February 1981, noted that any residual costs in the P. & A. Campbell Ltd name would fall to his European Ferries Marine Superintendency Division.

Stylish publicity with newly-commissioned artwork was prepared for the 1981 season, which projected the image of the paddle-steamer **Waverley** and **Prince Ivanhoe** linking south Wales and the West Country, with the customary emphasis on the link with Lundy which P. & A. Campbell Ltd had themselves adopted. The company, at its Bristol address at Alliance House in Baldwin Street, was now described as being the Agents for The Waverley Steam Navigation Co. Ltd and for The Firth of Clyde Steam Packet Co. Ltd, which latter body had been formed to own and operate the revitalised former **Shanklin**. A lot of thought went into the promotion of excursions by **Prince Ivanhoe** and there were a variety of coach-links from south Devon and more locally around north Devon to feed into Lundy sailings from Ilfracombe, which were advertised as being at frequencies of up to four times per week in the high summer. Fares were typically only

Opposite: **Attractive new artwork was commissioned to market sailings by** **Prince Ivanhoe** **and** **Waverley** **in the Bristol Channel in 1981. The front of the bill listed Ilfracombe sailings, the obverse listed departure times from Minehead and Watchet, and from Lynmouth. P. & A. Campbell Ltd continued in business in 1981 (from Alliance House in Baldwin Street, Bristol and also at 10, The Quay, Ilfracombe) as the Bristol Channel agents for** **Prince Ivanhoe**, **perpetuating the operating and commercial arrangements which had been in place for** **Balmoral** **up until the 1980 season.**

Author's collection

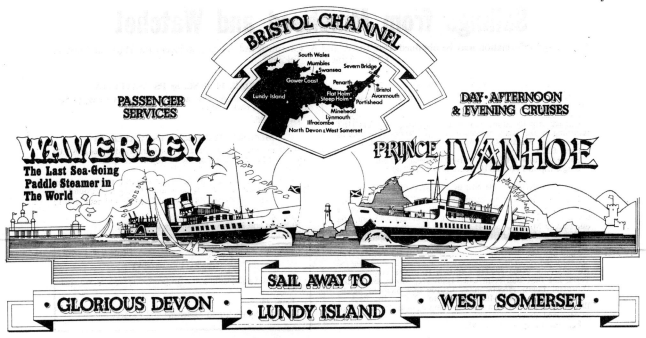

1981 Early Season Sailings
From Ilfracombe Pier

ALSO FROM MINEHEAD AND LYNMOUTH (*SEE OVERLEAF*)

TICKETS may be obtained from P. and A. Campbell Ltd, 10 The Quay, Ilfracombe, Tel 62687, or aboard the vessels.

FARES. Day return fares are shown against all sailings. Single fares are charged at the same rate as for day return. Child fares, applicable to children aged 3 and under 16 years, are approximately half the adult day return fare.

SUNDAY, 3 MAY, by MV 'PRINCE IVANHOE'

2.00 pm. Afternoon cruise to Lundy Island Roads, passing Capstone Hill, the Tunnels, the Torrs, Lee Bay, Bull Point and Lighthouse and viewing on the East Side of the Island, the Lighthouses, Landing Beach, the Church of St Helena and other points of interest. Back 5.20 pm.
Fare: £5.95.
5.30 pm. Single trip to Penarth.

BANK HOLIDAY MONDAY, 4 MAY by MV 'PRINCE IVANHOE'

2.30 pm. Afternoon cruise along the Coasts of Devon and Somerset, passing Hillsborough Hill, Hele Bay, Watermouth Castle and Harbour, Combe Martin, Hangman Hills, Heddonsmouth, Wooda Bay, Castle Rock and off Lynmouth. Back about 4.45 pm.
Fare: £2.95.
5.00 pm. Single trip to Penarth and Portishead.

SUNDAY, 17 MAY, by MV 'PRINCE IVANHOE'

2.00 pm. Afternoon cruise to Lundy Island Roads, passing Capstone Hill, the Tunnels, the Torrs, Lee Bay, Bull Point and Lighthouse and viewing on the East side of the Island, the Lighthouses, Landing Beach, the Church of St Helena, and other points of interest. Due back at Ilfracombe 5.30 pm.
Fare: £5.95.
5.30 pm. Single trip to Penarth.

TUESDAY, 19 MAY, by MV 'PRINCE IVANHOE'

2.30 pm. Afternoon cruise along the Coasts of Devon and Somerset, passing Hillsborough Hill, Hele Bay, Watermouth Castle and Harbour, Combe Martin, Hangman Hills, Heddonsmouth, Wooda Bay, Castle Rock and off Lynmouth. Back about 4.40 pm.
Fare: £2.95.

MONDAY, 8 JUNE, by PS 'WAVERLEY'

2.30 pm. Afternoon cruise along the North Devon Coast, passing Capstone Hill, The Tunnels, The Torrs, Lee Bay, Bull Point and Lighthouse, Morte, Baggy and Downend Points, Woolacombe, Croyde and Saunton Sands, Westward Ho, Bucks Mills etc and to off Clovelly. Back about 5.15 pm.
Fare: £3.95.
5.30 pm. Single trip to Lynmouth and Penarth.

THURSDAY, 11 JUNE, by PS 'WAVERLEY'

11.40 am. Day trip to Lundy Island (to land), due Lundy 1.20 pm. Return from Lundy 4.40 pm. Due back at Ilfracombe 6.20 pm.
Fare (including landing charges): £7.95.
(*Please see notes overleaf about landing at Lundy*).
6.30 pm. Single trip to Mumbles and Swansea.

WEDNESDAY, 17 JUNE, by PS 'WAVERLEY'

2.30 pm. Afternoon cruise along the Exmoor Coasts of Devon and Somerset, passing Hillsborough Hill, Hele Bay, Watermouth Castle and Harbour, Combe Martin, Hangman Hills, Heddonsmouth, Wooda Bay, Castle Rock, Lynton and Lynmouth, the Foreland Point and Lighthouse, Glenthorne, etc and to Porlock Bay, calling off Lynmouth. Back about 5.20 pm.
Fare: £3.95.
5.30 pm. Single trip to Mumbles, Swansea and by coach to Barry.

THURSDAY, 18 JUNE, by PS 'WAVERLEY'

11.40 am. Day trip to Lundy Island (to land), due Lundy 1.20 pm. Return from Lundy 4.40 pm. Due back at Ilfracombe 6.20 pm.
Fare (including landing charges): £7.95.
(*Please see notes overleaf about landing at Lundy*).
6.30 pm. Single trip to Porthcawl and by coach to Swansea.

SATURDAY, 20 JUNE, by PS 'WAVERLEY'

2.30 pm. Afternoon cruise along the North Devon Coast, passing Capstone Hill, The Tunnels, The Torrs, Lee Bay, Bull Point and Lighthouse, Morte Point, Woolacombe, Baggy Point and to Bideford Bay. Back about 4.15 pm.
Fare: £3.95.
4.30 pm. Single trip to Penarth and Portishead.

SUNDAY, 21 JUNE, by PS 'WAVERLEY'

1.45 pm. Afternoon cruise around Lundy Island, passing Capstone Hill, the Tunnels, the Torrs, Lee Bay, Bull Point and Lighthouse and viewing on the Island, the Lighthouses, Landing Beach, the Church of St Helena, Logans Stone, Jenny's Cave, the Devils Slide and other points of interest. Back 5.20 pm.
Fare: £5.95.
5.30 pm. Single trip to Penarth and Portishead.

The end. **Balmoral** *and* **Devonia** *laid up together in the centre of Bristol, at The Grove, pending disposal after P. & A. Campbell Ltd had ceased to operate excursion sailings.*

Martin Oatway

slightly higher than those that had been charged in 1980 for **Balmoral**, at around 6% or 7% which largely reflected inflation, although what been the excellent bargain of a weekly ticket was increased from £15 to £25, and one would really need to travel for at least four days to 'break even' rather than three in P. & A. Campbell Ltd days if one had the time and dedication: it was nonetheless still a good bargain for the enthusiast and demonstrated that careful marketing had been applied.

As the early season got underway there was much positive reaction to the new image of Bristol Channel cruising, although it was said that **Prince Ivanhoe** needed a degree of structural enhancement to properly fit her for a long-time role in these waters, where she was inevitably subject to more demanding conditions than those for which she had been designed. Her generous accommodation was impressive, as was her excellent open-deck space and all in all her arrival generated considerable excitement, as well as good crowds at Penarth Pier and elsewhere.

Alan Brown described the story of **Shanklin**, and her rebirth as **Prince Ivanhoe**, in fastidious detail. Insofar as P. & A. Campbell Ltd are concerned the company might have continued, at least in name, for a few more years had not **Prince Ivanhoe** met with disaster very early on in her new career, being lost on Monday 3rd August 1981 off the Gower coast at Port Eynon. Words can scarcely describe this loss after such a promising start, and it has to be said that during her brief reign the positive new image she created only emphasised just how shabby the final years of P. & A. Campbell Ltd sailings had actually become. Even the most dedicated enthusiasts, who put tradition first and valued the continuity with the past that **Balmoral** represented, were obliged to concede that the former Denny-built Isle of Wight railway ferry was a hit. Yet all of a sudden, what might have been a promising and profitable new venture had come to an end. More specifically, income crucial to the survival of P. & A. Campbell Ltd was abruptly cut off, which necessitated Tony McGinnity and Clifton Smith-Cox having to face the unpalatable truth that it really was now all over. The ship-broking side had been holding its head above water, just, but a major contract for P. & A. Campbell Ltd to manage two motor cargo vessels owned by John Laing, **Northumbrian Lass** and **Northumbrian Rose**, being negotiated in March 1981 – and which would have generated a vital income stream – fell through a couple of months later.

The blow caused by the loss of **Prince Ivanhoe**, coupled with this setback, proved to be fatal for P. & A. Campbell Ltd. Severe cashflow

problems arose and although European Ferries assisted this situation as backers it was solely on the basis that the Bristol company would now close down completely, and remaining activities be dispersed elsewhere as appropriate. Tony McGinnity put three alternatives to the European Ferries, namely that (a) P. & A. Campbell Ltd be sold as a name, with its remaining business, (b) Campbell activities be transferred to the Marine Division of the parent company at Tonbridge or (c) that these activities be instead transferred to West Marine Surveyors (by this time owned by Campbells themselves). The response of the Managing Director of European Ferries on 19th October 1981 was simple and predictable, given that option (a) was scarcely practical except at a purely nominal figure: P. & A. Campbell Ltd would finally close down as no commercial logic was seen in its retention in any form.

What actually happened was that P. & A. Campbell Ltd ceased actively trading after 31st January 1982, and West Marine Surveyors was sold back to its partners, including Tony McGinnity. The Campbell name, as a legal entity but one which had ceased to trade, lingered on a little longer. The remaining employees were made redundant and the office premises surrendered.

Devonia had been sold late in 1981, to another West Country venture, Torbay Seaways, for £90,000 'as is', for a new role which involved running coastal excursions from Torquay and trips to the Channel Islands as **Devoniun**. She still had plenty of life in her, it seemed, as she went on to see different uses in the 1980s and enjoyed a number of subsequent name-changes, during a long and diverse existence.

It merely remained for the efforts to sell **Balmoral** to be concluded, the final act of Tony McGinnity as the Joint Managing Director being to bank a cheque for £30,000 from Craig Inns of Dundee into the European Ferries account at Lloyds Bank in Avonmouth as the Bristol office of P. & A. Campbell Ltd had closed by then. Her destiny then seemed to be that of a static exhibit only, far away from the area in which she seemed to belong, and she left Avonmouth on 25th March 1982, under her own power.

Although nomadic appearances by **Waverley** in the Bristol Channel during the next few years were to keep hopes alive, the future for regular coastal cruising in those waters seemed bleaker than ever. **Balmoral**, the last operational P. & A. Campbell Ltd ship, had escaped the breakers, but nobody would then have seriously predicted any future revival of Bristol Channel excursion sailings by a 'resident' ship again. Happily, events were to prove otherwise.

*The paddle-steamer **Waverley** had made her Bristol Channel debut during 1979, by arrangement with P. & A. Campbell Ltd. Not long after this picture was taken on 1st June 1980 **Balmoral** would be withdrawn as the charter to White Funnel Steamers Ltd ended after that season, and a commercial undertaking was replaced by the preservation movement.*   Author

Acknowledgements

As noted in the Introduction, it was the renaissance in 1986 of **Balmoral** that triggered the research for this book, and I must pay tribute to all those responsible for that initiative which perpetuated Bristol Channel cruising after the end of P. & A. Campbell Ltd operations in 1980 closely followed by the loss of **Prince Ivanhoe** in 1981. The late Jon Holyoak was an ardent follower of the Campbell concern and had a great deal to do with fund-raising and generally providing inspiration, and within the PSPS movement was a key instigator of the Balmoral Restoration Fund. Since I met Jon in the mid-1970s, I personally look back to him as a key person who helped me with, and suggested new directions for studying the late years of P. & A. Campbell Ltd as well as collaborating in Barry Railway Company steamer research. Terry Sylvester, the long-serving Commercial Director of Waverley Excursions Ltd also encouraged these endeavours, as did Nigel Coombes, Richard Clammer and Chris Collard and others in the PSPS.

It is my hope that taking the story beyond the paddle-steamer era will be seen as a worthwhile endeavour, and one that furthers understanding of how P. & A. Campbell Ltd functioned as a business. I have aimed to build on the comprehensive writings of Chris Collard covering operational matters recalled from his first-hand association with the steamers from the 1950s. My thanks also go to Iain Hope who, through his work *The Campbells of Kilmun*, further stimulated the desire to get to the roots of the Bristol Channel pleasure-steamer scene. Although I did not know the Bristol Channel paddle-steamer 'Queens' myself, the work of Nick James (past Chairman of the PSPS) in documenting **Cardiff Queen**, and Norman Bird likewise for **Bristol Queen** has been a further cue for delving into the activities of the motor-vessels which replaced them.

In seeking to blend company history with reminiscences I have relied heavily on documents made available by Peter Southcombe. Peter comes from an old Ilfracombe family and his influence within the company was fundamental, particularly away from the mainstream Bristol Channel business, and all of my extensive questions to Peter have been helpfully and thoroughly addressed in his good-humoured manner, over the last fifteen years or more. Similarly I have relied on old company papers made available to me by the late Tony McGinnity, as well as his concise recollections of what it meant to run the company with Clifton Smith-Cox in the 1970s when relationships with the parent company were rapidly changing. I thus hope to have achieved a balance between company history as gleaned from surviving officially documented sources, as well as from the personal and professional memories of the ships officers, notably George Gunn. The death of Tony McGinnity in 2008 so soon after his retirement was a huge loss, particularly after the satisfaction of working with him at his Isle of Wight home to finalise the details of his lengthy involvement in the business.

Over a quarter-century on from the end of the White Funnel Fleet, many PSPS Bristol Channel members today were the customers of P. & A. Campbell Ltd in the late years of the company, some of whom recorded their experiences then in a manner which has proved invaluable to complement the above sources. I therefore record my gratitude to Donald Anderson, who edited the excellent World Ship Society journal *Ship Ahoy*, to Sid Robinson, and numerous contributors, notably John Brown and Norman Bird. Miss Gwyneth White of Penarth had a particular gift for recalling how it was before the Second World War as well as afterwards, and it is through actually having been privileged to know such characters that – to me – the past has been illuminated over and above that which has merely been written down. The late George Owen was a particular source of inspiration particularly regarding the earlier life of the company, and pointed me towards the excellent Ilfracombe Museum, whose resources enabled a wider appreciation of the Campbell business from a north Devon perspective. Pat Murrell of Bristol and Howard Jones of Cardiff have, in many ways, filled out the story of what went on in the 1960s and 1970s, as has Ken Jenkins (son of William Jenkins, one-time Company Secretary), Philip Tolley, Robin Wall, Jack Rowles and Martin Oatway, all of Bristol, as well as Ian & Margaret Boyle and John Spears.

I must finally thank those who have enabled me to document the north Wales years of the White Funnel Fleet 1963-1969, notably George Boswell (and the CCA journal Cruising Monthly) and Malcolm McRonald, as well as Stan Basnett for the Isle of Man photographic connection. I am also indebted to Richard Clammer for having read the entire manuscript, although of course the responsibility for any errors is my own.

Sources & Bibliography

Sources

Unpublished

Minute Books of P. & A. Campbell Ltd (held at the Bristol City Record Office), also Ships Log Books, Memorandum Books, and other miscellaneous company records, Accession nos.

Newspapers & periodicals

Newspapers

Bristol Times & Mirror; *Caernarfon & Denbigh Herald*; *Ilfracombe Chronicle*; *Ilfracombe Gazette and Observer*; *North Devon Journal*; *North Wales Weekly News*; *South Wales Argus*; *South Wales Echo*; *Western Daily Press*; *Western Mail*; *Weston Mercury & Somersetshire Herald*.

Journals/Magazines

Ship Ahoy, published 1955-69 by the South Wales Branch of the World Ship Society, in particular 'The Bristol Channel and the Bristol Queen', series by Norman Bird.
NB *Best of Ship Ahoy*; a compilation of articles from *Ship Ahoy* was published April 1999 by the Bristol Channel Branch of the Paddle Steamer Preservation Society.
Cruising Monthly, 1960s-date
Paddle Wheels, journal of the Paddle Steamer Preservation Society

Shipping company guidebooks & handbooks

The Bristol Channel District Guide (various editions), published for P. & A. Campbell Ltd, by F. G. Warne of Bristol.
The Red Funnel Steamers Illustrated Handbook (various editions), published for Red Funnel Steamers Ltd, by Ed. J. Burrow &Co. Ltd.
North Wales Coast – Official Guide (various editions), published by the Liverpool & North Wales Steamship Company Ltd.
Seawards: Official Souvenir Handbook of the Eagle & Queen Line Steamers, published by the General Steam Navigation Co. Ltd.
Ilfracombe Devon by S. P. B. Mais, official publication of Ilfracombe Urban District Council, 1930s (various years)

Scrapbooks from individual collectors

John Brown, Sid Robinson, the late E. R. Keen (courtesy of Phil Tolley)

Bibliography

Brown, A., *Shanklin: Ill Fated Prince*, Waverley Excursions Ltd., Glasgow, 1985
Burton, S. H., *The North Devon Coast*, Werner Laurie,London, 1953
Collard, C., *White Funnels: The story of Campbell's steamers, 1949-68*, Baron Birch, 1996
Collard, C., *P. & A. Campbell Pleasure Steamers from 1946*, Tempus, Brimscombe, 1999
Colver, Hugh, *This is the Hovercraft*, Elm Tree Books, 1972
Coombes, N., *Passenger Steamers of the Bristol Channel: a pictorial record*, Twelveheads Press, Truro, 1990
Coombes, N., *White Funnel Magic*, Twelveheads Press, Truro, 1995
Cowsill, M. & Hendy, J., *The Townsend Thoresen Years: 1928-1987*, Ferry Publications, Dyfed, 1988
Cowsill, M. & Hendy, J., *The Townsend Eight*, Ferry Publications, Ramsey, IoM, c2000
Danielson, R., *The Honourable Balmoral: Her Peers and Piers*, Maritime Publications, Laxey IoM, 1999
Duckworth, C. L. D., & Langmuir, G. E., *West Coast Passenger Steamers*, Stephenson, Prescot, Lancs., 1966
Farr, G., *West Country Passenger Steamers*, Stephenson, Prescot, Lancs., 1967
Grimshaw, G., *British Pleasure Steamers, 1920-1939*, Tilling, London, 1945
Gunn, Capt. G., *White Funnel Memories*, Gomer Press, Llandysul, 1997
Gunn, Capt. G., *Ships & Short Splices*, Gomer Press, Llandysul, 2002
Hendy, J., *Ferry Port Dover*, Ferry Publications, Kent, 1997
Hope, Iain, *The Campbells of Kilmun: Shipowners 1853-1980*, Aggregate Publications, Johnstone, Renfrewshire, 1981
James, Nick, *Cardiff Queen – the Ultimate Coastal Paddle-Steamer*, author/PSPS, 1988
Shepherd, J., *The Liverpool & North Wales Steamship Company*, Ships in Focus Publications, 2006
Thornley, F. C., *Steamers of North Wales*, Stephenson, Prescot, Lancs., 1952
Thornton, E. C. B., *South Coast Pleasure Steamers*, Stephenson, Prescot, Lancs. 2nd edition, 1969
Wall, R., *Bristol Channel Pleasure Steamers*, David & Charles, Newton Abbot, 1973
Waters, B., *The Bristol Channel*, J. M. Dent & Sons, London, 1955

Balmoral at Dundee in 1983 where she served as a restaurant prior to her restoration for the 1986 season.   Ian Pope

P.S. "CARDIFF QUEEN   P. & A. CAMPBELL, Ltd.

An official postcard of the **Cardiff Queen** *approaching Ilfracombe.*   A.K. Pope collection

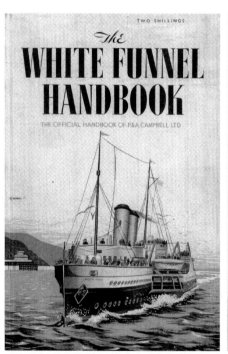
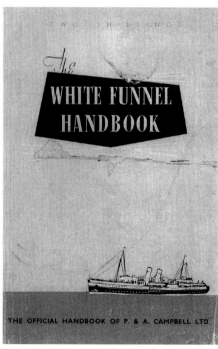

Before the Second World War the official handbook of P. & A. Campbell Ltd was published at least annually, and was known as the Bristol Channel District Guide. Starting out in 1893 it continued until 1938 when a new publication, the White Funnel Handbook, combining Bristol Channel and South Coast information, took its place, and was revised for 1939. After a wartime absence a new edition was produced for 1954, the Centenary Year, (left), based on the 1939 book but with substantially different fleet details. It was re-published in 1957, (middle), after the fleet had contracted somewhat, and sold at the same price of two shillings. A different style of booklet (right) appeared for the 1964 season, rather smaller, and sold for the lower price of one shilling and sixpence. The final White Funnel Handbook was produced for 1968, (back cover), with a very different fleet description as the paddle-steamers had gone, there had been hovercraft until 1967, and the South Coast could be included again on account of the cross-channel coach excursions, and north Wales was added too. Stocks of this booklet were still on sale throughout the 1970s even though **Balmoral**, *the last of the line, was not mentioned.*

Author's collection

Appendix One
THE CONTEXT OF FINANCIAL RECONSTRUCTION

Explanatory note The author was fortunate to acquire, via the late H. G. Owen, some of the papers of the late Cyril Hawkins-Garrington, who had been a P. & A. Campbell Ltd shareholder of long-standing. These included official letters to shareholders, which complemented the statutory Accounts of the company and Chairman's Reports that shareholders would have received.

From these official communications (*a number of which are referred to in part in the text, and some of which are reproduced in full here*) it has been possible to build up a picture of what shareholders were told as the Company went through the periods of financial difficulty already described, culminating in Chancery proceedings and the successful conclusion to the financial reconstruction.

Taken together the first five items illustrate the officially-communicated message, whilst the sixth takes a more technical look – with hindsight – at the figures which had formed the basis of what shareholders, creditors and others were being told, from a practical accountancy perspective. Some brief explanation of the significance of the company statements is possibly useful here. Item 1 practically amounted to the first formal postwar admission by the Company that all was not well financially, despite new initiatives that had been taken. Time went by in the mid-1950s, but item 2 pointed to the continuing seriousness of the trading position of P. & A. Campbell Ltd, whilst expressing hope that the company might yet pull through. One year later, item 3 explained and justified the actions that the Board had taken in 1956, it being hoped that enough had now been done to arrest the decline. I have added annotations of my own here to further develop the themes emerging at this challenging time. But a year later the company was in Receivership, and item 4 practically illustrates the line that came to be drawn through the 'old company' and pointed towards the inevitability of financial restructuring. Later in 1958 another communication from the Chairman, item 5, clarified the belief that things had now reached their nadir and expressed the hope that a brighter but modest future lay ahead.

I am indebted to Keith Adams for item 6.

Item 1
Letter, dated 24th September 1954 sent to all shareholders from the P. & A. Campbell Ltd registered offices at Britannia Buildings in Bristol.

TO ALL SHAREHOLDERS

Dear Sir or Madam,

I regret to have to inform you that your Directors have decided that payment of the Preference Dividend normally payable on 1st October next cannot be recommended.

I doubt whether any shareholder will be surprised to learn that the deplorable weather which has characterised the Summer of 1954 – by all accounts the worst encountered within living memory - will inevitably result in a serious loss being shown when the Company's Accounts for the year are completed. Unfortunately the benefits which might under average conditions have been expected to accrue from the improvements and innovations forecast in the statement which I circulated earlier in the year and most of which have been successfully carried out, were largely negatived by the bad weather.

This ill fortune, following as it does four successive years of poor summer weather, will be a bitter disappointment to all those who have this year - in many cases gratuitously – made special efforts to make the year a success and to maintain a public interest in the Steamers. I refer in particular to Management, Staff, Officers, and Crews of vessels, many of the Company's old friends and customers, and certainly to the Press on both sides of the Bristol Channel.

In the light of the above I can understand that the situation must occasion anxiety to all shareholders, and I have no doubt that many must be wondering what the future prospects of the Company really amount to.

Your Directors had hoped that one period at least of settled weather would prevail in July or August so as to enable reliable data to be gained as to the present Company's earning potential and the effect of introducing new Ports of call, sailings and other innovations to be gauged. Unfortunately this did not occur, and in expressing opinions about future prospects we are compelled to base them upon such data as the weather has permitted us to obtain and upon the observations and opinions of the Managing Directors and Senior Executives of the Company.

With this reservation, we believe that given reasonable weather and notwithstanding the existence of other means of travel and holiday attractions, the Company still has a reasonable chance of showing satisfactory results. Indeed, we consider that with the innovations and improvements which have been effected and with further improvements and adjustments which are planned it should not be necessary for the Company to have to rely solely upon brilliant summers for successful results. We believe that in future even if the weather is merely reasonable as distinct from deplorable as has been the case in 1954 results will at least be passable.

In these circumstances in our view the interests of Shareholders are best served by the Company continuing to trade, and we are doing our best to ensure that it does so efficiently and profitably in 1955.

Yours faithfully,

A. R. BOUCHER,

CHAIRMAN

Item 2

The following document accompanied the 1955 Accounts, and was issued from the Company Headquarters at Britannia Buildings, Bristol, dated 3rd July 1956. It has been reproduced exactly as it was issued except that for the purposes of analysis certain annotations are made and discussed below. It was an important document as it linked the 'poor' 1954 results with the somewhat 'better' 1955 ones, although worse was to come.

P. & A. CAMPBELL LIMITED

Statement by the Chairman

At last year's Annual General Meeting I could say little that was encouraging but I did express the hope that the innovations explained in some detail in my circulated statement, coupled with a fine summer, might enable our services to regain their popular appeal. The weather in 1955 was good, the majority of the innovations proved to be successful and as a result the trading loss of £48,102 of 1954 has been turned into a trading profit of £26,656 in 1955.

Two other features of the Accounts merit special mention. It will be observed that a further sum of £6,084 has been provided for depreciation, the effect of which is that after making the necessary adjustments covering the sales of the **Empress Queen** and the **Ravenswood**, the present net value of the five steamers now comprising the White Funnel Fleet stands at £120,000. It will also be noted that £10,000 has been reserved as "provision for special repairs". Shareholders may be aware that on order to retain her passenger certificates each steamer is subjected to an official quinquennial survey. On the basis of data gained from the latest survey of the **Glen Usk** - an excellent vessel from an operational point of view, but one no longer young - it has been deemed prudent to reserve this amount mainly in respect of _the next quinquennial survey of the Britannia which is due in 1957._ [Note 1]

The Board are doubtful whether any profit would have been made in 1955 had not the Company's _outlook and methods been radically revised_ [Note 2] as outlined in my last circulated statement. High and increasing costs affect almost every branch of the Company's activities and to give shareholders a practical idea of this I may say that our costs are now some four or five times higher than they were in 1922, and that it cost approximately £70,000 more to run five steamers in 1955 than it cost to run seven in 1947. In order to offset this, fares were increased in 1955 and have been further increased in 1956, but it is obvious there are limits to what can be done in this direction, particularly at a time when the Company is facing intense competition from other sources of entertainment and means of transport and is seeking to _re-establish its popularity_ [Note 3] with the public and particularly with the younger generation. Even now fares are little more than double the 1922 fares. It is clear, therefore, that if the present services are to continue, the only answer is to increase the number of passengers carried per steamer and I am glad to be able to say that in 1955 the average per steamer was in excess of any previous figure. _The numbers carried_ [Note 4] on excursions from Ilfracombe were the highest since 1924, when eight steamers were operating in the Bristol Channel, and the numbers carried from Swansea were double those of 1954 and equal those of the best pre-war years. We are attempting to improve on this and the evidence now available from the working of the various innovations indicates that an improvement is not impossible. Nevertheless I must warn shareholders that the question of increasing costs is by far the most serious problem which we have to face and is one to which, for the reasons which I have already given, the Company is particularly vulnerable. Even since last year costs have increased by some 10% and if this tendency continues unchecked _repercussions upon the Company will be inevitable and serious._ [Note 5]

In view of the Company's position at the end of 1954, I felt it was my duty to inform shareholders in great detail in my last circulated statement of the various steps which were being taken and innovations initiated to re-organise the Company's business and business outlook. On that occasion I dealt with such questions as improved services between Cardiff and Weston, the opening of new ports, the inclusion in many cases of Pier tolls in fares, the improvement of advertising and publicity, the provision of entertainments afloat, the opening of new agencies and the improvement in liaison with British Railways and the Motor Coach Proprietors, together with numerous other matters of a similar character. I also explained the situation with regard to the limited 'no-passport' service which it was proposed to open. With minor exception all these innovations and improvements were successfully brought into being last year and all played their part not only in encouraging more people to travel but also in attracting the interest of the younger generation. I am pleased to be able to say that a marked increase in the numbers of the latter is now obvious to anyone who travels on any of the Company's steamers. In this statement I do not propose to burden shareholders with another detailed account of how all these innovations and improvements are working except in the case of the "no-passport" services and the new Sailings Bills which I think merit special attention. So far as the remainder are concerned it suffices to say that in pursuance of our policy of endeavouring to encourage more people to use the steamers we are intensifying our efforts in all the directions set out in my 1955 statement.

With regard to the 'no-passport' trips, shareholders will remember that _authority was given last year_ [Note 6] for the first time since the War for the opening of a limited 'no-passport' service between Newhaven and Eastbourne and Boulogne and I may say that the Board takes some satisfaction in knowing that it was their efforts which pioneered this concession not only for the Company but for other passenger steamer proprietors. The service proved to be an unqualified success, the administrative difficulties forecasted in some quarters were not present in practice and some 16,000 passengers were carried on the 37 trips. Despite the fears expressed in some quarters the concession was not abused and as a result "no-passport" facilities are now available from Brighton, Hastings and Eastbourne, as in the early pre-war years. The number of crossings scheduled for 1956 is in consequence nearly twice the number scheduled for 1955.

With regard to Sailings Bills, the more attractive design of Sailings Bill outlined in 1955 proved popular and has been further improved in 1956 by the use of a new system of Columnar printing. As a result _much longer notice_ [Note 7] of sailings is available to intending passengers. On the subject of early publication of Sailing Schedules I referred in my 1955 Statement to the fact that we had managed to produce the Sailing Schedules for 1955 rather earlier than usual and that we hoped in the case of 1956 to do better still. In actual fact the schedules for 1956 were completed by early January 1956 which was a remarkable achievement on the part of the Company's staff headed by Mr S. C. Smith-Cox and _Mr J. Guy._ [Note 8]. As a result of this it was possible to circulate details well in advance. Undoubtedly the acceleration of the preparation of the Sailing Schedules played its part in the increased part business secured in 1955, particularly on the Cardiff-Weston services where the 1954 figures of total passengers carried between the two places were exceeded by 40,000 in each direction. Undoubtedly this factor has contributed to the even better figures for party business in 1956.

Finally, I would like to express my best thanks to everyone employed by the Company whether afloat or ashore for the support given to the Board in 1955. The _tempo_ [Note 9] of the Company's operations has been much accelerated and the Board is well aware that the Company's employees have almost without exception worked long hours and sometimes under considerable strain. We have received help and goodwill from so many other persons, newspapers, firms, companies and authorities, some closely connected with the Company and others comparative strangers, but nevertheless good friends, that it is really impossible for me to list them all. I can, however, assure them that the help and assistance which has been extended to us has been greatly appreciated.

Analysis of the 1956 statement (which accompanied 1955 Accounts)

What was this detailed statement really saying ? In essence, it appears to be an acknowledgement of the vulnerability of P. & A. Campbell Ltd as a going concern operating pleasure steamers on a seasonal basis, in terms of sensitivity to the weather, market forces and the ageing nature of the assets of the Company. Particular items thought to be worthy of comment have been highlighted (in italics) and are discussed below:

1. The reference to the imminent quinquennial survey of **Britannia** was ominous, and suggests that her future was uncertain even at that stage as another 5-year survey would have been a major cost.

2. A reference to the increased marketing activity in 1954 (the Centenary Year) and a more rigorous business-management attitude plus enhanced publicity, catering efforts, etc. Maybe this was also a veiled reference to the departure of W. G. Banks as erstwhile Managing Director.

3. This prompted the question of the extent to which the management accepted the trend of declining demand, and acknowledged the need to appeal to a wider market.

4. A reference to enhanced fleet/resource utilisation in the general sense.

5. Again, an acknowledgement of the vulnerability of the Company despite the measures already taken.

6. 'No-passport' trips began in 1954 (Newhaven-Boulogne only), embraced Eastbourne in 1955 and were to incorporate Brighton (Palace Pier) that year, in 1956.

7. It seems remarkable nowadays that this was seen as innovative then.

8. Jack Guy held the position of Traffic Manager for P. & A. Campbell Ltd, in succession to Alec Taylor.

9. A fascinating remark, suggesting that maybe the Company was just beginning to wake up to the fact of years of unprofitable trading, although were very determined to survive despite the perceived adversity facing them.

This statement did not mention one other very important point regarding the finances of the Company by then, namely that during the previous year the bankers to P. & A. Campbell had placed a Financial Controller within the management structure. A positive note was put to this arrangement, which would nowadays be looked on as somewhat unusual, and the Chairman Mr A. R. Boucher had said in July 1955 that:

'... after half a century of friendship, they (i.e. the Bank) have shown that they are still our friends today, despite our difficulties'.

Item 3

This statement was dated 1st August 1957.

P. & A. CAMPBELL LTD.

(1957) STATEMENT BY THE CHAIRMAN

... While in the interim report which I then gave to Members I outlined some of the practical results of the reorganisation, I am now able to do this in rather more detail and to explain the reasons why reorganisation had become necessary and what its results are likely to be. It had become apparent to your Board that the vastly increased costs which, unfortunately, have shown no signs of falling during the last two years were making the continued operation of steamers on *the basis that had been so successfully adopted* [Note 1] for so many years quite impracticable. It was therefore essential that all services not likely to prove profitable should be eliminated and that fewer ships should be operated, but operated more intensively and economically by selecting routes upon which they could be kept busy for three or four months. This meant of course that the whole organisation of the Company from top to bottom would have to be completely altered.

As part of this alteration it was considered essential to transfer the business to Cardiff and that has now been done. In other words the stores and engineering yard in Bristol which, with few ships to maintain, had become uneconomic have been closed and the Head Office which operated in Bristol divorced from the main centre of the Company's activities at Cardiff has been moved to its present address. Sailings from Bristol, particularly on poor tides, have been reduced and the Newport service which, *largely for tidal reasons* [Note 2] and due to the proximity of Newport to Cardiff was proving unprofitable, has been entirely suspended. As a result of these changes it has been possible to effect material reductions in the numbers of persons employed, but we are happy to be able to say that those who have been displaced have, in almost every case, been able to find alternative employment. To most of those who served the Company for many years and thus became redundant, small allowances are being paid. In addition the arrangements which were in force in the case of certain employees to provide a capital superannuation payment have been continued by the Company on their behalf in the case of older employees so affected and transferred to the employee in the case of the younger.

(Information here concerning the South Coast in 1956 was reproduced in Section 4.3)

... I would like now to refer to future prospects. If the Company were so unfortunate as to sustain further reverses its present organisation is such that its activities could easily be reduced to the simple operation of the Cardiff-Weston Ferry Service, but we hope and think that the necessity for this will not arise since as far as one can reasonably foresee there is every prospect of making a success of the routes now being operated.

The **Bristol Queen** serves Bristol and Cardiff so far as trips to Ilfracombe and elsewhere are concerned: the **Glen Gower**, which has been altered for the purpose, is now stationed on the Cardiff-Weston service and on this vessel a large bar has replaced the old dining saloon, as meals are not required on this short route and a milk bar and sweet shop have been introduced. The **Cardiff Queen** operates from Swansea to Ilfracombe, thence to Lundy Island and elsewhere with frequent calls at Tenby and Porthcawl. The effect of this is that these three vessels are now regularly employed on routes where satisfactory revenue can be secured and the heavy drain occasioned by *the operation of unsatisfactory trips on poor tides* [Note 3] is avoided. As a result I now have reasonable hope that in a poor year the Company should at least 'break even', and in a reasonable year should make a profit. Our Profit and Loss Accounts which are now available to us within a fortnight of the end of each month show that, so far this year, our estimates have been in accordance with expectation.

At the end of 1956 the **Britannia** was sold, as she had reached the age where it had ceased to be economic to keep her in repair or to operate her; apart from this we had no further use for her services.

Extensive publicity is still being undertaken; the whole of the schedules for the year 1957 were circulated well in advance of the season: factories, clubs and the like have been approached throughout the winter months and well over a hundred special train connections have been arranged. In addition, regular through bookings from the Bristol and Bath area via Weston *by rail*; [Note 4] also from Swindon and elsewhere, have been introduced and combined steamer and coach tours have been greatly increased from Bristol, Clevedon and Weston via Cardiff and Barry to Porthcawl and the Welsh Mountains and from Swansea, Cardiff and elsewhere, via Ilfracombe and Minehead to various beauty spots in Devon and Somerset. With a view to improving further this type of business, the schedules for 1958 have already been put in hand and meetings have already taken place with British Railways in regard to a further augmentation of these services in 1958.

It only remains for me to say that everything humanly possible has been done to reorganise this Company and I am very hopeful that results may now be obtained which will justify the effort that has been made.

Shareholders will, of course, appreciate that, in due course, a scheme for *the reconstruction of the capital of the Company* [Note 5] is inevitable, and steps will have to be taken in due course to submit this for the approval of Members. Our thanks are due to the Financial Controller for his assistance and encouragement in a particularly difficult year. Once again I find it difficult to particularise the many other friends of the Company to whom we are grateful for help, but I would not wish to forget the press, the Members and Staffs of the Pier and Harbour Authorities and Municipalities and of the Railways and Dock Authorities with whom we are in regular contact and also the many enthusiasts who support us in fair weather or foul.

In conclusion, I offer my best thanks for their assistance and loyalty to the Managing Director and all Members of the Company's staff afloat and ashore. I realise that a great deal has been asked of them in the past 12 months. I believe that your Company is now regarded by them as well as by me as having a *young and progressive outlook* [Note 6] with prospects for a better future.

A. R. BOUCHER, Chairman

25 BALDWIN STREET
BRISTOL.
1st August 1957.

Despite the address quoted on the statement, what was to be the Sixty-Fifth Ordinary General Meeting of the Company did take place in Cardiff, on Friday 23rd August 1957, at The Coal and Shipping Exchange Building in Mountstuart Square, Bute Square, Cardiff Docks, a short distance from the new HQ in Dock Chambers, Bute Street.

Analysis of the 1957 statement (which accompanied the 1956 Accounts)

Rather like the Statement issued by the Chairman in 1956 accompanying the 1955 Accounts, this message was interesting in its balance of defensiveness and optimism, as well as the recognition that things were still going to have to change further. Particular items singled out for comment are:

1. A defensive remark, and hard to understand as losses had been sustained for six out of the previous seven operating seasons.

2. Not altogether true, as the evidence in the records of the Newport Harbour Commissioners shows that the condition of the Landing-Stage, and the need for major refurbishment, was critical in terms of its demise. It was demand that was the variable: the tidal factor would not have changed since the construction of the Landing Stage in the previous century !

3. An interesting remark: why did the Company feel obliged to run such trips at all if they were going to produce unsatisfactory results?

4. Through rail and bus/steamer bookings were a notable feature of the services on offer from the White Funnel Fleet, and Norman Bird noted that the increase in variety of these from around 1954 onwards was well received by passengers, and evidence of a more enterprising approach being developed.

5. In simple terms, this can be interpreted as acknowledging that the Assets side of the Balance Sheet no longer adequately reflected the reduced number of steamers or their realisable values.

6. A revealing remark, it is very difficult to imagine that employees saw much future in a company which had so reduced the numbers it employed.

Item 4
The letter sent by the Chairman announcing receivership read as follows:

P. & A. Campbell Ltd., 4 Dock Chambers, Bute St., Cardiff

Receiver & Manager
W.Walker, F.A.C.C.A.   18th August 1958

TO THE MEMBERS AND CREDITORS

As you will be aware, this Company has been passing through an extremely difficult period and a succession of bad summers, in 1956 and 1957 in particular, has greatly aggravated the situation. Steps were taken at the end of 1956 to effect a complete reorganisation, the full results of which have only become apparent during 1958. As a result of this reorganisation, costs have been very much reduced, unprofitable services eliminated and steps taken to operate the vessels to the greatest possible advantage.

By the start of 1958, it seemed certain that the services had been put on a profitable basis, and it was the intention of the Directors to formulate proposals for the complete re-organisation of the capital structure of the Company. Until the middle of July, although the most appalling weather had attended our activities, particularly at Easter and Whitsun, it still appeared that such a result would be achieved. Between the middle of July and the present time, the position has been made acute by the worst possible weather during the high season that has occurred, probably within living memory. As a result, the situation of the Company has become serious and only exceptionally fine weather for the remainder of the Season could obviate a loss being incurred during 1958. Bad weather would undoubtedly result in a loss, though probably a much diminished loss in comparison with the experience of former years having regard to the drastic economies which have been effected.

This being the case, the Directors have immediately given consideration to the position and feel that these facts must be put before the shareholders and the creditors. They have a number of suggestions as to what ultimately may be done. In the meantime, in order to ensure that these suggestions can be considered and, if any of them are found practicable, put into operation, they feel the position can only satisfactorily met by the appointment of a Receiver. In order to preserve the position in the interests of all concerned, your Directors have requested the Bank, as debenture holder, to appoint a Receiver which has been done. The proposals which the Directors have in mind will be communicated to the Receiver at an early date.

I think you will readily appreciate that the Directors have taken the first possible opportunity since the position to which I have referred above arose to deal with it and to acquaint you with the facts and I feel sure that they will have your full support in the action which they have taken. The Accounts for the year ended 31st December 1957 will shortly be presented to the shareholders and at the resultant meeting the maximum information will be given as to the position which by then will have become more clear in respect of 1958.

The present Directors have tried, for several years now, in most cases without remuneration, to do everything possible to enable the passenger steamship services to be successfully operated in the Bristol Channel and indeed in the interest of both creditors and shareholders are anxious to continue to do all that they are able to that end. I feel that, in the exceptional circumstances that have arisen, my colleagues and I can look for your understanding and support in the efforts which we are making.

The Receiver has authorised me to say that for the remainder of the 1958 season the services will be operated in accordance with the advertised timetables.

A. R. BOUCHER,
Chairman

Item 5
Extract from Chairman's Speech, 14th November 1958.

While, as I have stated, we have always thought three vessels could be profitably operated in the Bristol Channel in normal circumstances, there is no doubt that in the event of a bad summer, the operation of a steamer from Swansea carries an undue element of financial risk. From all other ports in the Channel services have been reduced until they now appear to provide the facilities for which there appears to be a reliable demand. In the case of Swansea, however, no reduction is possible on the prewar service since a steamer based at Swansea must inevitably sail from Swansea as it is not practicable to interchange her at Ports further up-Channel. Consequently, a daily service is provided and only in good weather can sufficient passengers be found to justify this. A good deal of revenue derived by that steamer is obtained on her arrival at Ilfracombe from whence she journeys to Lundy Island or Clovelly or some other resort. Your Directors decided that they could not recommend the continuance of this risk in present circumstances and the Receiver likewise arrived at the same conclusion. Your Directors, however, are of the opinion that the operation of two vessels along lines which I will set out below should prove profitable and the Receiver has intimated that it is his present intention, in the absence of any unforeseen circumstances and subject to it being possible to make satisfactory arrangements with the various Ports concerned, to operate two vessels during 1959. These will be the **Cardiff Queen** and the **Glen Usk**.

The effect of this will be that the number of sailings from Bristol will be reduced while the number of coach connections from Bristol via Weston will be increased. The service from Cardiff, Penarth, Barry and Weston will be approximately as this summer. The service from Swansea, except for one or two occasions during the summer, will be suspended, but on many Saturdays a service leaving Ilfracombe about midday will operate to Mumbles returning from Mumbles to Ilfracombe sometime during the afternoon, thus enabling tourist passengers to cross from one side of the Channel to the other, when going on holiday. The steamer from Cardiff to Ilfracombe will be so timed as to enable at least two journeys a week to be made from Ilfracombe to Lundy Island, one to Clovelly and one to Porlock Bay, thus providing for the requirements of holidaymakers in Ilfracombe. As a result, a considerable portion of the revenue at present earned by the Swansea steamer will be transferred to the steamer operating from Cardiff.

... It would seem that the limited services which are now proposed may well be operated with a prospect of success ... I can only express the hope that the next time we meet, given the continuance of the understanding so far shown by both creditors and shareholders, the story we have to tell may prove to be a happier one and that a beginning may by then have been made towards ending the troubles with which we recently been surrounded.

A. R. BOUCHER, CHAIRMAN

Item 6

An accountancy perspective: As stated in Chapter 1, the technical accountancy issues involved with the processes of receivership, insolvency, liquidation and so on in this case-study were complex and not easily understood by the layman. This analysis by Keith Adams, a professional accountant, relates to the summarised Annual Results from 1950 set out below in tabular form, and other financial documents relating specifically to the period of receivership, broadly covering the five-year period 1956-1960, which comprised items 1-5 of this appendix.

The Company's published financial information showed a steadily deteriorating position. In every year except 1955, a summer of good weather, a net loss was recorded in the annual accounts.

The cumulative effect was that by 31 December 1956 the company's net deficit was £817. The amount seems small in todays terms, but the importance should not be underestimated because the company had become insolvent. The value of its assets at book value were exceeded by its known liabilities. The question of steamers being shown at book value is important. The accounting convention is to show fixed assets (i.e. steamers) in the accounts at cost less depreciation. Depreciation reduces the net book value of steamers and results in a charge against trading results, representing the use of the assets during the year. The net book value (i.e. cost less cumulative depreciation) does not set out to show the realisable value of the asset if it was to be put up for sale. In normal trading conditions, where a company is clearly a going concern, and is solvent, this is of no real concern to shareholders or to the creditors.

However, when the accounts for the year ended 31st December 1956 were presented to the shareholders in August 1957 the Directors would have been well aware of the seriousness of the company's situation, and their legal responsibilities towards the company's creditors, i.e. its bank and its suppliers. There is a convention, unfortunately often abused, that Directors should not cause their Company to borrow funds unless they are able to repay the debts in due course. The 1956 Accounts show that the Westminster Bank had lent the company £125,260 and had secured the overdraft by a legal charge (the debenture) over the company's whole undertaking. This meant that in the event of a liquidation the assets would be realised and the Bank would have first call to retrieve its money. The Directors, and the Bank, would be content with this arrangement until there were signs that the value of the company's assets might be insufficient to repay the banks lending. The Chairman acknowledged the inevitability of the need for reconstruction of the capital of the company.

In normal circumstances the company's results for the year ended 31st December 1957 would have been made public in August 1958. They were delayed, and were not published until 20th October 1958. Instead of the usual Report & Accounts, shareholders received a short statement from the Chairman dated 18th August 1958, which announced the appointment of the Receiver and stated that it was intended to operate the remainder of the 1958 season as advertised. The Receiver subsequently wrote to shareholders and creditors on 4th December 1959, summarising the detailed state of affairs which he had filed at Companies House, and making it clear that nothing was available for unsecured creditors. This summary stated that, as at 15th August 1958, stock, debtors, plant etc at net realisable value were estimated to be worth £45,013, together with book value of steamers at £107,533, which gave total assets of £152,546. The amount due to the Bank was given as £135,588. On the face of it the Bank's situation was covered, but it was clear to the Receiver that the book value attributed to the four steamers (**Glen Usk**, **Glen Gower**, **Bristol Queen** and **Cardiff Queen**) was overstated. He stated: 'In the event of individual sales I should not expect to receive that total figure'.

The official proposals for the 'Scheme of Arrangement' were separately circulated by the Chairman on 7th December 1959. The covering letter referred to the Directors having '*had conversations with the Directors of Townsend Bros. Ferries and Shipping Limited*' prior to the Receiver's appointment and these were recommended by the Receiver towards the end of 1958 when arrangements were made for the undertaking to be disposed of as from 1st January 1959 as a 'going concern'. The document ended by confirming the new owners

intention that there would be no changes to Management or Staff, indeed '*they would not have been interested in the acquisition had not the present Managing Director agreed to continue to make his services available*'. In fact Mr Smith-Cox was to serve P. & A. Campbell Ltd until the companys eventual demise as steamer operators in 1980.

The proposed reconstruction had to be approved by the High Court. There was nothing unusual in this procedure, it is normal for the Court to review such proposals to ensure that no party is disadvantaged by the arrangements agreed by the Receiver. With the benefit of hindsight the Receiver had clearly negotiated a very satisfactory situation for the Bank. The overdraft stood at £135,588 and the proposal was that it should receive £95,000 and release its legal debenture. Had the Bank had to force the sale of the steamers, it is likely that they would have been scrapped and the banks loss would have been considerably greater. The deal also allowed the ordinary shareholders to retain a small interest in the company by receiving a lesser number of 6% preference shares in lieu of their ordinary shareholdings. (Again, with hindsight, the shareholders might be thought fortunate to have received anything out of their insolvent investment). Preferential creditors would be paid in full, with ordinary creditors receiving five shillings in the pound.

The proposals were formally approved by the shareholders at an Extraordinary General Meeting, held in Bristol on 31st December 1959, and confirmed by the Court on 25th January 1960. The company then became a subsidiary of George Nott Industries Ltd. In order to bring the accounting arrangements into line with its new owners procedures, the P. & A. Campbell year-end was changed to 30th April.

Returning to the Annual Results, the net loss for the year to 31st December 1957 was £49,402. These results were published in October 1958. The Directors were clearly aware of the deficit earlier in the year and this would have influenced their decision to call in a Receiver in August. The next published figures covered the sixteen-month period to 30th April 1959 when a net loss of £55,246 was recorded. The Directors Report noted that during this 16-month period two winter refits had been undertaken with only one summers income to set against these costs. The effect of this was to cause the loss to be approximately double that which would have been recorded had the year remained at 31st December. The Board thanked Mr Walker for his assistance as Receiver and also for his previous duties as Financial Controller over '*a period of some years*'. This was the first mention in documents that Mr Walker had been previously connected with the Company. This arrangement may not have been unusual at that time, but by todays standards it would be most unusual for a Company Officer to be appointed as Receiver because his independence and objectivity would be questioned, particularly with regard to reporting to the shareholders about any dubious or unusual practices entered into by the past management.

P. & A.Campbell Ltd Financial Results prior to reconstruction y/e 1959

Year	Trading Profit/(Loss)	Net Profit/ (Loss)	Profit/(Loss) after Preference Dividend	Cardiff prices of Ordinary shares Highest Lowest	
1944	26,628	11,600	10,700		
1945	21,043	9,888	8,988		
1946	57,930	19,665	18,697		
1947	106,181	38,393	37,403		
1948	36,966	7,405	6,415		
1949	63,814	13,871	12,881		
1950	(34,834)	(28,702)	(29,692)		
1951	(7,410)	(14,825)	(15,781)		
1952	4,982	(2,873)	(3,818)	17s 6d	14s 0d
1953	(12,627)	(21,698)	(22,677)	14s 9d	11s 0d
1954	(47,981)	(57,609)	(57,857)	13s 0d	5s 9d
1955	26,761	8,742	(a)	10s 6d	4s 11d
1956	(54,779)	(70,8950)	(a)	7s 3d	4s 6d
1957	(35,865)	(49,402)	(a)	4s 9d	2s 9d
30.4.59	(44,249)	(55,246)	(a)	–	–

Notes

No share-price information available prior to 1952

(a) No Preference Dividends paid in these years.

Authorised Share Capital, Issued

Appendix Two
OPERATIONAL

The following data was extracted from ships log-books which form part of the P. & A. Campbell Ltd archives held at the Bristol City Records Office.

Notes (numbered 1-13) refer to noteworthy features of steamer operations during the week, (special) boat-train connections at Barry Pier, and rail connections between Swansea & Mumbles by the Swansea & Mumbles tramway. Extension of the normal train service between Cardiff General and Barry Island, onwards to the station at Barry Pier specifically provided for boat-trains to serve the pontoon-berth, was by arrangement between British Railways and P. & A. Campbell and linked to the extensive advertising/promotion of through rail & steamer fares from Welsh valleys and other local stations that then took place.

Notes (lettered A-N) describe the range of Coach Tours advertised throughout the whole week in connection with specified steamer journeys, and for which inclusive fares were marketed. These were of two types:

a. *From a port unserved that day by steamer, to the nearest appropriate port in order to join a steamer.*
b. *On arrival of the steamer at a port, in order to visit local beauty or other spots.*

In addition, 'Circular Trips' were advertised as being generally available at Lynmouth, Ilfracombe & Minehead whenever a steamer sailing permitted an outward journey by steamer and return by ordinary bus, or vice-versa. Specific days during w/c 24th August on which such Circular Trips were possible have been annotated.

Finally, empty positioning runs have been highlighted thus.

Two-Vessel operations, Bristol Channel, 1959
Cardiff Queen & Glen Usk, w/c Monday 24th August

Monday 24th August		Scheduled		Actual
Cardiff Queen				
Bristol		0900		0905
Clevedon		1020		1024-1032
Weston	(Note A)	1100		1110-1113
Barry	(Note B)	1150	(Note 1)	1202-1206
Lynmouth	$	1315		1339-1345
Ilfracombe	#	1430	(Note 2)	1430-1440
Lynmouth		1515		1531-1538
Cruise Porlock Bay				
Ilfracombe	#	1700-1715		1705-1716
Lynmouth		1745		1759-1807
Barry		1930	(Note 3)	1941-1945
Weston		2020		2030-2035
Clevedon		2100		2109-2113
Bristol		2205-2220		2220-2224
Cardiff		0015 (Tues)		0025

Glen Usk				
Cardiff		0730		0730
Minehead	(Note C)	0940		0942-0950
Cardiff	(Note D)	1130		1126-1140
Penarth		1140		1150-1153
Weston		1240		1235-1242
Cardiff		1345		1334-1345
Penarth		1355		1359-1403
Weston		1455		1442-1445
Barry		(1555)		1550
(idle)				
Barry		1750	(Note 4)	1755
Weston		1850		1852-1905
Cardiff		1950		2000-2010
Penarth		2000		2025-2028
Minehead		2205		2225-2235
Penarth		2345		0008-0011
Cardiff		(midnight)		0020

Also, 0940 steamer Minehead to Weston, return by any train.
(D) 1130 steamer to Weston, then Coach Tour to Cheddar Gorge.

Tuesday 25th August		Scheduled		Actual
Cardiff Queen				
Cardiff	(Note E)	0845		0847
Penarth		0855		0902-0904
Barry		0930	(Note 5)	0934-0936
Porthcawl	(Note E)	1100		1113-1118
Ilfracombe		1250		1256-1308
Lundy		(1415)-1645		1432-1650
Ilfracombe		1815-1910		1821-1913
Porthcawl		2100		2113-2124
Barry		2215	(Note 6)	2247-2250
Penarth		2250		2322-2324
Cardiff		2300		2335

Glen Usk				
Cardiff		0930		0930
Penarth		0940		0940-0949
Weston	(Note F)	1040		1031-1045
Cardiff		1140		1135-1153
Penarth		1150		1205-1209
Weston		1315		1251-1318
Cardiff		1415		1410-1418
Penarth		1425		1430-1434
Weston		1530		1517-1535
Barry		(1630)		1626
(idle)			(lifeboat drill, etc)	
Barry		1755		1800
Weston		1900		1904
Cardiff		2000		2022-2038
Penarth		2010		2050-2055
Weston		2115		2140-2145
Penarth		2205		2230-2233
Cardiff		(2215)		2245
				(2300 to bunkers)

Notes
(1) Train connection, 1041 Cardiff General to Barry Pier.
(2) Highlighted as the 'Ilfracombe Publicity Cruise', viewing Devon & Somerset coasts.
(3) Train connection, 1841 Cardiff General to Barry Pier, and from BP to Cardiff.
(4) Train connection, 1641 Cardiff General to Barry Pier.
Circular trips, out by steamer to Lynmouth, return by Southern National bus.
$ Circular trips, out by steamer to Ilfracombe, return by Southern National bus.
(A) 0945 Coach ex-Burnham, 1000 ex-Brean, to meet 1100 steamer to Lynmouth, (WEMS Coaches).
(B) 1005 Coach Porthcawl to Barry, for 1150 steamer to Ilfracombe.
(C) 0940 steamer Minehead to Cardiff, then Welsh Mountains Coach Tour.

Notes
(5) Train connection, 0841 Cardiff General to Barry Pier.
(6) Train connection, from BP to Cardiff.
(E) 0845 steamer Cardiff to Ilfracombe, Coach Tour to Clovelly & Westward Ho! Also advertised from 1100 steamer from Porthcawl.
(F) 0910 Coach from Bristol (Anchor Road) to Weston, 1040 steamer to Cardiff, for Welsh Mountains Coach Tour, due back at Bristol 2010 (Also bookable from Weston).

Wednesday 26th August Cardiff Queen		Scheduled	Actual
Cardiff		0930	0931
Penarth		0940	0945-0949
Weston		1040	1029-1042
Cardiff	(Note G)	1140	1129-1145
Penarth		1150	1200-1203
Weston		1405	1238-1412
Cardiff		1500	1458-1507
Penarth		1510	1521-1525
Weston		1610	1600-1612
Barry		(1710)	1658
(idle)			
Barry		1820	1825
Weston		1920	1923-1939
Penarth		2010	2020-2024
Cardiff		2020	2040
	Cardiff		d. 2206 empty
	Swansea		a. 0105 (Jetty)
	Swansea		a. 0129 (Swung & moored)

Glen Usk

Off-service day at Cardiff (Painting, varnishing, scrubbing vessel's side, etc)

Notes

(G) 1140 steamer Cardiff to Weston for Coach Tour to Bristol Zoo.

Thursday 27th August Cardiff Queen		Scheduled		Actual
Swansea	(Note H)	0830		0830
Mumbles		0850		0900-0904
Ilfracombe	#	1040	(Note 7)	1040-1100
Clovelly		1210		1228-1317
Lundy		d.1600		1420-1445 (Note 8)
Clovelly	$	1710		1635-1741
Ilfracombe		1830-1930		1908-1934
Mumbles		2110		2110-2117
Swansea		2130		2138
	Swansea			d.2215 (empty)
	Barry (lock)			0039-0059 (Fri)
	Barry Berth 19			0134 (moored)

Glen Usk

Cardiff		0905	0905
Penarth		0915	0921-0924
Weston	(Note I)	1015	1006-1020
Cardiff	(Note J)	1120	1115-1135 (Note 9)
Penarth		1130	1150-1154
Weston		1240	1240-1250
Cardiff		1345	1342-1350
Penarth		1355	1404-1408
Weston		1500	1454-1504
Cardiff		1600	1600-1615
Penarth		1610	1626-1631
Weston		1715	1714-1727
Barry		1815-1915 (Note 10)	1822-1918
Weston		2020	2014-2028
Penarth		2110	2112-2116
Cardiff		2120	2135
			(2150 to bunkers)

Notes

(7) Non landing cruise viewing Clovelly & Lundy also offered from Ilfracombe (although late running appears to have led to landing of single passengers only at Lundy).

(8) Steamer ran to North end of Lundy then returned directly to Clovelly.

(9) Minor collision with 'Burnham berth', 'Full Ahead' rung in error, no apparent damage recorded.

(10) Train connection 1811 Cardiff General to Barry Pier.

\# Circular trips, out by steamer to Clovelly, return by Southern National bus.

$ Circular trips, out by steamer to Ilfracombe, return by Southern National bus.

(H) 0830 steamer to Ilfracombe, Coach Tour (at 1415) to Lynton & Valley of the Rocks (Described as 'The English Switzerland').

(I) 0900 ex-Burnham, 0915 ex-Brean, to meet 1015 steamer to Cardiff (WEMS), Welsh Mountains Coach Tour from Cardiff, (also offered from Weston).

(J) 0950 coach Porthcawl to Cardiff, 1120 steamer to Weston (returning at 1715).

Friday 28th August Cardiff Queen		Scheduled	Actual

Off-service day at Berth 19, Barry Dock (Workmen renewing bushes to starboard paddle-wheels)

Glen Usk

Cardiff		0940	0945
Penarth		0950	0957-1000
Weston	(Note K)	1050	1043-1050
Cardiff		1150	1145-1155
Penarth		1200	1209-1212
Weston		1400	1255-1400
Cardiff		1500	1453-1500
Penarth		1510	1514-1517
Weston		1615	1603-1615
Penarth		(1705)	(omitted)
Cardiff		1715	1714-1725
Penarth		1725	1740-1745
Weston		1830	1830-1835
Barry		(1930)	1930
			1940 crew cease duty

Notes

(K) 1050 steamer Weston to Cardiff for Welsh Mountains Coach Tour, return by steamer at 1715 from Cardiff.

Saturday 29th August Cardiff Queen		Scheduled		Actual
		Empty		dep. Barry 0515 (Berth 19)
			Locks	0540-0550
			Swansea	0825 (moored
Swansea	(Note L)	0930	(Note 11)	0935
Mumbles		0950		1002-1009
Ilfracombe	#	1145	(Note 12)	1152-1207
Lynmouth		1215		1256-1319
Barry		1425		1450-1455
Penarth		(1510)		1528-1531
Cardiff		1520		1542-1552
Weston		(1600)		a.1637
(idle)				
Weston		1730		1733
Penarth		(1820)		omitted
Cardiff		1830		1818-1834
Penarth		1840		1847-1849
Weston		1945		1926-1946
Barry		(2045)	(Note 13)	2030

Glen Usk

Barry		0925	0925
Weston		1025	1025-1035
Cardiff		1130	1135-1152
Penarth		1140	1205-1209
Weston		1255	1250-1305
Cardiff		1400	1357-1410
Penarth		1410	1422-1427
Barry		1445	1502-1508
Lynmouth	$	1705	1705-1713
Ilfracombe		1805-1900	1804-1900
Mumbles		2050 (Note 14)	2117-2135
Barry			0014-0020 (Sun)
Penarth		0035	0100-0104
Cardiff		0045 (Sun)	0120
			0135 to bunkers

Notes

(11) 'Grand Long Day Sea Cruise' offered from Swansea to Barry & rtn. (Change steamers at Barry for return voyage).

(12) As (11), but from Ilfracombe to Barry, and change steamers to return.

(13) Train connection, from Barry Pier to Cardiff.

(14) Free rail journey from Mumbles to Swansea.

\# Circular trip, out by steamer to Lynmouth, return by Southern National bus.

$ Circular trip, out by steamer to Ilfracombe, return by Southern National bus.

(L) 0930 steamer to Ilfracombe, Coach Tour to Clovelly & Westward Ho!

Sunday 30th August	Scheduled	Actual
Cardiff Queen		
Barry	1115	1121
Weston	1210	1215-1221
Penarth	1300	1300-1301
Cardiff	1415	1315-141
Penarth	1425	1430-1434
Weston	1530	1511-1535
Cardiff	1630	1617-1633
Penarth	1640	1645-1650
Weston	a.1730	1724
(idle)		
Weston	1915	1917
Penarth	(2005)	1954-2001
Cardiff	(2015)	2015

Glen Usk		
Cardiff (notes M,N)	1240	1245
Penarth	1250	1303-1310
Weston	1350	1353-1405
Clevedon	1435	1440-1448
Bristol	1600	1615-1630
Walton Bay cruise		(turned off Avonmouth 1727)
Bristol	1800-1815	1836-1845
Clevedon	1920	AGROUND (See text)
Penarth	(2015)	
Cardiff	(2030)	

Notes

(M) 1240 steamer Cardiff to Clevedon, Somerset Mystery Coach Tour.

(N) Coach at 1110 from Porthcawl to Cardiff, 1240 steamer to Weston, or to Clevedon, or to Bristol to land, or stay on for Walton Bay cruise.

EASTER MONDAY 1967

SPECIAL

DAY TRIP TO DEVON

(ILFRACOMBE)

A Combined Land and Sea Excursion by

"STRATFORD BLUE" and the **"WHITE FUNNEL FLEET"**

Leave	Time		Due Ilfracombe	Leave Ilfracombe
Kineton (Church)	*6.30 a.m.		2.00 p.m.	4.45 p.m.
Ettington (Stores)	*6.40 a.m.			
Wellesbourne (Post Office)	*6.45 a.m.			
Tiddington (Crown)	6.55 a.m.			
Stratford-on-Avon (Bus Station)	7.00 a.m.		The coaches are due	
Luddington (Church)	7.10 a.m.		back at the starting	
Welford-on-Avon (Maypole)	7.15 a.m.		points between 10.45 and 11.15 p.m.	

Fares: (day return) ADULTS 40/- CHILDREN (3-14 years) 23/6d.

NOTE: The normal small excess mileage charges will apply from the starting places indicated by "*" above.

THE TOUR

Passengers commence their journey by "Stratford Blue" luxury coach from the places and at the times stated above. The coaches travel via the Vale of Evesham, Tewkesbury, Gloucester and Bristol to Weston-super-Mare, where passengers are taken direct to the Birnbeck Pier for embarkation in the steamer sailing at 10.45 a.m. During the voyage down the Bristol Channel the steamer passes the Flat and Steep Holm Islands, the towering cliffs of the North Somerset and Devonshire coasts and the small towns of Lynton and Lynmouth as well as numerous other coastal villages and places of interest. It is generally acknowledged that the coastal scenery on the south side of the Bristol Channel is among the finest to be seen in the British Isles.

The steamer is due to arrive at Ilfracombe at 2.00 p.m. allowing passengers over 2½ hours in this delightful Devonshire resort.

The return journey commences at 4.45 p.m. (PROMPT) from Ilfracombe Pier, the steamer being due at Weston at 7.40 p.m., where the coaches will be waiting for the return journey to their destinations.

— see overleaf —

Three-Vessel operations, Bristol Channel, 1966

Notes

Duration of operating season, by vessel:

Westward Ho	Wednesday 6th April to Monday 17th October
Bristol Queen	Wednesday 25th May to Thursday 8th September
Cardiff Queen	Saturday 11th June to Wednesday 21st September

Sunday 10th July	Scheduled	Actual
Bristol Queen		
Cardiff	0830	0845
Penarth	0840	0903
Barry	0915	0935-0938
Ilfracombe	1150-1200	1202-1211
Milford Haven	1545	1600
(Cruise)		(Southerly gales, cruise cancelled)
Milford Haven	1705	1705
Ilfracombe	2040-2045	2107-2118
Barry	(2300)	2326
Penarth	(2325)	2358
Cardiff	2340	0015 (Mon)

Westward Ho		
Swansea	0945	0947
Mumbles	1010	1010-1016
Porthcawl	1110-1115	1118-1125
Ilfracombe	1305-1445	1325-1450
Porlock Bay cruise	(No time quoted turning)	
Ilfracombe	1845	1805-1847
Mumbles	2035	2048-2054
Swansea	2105	2115-2120
Porthcawl	2215	2235-2245
Barry	2350	0030 (Mon)

Cardiff Queen		
Weston	0800	(0745)-0802
Penarth	(0850)	0838-0850
Cardiff	0930	0910-0935
Penarth	0940	0951-0954
Weston	1035	1030-1042
Cardiff	1130	1125-1141
Penarth	1140	1155-1157
Weston	1240	1232-1241
Cardiff	1340	1330-1341
Penarth	1350	1355-1357
Barry	1425	1420-1425
Ilfracombe	1640-1650	1637-1651
Barry	1915-1920	1910-1921
Weston	2020	1954-2015
Cardiff	2120	2115-2128
Penarth	2130	2140-2145
Weston	2225	2230-2237
Cardiff	2320	0008-0012 (Mon)
Penarth	2330	0008-0012
Weston	0020	0100-0110
Cardiff	(0110)	0150

Not just a sailing bill: the Warwickshire bus company Stratford Blue, serving the heart of England, jointly promoted Bristol Channel excursions via Weston-super-Mare, reasonably accessible by relatively newly-built motorway in 1967. In the early season this trip involved the motor-vessel **Westward Ho** *from Birnbeck Pier rather than the surviving paddle-steamer* **Bristol Queen**, *on a very long day out of almost 18 hours. The bus company retained its independence until absorbed by Midland Red in 1971.* Author's collection

Appendix Three
TICKETS

Despite the general contraction of P. & A. Campbell Ltd business activity in the 1970s, in comparison to the 1950s when a much bigger fleet had been operated on the south coast as well as in the Bristol Channel, the company continued to maintain a small number of ticket sales outlets for *Balmoral* excursions, either manned by their own staff or through agency arrangements. Handbills describing sailings listed fares, and referred to the availability of tickets at 'the Company's Offices' but made it clear that these could also be purchased 'on board the steamers', and listed the general conditions which applied. After the cutbacks of the 1971 season, the three places which offered most sailings were Penarth, Swansea and Ilfracombe. The offices of the company remained at 4, Dock Chambers, in Bute Street in the docks quarter of Cardiff, and also those of The Agent at 10, The Quay, Ilfracombe. In addition to the facility to buy tickets at the pier offices at Penarth and at Weston (Birnbeck, or 'Old Pier'), Clevedon Pier being out of the picture by this time, a considerable network of agency outlets had been set up in west Wales reflecting the new-found importance of this region after the demise of sailings from Cardiff Pier Head and Bristol on a regular basis. Over at Ilfracombe, a ticket booth at the pier entrance complemented the Agency premises of long-standing, where stalwart Fred Birmingham could still be found dispensing timetables and keeping an eye on the companys affairs in north Devon generally. This perpetuated a family connection established as far back as the 1890s.

Penarth handbills provided telephone details for the pier and the Cardiff head office, as well as for the Western Welsh bus company at Newport Bus Station, harking back to the late-1950s when Campbell sailings had still operated from the heart of Newport. Swansea bills listed a remarkably wide range of sales outlets, including the offices of the then local bus company South Wales Transport at Singleton Street, Swansea. Local Agent George Gunn oversaw other outlets including Libbys Travel Agency at the Mumbles, Clay Travel at Dunraven Place, Bridgend, W. B. Trick Son & Lloyd at Neath, Owen Travel at Llanelly, and at Carmarthen, and the Porthcawl Omnibus Company at Porthcawl.

On the other side of the Bristol Channel, apart from the aforementioned commercial arrangements at Ilfracombe, it fell to the Western National bus company to handle P. & A. Campbell Ltd enquiries and sales at Minehead. At Weston super Mare, in recognition of the invisibility of Birnbeck Pier to a percentage of visitors, an information bureau at the centrally-sited Grand Pier (which obviously had no steamer services of its own) promoted the White Funnel Fleet. Mr J. Headon of Clovelly acted as agent there, in addition to being the boatman. Similarly, Mr K. Oxenham did the honours at Lynmouth. All in all, a fairly comprehensive presence was still apparent even if the company did only operate one, very hard-worked steamer around the Bristol Channel by then. One must not here forget the 1960s presence in north Wales, too, where to a degree Clifton Smith-Cox relied on the same outlets that had promoted Liverpool and North Wales Steamship Company sailings until 1962, and carried on in much the same way for *St. Trillo* when she operated alone after 1963, principally at Llandudno Pier and Menai Bridge, and via the Crosville Bus Company and their

extensive sales network in the north Wales region.

What of the tickets themselves? Compared to queuing at the Pursers Office nowadays 'on the Promenade Deck, behind the funnel' for a modern-style ticket, often paid for by plastic, a visit below to extract a ticket from long-standing P. & A. Campbell Ltd. Purser Vic Taylor down on the main deck on *Balmoral* was a somewhat different experience in the 1970s. Tucked away in a cramped corner aft, near what used to be the cocktail bar, the ticket office was not a place one could actually see into. If Vic was in a good mood one might succeed in acquiring a timetable, unceremoniously ripped off from a loop of string threaded through the top left-hand corner, but which was tantamount to him doing you a favour. I often wanted a single ticket, say from Weston to Penarth in the evening, probably after he had already cashed up for the day, and hence the occasional taciturn tendency. One could just make out racks of dusty card tickets, railway booking-office style, and many of the more esoteric ones – say, Minehead to Lundy, a distinctly rare sailing by the 1970s – seemed to have been printed before the war in vast quantities, which never quite got used up three or four decades on. Some of the more common journeys had more recently-printed styles, although every now and then a request for a ticket for an unusual journey might result in the issue of a ticket that actually said something quite different. Any ensuing accountancy checks must have been quite a nightmare.

Just to frustrate would-be collectors of such items, it was customary for all tickets to be gathered from passengers as they disembarked. It was not until after the closedown of P. & A. Campbell Ltd that the author acquired a batch of surviving, unused tickets which had narrowly avoided being thrown in a skip as 4, Dock Chambers was being evacuated. A selection of these is illustrated here.

As mentioned in the text, a weekly ticket was a bargain if one wanted to sail on three or more days in a seven-day period, but these had to be purchased from one of the Company's Offices, to quote the handbills. Furthermore, as a cost-conscious means of not parting with cash on a sailing, pre-purchased coupons were a commercial item of long-standing and enabled users to enjoy a worthwhile amount of discount in return for investing in a book or more of these before the season, also illustrated here.

Finally, the reasonably comprehensive through-booking arrangements with the railway, principally in south Wales, must be mentioned. Through fares from, for example, Rhymney Valley stations via Penarth Pier to Weston super Mare were offered right to the end, as well as from Carmarthen and other west Wales stations, via Swansea on days when sailings operated. This arrangement largely relied on P. & A. Campbell Ltd supplying the BR Divisional Manager, Cardiff with sufficient supplies of bills which would be supplied from the Cardiff Riverside bill-store to stations which participated in the scheme. For their part, BR also printed Seafarer pamphlets for display at travel centres and booking offices throughout South Wales. This went back a long way, to the early days when the cooperation of the Taff Vale Railway, the Rhymney Railway and the Barry Railway Company was prized to get South Wales folk onto the White Funnel steamers.

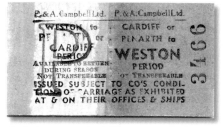

Day return, Ilfracombe to Mumbles or Swansea. The return portion was pink, outward white with blue stripe.

Period return, Cardiff to Weston. Return portion pale blue with mid-blue stripe, outward darker blue.

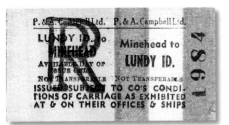

Day return, Minehead to Lundy Island. Return portion yellow, outward white with grey stripes.

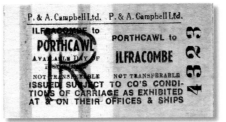

Day return, Porthcawl to Ilfracombe. Return portion white with purple stripes, outward, pink.

Single, Cardiff to Weston. Blue card ticket with green stripes.

Party, Cardiff to Weston. Black print on white card.

The White Funnel Fleet

COUPON BOOKS

Coupon Books, offering patrons an opportunity of securing reduced rates for steamer travel during the summer months, are now available at the following prices :

Book One costs £2 15s. 0d. and contains coupons to the value of £4.

Book Two costs £2 5s. 0d. and contains coupons to the value of £3.

Book Three costs £1 10s. 0d. and contains coupons to the value of £2.

Each book can be used to obtain steamer tickets for the holder or other members of his family, including children, and affords an advantage over the ordinary traveller who, at the normal fare, pays more for his steamer travel when the season commences.

General sales for the forthcoming season will start on December 1st and continue until the end of the month. Application by post however, can be made immediately on receipt of this order form, and intending purchasers are recommended to take up their full order at this stage, since no further issues for the season will be made after December 31st.

The form overleaf should be completed and returned to this office at the earliest convenient date. Payment should be included with the order, and it will greatly assist our staff in ensuring that books are forwarded correctly, if names and addresses are printed in Block Capitals.

Application form for coupon books, for advance purchases by 31st December of the year before the sailing season, to obtain discount.

Right: Specimen coupon booklet reproduced at half full-size. This one contained four fifty pence coupons, eight for twenty pence each, and four for ten pence each, amounting to £4.00 value in total, which could be individually detached to pay for tickets in any multiple of 10p.

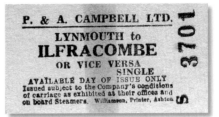

Single, Lynmouth to Ilfracombe (or vice-versa). Pink card ticket with orange printed stripe.

Dog return. Buff card ticket.

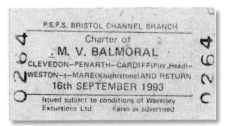

Special PSPS charter sailing on Balmoral, 16th September 1993, before completion of Cardiff Bay. Buff card ticket.

Appendix Four
THE LATE YEARS FLEET & GENERAL ARRANGEMENTS

Built	Acquired	Name	Length (ft)	Breadth	Depth	GRT	cl.III pass.	Last season	Disposal
1891	1891	p.s. **Ravenswood**	215	21.2	8.5	345	695	1954	1955, scrapped
1896	1896	p.s. **Britannia**	230	26.6	9.6	459	887	1956	1956, scrapped
1914	1914	p.s. **Glen Usk**	224.3	28.1	8.9	532	1,005	1960	1963, scrapped
1922	1922	p.s. **Glen Gower**	235.1	28.5	9.1	553	1,079	1957	1960, scrapped
1940	1947†	t.s. **Empress Queen**	269.5	37.5	12.0	1,781	1,300	1951	1955, sold
1946	1946	p.s. **Bristol Queen**	244.7	31.2	10.5	961	1,014	1967	1968, scrapped
1947	1947	p.s. **Cardiff Queen**	240	30.1	9.75	765	883	1966	1968, scrapped
1938	–	m.v. **Crested Eagle**	143	25.2	7ft dr	249	408	chartered 1957 season	
1936	1963	m.v. **St. Trillo**	149.2	27.1	10.0	314	568	1969	1975, scrapped
1939	1965	m.v. **Westward Ho**	199.5	30.2	6ft dr	623	855	1971	1972, sold
1965	–	m.v. **Queen of the Isles**	156.2	29.0	9ft dr	600	300	chartered 1967-9 seasons	
1949	1969	m.v. **Balmoral**	203.5	30.0	6.5ft dr	688	892	1980	1981, sold
1956	1977	m.v. **Devonia**	199.5	30.8	19.3	921	855	1978	1981, sold

Notes

Pre-war fleet all owned by P. & A. Campbell Ltd., † **Empress Queen** not delivered until post-World War Two
St. Trillo owned by Townsends, chartered to P. & A. Campbell Ltd.
Westward Ho (built as **Vecta**), purchased from Red Funnel Steamers
Queen of the Isles on charter from Isles of Scilly Steamship Company
Balmoral purchased from Red Funnel on demise charter, owned in European Ferries name
Devonia (built as **Scillonian**) purchased from Isles of Scilly Steamship Company.

The above table has been compiled from various sources, mainly articles in technical journals such as *The Shipbuilder and Shipping Record*, or company publications. Draught figures (rather than depth) are quoted for most of the motor-vessels.

The passenger capacity figures quoted (for the older paddle-steamers) are those that P. & A. Campbell Ltd published in the 1935 edition of the *Bristol Channel District Guide*, cl.III limits then applying broadly between Bristol and Lundy. The figures quoted for the two former Red Funnel motor-vessels are those which that company stated in a 1950s handbook, and refer to their Solent limits, whilst their respective car-capacities then quoted were 12 (**Vecta**) and 10 (**Balmoral**). By 1978 the Bristol Channel passenger certificate for **Balmoral** mentioned a capacity of 733. For interest, the figure quoted for **Crested Eagle** (on charter to P. & A. Campbell Ltd. for a short summer season in 1957, on the south coast) was that given in the General Steam Navigation handbook of the period.

By way of comparison between the paddle-steamers and motor-vessels, the crew figures for **Bristol Queen** and **Cardiff Queen** were 41 and 39 respectively. The 1978 passenger certificate for **Balmoral** quoted a figure of 23 crew.

This fleet was interesting inasmuch as the seven vessels were built by only three shipyards, coming from the Clyde (Fairfields, **St. Trillo** and **Cardiff Queen**), the Solent (Thornycrofts, **Vecta**, **Balmoral** and **Scillonian**) and Bristol itself (Charles Hill, **Bristol Queen** and **Queen of the Isles**). Each vessel had different specifications, the two modern, broadly comparable postwar paddle-steamers being equipped with full restaurant facilities and geared to long-day excursion use. The two Southampton-built Isle of Wight car-ferries (car-deck forward on **Vecta**, aft on **Balmoral**) likewise had full restaurant facilities, but were

SHIP OWNERS SINCE 1854

A 1970s letterhead for the company.   Author's collection

P&A CAMPBELL LTD

Ship Owners, Ship Managers, Ship & Insurance Brokers
HEAD OFFICE: Alliance House, Baldwin Street, Bristol, BS1 1SA
Telephone Bristol (STD 0272) 20218. Telex 444129
Out of hours telephone Wells (STD 0749) 72522

intended for the short, one-hour long Southampton to Cowes Solent run. The other three lacked such facilities, *St. Trillo* being the most basic of the trio.

The SRN-2 hovercraft was used for short periods in 1963 and 1964. The SRN-6 hovercraft was used in 1966 and again in 1967.

Historically, most vessels owned by P. & A. Campbell Ltd had not, when they finished their careers, been sold on for further use. The youthful **Empress Queen** was an exception, going to Kavounides, and surviving (after dieselisation) into the 1960s. **Westward Ho** survived,

in static form, for a good few years after her withdrawal. **Devonia** was notable for the range of her successive owners after she was sold out of the Bristol Channel fleet : these were Torbay Seaways (1982-84, as **Devoniun**) and Norse Atlantic Ferries (1984-85, as **Syllingar**) before disposal to the Greeks, initially Hellenic Cruising Holidays who ran her as **Remvi**.

Balmoral lay at Dundee as a static restaurant/nightclub attraction between 1982-1985 before her rescue and reincarnation in 1986 as the consort to the 'World's Last Sea-Going Paddle-Steamer' **Waverley**.

St. Trillo

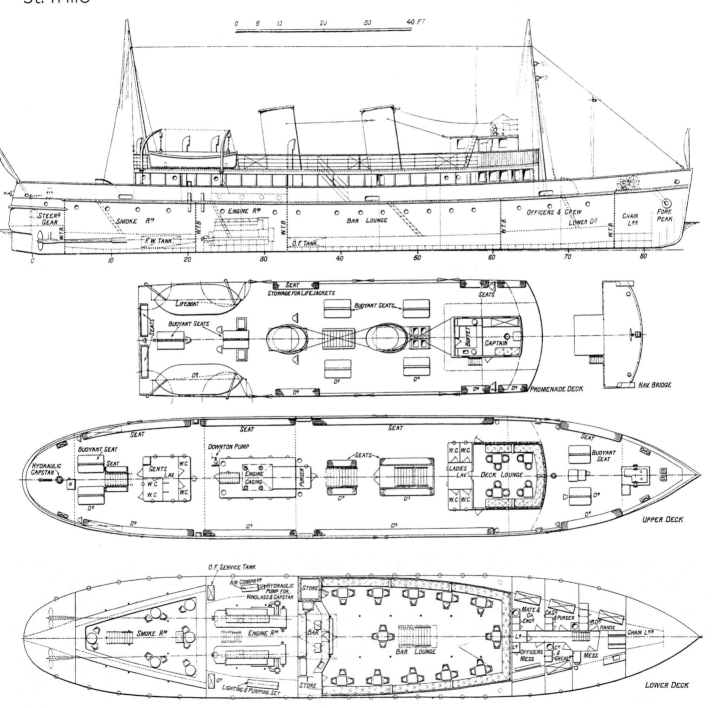

The GA drawings of the motor-vessels *St. Trillo*, *Queen of the Isles* and *Balmoral* here (together with the cutaway of *Vecta*, later **Westward Ho**, included within chapter 2) illustrate the larger part of the White Funnel Fleet in the 'Late Years' of P. & A. Campbell Ltd during the 1960s & 1970s, after the last of the veteran prewar paddle-steamers had gone, once the Ailsa-built *Glen Usk* was finally displaced on Cardiff-Weston-super-Mare ferry duties in 1960.

Queen of the Isles

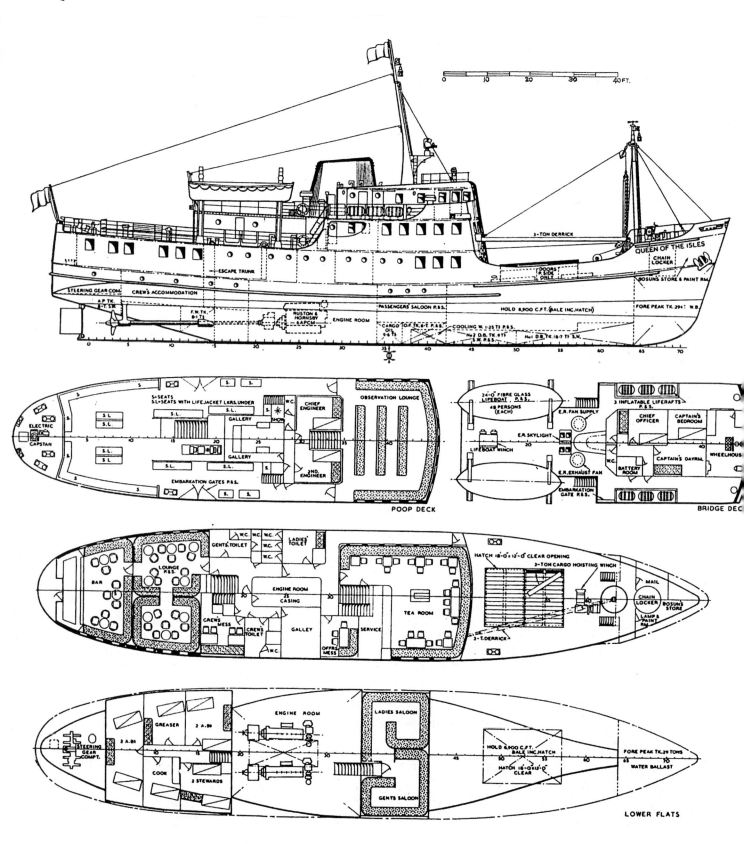

Balmoral

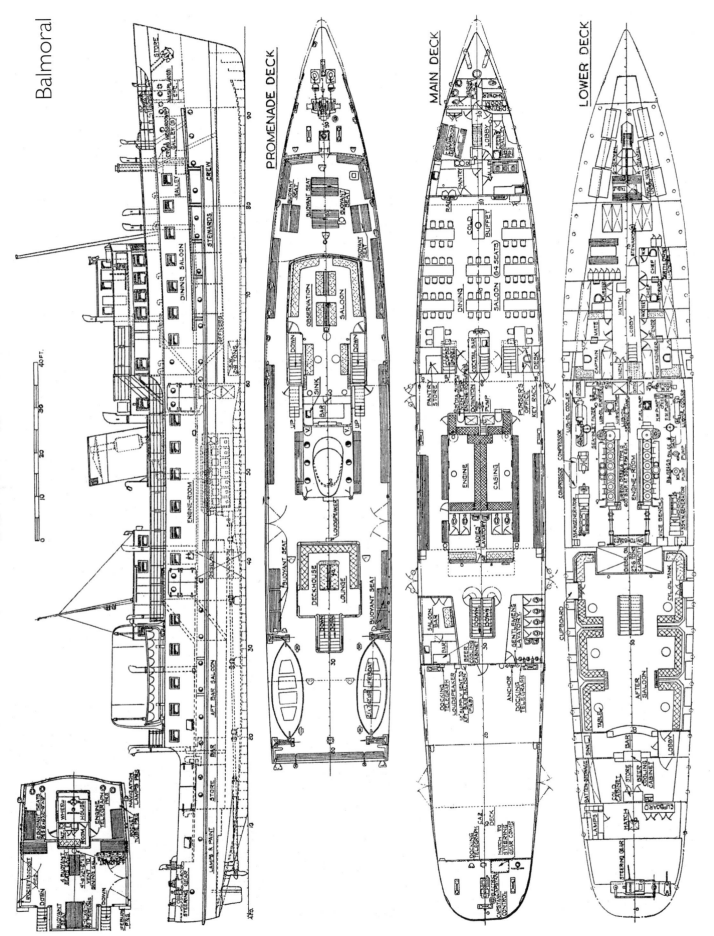

PROMENADE DECK

MAIN DECK

LOWER DECK

Captain Cyril Smith of Balmoral (right) and Captain David Neill of Waverley, at Ilfracombe, on the evening of Sunday 1st June 1980, prior to their respective return departures for Penarth and Swansea, during the last year of commercial operation of Balmoral by P. & A. Campbell Ltd, on charter to White Funnel Steamers that season. The paddler had circumnavigated Lundy whilst the motor-vessel had carried passengers to and from the Atlantic island that afternoon. Author